D1326259

Bonds Without Borders

For other titles in the Wiley Finance series please see www.wiley.com/finance

Bonds Without Borders

A History of the Eurobond Market

CHRIS O'MALLEY

WILEY

Registered office

John Wiley & Sons Ltd, The Atrium, Southern Gate, Chichester, West Sussex, PO19 8SQ, United Kingdom

For details of our global editorial offices, for customer services and for information about how to apply for permission to reuse the copyright material in this book please see our website at www.wiley.com.

Library of Congress Cataloging-in-Publication Data

O'Malley, Chris.
  Bonds without borders : a history of the Eurobond market / Chris O'Malley.
    pages cm
  Includes bibliographical references and index.
  ISBN 978-1-118-84388-8 (cloth)
 1. Euro-bond market–History.   I. Title.
  HG3896.O43 2015
  332.63′23094–dc23

                                                          2014029870

A catalogue record for this book is available from the British Library.

ISBN 978-1-118-84388-8 (hbk) ISBN 978-1-118-84387-1 (ebk)
ISBN 978-1-118-84386-4 (ebk) ISBN 978-1-119-01084-5 (ebk)

Cover Design: Wiley
Cover Images: top photo: ©iStockphoto.com/peepo
              bottom photo: ©iStockphoto.com/ricardoinfante

Set in 10/12pt Times by Aptara Inc., New Delhi, India
Printed in Great Britain by TJ International Ltd, Padstow, Cornwall, UK

To my dear sister Kath, and sister-in-law Jan, who lost their battles with cancer during the writing of this book.

Contents

Foreword by Hans-Joerg Rudloff   ix

Introduction: Fifty Years of the Eurobond Market   xi

Chapter 1
Before the Beginning   To 1962   1

Chapter 2
Building the Base   1963–1969   21

Chapter 3
Oil and Turmoil   1970–1979   47

Chapter 4
Masters of the Market   1979–1984   73

Chapter 5
Going Global   1985–1989   99

Chapter 6
The Derivatives Dash   1990–1995   125

Chapter 7
Convergence and Credit   1995–1999   145

Chapter 8
Of .Com's and Cons   1999–2004   163

Chapter 9
Mark-to-Model   2004–2007   187

Chapter 10
Busts and Bailouts   2007–2010   207

Chapter 11
  Sinking Sovereigns   2011–2013   **229**

Postscript   **247**

Glossary   **251**

Index   **259**

Foreword

*B*onds Without Borders is a testimony to a fascinating period in the development of the international financial markets. Chris O'Malley in his different positions at Credit Suisse First Boston and Samuel Montagu was an active participant in the fastest growing securities market in the world. He has undertaken the difficult task of describing the different stages of the history of modern international bond markets. His painstaking research into the defining moments of the market deserves great applause and most importantly gives the reader a fascinating picture of the dynamic pioneering work of investment banks and their people. It shows their unlimited commitment to the expansion and creation of a borderless world in which capital is moved to where it is most needed, with the best risk adjusted returns. The missionary spirit of people like Chris helped to put together, piece by piece, a market that today provides US$2.5 trillion to supranationals, governments, and corporations alike.

Chris's insights into the workings of the market have allowed him to concentrate on the essentials and enable the reader to understand the enormous progress achieved over the years in allocating capital through free markets. This book catches the spirit which drove the markets towards globalisation; providing an enormous benefit to emerging countries, and helping billions of people to achieve economic progress. This book offers a very timely reminder of how important open markets are for the unrestricted flow of ideas, goods, people and capital. Chris O'Malleys' book makes a significant contribution to a better understanding of the great benefits open financial markets have brought to the world.

In addition, this book demonstrates how important it is for the actors in the market to exercise their profession with the necessary care and prudence.

Hans-Joerg Rudloff
Chairman of Kidder Peabody 1978–1980,
Chairman of Credit Suisse First Boston 1989–1998 and
Chairman of the investment bank at Barclays from 1998 to 2014

Introduction: Fifty Years of the Eurobond Market

It was Paul who came up with the idea. Instead of singing the usual love song lyric of 'I love you', it should be in the third person 'She loves you' and other band members would respond with the refrain 'yeah, yeah, yeah'. A few days after writing the song, The Beatles gathered at Abbey Road Studios, London, on 1 July 1963 to record 'She Loves You' for release as a single. Released in the following month it was a gigantic success, becoming the best-selling single of 1963, and remains the best-selling Beatles' single in Britain. It was the breakthrough that led The Beatles to international success.

As that recording session in Studio 2, Abbey Road was getting under way, five miles away in Gresham Street in the City of London a group of senior international bankers and lawyers were signing a subscription agreement for an international bond issue for Autostrade, an Italian road builder. It was the first of a new type of financing targeted at international investors. This new 'Eurobond', as it came to be known, represented an historic breakthrough in the international financial markets.

*   *   *

The Eurobond market, the largest international capital market the world has known, has a confusing name. Eurobond doesn't refer exclusively to bonds issued in Europe or indeed, bonds denominated in the euro currency. (Nor does it refer to the term chosen by the authorities during the current financial crisis to describe a possible European sovereign bond underwritten jointly and severally by all Eurozone governments.) The term Eurobond defines the type of security rather than the currency or domicile of the obligation.

A web search reveals the popular, but imprecise, definition that it is a bond issued in a currency other than the currency of the borrower. But this could also describe a 'foreign bond'. A foreign bond issue is one offered by a foreign borrower to investors in a national capital market and denominated in that nation's currency, for example, the Kingdom of Norway issuing a dollar bond in New York. Helpfully, foreign bond markets have all attracted nicknames: so a foreign bond in the US market is a 'Yankee bond', a foreign bond in the Japanese domestic market is a 'Samurai bond', and a foreign bond issued in the Australian market is a 'Kangaroo bond', and so on. A foreign bond issue will always follow the rules and practices of the relevant domestic securities market.

Whereas a Eurobond issue is one denominated in a particular currency, but sold to investors in national capital markets other than the country of issue. It is a bond issue specifically targeted at cross-border distribution, hence the title of this book. It does not follow the rules of a particular domestic market. In the modern era this cross-border status is protected by documentation which protects the investor's right to receive payment free of any national withholding taxes. However in earlier times, before national tax regimes, this cross-border characteristic was less clear.

Over half a century the Eurobond market has grown into the world's largest international capital market, with approximately $20trn equivalent of bonds outstanding as at mid-2013. For many years it grew at a compound rate of 20%. The market has played a pivotal role in the worldwide flow of capital. Indeed such has been the success of the market in Europe that it has replaced most domestic bond markets and even foreign bond markets. Visiting regulators from Asia, for example, are surprised to find that the UK does not have a domestic corporate debt market nor indeed an active foreign bond (i.e. 'bulldog') market. Such is the efficiency and depth of the Eurobond market, with its opportunity for worldwide distribution, that issuance in the UK domestic market has become redundant and all financing is channelled via the Eurobond market. This is the case in most European jurisdictions.

The Eurobond market has offered an ever-increasing range of instruments, currencies and innovative product structures. The response of certain domestic markets might be to limit the range of permitted currencies and products, whereas the Euromarkets characteristic response has been to remain flexible and open to innovation and change. Indeed the Eurobond market has benefited by exploiting the inefficiencies in individual domestic markets. This book describes the developments, the market practices, the challenges and the innovations in the Eurobond market during its first half-century. The story, of course, is a cumulative one. Innovations arrive, but they stay and are developed further and create new markets of their own with new customers and new expertise. It is difficult to take in the immense size, complexity and interdependency of the modern debt capital markets. The founding fathers probably had a pretty clear overall picture of the workings of the debt capital markets, whereas today's market participants are typically focused on small areas of those complex markets. Their expertise and understanding are largely limited to those sectors.

The generation that developed the Eurobond market are long retired. Today's practitioners know little of the origins of today's global market; indeed many have only known markets in the midst of the financial crisis. After more than a decade training capital market practitioners I have found that today's market participants tend know *what* to do, but have little grasp of *why* things need to be done the way they are. For example, they will know what the requirements of SEC Rule 144A are, but have little understanding about why and for what purpose it was introduced. So the 50th anniversary of the market seems a good point at which to pause and look back on the market's history and answer some of the 'whys?'. To this end this text is targeted at students and new market participants; although I hope it will also be read by older or former market participants, as a source of interest and, perhaps, nostalgia.

*   *   *

Any breakdown of the history of the Eurobond market is inevitably arbitrary, but there are some clearly defined stages in the market's development. The period from the inception of the market until 1984 saw the gradual opening up of the international markets and a period of deregulation. This regulation had resulted from the protectionist attitudes in the post-war era. Economies had shielded themselves from outside economic forces by exchange controls, restrictive fiscal regimes, and domestic markets closed to outsiders. By the end of 1984 in

Europe, most of these national barriers had been removed. Arguably, the mid-1980s was the most liberalised and unfettered period for international securities markets in modern history. There were few securities market regulators and concerns about investor protection were still some way off.

The next discernible period is from 1984 until 1999, or until the introduction of the euro. As markets liberalised in Europe and opened up to foreign competition, the need to put in place codes of conduct and measures to protect the interests of individual investors grew. Europe was building the foundations of the single market. Increasingly, governments and regulators were concerned about the globalisation of the markets and the integrity of the financial system. The Basel Accord was one of the early products of this concern, and the Group of 30 report on derivatives in 1993 a further signal. These concerns were well justified as market crises continued, threatening the financial system as capital flowed increasingly freely across international borders. There were times when the old protectionism looked attractive again, as evidenced by Malaysia closing its economy in response to the Asian crisis in 1998.

The introduction of the single European currency in 1999 heralded the modern era of the markets and resulted in the conversion of the international debt market into a largely dual currency market. With the disappearance of the legacy currencies, market convergence plays and currency plays became redundant and investors focused on credit. The rise of this credit market occurred in a low nominal interest rate environment, which followed a long period of high interest rates. Investors, hungry for high returns, were enticed to consider riskier credits or looked to invest in structured derivative products which would provide, higher, leveraged returns. This pursuit of high, if not excessive, returns inevitably led to a crisis which has shaken the global financial system to its roots; first in the form of a global banking crisis then leading on to a disturbing sovereign debt crisis.

This then raises the issue of regulation. Previous histories of the Eurobond market have either pre-dated, or chosen to ignore, the development of financial markets regulation. But our story would make little sense if we did not cover regulatory matters, and the profound impact of regulation on the Euromarkets both now and in the future. Key landmarks in the development of European, and where relevant, US regulation are addressed in the text.

* * *

But what is history? The eminent historian Professor E.H. Carr, in a series of lectures under the same name, argued that the 'facts' of history are simply those which historians have selected for scrutiny. Historical facts come to us as a result of choices by historians influenced by their own perspective and experience. So it is with the current volume. This is not a comprehensive history of the cross-border debt markets, although it is an attempt to catalogue the development of the investment grade bond market over the last 50 years. Many related areas of the international bond and money markets only receive a cursory mention or, indeed, no mention at all; from commercial paper to repo, to emerging markets, high yield or Islamic sukuk. The path the reader treads is, to a degree, the path the author trod, and the areas of focus in the text reflect the bias of the author's own interests.

My own career in 'high finance' came about somewhat by accident. In the early 1970s the City was still largely dominated by alumni of the British public school system and 'Oxbridge'. I was an economics undergraduate at Manchester University. The university had just embarked on the pioneering idea of an 'Appointments Bureau'; a special office to assist graduates in getting employment when their studies finished. Central to the Appointment Bureau's services was a computer dating facility which matched undergraduates up with suitable companies. I had little interest in the prospect of work after my studies but was obliged to participate in the service and was matched with Dunlop, the tyre and sports equipment manufacturer. Having come from an area of Birmingham where Fort Dunlop, the original tyre factory, was a major employer, this appeared to me to be an uninspiring choice and I did not take up the offer to pursue the match. However as my time at university drew to a close I was summoned to the Appointments Bureau to give an account of my job search. Of course I had done nothing; student life in the 1970s was far too much fun to bother about a career.

The afternoon arrived when I must visit the bureau and I began to panic. Then, by chance, on afternoon television the then Chancellor of the Exchequer, Denis Healey, was speaking at a conference about curbing the excessive pay, or taxing more heavily, stockbrokers and merchant bankers. That was it! I turned to my girlfriend and said, 'I don't want to work, but if I have to, I want to earn a lot of money!' The manager at the Appointments Bureau was somewhat taken aback when an hour later I announced to him that I wanted to be a stockbroker or merchant banker. He knew little of this profession but recalled that one such company had approached the University. After a search, he found details of a stockbroker called Phillips and Drew, and, what's more, they were having an open day for graduates the following day. As the university would pay my expenses I found myself early the next morning on the train to London.

I joined Phillips and Drew in July 1974 and began working on Local Authority Bonds. This was a very active market in which Phillips and Drew had a dominant position. (Unfortunately the Hammersmith and Fulham swap fiasco in 1988 would effectively close the market down.) My destiny was to move into the government bond or 'Gilt-edged' department. However in July 1977 Phillips and Drew decided to enter the burgeoning Eurobond market and hired Philip Howard from Deltec to set up the business. I was offered a role to be Philip's assistant, which sounded a far more exciting prospect to me than a life in long gilts. As the department grew, with further recruits, my prospects of partnership seemed to grow more remote, so I moved to another stockbroking company, Savory Milln where I set up a Eurobond desk myself. In time my sales activities in this minnow of a player became well known to Brian Berry, head of trading at Crédit Suisse White Weld and ultimately to his boss, Oswald Gruebel. At the AIBD's Venice AGM, Mr Gruebel hired me as head of sales for Crédit Suisse First Boston (CSFB). (Mr Gruebel would go on, of course uniquely to be CEO of both major Swiss banks, Crédit Suisse and UBS.) These were vintage years for CSFB when they dominated the new issue league tables under the inspired guidance of Hans-Joerg Rudloff. But CSFB was a highly competitive and aggressive environment and three years later when approached by Samuel Montagu I moved to the UK merchant bank. Samuel Montagu was one of the original Eurobond houses and at this time had hired David Potter from CSFB to lead a renewed thrust into the Euromarkets. The bank was also attractive as, through its partial ownership by Midland Bank, it gave access via Midland's controlling interest, to Trinkaus and Burkhardt, the German private bank; which was key as the deutschemark primary market was just opening up in 1984. I became head of global bond sales for Samuel Montagu, running teams in London, New York, Hong Kong and Tokyo and serving on the bank's Board for nine years. In time, Midland Bank took full ownership of Samuel Montagu and thereby became the first British clearing bank to own a London merchant bank, now renamed Midland Montagu.

Midland Bank's fortunes waned after its disastrous purchase of a majority share in Crocker National Bank of California in 1980. In 1987 HSBC took a 15% investment in Midland and in 1992 HSBC Holdings plc acquired full ownership of Midland Bank. As my sales role would now be confined to Europe, I suggested to management that I change direction and establish a department for capital markets coverage for the Middle East, India and Africa. This business grew steadily over subsequent years with an increasing number of bond and loan issues for borrowers from the region until the Asian crisis blew up in 1998. In the belt-tightening which followed, HSBC closed many peripheral operations and my department fell victim to the cuts.

Before long, Robert Gray, Managing Director of HSBC, and Chairman of the International Primary Market Association (IPMA) approached me to work as a consultant to IPMA covering membership and IT initiatives, in particular developing a cross-market bookbuilding system, IPMA Match. As IPMA's finances were strained I also developed and ran a training course for the primary markets, the IPMA Diploma. When IPMA merged with ISMA in 2005 to form ICMA, I became a Senior Advisor to ICMA and the IPMA Diploma joined the suite of courses run by ICMA Executive Education as the Primary Market Certificate. I now run courses on a wide range of topics from the Debt Capital Markets to European Regulation. This background has left me well placed to embark upon the current text.

One of the original plans, particularly for the earlier part of the book, was to interview prominent market participants to record their experiences. While interviews are used, their use was limited as it became apparent that people's memories over a span of fifty years can be hazy; oft repeated stories contained different details or numbers each time they were recounted. It therefore proved a more fruitful strategy to search out as much available source material as possible, hopefully recorded closer to the time of the actual events, to make the narrative as accurate as possible. Yet even amongst source publications there are often discrepancies in the information, for as simple a matter as the coupon and term of a particular bond issue. *Euromoney*, *EuroWeek* and IFR (*International Financing Review*) articles written at the time proved an immense help. Any inaccuracies that still remain are my responsibility.

Completing this volume would have been nigh on impossible without the kind assistance of the Board and senior management of the International Capital Market Association, both in terms of their generous support and advice and the access they afforded to ICMA's internal archives and publications.

Further thanks must go to Euromoney Publications with their flagship publications *Euromoney* and *EuroWeek* (now renamed *Global Capital*), and Thomson Reuters with 'IFR'; they have chronicled every development in the Eurobond market since the 1970s. They are an essential and often quoted source of detailed bond market information.

Special thanks also go to Stanilas Yassukovich and Robert Gray for reviewing the text and for Hans-Joerg Rudloff for kindly agreeing to write the Foreword.

My thanks must also go to colleagues and friends in the market, and participants on my training courses, who have encouraged me to stick with the book when occasionally my enthusiasm waned.

Most importantly I must thank my long-suffering wife, Brenda. Throughout my career in the market, when I worked long hours in London or spent extensive periods abroad, she managed to bring up a large family without a great deal of help from me. And now for more almost three years she has put up with me huddled every day in my office at home while the house and garden fell into neglect.

On finishing the narrative, my wife, who had been clearing out her parent's home, presented me with a booklet entitled, *A Guide to the Eurobond Market*, dated 1979. This was an internal publication from Phillips and Drew. I had been one of its authors 35 years ago, and had not seen the document in 30 years. Yet here I was many years later undertaking the same task but on a bigger scale. Why?

Perhaps it is the sense of good fortune for having lived through such an exciting time in international finance, to have been given so much responsibility, to have travelled the world, and been well rewarded for doing so. I only need reflect on the gulf between my career and the working life of my own father; a semi-skilled welder in a Midlands car factory for 40 years; more than 10 years of which were spent on the night shift.

Perhaps it is a sense of fellowship. At the end of the day markets are simply about people, and I have been lucky enough to work with many fine and talented people in the cross-border markets; many are friends still. I cannot express it better than Stanislas Yassukovich did years ago in the *AIBD Gazette* in April 1982 on the occasion of the passing of the eminent euromarketeer, André Coussement:

> *No-one can fail to be impressed by the statistical evidence of the Eurobond market's importance in the world financial scenery. Statistics only tell part of the story, however. At the end of the day, regardless of the league tables, the rankings, the size of the issues, or the turnover which may illustrate the contribution of a particular institution or group of firms to the market as a whole, it is still the people who count: it is the individual operators who have influenced the general course of the market and its tone at any particular moment in its evolution.*

CHAPTER 1

Before the Beginning

To 1962

The origins of bond markets can be traced back to governments and their need to borrow, particularly in times of war. In the late Middle Ages, the Republic of Venice was involved in recurring conflicts with neighbouring states. The authorities, concerned about the strains on the state treasury, took to drawing forced loans from their citizens in proportion to their wealth. Such debt paid 5% interest per year and had an indefinite maturity date. Initially regarded with some suspicion, they came to be seen as valuable investments that could be bought and sold. The bond market had begun.

From the medieval Italian city states to warring European powers looking to finance military campaigns, the issuance of interest-bearing debt has enabled them to pursue their ambitions. Much of this debt, like that of Venice, was undated with governments creating a permanent funded debt burden. The amount of debt that could be issued depended on the investor's confidence in the ability and commitment of the issuer to make the required payments under the contract. Unfortunately sovereign issuers were prone to renege on their debts or change the terms substantially, so the investor's preference was originally for short-dated, high interest loans.

During the latter part of the 16th century the Dutch attained an increasingly dominant position in international trade, especially the lucrative spice trade, a position previously occupied by the Portuguese and Spaniards. Amsterdam became the city where merchants and bankers could obtain bills of exchange to settle their trading activity.[1] At the time, it was customary for a trading company to be set up for the duration of a single voyage, financed by a small group of merchants, and to be wound up upon the return of the vessels. Investment in these expeditions was a high-risk venture, not only because of the dangers of sickness, piracy and shipwreck, but also because of changing market conditions for the imported goods. The further a trading expedition ventured, the greater the risks involved, and the greater the number of investors required to finance it. In 1602 the Dutch government sponsored the formation of the Dutch East India Company, which was given a monopoly over Asian trade for a continuous period of 21 years. It was the first company to issue shares and the offering attracted more than a thousand Dutch investors. As the financial outcome of voyages was not known until a particular expedition was completed, the shares varied widely in value and a secondary market soon developed between merchants, investors and speculators. As Asian spices were

1

imported in bulk to meet the seemingly insatiable appetite in Europe, huge profits accrued to the shareholders.

The Dutch came to dominate trade in Europe. They were favourably positioned at the centre of a network of European trade routes. Dutch traders shipped wine from France and Portugal to the Baltic countries and returned with grain for countries around the Mediterranean. By the 1680s, an average of nearly 1,000 Dutch ships entered the Baltic Sea each year. The Dutch were also able to gain control of much of the trade with the young English colonies in North America.

The accumulation of capital in the enormous amounts generated in this period caused a demand for productive investment opportunities. Wealthy investors with cash balances found that investing in loans and securities was a more portable and flexible way of managing their wealth, rather than relying solely on the revenue from their estates or their trading ventures. So it was among the merchants of Amsterdam that active trading in securities first developed and led to the establishment of the Amsterdam Stock Exchange and the Bank of Amsterdam.

With only a modest domestic government bond market, wealthy Dutch investors became interested in loans issued by foreign governments. Dutch public loans offered yields of only 2–3% whereas foreign government loans offered 4–6% yields. Consequently European states became accustomed to funding part of their budget deficits by selling bonds to wealthy international investors through specialist intermediaries, based in Amsterdam.

Prominent amongst these intermediaries was Hope & Company. The firm was founded in 1762, but members of the Hope family – originating in Scotland and arriving in Amsterdam via Rotterdam – had already been involved in the money and commodity trade since 1720. In the aftermath of the Seven Years War (1756–1763), after Henry Hope had joined the firm, Hope & Co. arranged numerous loans for the governments of Sweden, Russia, Poland, Portugal and Bavaria. Many of these loans were made in exchange for trading privileges. The Portuguese loan was made in return for an exclusive concession to market diamonds from the Portuguese colony of Brazil. Hope & Co. sold the diamonds on the Amsterdam market, and the sale proceeds provided the interest and principal on the loan. This activity contributed to Amsterdam becoming the leading diamond centre of Europe.

The bank floated 10 loans for the Kingdom of Sweden between 1767 and 1787 and 18 loans for Russia from 1788 to 1793.[2] The first loan to Catherine the Great's Russia was for Fl.3m in 1788 at a rate of 4.5% and many more followed. In return for these loans, Hope & Co. obtained the right to export sugar to Russia, and sell Russian wheat and timber to countries throughout Europe. In fact Hope and Co. remained bankers to the Czars until 1917.[3]

The bank was also involved in financing plantation owners in the West Indies, taking payment in kind: sugar, coffee or tobacco, which Hopes would then sell on the Amsterdam market. For the majority of these loans, Hope led a syndicate of prominent English and Dutch investors who provided the funds, while Hope & Co. collected a handsome commission of 5–9%.*

---

*In 1962, with the increasing consolidation of the banking industry, Hope & Co. sought an alliance with R. Mees & Zoonen, initially as a joint venture and then as a fully merged company under the name Mees & Hope, Bankiers. In 1975 Bank Mees & Hope became a wholly owned subsidiary of ABN. It was subsequently sold to Fortis Bank in 1991 but acquired back when Fortis Bank Nederland merged with ABN AMRO in 2010. The private banking business of the combined bank was renamed ABN AMRO MeesPierson.

The securities trading methods and practices established in Amsterdam spread to other financial centres. As markets grew rapidly, speculative booms developed, most notably, the South Sea Bubble in London and the Mississippi Bubble in Paris. The first led to restrictions on joint-stock companies in England while the second led to the French government establishing the first formal stock exchange in Paris in 1724. Paris and London continued to vie with Amsterdam as growing financial centres throughout the 18th century although their focus was on domestic government stock and issuance by domestic joint-stock companies. Amsterdam remained the principal centre for international trading.[4]

* * *

From 1789 to 1815 revolution, then war, spread through Europe with profound consequences for the developing securities markets. The French Revolution of 1789 had a significant impact throughout Europe, with the proclamation of a Republic in 1792 and the execution of King Louis XVI the following year for 'crimes of tyranny' against the French people. The outbreak of European wars, originally intended to defend and then spread the influence of the French Revolution, prompted the Republican government in France to renege on a major part of the previous monarchy's debts.

Napoleon Bonaparte seized power in 1799 after overthrowing the French revolutionary government. There followed a series of wars where French forces battled various coalitions of European nations between 1803 and 1815. French power rose quickly as Napoleon's armies conquered much of Europe.

But as the conflict spread, other governments also ceased to pay interest on their debts and in some cases even acknowledge their indebtedness, all the more so if such debts were owed to foreign investors. Numerous sovereign defaults ensued and the international securities markets collapsed.

In 1803 Britain declared war on France and, aided by its island status and naval supremacy, remained at war until 1815. The British government, in addition, paid out large sums of money to other European states, so that they would remain at war with France. But the cost of war drained Britain's resources, and ran up a considerable national debt. The British government was borrowing heavily, not only to build up her own forces, but also to subsidise her European allies whose capital markets were no longer operating.

Between 1810 and 1814, the Netherlands was annexed to France and the French franc circulated in place of the 'gulden'. International trading links broke down. As the Amsterdam market suffered, so that of London prospered. International trade increasingly gravitated towards British merchants.

Yet during this period of turbulence a landmark bond transaction took place involving for the first time on a major scale, cooperation between the financial markets. This was 'the Louisiana Purchase'. Spain had secretly granted the Territory of Louisiana, in North America, to France in 1801. The territory stretched across the entire Mississippi Valley, to the Rockies in the west, to Canada in the north and southwards to the Gulf of Mexico. An area roughly equivalent to a third of the United States today, encompassing all or part of 15 US states. Louisiana was of diminishing strategic importance to France and Napoleon believed that it could be a liability in any future war with Britain. When approached to sell it to the US government, he agreed.

The sum needed for the purchase was beyond the means of the US government and so help was sought from the two leading merchant banks at the time, Hope & Co. of Amsterdam and Barings of London. Barings had well-established connections with both the US and France, and Hopes were the leading issuer of sovereign loans, and the banks themselves were linked through family connections. Negotiations were conducted during a brief period of peace between Britain and France. The size of the transaction was unprecedented, as France demanded FF100m for the territory. The parties agreed that the financing could only be achieved by the issue of US government bonds and the price finally agreed was FF80m (equivalent to $15m). After the American bonds had been issued, the French government then sold them on to Hopes and Barings at a discount of 87\frac{1}{2}$ per $100. The bonds were issued in 1804, and rank among the first US securities issued in the international markets. The coupon of 6% was payable half yearly in Amsterdam, London or Paris. In fact Napoleon was so desperate for funds that the bankers advanced FF10m of the funds ahead of the bond issue. The issue was an evident success for the underwriters with all bonds placed at or above par.[5]

* * *

A rapidly expanding industrial economy and the success of the new income tax (introduced to finance the war against France) meant the London market was growing as the fortunes of the international securities markets waned. For foreign investors at a time of widespread sovereign default, British government debt was viewed as a safe haven. Bankers and brokers from other financial centres moved to London as the only centre still operating normally. One noteworthy immigrant was Nathan Rothschild.

Mayer Amschel Rothschild founded the house of M.A. Rothschild in Frankfurt in the 1790s. Starting out as a coin and bill dealership, his business developed into offering financial services to wealthy German clients and Prussian nobility. 'Court Jews' as they were known, were opportunists operating on the principle that courtly patronage would lead to a range of advantageous state and commercial benefits. In 1816 Amschel advised his brother 'Business transactions with royalties always end in a profitable way. Please do not let the smallest business go by.'[6]

In the early 19th century the five sons of Mayer Amschel Rothschild set out from their home in Frankfurt to establish businesses in Europe's principal financial centres: London, Paris, Frankfurt, Naples and Vienna. His third son, Nathan, at the age of 21, left Frankfurt for England. After 10 years working as a textile merchant in Manchester, he took a small office near the Bank of England in London, where, with a large sum of money given to him by his father, he set up a banking house. His brothers followed his example and in time they had established a family network of banks in Europe's financial centres.

By 1811 Nathan Rothschild had begun to involve himself in British war finance. The British government used the Rothschild family network to relay funds to troops in the field and subsidy payments to Britain's European allies.

After the peace of 1815 the first big international financial transaction was an 1817 loan to France, however Rothschild was excluded from the deal. It was a loan to allow France to pay war indemnities and so facilitate the evacuation of foreign troops and was arranged by the experienced partnership of Barings and Hope & Co.

When the British wartime subsidies ran out as the conflict ended, so her allies, particularly Austria, Prussia and Russia, the so-called 'Holy Alliance', found themselves in financial straits. The post-war Prussian deficit amounted to Thaler 188 million (£32 million). Their own continental markets were not capable of raising sufficient finance so it needed to be raised in London. In fact the idea for a London loan came from the Prussian Seehandlung Bank in

London, but they had proposed it be raised in Prussian Thaler.[7] Nathan Rothschild took a different view.

The end of the Napoleonic Wars found English merchants and aristocracy with substantial sums to invest. As the financial momentum had swung towards London so Nathan Rothschild decided that future foreign government borrowings should be denominated in sterling to attract these investors. Heavy domestic government issuance had crowded out foreign issuance in the past. Interest would be payable in sterling in London rather than in Prussian Thaler in Berlin. Seehandlung Bank would be responsible for ensuring the necessary payments were transferred to Rothschilds in London. He insisted the bonds should be in bearer form rather than in the registered form favoured by some European governments and included a British style sinking fund to ensure the amortisation of the loan.[8] These features would attract British investors, along with the bond providing a more attractive yield than the 3% available on British 'Consols' (Consolidated government stock) at the time.

The new loan was not just offered in London but throughout Europe via the Rothschild network of offices. Despite the initial opposition in Berlin, particularly from the German bankers, the £5 million Prussian loan of 1818 was an outstanding success attracting both British investors and major European financiers. With this initial success Nathan was able to raise a further Prussian loan in 1822.

Despite the obvious success of the sterling loans not all governments were enthusiastic about following the Prussian example. Cash-strapped Russia favoured a rouble transaction. Rothschild came up with a sterling loan similar to the Prussian loan but with the option to pay interest in sterling in London or roubles in St Petersburg with the exchange rate fixed at the outset.[9] Before long, the overwhelming majority of sovereign issuance was launched in sterling via London; either as a straight sterling loan targeted at British investors or with the ability to pay interest in foreign currency to attract both domestic and foreign investors. These bond issues of 1818 and 1822 became the template for sovereign bond issuance for more than a century. The economic historian Niall Ferguson declares these Prussian and Russian loans to be among the first, if not *the* first, Eurobonds.[10]

Between 1822 and 1825 British merchant banks issued 20 foreign loans totalling £40 million. Of these, 12 were for new Latin American Republics, largely building on the template Rothschild had set. Many featured a syndicate of European merchant banks looking to attract subscriptions from as wide an investor base as possible. To accommodate trading in the new loans the London Stock Exchange established a 'Foreign Funds' market which was absorbed into the main market in the 1830s.[11] In England it became the custom to underwrite issues at fixed prices by having banks enter into purchase contracts with issuers, thereby assuming the market risk of success or failure. The need for syndication was expressed by Nathan Rothschild to London colleagues in 1865: 'I think you will not only require your friend Baring, but likewise some of the joint-stock banks to unite with you, and however disagreeable it may be to have such partners, if it is the means of making the affair go down, you ought not to mind it.'[12]

$$* \quad * \quad *$$

The dominance of government issuance in the securities markets came under threat as the 19th century progressed. From the middle of the 18th century, British industry increased rapidly because canals provided the means for the movement of raw materials and manufactured goods. The needs of the new industrial age required development and infrastructure projects necessitating substantial up-front investments. The canal companies had sought capital before

1800 but now they were joined by the needs of gas and water network projects and by the railway 'mania' of the 1840s.

The British railway network, the oldest in the world, was developed in a piecemeal fashion by small private railway companies. In 1825 the government had repealed the Bubble Act, brought in after the South Sea Bubble fiasco, which restricted new business ventures and had limited joint-stock companies to a maximum of five investors. With these limits removed the newly emerging middle class could invest their savings in new industries and railway companies presented an exciting opportunity. During the railway boom of the 1840s the proliferation of competing small railway companies were linked up to form a national network.

The new railways reduced the cost of shipping by carriage by 60–70%, so it was not long before railway 'fever' spread to other countries. Large numbers of bond issues were launched for British and foreign railways from the United States, China, France and other countries throughout the 1840s and 1850s. In the United States new 'railroads' developed swiftly across the vast continent and European banking firms forged alliances with US securities firms to participate in the business.[13] In 1860 Henry Varnum Poor, a financial analyst, published a *History of Railroads and Canals in the United States*. This book was an attempt to compile comprehensive information about the financial and operational state of US railroad companies and was annually updated. This would evolve into the financial analysis company and rating agency Standard & Poor's.

So by the middle of the century corporate securities were beginning to challenge the dominance of government debt. While the railways led the way, they were closely followed by other public services. In addition the growth of the banking and insurance industries bolstered the securities markets. But key to the development of the international securities markets was the development of international communications.

In 1832 Samuel F.B. Morse, among others, worked on the idea for an electromechanical telegraph. The flow of electricity through a wire was interrupted for shorter or longer periods by holding down the key of the device. The resulting sequences of dots or dashes enabled messages to be transmitted. The first commercial telegraph lines were completed between Washington, Philadelphia and New York in the spring of 1846. This enabled links between stock exchanges on the US east coast. The *New York Herald* of 3 March 1846 records 'certain parties in New York and Philadelphia were employing the telegraph for speculating in stocks.'[14] At this time other telegraph systems based on rival technologies were being built. Amsterdam and Rotterdam were connected by telegraph in 1847 and Berlin and Frankfurt linked in 1849.[15] With messaging between markets now taking minutes rather than days, national markets became increasingly internationally connected via telegraph. A trans-Atlantic cable was successfully completed in July 1866 and four days later the *New York Evening Post* published price quotations from the London Stock Exchange.[16]

Throughout the second half of the 19th century, London and Paris were the principal financial centres in which large foreign bond markets existed.[17] One of Rothschild's principal rivals in France, and similarly well-connected with foreign governments, were the Paris-based bankers, Erlanger et Cie. They played a major role in channeling French capital into railroads and land development in the southern states of the US during and after the American Civil War. Baron Frederic Emile d'Erlanger was married to Matilde Slidell, the daughter of Louisiana merchant, lawyer and politician, John Slidell. Slidell was the Ambassador of the Confederate States of America at the court of Emperor Napoleon III. The Confederate States had relied heavily on import tariffs and taxes on exports to finance their war effort. However they introduced a trade embargo on cotton exports in 1861 in an attempt to starve Europe of cotton and thereby try to force international diplomatic recognition of the Confederacy. Meanwhile the Union Navy blockaded southern ports. With dwindling revenues from exports, the Confederate government raised taxes and increasingly printed money.

Foreign debt finance was an alternative, but the Confederate currency was considered worthless in Europe. Moreover the principal merchant banks in London were reluctant to be seen as supporting the Confederacy, particularly as they were suffering repeated defeats in the conflict. The Confederate government therefore entered into an arrangement with Emile Erlanger et Cie. for the so-called Erlanger Loan or 'Cotton Bonds'.

The loan for £3m or FF75m was issued in five European cities, London, Liverpool, Paris, Amsterdam and Frankfurt with a fixed coupon of 7%. *The Times* of London commented on 18 March 1863:

> *One of its peculiar features is that the bonds are to be exchangeable against cotton, the latter being taken at the fixed price of 6d per pound. This arrangement is of course designed by way of attraction to the speculative appetite; for supposing it were possible to get the cotton away and sell it at Liverpool at 12d per pound (which is less than half the present price,) the holder of a bond which has cost £90 might get from £180 to £200. In every respect this is a very remarkable operation … As a matter of course, the security of the bondholders will depend entirely upon the ability of the South to maintain its independence.*

The bond issue was allegedly over-subscribed five times with even the British Chancellor of the Exchequer at the time, William Gladstone, a willing investor. All this, despite the fact that cotton shipments would need to be collected in the blockaded southern ports.

Erlanger did very well out of the issue which they had purchased at a face value of £77 to offer at £90 plus taking a 5% fee for their efforts. In addition they established the European Trading Company, a shipping company targeted at evading Union ships and breaking the blockade in the Gulf of Mexico. For a significant fee, cotton would be delivered to Bermuda, the Bahamas or Cuba for transport onwards to anxious European bondholders. After the Confederate forces defeat at Gettysburg, the bond price collapsed. Some commentators claim these 'Cotton bonds' as the first true Eurobonds.

*   *   *

As international markets became more connected what could be done about foreign exchange risk? From the earliest times, gold and silver had provided a common medium of exchange with goods being exchanged for gold and silver coins. If the coins were unfamiliar, then a merchant simply weighed the coins, assessed or rather 'assayed' their purity, then calculated what weight of pure gold or silver they represented. In Britain, the Anglo-Saxons introduced silver pennies or 'sterlings' and 240 of these weighed exactly one pound weight. As trade proliferated it became unwieldy to carry around vast quantities of coins or bullion so bankers began to issue paper notes representing a particular quantity of gold or silver. Goldsmiths had issued bank notes – promises to pay set against gold deposits – from the 16th century. In 1717 Britain fixed £1 to 113grains (7.32g) of fine gold, rather than its original silver. This so-called 'gold standard' fixed the value of money by allowing it to be converted into a certain amount of gold. People could now have faith in 'paper money'. In the 1870s Germany joined Britain on the gold standard and by the end of the 1870s nearly the whole world was on the gold standard. As a result exchange rates only moved after an agreed adjustment which largely removed foreign exchange risk. Trade expanded rapidly under the gold standard, as did international capital markets.

But there was a down side to the gold standard in that it would transmit economic cycles and financial crises around the world as fast as the telegraph could carry them. Governments faced with the need to fund high levels of expenditure, but with limited sources of tax revenue, suspended convertibility of currency into gold on a number of occasions in the 19th century. The British government suspended convertibility during the Napoleonic wars and the US government during the US Civil War. In both cases, convertibility was resumed after the war.

* * *

By the dawn of the 20th century national stock exchanges proliferated but they were no longer confined by their national boundaries. The international securities markets had become a significant source of corporate financing for developed economies. With an absence of major conflicts, government borrowing declined while corporate issuances grew. In general by 1914 corporate stocks and bonds had overtaken government debt in importance, with around 60% of the securities in existence having been issued by companies, compared to only 40% by government.[18]

Before the First World War the British pound sterling was the most important international currency, and the City of London was the world's most important financial centre. More than 60% of global trade was financed, invoiced and settled in sterling, and the largest proportion of official reserves, apart from gold, was held in sterling. The City of London was the undisputed centre of international finance with 387 loans issued for 54 different sovereign borrowers in the period from 1866 to 1914. The London market was attractive because interest rates were generally lower than elsewhere, and restrictions on foreign loans were less in London than in competing financial centres.[19]

However the period before the First World War was one of increasing political tension among the European powers. From 1815 onwards the major European nations had gone to considerable lengths to maintain a balance of power throughout Europe, resulting by 1900 in a complicated network of political and military alliances across the continent. But with a host of unresolved territorial disputes, a mood of growing nationalism and increasing militarism was developing. On 28 June 1914, the Archduke Franz Ferdinand, heir to the Austrian throne, was shot and killed by a Serb terrorist, while visiting Sarajevo. Austria was already hostile towards Serbia, and now it decided on retaliation. On 28 July 1914, Austria declared war on Serbia.

Now the alliance system swung into play. On 30 July, Russia started mobilisation in support of Serbia. In reaction, Germany, in support of Austria, declared war against Russia on 1 August. Germany declared war on France, and demanded free passage across Belgium. Britain was a particularly reluctant participant in the growing tensions, more concerned with the troubles in Northern Ireland. Nonetheless Britain pledged to support Belgium and on 4 August a British ultimatum to Germany was refused. Britain therefore declared war on Germany, while Germany declared war on Belgium, and launched an invasion of the country. Finally, on 5 August, Austria declared war on Russia. The horrors of the First World War were about to unfold.

A government can finance a war in only three ways: it can raise taxes, it can borrow or it can print money. Increasing taxes is the most painful and unpopular, while opportunities for debt financing may be limited and put pressure on interest rates. Printing money, however, makes war seem costless to the average person. The economic situation in Europe when war broke out led many to believe an extended conflict would be ruinously expensive and therefore the war would be over in weeks or months at worst. Unfortunately ways were found to fund the fighting.

In August 1914 the gold reserves of the Bank of England amounted to nine million pounds (at the time £1 = US\$4.85). The banks feared the declaration of war would trigger a run on the banks, so the Chancellor, David Lloyd George, extended the August bank holiday for three days to allow time for the passing of the Currency and Bank Notes Act, by which Britain left the gold standard. Most belligerent countries followed the UK in leaving the gold standard during the war, and as a result suffered significant inflation.

The international securities markets were not prepared for a major European war and it came as a considerable shock. Markets collapsed as investors panicked and looked to sell whatever securities they could. In response, to avoid a meltdown, authorities closed down stock exchanges around the world. Only the New York Stock Sxchange remained open and only the US dollar remained convertible into gold.

But while markets for corporate stocks remained subdued, the supply of government bonds in national markets exploded, as authorities looked to tap domestic savings to finance the war effort. The international securities market shrank and gravitated to New York as domestic government paper swamped investors. Investors were either enticed or forced to sell foreign investments and support the home war effort. American investors purchased more than \$3bn of US securities previously held in Europe. Between 1917 and 1919 they were also called on to absorb \$17bn of US Liberty Loans and a victory loan of \$4.5bn.[20] And it was to the US market that Britain and her allies looked to for much needed funds. In the period August 1914 to April 1917 Britain borrowed \$1,250m, France \$640m and Russia \$107m.[21]

Before the First World War the US was a substantial debtor country and its growth was financed in large part by European capital. When the war began the US economy was in recession. But the war stimulated the US economy, increased employment and raised the profitability of US industry as the demand for US materials in Europe escalated. Steel production reached twice its pre-war level by 1917. US farmers enjoyed boom years as agricultural prices rose and the international market for their products expanded. Annual incomes rose steadily, from \$580 in 1914 to more than \$1,300 by 1920. Now US citizens had money to invest. By the 1920s the US found itself as the world's largest creditor nation, being owed significant sums of money by most of the combatant nations involved in the First World War. After the war the US began investing large amounts overseas, particularly in Latin America, taking a role previously played by London.

Following Germany's defeat, reparations were set by the Allied victors at the Treaty of Versailles in 1919 – as compensation and punishment for the 1914–18 war. Most of the money was intended to go to Belgium and France, who had suffered the greatest devastation from the war, and to repay the Allies some of their war expenditure.

The victors in 1919 were in no mood to be charitable, and the initial sum agreed upon for war damages was 226 billion gold marks, the equivalent of around 100,000 tonnes of pure gold. This 100,000 tonnes of gold was clearly beyond the means of the Germans to pay. Consequently their only way of paying back the debt was in foreign currency, but attempts to purchase foreign currency with the devalued paper Marks in circulation led to hyperinflation.

The principal representative of the British Treasury at the Paris Peace Conference, John Maynard Keynes, resigned from the Treasury in June 1919 in protest at the scale of the reparations demands, and subsequently protested publicly in the best-selling book *The Economic Consequences of the Peace* (1919). Keynes exposed the folly of imposing on Germany a debt of more than three times its pre-war annual GDP, which was to be repaid over a period of decades. He warned that the reparations threatened to destabilise the German economy, and German politics: 'If we aim deliberately at the impoverishment of Central Europe, vengeance, I dare predict, will not limp.' The 1924 Dawes Plan modified Germany's reparation payments and in May 1929, the Young Plan reduced the payments further to 112 billion gold marks.

*   *   *

The United States was now a financial superpower eclipsing that of Britain. Yet after the war Britain sought to return to its former pre-eminence, ignoring the consequences of the war. Winston Churchill returned sterling to the gold standard in 1925 at the pre-war rate of £4.86 to the dollar. This rate of exchange for sterling had been unchanged since Sir Isaac Newton, Master of the Mint, set it in the 18th century, and now was seriously overvalued. The dollar's growing dominance was reducing sterling's importance as a reserve currency.

The financial imbalance between the US and Europe was growing and the Federal Reserve maintained a low interest rate policy to support the dollar sterling exchange rate. Encouraged by the low US rates foreign borrowers were attracted to the New York market. It is estimated that US investors absorbed US$3.6bn in European securities between 1921 and 1926 for both sovereign and corporate borrowers.[22] Much of the debt offered in the foreign bond market during the 1920s and early 1930s defaulted during the Second World War. Investors in new issues like the First Bohemian Glass Works (of Czechoslovakia) 7.5% due 1957 issued in 1927 or the City of Warsaw 7% 30-year bonds issued in 1928 could not imagine the devastation that was to be wrought on those countries in the subsequent conflict.[23]

The US was now enjoying a great sense of confidence, optimism and prosperity. By the mid-1920s the economic boom was fuelling a speculative frenzy on Wall Street. US investors were being tempted by the increasing returns available on the New York Stock Exchange. A significant number of them were borrowing money, at the prevailing low rates, to buy more stocks. By August 1929, brokers were routinely lending small investors more than two-thirds of the face value of the stocks they were buying. Over $8.5bn was out on loan, more than the entire amount of currency circulating in the US at the time. From 1921 to 1929 the Dow Jones rose from 60 to almost 400.

Because of margin buying, investors stood to lose large sums of money if the market turned down – or even failed to advance quickly enough. On 24 October 1929, with the Dow just past its 3 September peak of 381.17, the market finally turned down, and panic selling started. The falls in share prices on 24 and 29 October 1929 prompted panic and price falls in all major markets. During November alone the Dow Jones collapsed from close to 400 to 145. The 1929 Wall Street crash brought the 'Roaring Twenties' to a grinding halt.

The decline in stock prices caused bankruptcies and severe economic difficulties including contraction of credit, business closures and redundancies. Banks began to fail as debtors defaulted and depositors attempted to withdraw their deposits en masse, triggering multiple bank runs. Bank failures multiplied as desperate bankers called in loans which the borrowers did not have time or money to repay. With future profits looking poor, capital investment and construction slowed or completely ceased. The liquidation of debt could not keep up with the fall of prices which it caused; eventually turning a recession into a depression.

One response to shore up the ailing US economy was the protectionist Smoot Hawley Tariff Act of 1930, which raised US tariffs on over 20,000 imported goods to record levels. This Act prompted retaliatory measures by other countries and is often considered as marking the beginning of the Great Depression when international trade plunged by 50 % and where, by 1932, US unemployment reached 25%.

It was the longest, most widespread, and deepest depression of the 20th century, leading to mass unemployment and mass poverty. The majority of countries set up relief programmes, and most underwent some sort of political upheaval, pushing them to the left or right. In Germany the emergence of the National Socialist Party, out of the chaos of hyperinflation, would set the stage for the Second World War in 1939.

Many believed that the depression was spread around the globe by the rigidities of the gold standard. Accordingly every major currency left the gold standard during the Great Depression as countries tried to stimulate domestic demand by devaluing their currencies. Exchange controls were introduced, isolating one economy from another. The liberal global securities market of 1914 was now replaced by a series of restrictive compartmentalised markets under domestic government supervision.

When sterling left the gold standard in 1931, many other currencies – about half the world's total – chose to leave with it and many countries opted to remain pegged to sterling. This gave rise to the 'sterling bloc', which during and after the Second World War would evolve into the sterling area.

*   *   *

Crisis always brings regulation in its wake. In reaction to the Wall Street crash and the ensuing depression, and at President Franklin Roosevelt's instigation, Congress set out to enact laws that would prevent further speculative securities frenzies. After a series of hearings that brought to light the severity of the abuses leading to the crash, Congress enacted the Securities Act of 1933 (the 'Securities Act') governing the issue of securities, and the Securities Exchange Act of 1934 (the 'Exchange Act') which regulated the trading of securities. The key theme of the new federal securities law was the need to give investors access to information about the securities they buy and the companies that issue securities. Federal securities laws primarily accomplished this by putting the burden on companies to disclose information about themselves and the securities they issue and the adoption of GAAP (Generally Accepted Accounting Principles). Companies looking to issue securities publicly must disclose important financial information through the registration of securities. These disclosure requirements are backed up by broad liability for fraud under the Securities Act and the Exchange Act for both issuers and sellers of securities.

The 1933 Act was the first major federal legislation to regulate the offer and sale of securities. Prior to the Act, regulation of securities was chiefly governed by state laws, commonly referred to as 'blue sky' laws. In addition, the Exchange Act created the Securities and Exchange Commission (SEC), a federal agency that had the authority to enforce federal law and its own rules. The SEC also regulates the securities business. Under the Exchange Act, the SEC has the authority to register, regulate and discipline broker-dealers, regulate the securities exchanges, and review actions of the securities exchanges' self-regulatory organisations (SROs).

In addition to the new securities laws, new banking laws came into force to reform the banking system and control speculative activity. The Banking Act of 1933 sometimes referred to as the Glass-Steagall Act (although only four sections directly relate to Glass-Steagall), prohibited commercial banks from engaging in the investment business. It protected bank depositors from the additional risks associated with security transactions. It was enacted as an emergency response to the failure of nearly 5,000 banks during the Great Depression. It gave tighter regulation of national banks to the Federal Reserve System; prohibited bank sales of securities; and created the Federal Deposit Insurance Corporation (FDIC), which insures bank deposits.

Banks were given a year to decide on whether they would specialise in commercial or in investment banking. Only 10% of commercial banks' total income could stem from securities. As a result banks such as J.P. Morgan decided to remain as a commercial bank but with a group of managers leaving to set up a securities business as Morgan Stanley. First National Bank of Boston decided to go down the commercial banking route while setting up a separate securities company, First Boston Corporation, in conjunction with Mellon Securities Corporation.

Another development at this time which would have considerable long-term effects on the debt markets was that bank regulators, eager to encourage banks to invest in only safe bonds, issued a set of regulations culminating in a 1936 decree that prohibited banks from investing in 'speculative investment securities' as determined by 'recognised rating manuals'. This put the rating agencies at the heart of investment decision making in the US.

*   *   *

Unlike the First World War, the Second World War was widely expected in Europe. Indeed the armaments expansion ahead of the anticipated conflict went some way to drag countries out of their economic depression. When war finally arrived, securities markets did not experience panic as they had in 1914. Domestic securities markets were now managed by national authorities with little exposure to international markets. Any foreign securities that still commanded a value had been sold if buyers could be found. As in the First World War there was some evidence of a flight of capital to New York during the war but the evidence suggests that much of this was put on deposit with US banks rather than invested in the securities markets.[24]

The Second World War had put an end to any sense of a global securities market. Governments controlled their domestic markets and any foreign assets had been sold.

Yet in 1944, while still at war, 730 delegates from 44 allied nations met in the US resort of Bretton Woods, looking to rebuild the global financial system when the conflict ended. While 44 countries participated, negotiations were largely driven by the US and the UK. The Bretton Woods Agreement sought to regulate international finance and foreign exchange trading to prevent economic collapses like the 1930s Depression. The principal architect of the agreement, the celebrated economist, John Maynard Keynes, argued that capital controls were necessary to preserve and protect industry and society. He advocated the use of fiscal and monetary measures to reduce the effects of economic recessions and depressions. Similarly he stressed that no economy was independent of other economies and argued for a world currency and a world central bank. Two new institutions, later known as the World Bank and International Monetary Fund (IMF), were founded as a compromise to Keynes's plans, reflecting the more conservative American vision.

An attempt was made to return to a system of fixed exchange rates. The chief features of the monetary system agreement were an obligation for each country to adopt a monetary policy that maintained the exchange rate by tying its currency to the US dollar, with the IMF offering short-term help to avoid devaluation. The fixing of exchange values or parities permitted only a 1% appreciation or depreciation from the exchange value agreed. The United States agreed separately to establish and maintain the international value of the dollar at $35 per ounce of gold, making the system a modified form of gold standard. Foreign nations would use the dollar as an intervention currency, and would keep their reserves in dollars as well as gold.

At the conference's farewell dinner, Keynes told the assembled delegates that thanks to their work 'the brotherhood of man will … become more than a phrase'.

The Bretton Woods conference in 1944 effectively marked the end of sterling's predominance in international trade, and its replacement by the US dollar. While the agreement defined both the dollar and the pound as reserve currencies, given the UK's very large balance of payment deficit caused by the war, this was more 'a sop to British pride rather than a reflection of the truth'.[25] By September 1949 the UK's balance of payments deficit finally proved untenable and the pound was devalued by 30%.

As devaluation pressures were most prevalent, European countries were incentivised to build up significant dollar reserves which could be used, if necessary, to support the external value of their currencies. Exchange control regimes were extensively introduced by countries either during the Second World War or put in place in the immediate post-war period. Many of these capital controls persisted throughout the 1950s and beyond.

After the war the allied nations desperately needed US assistance to rebuild their war-torn economies. The United States at the time was running huge balance of trade surpluses, and the US reserves were substantial and growing. In response the United States set up the European Recovery Program (popularly known as 'the Marshall Plan') to provide large-scale financial and economic aid for rebuilding Europe. From 1948 to 1954 the United States provided 16 Western European countries with $17 bn in grants and a further $4.4bn to Japan. Between 1947 and 1958, the US deliberately encouraged an outflow of dollars, and, from 1950 on, the United States ran a balance of payments deficit with the intent of providing liquidity for the international economy. These deficits were exacerbated by the strong international demand for dollars, which kept the exchange rate high, thereby making US exports less competitive.

Over time the quantity of US dollars outside the United States increased significantly, as a result both of the Marshall Plan and US imports. Consequently, large sums of US dollars were in the custody of foreign banks outside the United States. The surplus dollars were mostly kept on deposit by European banks, which in turn held this currency in their New York branches, subsidiaries or correspondent banks.

As Cold War tensions increased, particularly after the invasion of Hungary in 1956, the Soviet and East European countries transferred much of their dollar holdings to Paris and London from New York. This was to prevent the US government confiscating or freezing those deposits. The first transfer by the Soviet Union of a dollar account to a European Bank was to the Banque Commerciale pour l'Europe du Nord, whose telegraphic address was Eurobank. It is suggested that this was the first time in which 'euro' was used in a financial market, and in time a dollar deposit held in Europe became known as a 'Euro-dollar' deposit.[26]

There were more than enough of these Eurodollars for the banks receiving them to lend them on, or redeposit them with other financial institutions. There were no US reserve requirements for Eurodollar deposits. In addition they were outside the jurisdiction of the Federal Reserve Board's Regulation Q, which controlled the rate of interest that could be paid on domestic dollar deposits. From 1935 to 1956 the maximum rate payable in the US on 30-day deposits was 1%, and 2.5% on three-month deposits. With no such restrictions in Europe, banks bid competitively for dollar deposits and the Eurodollar market flourished.[27] US bank expansion overseas naturally followed the rise in offshore dollar activity.

When UK interest rates rose above US rates in mid-1955, Midland Bank decided to offer non-UK residents dollar deposit facilities. Midland offered $1\frac{7}{8}$% interest for 30-day dollar deposits, which was $\frac{7}{8}$% more than the maximum rate payable in the US according to Regulation Q. Midland then sold the dollars spot for sterling and bought them back in the forward market paying a premium of $2\frac{1}{8}\%$. The net result was they acquired sterling funding at 4% at a time when the Bank Rate was fixed at 4.5%.[28] The Bank of England appeared to reluctantly tolerate this development so other banks, including US banks in London, followed Midland's lead. This attracted new customers with more US dollars to the UK. By the late 1950s the growing pool of externally held dollars had encouraged the development of a market between banks lending money to each other in the form of dollar deposits at competitive rates of interest, i.e. the 'interbank market'.

Meanwhile US multinational companies were expanding and making sizeable overseas investments. Between 1950 and 1957 US deficits were modest but from 1958 to 1962 US deficits reached levels of between \$2.5bn and \$3.8bn.[29] By 1961 the Federal Reserve was expressing concerns about the Eurodollar market's growth suggesting it may 'constitute a danger to stability', whereas the Bank of England felt the market had value in developing international trade.[30] A key supporter of these developments at the Bank of England was Sir George Bolton. He lobbied tirelessly for the abolition of exchange controls in Europe and the promotion of London as an international financial centre. By 1963 the Bank for International Settlements estimated the overall size of the Eurocurrency market to be US\$12.4bn, of which \$9.3bn were US dollars.[31]

In the post-war period foreign borrowers naturally turned to New York in search of much needed funds. The US was the leading centre of wealth creation and the US dollar was the pre-eminent international currency for trade and finance. During most of the depression and the Second World War there had been very little activity for foreign bond issuers in the New York market. The first international bond issue after the war was issued in 1947 on behalf of the World Bank. It took time for such issues to develop but according to an estimate in Salomon Brothers' International Bond Manual some \$14bn of capital was raised in 'foreign dollar bonds' in the years 1946 to 1963. The market was almost entirely a public sector market. The issuers were largely governments, government agencies and municipalities: Australia, Belgium, New Zealand, Denmark, the Japan Development Bank, the European Coal and Steel Community, and entities of the Italian and French governments. Naturally such issues had to be compliant with the Securities Act of 1933 and registered with the SEC. In addition, offering these foreign dollar bonds in New York required using a US investment banking house as lead manager and a US domestic underwriting syndicate. The lead managers included Kuhn Loeb, First Boston, Lazard Freres and Morgan Stanley.[32]

These foreign dollar bond issues (later to attract the title 'Yankee bonds') were targeted at US domestic investors but US underwriters had little interest in trying to distribute such paper as foreign issuance was insignificant compared to the mainstream mass of domestic offerings. In addition two key groups of institutional investors were limited in their ability to buy foreign bonds. Many US public pension funds could buy no foreign securities at all, while US insurance companies were also limited in the amount of overseas investments they could make. Increasingly these securities were purchased by European investors attracted by dollar-denominated investments for familiar names. By the late 1950s more than 75% of those New York issues were being placed in Europe. They were taken up by 'discretionary accounts managed by Swiss, Dutch or Benelux banks, or London brokers'.[33] Increasingly New York issues were also listed in Paris, Brussels and Luxemburg reflecting European investor interests. By 1958 the European Coal and Steel Community were undertaking multiple listings.[34]

These European intermediaries found it particularly galling that the US underwriters earned most of the new issue fees while the distribution was largely handled by a European selling group. Over time European distributors would seek ways to handle the entire new issue process themselves. As distribution increasingly took place in Europe so did secondary market trading activity.

Most notable among these early participants in the foreign bond markets were White Weld and Strauss Turnbull.

White, Weld & Co. was founded in Boston in the 19th century, as a family office for the White and Weld families. Having taken on a wide circle of friends as clients, it moved to New York and became an NYSE firm before the First World War. White Weld had formed a close relationship with J.P. Morgan – which gave it a privileged position in Morgan Stanley foreign dollar bond issues after the Second World War.

White Weld had formed a foreign department in 1929 and was the first American house to re-establish an overseas presence after the Second World War– in Venezuela and Zurich. They set up an office in Zurich (rather than the more usual Geneva) in the 1950s – courtesy of a long relationship with Crédit Suisse, a relationship which would later develop into the successful joint venture, Crédit Suisse White Weld (CSWW), in the 1960s. Robert Genillard, a partner since 1958, moved from Caracas to Zurich as Chairman and Chief Executive of the new joint venture. Genillard is regarded as one of the main architects and developers of the Eurobond market in which the firm he led played a dominant role. 'White Weld wasn't one of those elite firms in New York doing foreign dollar bond business. White Weld started out in the secondary market in New York. It learnt who bought the bonds. It first just got a selling concession, then became a member of the underwriting group and ultimately manager.'[35]

Genillard gathered around him a formidable set of young bankers who would become key figures in the development of the Eurobond market. Stanislas Yassukovich joined White Weld in Zurich in 1961. His father, Dimitri Yassukovich, had been one of White Weld's partners and opened an office in London in 1933, first as a joint venture with Old Broad Street Securities, and then as a branch of New York: 'In those days, nepotism was not only rife, but okay' remarked Yassukovitch.[36] He was key in moving the market's focus to London. Yassukovich would become Deputy Chairman and CEO of the European Banking Company and a highly regarded Chairman of the Association of International Bond Dealers (AIBD). He would move on to become Deputy Chairman of Merrill Lynch Europe Ltd, Deputy Chairman of the London Stock Exchange and Chairman of the Securities Association, the forerunner to the FCA.

Another White Weld alumnus was David Mulford, Managing Director and head of International Finance. He went on to become senior advisor to the Saudi Arabian Monetary Agency in its key formative years. He served as Under-Secretary for Finance at the US Treasury presiding over the Brady Plan and in his later career served as US Ambassador to India.

White Weld's Zurich office was the leading distributor of foreign bonds – indeed White Weld produced the best known annual register of outstanding foreign dollar bonds – most having been issued in the 20s and 30s, and many in default. 'White Weld had a very privileged position in (foreign bond) syndicates and had a much higher retention than their underwriting always.'[37] 'The dominant takers of bonds in those very early days were the big three Swiss Banks for their own private clients, and at that time they were happy to be treated as simply sales agents and not seek to underwrite or certainly not manage issues.'[38]

White Weld also came to dominate secondary US bond trading in Europe. Yassukovitch explains: 'When we were trading in Zurich in the early days, the book would be handed back to New York for their opening, and they would trade it and then hand it back overnight.'[39]

The move of White Weld's trading from Zurich to London under Walter Koller was a critical event in the history of the market. White Weld, and others, believed foreign dollar bonds were exempt from Swiss stamp, not because the book moved to New York in the afternoon, but because all deals struck in Zurich in the morning were confirmed *by head office in New York. However when the volume had increased enormously, concern grew that this would be seen as an artificial construct. Bob Genillard wanted to move the trading to our Paris office. But Stancliffe and I had a young tax advisor in London who took us to see a senior Inland Revenue official. He pointed out that the UK tax code included a provision to facilitate inter-Empire trade (e.g. between South Africa and India) arranged through a London representative office but not involving a UK resident counterparty. The dollar premium rules at the time, excluded UK resident investment counterparties making foreign currency investments, however the official opined we could engage in foreign security market making in London, between non-resident counterparties, and continue to be taxed, as are all branches of overseas firms in the UK, on an expenses basis. The move to London of our market making brought the overwhelming bulk of the secondary market in foreign dollar bonds to London.[40]*

Walter Koller was White Weld's celebrated trader: 'If Walter came on, you better be sure you had the right price or he would smack you.'[41] The story is recounted of a Crédit Foncier de France deal in December 1959 where Koller noticed in the documentation that French investors could not buy the issue until January 1960. The deal had been issued at $95\frac{1}{2}$. So Koller bought up a significant holding in the issue and on 1 January deluged French investors with telexes offering paper at 100 or better which was eagerly taken up.[42]

The London stockbroking firm of Strauss, Turnbull & Co. was founded by Julius Strauss with his cousins Robert and Ronald in 1938. Strauss was born in Frankfurt but moved to England in 1933. Before the war Strauss had traded and distributed foreign dollar bonds, as he recalled:

[I]n the pre-war days we talked about foreign bonds, the principal issues being dollar obligations of countries like Australia, New Zealand, some Scandinavian countries, Argentina, Brazil, Chile and Mexico. They were issued and underwritten in New York, but the main investors were the British composite insurance companies. When I worked for a year in New York in 1934, I interested the banks in, what was then Palestine, in these bonds for investment purposes and carried on regular business for many years. I also discovered that some of the Canadian insurance companies were interested in the same market, and we began working the sinking funds actively, particularly in the few Japanese names then outstanding ... During the war years, UK residents were allowed to deal amongst themselves in Commonwealth foreign bonds denominated in dollars which proved very valuable investments, particularly with the eventual advent of the dollar Premium. During those years my firm was also privileged to re-purchase Norwegian dollar bonds for the Norwegian government in exile throughout the world thus putting their large shipping revenues to good use.[43]

Strauss continues:

After World War II, and once Marshall Aid was tailing off, very large amounts of funds were required to make good the ravages of war in the western world. Sterling was losing its role as a reserve currency and in those early days practically all borrowing was effected in US dollars through New York houses. With the increasing amount of Eurodollars in circulation, the majority of these bonds were eventually placed in Europe. A few selected European houses were invited by the American managers to join the selling groups but the allocations were very *restricted and most of the bonds could be obtained only less $\frac{1}{2}$% reallowance. The appetite grew, mainly through the intermediary of London, where a few of us spent a great deal of time and effort popularising this form of investment.*[44]

Strauss maintained these activities at Strauss Turnbull although this over-the-counter (OTC) market was very much outside the activities of traditional London brokers. Strauss was considered something of an outsider in the broking community, only gaining Stock Exchange membership after a period of many years.[45] Strauss proved to be a born trader and assembled fellow natural traders around him such as Paul Sherwood and Stanley Ross.

Ross, a bus conductor's son, left school at 15 and after a short time with the RAF headed for the City in 1951. In 1963 the young Stanley Ross was sitting in Strauss's office reading a translation of Proust's *A la Recherche du Temps Perdu*, volume four, recalls Ross, when Julius Strauss was making one of his routine tours of inspection. Strauss was so impressed by this display of intellect that he promoted him to Strauss Turnbull's equity trading department. From there, Ross moved to Eurobond trading from where he would go on to have a sparkling, if sometimes controversial, career, first at Kidder Peabody, and then at his own firm, Ross & Partners and finally as a Managing Director of Deutsche Bank.

$*\quad*\quad*$

But New York was not the only foreign bond market. The Swiss foreign bond market opened in 1947 and by 1963 totalled the equivalent of $790m – slightly more than that for European borrowers in the New York market.[46] The Swiss foreign bond market was particularly attractive to issuers because of the low Swiss interest rates. Eugene Rotberg, Treasurer of the World Bank, and a substantial issuer in the Swiss franc market, would later quip of the Swiss market 'the only place where the underwriting commission that was paid to the underwriters was higher than the interest rate for the bond itself'.[47] The German and Dutch capital markets were open to foreign issuers as long as they joined the central bank queue, and in the deutschemark market, also agreed to convert the issue proceeds into other currencies.[48]

In the wake of the Suez crisis in 1956 and the resultant severe foreign exchange pressures, the UK prohibited the use of sterling in third country financing and tightened exchange controls. So why then did the foreign bond market gravitate towards London?

Switzerland was the market's natural home as the majority of early issues were placed there. Switzerland, along with Germany, imposed a 35% withholding tax on domestic issues for non-residents, but not on foreign issues. In addition Swiss Federal issue tax of 1.2% discouraged Swiss banks from underwriting and managing issues in Switzerland themselves. But the killer stroke to the long-term development of the market in Switzerland was the Swiss authorities' refusal to exempt bond trading from Swiss stamp tax.[49]

US banks originally favoured Paris for tax reasons. Morgan Guaranty established Morgan et Cie with Morgan Stanley in Paris to undertake underwriting business. In the 1960s Morgan et Cie was second only to Deutsche Bank in the league tables. Dillon Read opted for Paris and Merrill Lynch initially set up their European headquarters there.

The UK was not an obvious candidate for a developing foreign securities market. John Craven, then of Warburgs, remembers: 'London was a pretty miserable place to be, beset with post-war gloom, exchange controls and the narrow parochial attitude of the City.'[50] The UK retained exchange controls from September 1939 until December 1979. During much of this time UK investors looking to purchase foreign investments had to go through a special pool of investment currency – or 'premium dollars' which traded at a large premium to the commercial rate (15% by 1965), and violators of the law were subject to criminal penalties. As a result, UK institutional investment abroad was typically less than 5% of total assets.

It was not possible to issue a prospectus in the UK or raise any money without the permission of the Treasury under the Control of Borrowing Order and the Capital Issues Committee.[51] In addition new domestic issues attracted a stamp duty of 4% and if issues were listed in London, the Stock Exchange ruled that 15% must be given to the jobbers – who had no placing power.

But, in its favour, the City of London shared a common language with the US, and its merchant banks had considerable experience and expertise in international corporate finance and syndication. The Bank of England was skilled at ensuring that exchange controls did not hinder the City of London's role as an international financial centre. White Weld's Yassukovitch explains 'Paradoxically it was because there was exchange control. As a result of the Exchange Control Act the Bank could allow traffic in foreign currency securities on its capital market, and activity in foreign currencies, because it was completely isolated from the management of the domestic currency mass.'[52] The UK Treasury and the Bank of England had created a highly regulated onshore domestic economy, but by tolerating the growth of the Eurodollar and subsequently the Eurobond markets they helped create a deregulated offshore market, with the City of London at its centre.

Other European countries were more fearful of the rapidly expanding stateless pool of Eurodollars and imposed restrictions on its growth. In the early 1960s Switzerland, France, Germany and Italy all took measures to restrict Eurodollar growth in their jurisdictions – principally by prohibiting interest payments on foreign deposits.[53] Herman Abs, the head of Deutsche Bank, warned the UK authorities that the Eurodollar market was not under any central bank supervision and urged great caution.[54]

Because of the heavy concentration of banks in London holding Eurodollar deposits the possibility of using Eurodollars for loans to foreign governments began to be discussed at the end of 1962. The Governor of the Bank of England declared at the Lord Mayor's Banquet in October 1962:

> The time has come when the City once again might well provide an international capital market where the foreigner cannot only borrow long term capital but where, equally important, he will once again wish to place his long-term investment capital. This entrepôt business in capital, if I may so describe it, would not only serve this country well but would fill a vacant role in Europe in mobilising foreign capital for world economic development.[55]

In mid-December the UK Treasury outlined the plan for a foreign currency loan, utilising the City of London's financing expertise and involving 'some of the very volatile Eurodollars at present in London'.[56] Belgium was looking for a $50m loan as were a group of Austrian public utilities and Norway was speaking with banks to place $15–20m in Europe.

Who would arrange London's first foreign currency loan?

NOTES

1. Ranald C. Michie, *The Global Securities Market: A History* (Oxford University Press, 2006) p. 24.
2. Samuel L. Hayes and Phillip M. Hubbard, *Investment Banking: A Tale of Three Cities* (Boston MA: Harvard Business School Press, 1990) p. 12.

3. *Handbook on the History of European Banks*, edited by Manfred Pohl and Sabine Freitag, European Association for Banking History (Edward Elgar Publishing Limited, 1994) p. 764.

4. Michie, *The Global Securities Market*, p. 46.

5. Baring Archive (online), www.Baringarchive.org.uk, *Exhibition: The Louisiana Purchase*.

6. Stanley Chapman, *The Rise of Merchant Banking* (George Allen & Unwin, September 1984) p. 36.

7. *The Origins of Value; The Financial Innovations That Created Modern Capital Markets*, edited by William N. Goetzmann and K. Geert Rouwenhurst (Oxford University Press, 2005) Chapter 18, 'The First Eurobonds' Niall Ferguson, p. 317.

8. Ferguson, *The First Eurobonds*, p. 318.

9. Ibid. p. 323.

10. Ibid. p. 325.

11. Michie, *The Global Securities Market*, pp. 66–67.

12. Chapman, *The Rise of Merchant Banking*, p. 156.

13. Hayes and Hubbard, *Investment Banking*, p. 16.

14. US Congress, Office of Technology Assessment, *Electronic Bulls & Bears: U.S. Securities Markets & Information Technology, OTA-CIT-469* (Washington, DC: US Government Printing Office, September 1990) p. 129.

15. Michie, *The Global Securities Market*, p. 81.

16. *Electronic Bulls & Bears*, p. 129.

17. Richard Benzie, *The Development of the International Bond Market*, BIS Economic Papers, No. 32, January 1992, p. 10.

18. Michie, *The Global Securities Market*, p. 125.

19. A.L. Mikkelsen, *The Market Practices and Techniques of London Issuing Houses in Connection with Sovereign Bond Issues and their Role in Facilitating Access of Sovereign Borrowers to the London Capital Market, 1870–1914*. PhD Thesis, Kings College, London 2014.

20. Hayes and Hubbard, *Investment Banking*, p. 24.

21. V.P. Carosso, *Investment Banking in America: A History (Study in Business History)* (Harvard University Press, July 1974) pp. 193–223.

22. Michie, *The Global Securities Market*, p. 179.

23. Michael H. Coles, Foreign Companies Raising Capital in the United States (1981) 3 *Journal of Comparative Corporate Law and Securities Regulation* 300–319 (North-Holland Publishing Company) p. 103.

24. Michie, *The Global Securities Market*, p. 212.

25. Kit Dawnay, A History of Sterling, *The Telegraph*, 8 October 2001.

26. Burk (1992). *Witness Seminar on the Origins and Early Development of the Eurobond Market*. Contemporary European History, 1, p. 67. © Cambridge University Press, reproduced with permission.

27. Catherine R. Schenk, The Origins of the Eurodollar Market in London: 1955–1963 (1998) 35(2) *Explorations in Economic History* 222.

28. Schenk *The Origins of the Eurodollar Market*, p. 226.

29. Hayes and Hubbard, *Investment Banking*, p. 28.

30. David Kynaston *The City Of London, Volume 4: A Club No More, 1945–2000* (Pimlico, March 2002) p. 269.

31. R.B. Johnston, *Economics of the Euro-Market: History, Theory and Policy* (Palgrave Macmillan December 1982) p. 11.

32. Hayes & Hubbard, *Investment Banking*, p. 31.

33. Peter Shearlock and William Ellington, *The Eurobond Diaries* (Brussels: Euroclear, 1994) p. 9.

34. Burk, *Witness Seminar*, p. 76. Reproduced with permission.

35. Ibid. p. 76. Reproduced with permission.

36. Stanislas Yassukovich interview for ICMA's 40th Anniversary Video, 2008.

37. Burk, *Witness Seminar*, p. 77. Reproduced with permission.

38. Ibid. p. 79. Reproduced with permission.

39. Ibid. p. 77. Reproduced with permission.

40. Yassukovich, Note to the author, 5 May 2014.
41. Stanley D.L. Ross interview for ICMA's 40th Anniversary Video, 2009.
42. Shearlock and Ellington, *The Eurobond Diaries*, p. 11.
43. Ian M. Kerr, *A History of the Eurobond Market: The First 21 Years* (London: Euromoney Publications, 1984) p. 8.
44. *AIBD Gazette*, Issue 3, April 1979, pp.10, 11.
45. Shearlock and Ellington, *The Eurobond Diaries*, p. 9.
46. Ibid. p. 9.
47. Eugene Rotberg interview for ICMA's 40th Anniversary Video, 2008.
48. Shearlock and Ellington, *The Eurobond Diaries*, p. 9.
49. Ibid. pp. 14, 16.
50. *Euromoney*, 30th Anniversary Edition, June 1999, p. 31.
51. Burk, *Witness Seminar*, p. 79. Reproduced with permission.
52. Ibid. p. 80. Reproduced with permission.
53. Schenk, *The Origins of the Eurodollar Market*, p. 234.
54. Kynaston, *City of London* Vol. 4 p. 283.
55. Recent Innovations in European Capital Markets, *Federal Reserve New York Monthly Review*, January 1965, p. 10.
56. Telegram to Commonwealth posts cited in Schenk, *The Origins of the Eurodollar Market*, p. 232.

CHAPTER 2

Building the Base

1963–1969

S iegmund Warburg was raised in Tubingham, Germany, a scion of the German banking dynasty which operated the second largest bank in Hamburg, M.M. Warburg. After his education, Siegmund Warburg joined the bank, gaining valuable experience in its offices in London, New York and Boston before settling to pursue his career in Berlin. He built influential relationships with senior bankers, amongst them Hjalmar Schacht, President of the German Reichsbank during the Weimar Republic, and a fierce critic of his country's post-World War I reparation obligations. Schacht, a supporter of Hitler and the Nazi Party, although not of German re-armament, served in Hitler's government as President of the Reichsbank and Minister of Economics, until 1937.

When the Nazi Party came to power they instigated their campaign to deprive all Jews of positions of influence. One day in 1933, Von Neurath, Hitler's first Foreign Minister, hinted to Warburg that he was a target of the regime and he should leave Germany at the earliest opportunity. Feeling an imminent war was unavoidable, Warburg with his wife and two small children emigrated to London in April 1934.[1]

In 1936, with the help of the Rothschilds and others, he set up a finance company in King William Street in the City of London with capital of £25,000. Called the 'New Trading Company' or 'Nutraco' for short, the company financed the growth of small businesses while quietly aiding German and Austrian refugees escape from Hitler and assisting them in recovering the assets they had been forced to leave behind. For more than ten years it comprised a small group of largely German-Jewish émigrés, where the principal members were known as 'uncles,' and the company's internal language was German. 'The Uncles of Warburgs were extremely formal and called each other by their surnames, even after several decades of acquaintanceship, in the best German tradition.'[2] The first decade, largely during the war years, was spent steadily building the business, principally offering financial advice to British companies, searching for any gaps not covered by other bankers.[3]

After the war, however, Siegmund Warburg and his partner, fellow German émigré and industrialist, Henry Grunfeld, felt confident enough to change the name of the New Trading Company into the merchant bank S.G. Warburg and Company. In 1956 Warburgs bought a small merchant bank, Seligman Brothers. The business acquired was not significant but Seligman

Brothers had been a member of the prestigious group of Accepting Houses recognised by the Bank of England. Now S.G. Warburg would be numbered amongst them.

Over the next few decades S.G. Warburg steadily gained a name for itself. But the transaction which put Warburgs firmly on the map as a leading merchant bank, took place in 1958, when S.G. Warburg engineered the first hostile corporate takeover the London market had experienced. For its clients Reynolds Metal and Tube Investments, Warburg clandestinely acquired 10% of British Aluminium, then advised its clients on a hostile bid for the firm – a manoeuvre that many in the City establishment found unsavoury (though, of course, it subsequently became commonplace).

Prior to the Second World War, a particularly close relationship had existed between the partners of Kuhn, Loeb & Co., the US investment bank, and M.M. Warburg & Co. Hamburg, through Paul and Felix Warburg, who were senior Kuhn Loeb partners. Following the Second World War, their cousin, Siegmund Warburg, would continue this relationship as a partner and Executive Director of Kuhn Loeb from 1953 until 1964.

Warburg and his colleague, Gert Whitman, once assistant to Hjalmar Schact and a fellow partner at Kuhn Loeb & Co., had both been involved in Germany in the 1920s with the Dawes Plan and the subsequent Young Plan – resolving German war reparations.[4] From that time they had been active in international loans. Whitman was seconded to Warburg by Kuhn Loeb due to his considerable expertise in the foreign dollar bond market. Both he and Warburg were well aware that foreign dollar bonds were increasingly purchased by European investors with the lucrative underwriting fees going to US investment banks. As far back as 1958, Warburg bemoaned the fact that US bond offerings were underwritten by American issuing houses whereas in practice European banks were the main distributors of the paper.[5] Why not raise a dollar bond issue in Europe? There was a liquid Eurodollar market available for European investors and dollars were increasingly in demand.

They now set about overcoming the impediments to launching a Eurodollar-denominated bond out of London for distribution to investors in Europe. Their deliberations became more urgent as another London merchant bank, Samuel Montagu, was trying to put together a transaction to raise $30m for Belgium. In mid-May Samuel Montagu did succeed in placing an issue of $20m 5% 3-year bonds for the Belgian government – the first non-sterling loan from London since the Second World War. The City Editor of *The Times* remarked: 'Bank of England consent to the actual placing has been given on the condition that Euro-dollars are used. This appears to be the first time that this form of currency rather than investment dollars has been used ... Other loans of this type, using a combination of City expertise and foreign currency funds, are probably in preparation.'[6] Technically, because the Belgium loan was a private placement and unlisted, with a limited secondary market, it is not generally attributed as being the first Eurobond – a somewhat unfair outcome.

Both Warburg and Whitman, from their experience with Kuhn Loeb in the US, were familiar with dollar bond syndication techniques and practices. If they were to issue a dollar bond in Europe then they would need a syndicate of European banks from different jurisdictions in order to promote distribution.

If a dollar-denominated bond was issued outside the United States then there was no requirement for registration with the SEC. If the new securities were to be in registered form, increasingly favoured in many national markets, in which jurisdiction should registration take place? Any arbitrary choice would impact investors from outside the jurisdiction. International bond issues before the First World War and in the interwar years had typically been in bearer form. In this case the bond is owned by whoever is holding the physical instrument. There is no registered owner, no records are kept of the owner, or the transactions involving ownership. It was felt that this should be the favoured format of any new instrument. Unfortunately, the UK authorities did not permit the issuance of bearer debt.

The most crucial and sensitive consideration was the question of withholding taxes. In many national bond markets it was common for bondholders to receive coupons paid net of tax. In the UK, tax was deducted at source from interest paid to British bondholders. In a cross-border environment this would be problematical. Investors in France would be reluctant to buy a Siemens bond, for example, if Siemens withheld tax from coupon payments due and remitted this to the German tax authorities. The French investor would be liable to the French tax authorities for declared investment income and so would be exposed to being taxed twice on the same instrument. The investor would be better off investing in the domestic French bond market and suffer tax in one country only. While double taxation treaties had started to emerge in the interwar years they were not widespread and even in the case of claiming tax deducted under a double tax arrangement this could take months. Therefore a 'sine qua non' for developing a cross-border international market was that bonds must be free of withholding tax at source.

With all these challenges to be resolved Warburg and colleagues needed to find a debut borrower.

The European Coal and Steel Community (ECSC) had been established in the aftermath of the Second World War as an initial attempt to bring European countries together to create a lasting peace. Six nations signed up to the treaty with the idea of pooling Franco-German coal and steel production. As the first European 'supranational', ECSC had become an experienced borrower in the foreign dollar bond market and had an ongoing requirement for funding. ECSC were sympathetic to the Warburg foreign dollar loan proposal as they were aware of the US Treasury Secretary's constant pleas for foreign borrowers to resist using the Yankee market and exacerbating the US budget deficit.

Negotiations with ECSC ran on for two months but eventually to no avail. Whether it was that subsequently ECSC did not need the money,[7] or they they did not want to tread on Kuhn Loeb's toes (as ECSC was a regular Yankee issuer),[8] or the burden of needing to acquire the approval from the Finance Ministers of all six ECSC members,[9] the Director of Credit and Investments, Hans Skribanowitz, decided not to go ahead.

However, Warburg's Ronald Grierson put the idea of a Eurodollar financing to Instituto per la Riconstruzione Industriale (IRI) the large Italian public holding company. IRI was established in 1933 with the objective to rescue, restructure and finance banks and private companies that went bankrupt during the Great Depression. IRI played a pivotal role in the 'Italian economic miracle' of the 1950–1960s. IRI was keen to test out the idea and awarded Warburgs a mandate. The dollar funds were urgently required by Societa Finanzaria Siderurgica (FINSIDER), the Italian steel company, to buy American equipment. Ian Fraser of Warburg explains:

> *That was fine, except that Finsider's statute did not permit it to pay interest on bond coupons without deducting Italian tax, a vital feature so Whitman persuaded us. Capanna, the Finsider finance director, therefore did a deal with another government company, Autostrade, which could pay coupons 'gross'. Accordingly Autostrade, the builder and owner of Italy's motorway network, was persuaded to act as front for Finsider, presumably for a fee, and we were asked, of course, not to mention this side of things.[10]*

Autostrade was exempt from all Italian taxes, as according to its prospectus, 'In lieu of taxes the company pays to the Treasury an annual royalty equal to Lit.50 for every Lit.1 million of the aggregate cost of the construction works.'

Extensive negotiations followed with the Inland Revenue, the Stamp Office, the Bank of England and the London Stock Exchange. Bankers warned the authorities that the 4% Stamp Duty would drive this potential new business activity from the City to rival aspiring financial centres in Europe. They insisted a new Eurodollar bond issue would be effectively an offshore instrument, targeting non-UK investors and would not present a means to UK investors of circumventing UK exchange controls. Sir George Bolton, then on the Court of Governors of the Bank of England, and a close friend of Siegmund Warburg, helped in convincing the relevant authorities of the worth of the project.[11]

Ian Fraser, attempting to structure the proposed issue, gave this account:

Whitman, who by now had joined as a director, was in charge of marketing our bonds and it was my responsibility to engineer their construction. Peter Spira made up the team and was an invaluable member of it. It took Peter and me six months to hack our way through the obstacles ... For instance there was a British stamp duty of 4% on the capital value of all bearer bonds in Britain: so we decided to issue them on Schiphol Airport in Holland, in which country there was no such impost. The British Inland revenue would insist on deducting $42\frac{1}{2}$ % income tax from all coupons cashed whether by UK residents or foreigners; so we arranged for the coupons to be cashed in Luxembourg and several other places abroad. Most of the banks in the syndicate that Whitman was putting together would not underwrite unless we put in place a listing on a major stock exchange such as London. After a lot of hard work we persuaded Throgmorton Street to admit our bonds to the official list even though they could not be 'delivered' (in settlement of a transaction) in Britain but only in Brussels or Luxembourg. Then we had major difficulties with the central banks of France, Holland, Sweden, Denmark and of course Britain, about the exchange control consequences of allowing the bonds to be underwritten, purchased, sold and coupons cashed and ultimately the bonds redeemed all in a foreign currency – US dollars. Finally we could not find any printing firm to do the security printing of the bonds to a standard required by the rules (written in the 1920s) of the London Stock Exchange, until at the last moment De La Rue, the playing card printers, came forward and said they had two aged Czech engravers whom they could bring out of retirement who could do it for us.[12]

After six months, due to the painstaking efforts of Ian Fraser with Geoffrey Sammons and Robin Broadley of Allen & Overy, relevant approvals were finally obtained and the necessary documentation drafted and on 1 July 1963 the first Eurobond for Autostrade was launched.

The bond issue was for US\$15m with a 15-year final maturity and an annual coupon of $5\frac{1}{2}$%. The principal was amortised over the last 10 years. The issue was guaranteed by IRI, Italy's state-owned industrial and financial holding company. S.G. Warburg was the lead manager of the issue while the co-managers were Banque de Bruxelles, Deutsche Bank and Rotterdamsche Bank. The issue was listed in London and Luxembourg. Definitive bearer certificates would be delivered to investors at Banque Internationale in Luxembourg following payment on 17 July. Fraser adds:

> *Whitman fixed the issuing price at* $98\frac{1}{2}$ *per cent and we, the banking group, were allowed to keep three and a half percentage points, US$ 525,000, for ourselves and the other members of the syndicate. The Italians seemed perfectly happy and Dr Obber, who signed for them, promised me a gold badge which would enable me to travel free on all the Italian motorways for my lifetime. Unfortunately the excitement of the issue was such that Obber had a heart attack and died and I never got my badge.*[13]

An article on the front page of the *Financial Times* on 2 July was headed 'UK Shares in $ Loan to Finance Italian Motorways'. The paper noted:

> *A further important step towards re-establishing London's pre-war position as the leading international money market was taken yesterday. An agreement was signed in the City by a consortium of European banks, headed by S G Warburg to float a US $15m (£5.35m) 5.5 per cent Guaranteed bonds 1972–78 of Autostrade, the public corporation owning and operating the principal Italian toll motorways. This is the first loan marketing to be arranged in London of a non-sterling area company since 1934, and it is also believed to be the first issue of dollar bearer bonds with a quotation in US Dollars to have been arranged here.*[14]

News of the transaction spread across Europe where 'even the normally derogatory newspapers of Germany and Switzerland had to admit that this was an important English coup.'[15]

While S.G. Warburg had originated the issue, their own ability to place paper with investors was limited and distribution relied heavily on the sales network of houses such as White Weld and Strauss Turnbull. Tradition has it that Julius Strauss first coined the term 'Eurobond' to replace the term 'foreign dollar bonds' or 'foreign loan in dollars' to emphasise the 'Europeanisation' of the market.[16] Opinions vary about whether the issue was a sellout with investors or took some time to be placed. Certainly the end buyers were largely high net worth individuals typically operating through private banks. In the secondary market, Stanley Ross, who first traded the paper at Strauss Turnbull, remarked that the issue was different from many Yankee bonds that had come before it, in that 'You could always get a quote … almost until a few years before the end of its life in 1978.'[17]

But one swallow does not make a summer. There were forces at play that would greatly add to the significance of this inaugural cross-border issue.

The outflow of currency from the US that created the Eurodollar pool reached worrying proportions by the early 1960s. Along with this outflow, there was a big surge in foreign investment by US companies looking to avoid import restrictions by setting up operations overseas. And all the time the issuance of Yankee bonds was increasing: $1.2bn in 1962 and in excess of $1.5bn in the first half of 1963. The US Administration was increasingly under pressure to find ways to stem this relentless outflow of dollars. In 1962 the US Treasury Secretary Douglas Dillon made speeches in both the US and Europe asking European borrowers to desist from raising funds in the United States and to raise capital in their own markets.

In July 1963, only months before his assassination, President Kennedy presented, as part of his 'Balance of Payments' message to Congress, a range of measures to address the situation. Key among these was the imposition of Interest Equalisation Tax (IET) for a period of two years. IET was a tax levied on the purchase price of a foreign bond or equity investment made by a US citizen. The rate of tax on debt varied according to maturity ranging from 2.75% for 3-year bonds to 15% for long-dated (over 28.5 years) paper. The rates were determined by adding 1% to the US interest rate to determine its equivalent present value. The administration's intention, therefore, was to increase the cost to foreigners of obtaining capital in the US by approximately 1% 'so as to place them more in line with the costs prevailing elsewhere. The end result, it is hoped, will be to substantially eliminate any incentive to obtain capital in the United States.'[18]

While the proposed tax would take time to be enacted (it was in fact signed into law by President Lyndon Johnson) it was applied retroactively to the day of President Kennedy's balance of payments message to Congress, 18 July 1963 – two weeks after the launch of Autostrade. Reaction to the development was swift. Henry C. Alexander, Chairman of Morgan Guaranty told bank colleagues 'This is a day you will remember for ever. It will change the face of American banking and force all the business off to London.'[19] In London *The Times* City Editor noted on 20 July that the probable 'isolation of the New York market' would provide for London 'an opportunity for a great expansion of its entrepôt capital issues business, particularly in dollar loans'.

By September the US press reported that a number of planned borrowings in the New York market had been cancelled by European issuers.[20] As a result of the imposition of IET United States investors reduced their purchases of new European and Japanese issues from $326m in the first half of 1963 to $110m in the second half and to under $40m in 1964.

Some bankers active in the markets in the 1960s have argued that while Autostrade has received all the attention, there had been earlier bond offerings laying claims to being the first Eurobond. In an attempt to circumvent the various controls that existed in national markets, experiments were made with multicurrency debt offerings. Petrofina, the Belgian oil company, launched a $25m issue as early as 1957 for international distribution. This offering allowed principal and interest to be payable either in US dollars, Belgian francs, Swiss francs or Dutch guilders – a structure which subsequently was to prove an expensive exercise for the issuer.[21] André Coussement of Kredietbank, Luxembourg, brought another oil company offering for SACOR of Portugal in 1961. The bonds were denominated in the composite currency, European Units of Account (EUA). With its link to gold, the EUA borrowing was less exposed to repayment in an appreciating currency and the offering was heavily oversubscribed.

However as the first widely distributed single Eurocurrency offering, with an active secondary market, Autostrade has always held pride of place.

In his budget in April 1963 the UK Chancellor permitted the issuance of bearer securities and reduced the 6% tax on the nominal value of bearer securities to 3% of the market value on securities issued by residents and to 2% on those issued by non-residents – changes which became effective in August 1963. That month the first post-war offering of sterling bearer bonds by a non-sterling country occurred with a £5 million refunding for the Government of Japan.

Later, in October 1963 the British Chancellor, speaking at the Lord Mayor's Banquet, exactly one year after his call for the re-establishment of the City of London as a financial entrepôt, observed that 'for the future, foreign currency loans, i.e. those which are no drain on the reserves, are being allowed almost without restriction'.[22] The UK authorities were now overtly pursuing a policy of re-establishing the City of London as an important exporter of long-term capital; a position they had held prior to 1914.

Ian Fraser recalls the immediate aftermath of the Autostrade transaction:

> *As soon as Uncle Siegmund saw that our first tentative step into the new arena was going to succeed, he went into top gear to line up more potential borrowers out of his huge personal connection. Warburg teams were despatched to Oslo, Tokyo, Luxembourg, Vienna, Stockholm, Milan, Rome, even Cologne, to capitalise on our competitive lead. Our competitors, Hambros, Rothschilds, Morgan Grenfell, Lazards limped far behind. In fact Lazards failed to understand that the secret of these issues of Euro-bonds (as they now came to be called) was that the bonds must be totally anonymous, coupons must be paid without any deduction of tax and the bonds at maturity paid off in full without any questions asked and that it must be possible to do this in several capitals. Morgan Grenfell did not do much better.*[23]

In October 1963 Morgan Grenfell launched a SFr60m Eurobond issue on behalf of the City of Copenhagen out of London. Unfortunately the Swiss National Bank was not consulted in advance of the offering. The Bank was unhappy with the issue and protested to the Bank of England. They were concerned it would interfere with Swiss controls over domestic liquidity and would contribute to the use of the Swiss franc as an international currency. This they felt was undesirable and any future foreign Swiss franc issuance would have to be in the domestic market.

Japanese companies took an early interest in the market with Canon Camera bringing the first convertible in December 1963, through M. Samuel & Co (later to become Hill Samuel). Takeda Chemical followed soon afterwards. This transaction was the work of Evan G. Galbraith at Morgan et Cie, Paris. An American investment banker who spent most of his career in Europe, Galbraith had pioneered the first international equity offering in Europe for the German mail order company Neckermann earlier that year. Later Galbraith would become the Chairman of Bankers Trust International, London where he would be lastingly associated with the invention of the Floating Rate Note. In his later career he was appointed the US Ambassador to France from 1981 to 1985 under Ronald Reagan and the Secretary of Defense Representative to Europe and NATO under Donald Rumsfeld from 2002 to 2007.

These early issues were made against the background of a dramatic fall in stock prices on the Tokyo Stock Exchange between 1962 and 1965. So much so that two state supported funds were set up to purchase shares in Japanese companies to stabilise equity markets.

New dollar-denominated Eurobonds rose from $35m in the second half of 1963 to $330m in January to June 1964 and an additional $180 million in the second half of 1964. Approximately two thirds of the total of $545m was arranged in London. The bonds were typically 15 to 20 years maturity carrying coupons of $5\frac{1}{2}$ to $6\frac{1}{2}$%. The major borrowers were governments, municipalities, European authorities and Scandinavian industrial companies. Japanese issuers accounted for 25% of the total.[24] In these early days US companies took little interest in the market.

1964 opened with a dollar transaction for Norges Kommunalbank guaranteed by the Kingdom of Norway. This issue of $10m for 20 years at $5\frac{3}{4}$% was lead managed by Hambros Bank. Hambros was a specialist in Anglo-Scandinavian business with expertise in trade finance and investment banking, and was the sole banker to the Scandinavian kingdoms for many years.

Rupert Hambro, who was later to succeed Stanislas Yassukovitch as Chairman of the AIBD, remembers the arrangements made for the issue in those pioneering days:

> *In 1963 Stamp Duty was payable at the rate of 2% in London which resulted in banks having to issue scrip certificates in bearer form with a life of six months, acceptable on the same basis as an allotment letter. Six months later the bonds were printed and delivered by the printers to Heathrow ... I was met there by the printers standing by the forward security hold of the aircraft. Beside them, containing the bonds were wooden zinc-lined crates (a requirement of the insurers) which were lifted into the hold, and, as the door shut, they became my sole responsibility ... We arrived at Luxembourg International Airport which consisted of one landing strip and two nissen huts. When the plane finally came to a halt, it was surrounded by police with sten guns at the ready, as well as television cameras ... I left the plane first and supervised the removal of the cargo from the front hold into a rickety old lorry with a canvas top. André (Coussement of Kredietbank) apologised for the security measures and television cameras explaining that this was also his first delivery of bonds to Luxembourg.*[25]

Another issue of note that month was an $18m offering for the Austrian government lead managed by Warburgs in conjunction with Hambros, Rothschilds and Creditanstalt. This issue had notably been scheduled for the New York market in the previous year but was prevented by IET.

Merchant banking firms in the City of London rapidly achieved leadership in issuing Eurobonds. As confidence in the market grew, so did issue sizes, with Hambros lead managing an issue for $25m for the Kingdom of Norway for 20 years and Banque Lambert issuing $25m of 15-year bonds with equity warrants for IRI. Subsequently Warburgs launched a $30m issue for the European Coal and Steel Community. By mid-1964 White Weld brought the first Eurobond transaction for a private sector borrower, a $12.5m 10-year offering for the Finnish logistics company Kesko Oy, albeit with a bank guarantee.

But dollar bonds were not the whole story in these early days.

The deutschemark returned to full convertibility in 1958 and the first foreign deutschemark bond was issued in the same year. The first issue was a convertible for Anglo-American Corporation of South Africa, lead managed by Deutsche Bank. Seven further foreign bonds were issued up till 1963. These issues all followed the standard domestic issue procedure and carried a slight premium over domestic bond yields. The transformation of the foreign bond market to a euro deutschemark market happened gradually. As non-German investors increasingly participated in the market, so non-German securities houses became active in underwriting and distributing these issues. Primary and secondary market practices came to resemble those of the dollar Eurobond market.

In order to curb the inflow of long-term capital and thereby alleviate the German payments surplus, the German authorities in March 1964 proposed a 25% coupon tax, or withholding tax, on non-residents' interest income from German bonds. However the tax would not apply to income from deutschemark issues of foreign borrowers. This stimulated demand by foreign investors and also enabled foreign borrowers to issue deutschemark paper more cheaply than domestic issuers. Foreign issues in Germany rose from $25m equivalent in 1962 to $40m equivalent in 1963 and almost $225m equivalent in 1964. The bulk of foreign issues in

Germany, like the dollar bonds, were for Scandinavian, Finnish and Japanese issuers, with Japan accounting for a third of the total. As with their Eurodollar equivalents the deutschemark issues were typically for 15 or 20 years with coupons between $5\frac{1}{2}$ and 6%.[26]

The first euro deutschemark issue with an international management group was in 1967 with a 5-year DM 100m offering for Argentina led by Deutsche Bank. The euro DM market grew naturally out of the DM foreign bond market with little difference in format other than that in a EuroDM syndication foreign banks would be included for wider international distribution. Both Eurobonds and foreign bonds had to join the queue system for issuance, be lead managed by a German bank and use the German settlement system.[27] The principal lead manager of EuroDM issues was Deutsche Bank with competition from Westdeutsche Landesbank, Dresdner Bank and Commerzbank.

Being cut out of the German market was a source of irritation to Siegmund Warburg. On New Year's Eve 1963 Warburg wrote to the Governor of the Bank of England that 'there might well be scope for issues to be made with a sterling/deutschemark option as the interest rates in Germany and the UK were not too far apart …'. The Bank gave its approval and in 1964 the City of Turin sterling/deutschemark issue was launched with a 6.5% coupon for 20 years. The rate of exchange was fixed at 9 marks to the pound. Peter Spira of Warburg remembers:

> [N]o-one had the slightest interest in the sterling aspect of it, but because it was sterling/deutschemark fixed option a UK house could appear as lead manager i.e. Warburgs. It was Warburgs who did it, outside the German new issue queue and you did not have to pay the extra 0.5 per cent Frankfurt Stock Exchange commission. So you could actually do a deutschemark issue, call it a sterling/deutschemark issue, and lead it, which was very good for you in the league tables apart from anything else.[28]

Exchange rate uncertainty was always a key consideration for investors in the new Eurobonds. To reduce this risk bonds were launched denominated in a basket of European currencies. This issuance was pioneered by André Coussement, a former colonial administrator in the Belgian Congo, and in the 1960s General Manager of Kredietbank SA Luxembourg, a subsidiary of Belgium's leading Flemish bank. A basket currency is a weighted average of a collection of currencies. The first basket to be used after the Second World War was the European Unit of Account (EUA). Units of account were first used by the former European Payments Union. Each of the 17 European currencies included – the reference currencies – bears a fixed relationship to the unit of account through its gold/dollar parity as communicated to the IMF. The EUA was a virtual currency and not a means of exchange so it could not be used for bond settlement. However the EUA concept was employed in the 1961 bond issue for the Portuguese borrower SACOR.[29] The recipient of a payment in EUAs, first the borrower and then the investor, could choose the currency of payment. Between 1963 and 1982 there were 96 issues denominated in EUA totalling around $2bn.[30]

Belgium and Luxembourg banks were the original sponsors of multicurrency issues. It is said that they profited less from marketing multicurrency bonds than from exchanging the coupons for domestic currency each year at the banks' counters in Luxembourg.[31] As a composite currency unit with no one currency representing a majority, there was no requirement for these lead managers to notify a central bank or seek prior approval for such issues.

*   *   *

Interest Equalisation Tax succeeded in reducing the outflow of private US portfolio capital into foreign securities. Sales of foreign securities to US investors fell from a total of $1bn in the first half of 1963 to $250m in the second half of the year.[32] Yet despite this, the total outflow of private capital in 1964 was the largest in six consecutive years. Direct investment abroad had soared in anticipation of further restrictions being imposed. Foreigners as well as US affiliates overseas switched from securities to bank financing, which was not subject to tax.

With the escalation of the Vietnam War exacerbating US balance of payments difficulties, President Lyndon Johnson took additional steps in February 1965 to try and eliminate the persistent deficit. Interest Equalisation Tax was extended for a further two years and extended to cover bank financing of more than one year. Voluntary restrictions were placed on the transfer of funds for investment abroad by US companies and on the foreign loans and investments of US financial institutions. US corporations that did invest overseas would need to show that they had made balance of payments savings in other forms, such as repatriating overseas earnings. The voluntary programme was designed to encourage US firms to borrow abroad to finance investments rather than restrict or limit the amount of such investments.

In addition the President required the Federal Reserve to put in place a set of guidelines, the 'Voluntary Foreign Credit Restraint Programme', to moderate the foreign lending and investing activities of US financial institutions. These voluntary arrangements continued to be basic policy until a sharp deterioration in the US balance of payments in 1967 led the President to tighten control on investments abroad.

These new measures persuaded US corporations to consider the new Eurobond market as a possible source of financing. The pioneering issue was for Mobil Oil, lead managed by Warburg featuring their sterling/deutschemark structure. Seemingly the deal was difficult to place with investors, with White Weld picking up about 60% of the issue. Brave investors who did take up bonds and held on to them would find their principal almost tripling over the 15 years.[33] Uniroyal followed soon after with a similar offering, proving again lucrative for investors; a nightmare for the borrower.

White Weld brought the first US dollar straight bond for a US corporation, a $20m offering for American Cyanamid. Thereafter there followed a rash of convertible issues for US companies which were eagerly taken up by European retail investors. A dozen US corporate borrowers issued paper in 1965 such as: Monsanto, IBM, Gulf, Du Pont, Amoco, Bristol Myers, Federated Department Stores and General Electric. In 1966 and 1967 a further 45 US corporates issued straight or convertible issues in the market – all good quality investment grade companies.[34]

As US corporates looked to finance themselves in Europe then US corporate financiers increasingly competed to win these mandates. From 1964 to 1967 leading US investment banks such as Morgan Stanley, First Boston, Smith Barney, Kuhn Loeb and Lehman Brothers all set up offices in Europe and started to appear in the Eurobond league tables. The London merchant banks did not welcome the competition. In early 1966 Siegmund Warburg complained to the Bank of England that the European capital markets were suffering from 'acute indigestion', because of US corporate borrowers avidly tapping the markets. The Bank was aware that US banks were increasingly reluctant to invite UK banks into new Eurodollar offerings as their distribution capability was poor. Indeed there was pressure from the US Treasury on the Bank of England for the automatic involvement of American banks in all dollar issues. The Bank rejected the US approach and made clear its view that a London-based offering should have a British lead manager.[35] Traditionally British merchant banks were strong in corporate finance but had little placement capability, relying on the stockbroking community for distribution. By the end of 1966 only two British banks were among the top seven issuing houses.

A similar situation arose with Japanese issuers who launched 11 offerings between December 1963 and April 1964. The principal Japanese securities houses of Nomura, Yamaichi, Daiwa and Nikko all set about establishing a presence in London.

Julius Strauss gives a flavour of these pioneering days:

> *The circle of borrowers widened practically daily and it was only a question of months until American borrowers availed themselves of the opportunity to tap this market as a new source of capital for their own requirements. These were hectic days in what soon became known as the Eurobond Market. A lot of midnight oil was burnt in scrutinising the prospectuses and the girls in Chelsea and the printers were kept busy providing proofs overnight. Syndicates were established and potential borrowers all over the world were intensively serenaded. Every issue was still an event and endless discussions took place as to correct pricing and as to what amount could be floated in each individual case.[36]*

The traditional new issue process was based on the assumption that the major investment force in the market was the high net worth individual, often operating through a bank rather than directly. It was therefore deemed necessary to allow a relatively long period of 10 to 14 days for completion of the marketing process. The traditional syndicate had a three-tier structure: a management group, an underwriting group and a selling group. Within the management group, the lead manager was responsible for the issue: for the preparation and documentation; for selecting the syndicate members; for negotiating the terms of the issue and for the allocation of bonds. Other members of the syndicate were selected primarily for their ability to take down and place a large part of the issue.

Syndication techniques varied widely in the early days. Hambros would first ask banks around Europe for their selling demand and only as a result of the process award underwriting positions. In time this process would be reversed, more in line with syndication in New York, where the underwriting came first and the selling afterwards with the roles rewarded separately. Invited institutions would be notified by telex of new offerings. By the late 1960s the typical offering would have 25 to 40 underwriters receiving an underwriting fee; these could be divided into special bracket underwriters, major underwriters and minor underwriters. Underwriting fees were paid according to the underwriting exposure undertaken by a firm rather than according to the number of bonds sold. The lead management might offer co-managers with good demand for paper 'protection' – the guarantee of a minimum allocation. Typically if deals went well, underwriters would receive negligible allotments, while if deals struggled, they would be allotted in full.

The underwriters would be assisted by a selling group of 50 to 75 firms receiving a selling concession. This large selling group might include end investors themselves. This was the position of the Swiss banks until they established offshore subsidiaries. This gave rise to lengthy 'tombstone' advertisements. For example, the $50m five-year bond offering for Standard Oil in May 1969 named 111 banks on the tombstone below the lead manager Morgan et Cie.[37]

The length of the selling period varied but was typically about two weeks. Being a bearer bond market with investor anonymity, underwriters and selling group members would indicate their demand for bonds in the issue but no investor names were revealed to substantiate their demand. Selling group members shared in a selling concession of $1\frac{1}{2}\%$ according to the amount of paper placed. As all participants wanted to convince the lead manager that they had strong investor placement, demand for deals was increasingly exaggerated. In time, as issues proved more difficult to sell, so syndicate participants started to pass on more than the agreed $\frac{1}{2}\%$ reallowance to other brokers to encourage placement. The choice of syndicate participants, and of final allotments, was often based on the whim of the lead manager and his relationships, rather than strictly based on investor demand.

Shepard Baker of Morgan et Cie's syndicate desks points out:

In some of the early Eurobonds, such problems as the decision to use an offshore financing subsidiary and its location, the language restricting offerings of new Eurobond issues from US citizens and residents and the use of a detailed offering circular were more time consuming and presented more difficulties than actually selling the issue. New problems had to be met and resolved by managers of almost every issue, but it is interesting to see how much of the format established in those early issues has remained to this day.

The major (perhaps the only) Eurobond purchasers in those early days were the Swiss, and what they did not get from syndicate allotments usually wound up with them later from the secondary market. A manager would have a lot more confidence in fixing the size and the indicated coupon of a new issue if he had visited and talked 'hypothetically' with Paul Lang, Richard Schait, Peter Sorg, Georges Streichenberg and Jean-Francois Vidouez, among others.[38]

The investor community was almost entirely retail based. As much as 75% of early issuance was sold to Switzerland with the Low Countries accounting for a proportion of the balance. Of course Swiss banks represented demand from high net worth investors from many countries. Gert Whitman believed the ultimate buyers 'were individuals, usually from Eastern Europe, but also from Latin America, who wanted to have part of their fortune in mobile form so that if they had to leave they could quickly with their bonds in a small suitcase'.[39]

Unfortunately the banks themselves could not participate in underwriting new issues because of Swiss Issuance tax, then 1.5% of the principal amount underwritten, and so could only participate in selling groups. Peter Spira of Warburgs remembered:

[O]ne of the great attractions of this market for all the banks was that there was a fixed commission structure which was not breached for a very long time. Certainly in the longer term issues over 7 to 10 years, of the total 2.5% commission, 0.5% went to the managing banks, 0.5% to the underwriters and 1.5% went to the selling group. The Swiss banks of course loved this because they kept 1.5% and stuffed their clients at the retail price (i.e. par) of the bond.[40]

European banks with a strong retail investor base supported the high commissions, as it was a means of compensating their branch distribution networks.

Initially the responsibility of underwriting issues was not taken fully on board by issuing banks:

> *[W]e paid 0.5% to a group to underwrite, and then if we didn't get sufficient demand from the selling group after we sent out the invitation telexes, we didn't stick the underwriters and say we've paid you 0.5% commission to stand up to your underwriting, we pulled the issue … or cut it down … It was a frightful racket for many years that we were paying out these commissions for nothing. And that meant it was extremely attractive to the investment bank community for many years.*[41]

While the underwriters were required to maintain the maximum permitted re-allowance at 0.5% they were soon exceeding this re-allowance to attract favoured clients.

John Craven, an alumnus of White Weld and Warburgs and later Chairman of Morgan Grenfell and a Deutsche Bank Board member, observed that 'at Warburgs, although we were one of the leading issuing houses we had in early years no distribution powers at all, so all we were doing was keeping the management fee and some of the underwriting. Moreover, we didn't make money, we never made serious money for years and years.'[42]

Siegmund Warburg had warned colleagues that once a new business was invented all competing banks would want to take a share in it and the result would be 'that profit margins for the banks went down or disappeared; this was bound to happen and it would soon happen with our Eurobond business'[43]

*   *   *

It is part of Eurobond folklore that the original buyer of Eurobonds was the archetypal 'Belgian dentist'. Why not a Swiss dentist? In Switzerland foreign bonds paid their coupons without the deduction of withholding tax whereas in Belgium, interest payments on domestic bonds were subject to tax at source. The Belgian dentist simply represents wealthy individuals who were tempted to invest in these new bearer Eurobonds probably via a bank account in neighbouring Luxembourg. The bank would clip the coupons and credit the dentist's account with the gross coupon payment. Protected by this veil of anonymity, the dentist may then fail to return this investment income to the Belgium tax authorities. There is little doubt that the core characteristics of Eurobonds attracted investors seeking to minimise their tax burden or evade it altogether. This was a state of affairs which sat uneasily with many national authorities.

As issues increased, so the demands for a secondary market grew. Richard Weguelin who instigated the first meeting to establish an association for bond dealers observed:

> *At the start it was assumed that Stock Exchanges would take on the secondary market functions for Eurobond dealings, and that local Eurobond markets would be established in each country where Eurobonds were listed. However, when issues were split internationally, each participating country often only received an allocation amounting to a few million dollars: insufficient for active Stock Exchange turnover. In addition, since the bond issues were international, it was necessary for the secondary market to be international also, in order to generate the turnover required for matching buying and selling orders. The bulk of secondary market trading therefore developed between finance houses and banks and in many ways the transactions*

were on lines more akin to the foreign exchange markets than to traditional Stock Exchange bond dealing.[44]

Numerous overtures were made to the London Stock Exchange to amend their rules to accommodate trading in the new securities. The two major hurdles were Rule 88 which required 15% of an issue to be offered to the jobbers to enable them to make a market, and a fixed $\frac{1}{2}$% stock exchange commission – typically higher than commissions charged by overseas trading firms. The Stock Exchange Council set up a special committee to look into the matter. Eventually they recommended a reduction in commission rates but rejected any amendment of Rule 88. Furthermore at Julius Strauss's suggestion, Hambros Bank offered to finance the stock jobbers' trading books in dollars so that they need not run any foreign exchange risk, but the discussions did not advance beyond a preliminary stage. Strauss concluded that the London jobbers 'were simply not that interested'.[45] Eventually the rules of the London Stock Exchange had to be altered to enable stockbroking firms rather than the jobbers, to make markets in Eurobonds.[46] Yassukovitch notes: 'Julius Strauss was able to interpret cleverly the regulation that required business to be shown on the market. He was a market-maker, the only member of the London Stock Exchange who understood how Eurobonds worked, and he was totally specialised in them.'[47]

Largely spurned by the Stock Exchange, banks and securities houses simply traded with each other over the telephone as they did in the money market or foreign exchange market. Investors would ring a broker or bank, who in turn would call several traders on their behalf. As with all major bond markets the convention in the Eurobond market was to quote a 'clean price' for the bond. This is the price of the bond as given by the present value of its future cash flows, but excluding interest that has accrued on the bond since the last coupon payment. Yields were the key metric (the concept of spreads was 15 years away) and were calculated from yield tables or using a slide rule. Stanley Ross gives some colour on early trading conditions:

Trunk calls to anywhere outside London, the long steel slide rules, the huge metal calculators, the quarter and half speed telexes, it was a totally different world … I used to have a steel slide rule … to make my calculations. The technology we had was our ears mostly. I would hear Sherwood sitting opposite me. I would be making something like 98 to $98\frac{1}{2}$ and I would hear him buy at 98 and immediately my price is $97\frac{3}{4}$ to $98\frac{1}{4}$. I've got a phone to each ear, he's got a phone to each ear. He hasn't said anything to me, but I've heard what he is doing and changed my price accordingly.[48]

Tom Beacham of Wood Gundy recalls:

[T]he infant market of 1963 developed very slowly and was for most participants a spare time occupation, with many companies playing some small part or other, but 4 organisations remain clearly in mind as the pioneers of the early years of secondary market trading. These were all involved to some degree in the foreign US bond market, trading in what we now know as 'Yankee' bonds long before the term was invented. They were naturally well placed to add to their trading lists. White Weld and Co. had Walter Koller trading from Claridenstrasse, Zurich with Alan Towner making the markets from their London office. Dominion Securities employed among

others, Armin Mattle, Bob Smith, Kurt Halter and Jo Tresch. Strauss Turnbull & Co. had Paul Sherwood and Stanley Ross working with the 'father' of the market, Julius Strauss, and finally Samuel Montagu & Co. (who having earlier bought out Hart Son & Co.) 'inherited' Georges Gason. These are without doubt the core of the houses who created and held the fabric of the early trading market together and without which we might not have the same story to tell.[49]

By the late 1960s there were more than a dozen self-proclaimed 'market-makers' although the *Financial Times* mentions the top six as being Kidder Peabody, Strauss Turnbull and Eurotrading in London, White Weld in Zurich, Merrill Lynch with Maurice Berger in Geneva and Bondtrade in Brussels. Other notable trading houses in the secondary market were Bank of London and South America (BOLSA), Deltec with Mike Scotcher in London, Dominion Securities and Weedon. Two characteristics emerge from this list of early trading houses: none had a strong, if any, primary business and most were brokerage houses rather than major banks. This being the case, the capital committed to the market was very modest with most traders needing to match buyers and sellers where they could. Secondary market trading sizes were modest, typically between $10,000 and $25,000 and trades as large as $100,000 were rare. In 1969 it was estimated that the combined capital of the market-makers was no more than $70m.[50]

Bondtrade and Eurotrading were consortium trading houses established to participate in the Eurobond market. Eurotrading was set up by three of the Rothschild family banks along with Pierson, Heldring, Pierson,and Banque Lambert. Within a few years Bondtrade would absorb Eurotrading. Bondtrade itself was set up in 1967 by Kuhn Loeb, Société Générale De Banque, Amsterdam-Rotterdam Bank, Crédit Suisse and a private Swiss bank. It was a combination of a US issuing house with banks representing the Swiss and Benelux retail client base. The shareholder banks originally agreed to direct all their trading business to Bondtrade. Armin Mattle, an experienced trader in both the foreign and Eurobond markets was hired from Dominion Securities to run the operation out of Société Générale's Brussels office. Over time, the shareholder banks would increasingly execute their business away from their consortium or establish their own trading presence to retain any profits. Bondtrade, themselves, ceased business in January 1981.

But dollars weren't the whole story. The euro-deutschemark sector was growing and in 1966 deutschemark bonds accounted for 25% of all primary issuance. With a further surge in issuance in 1968 a Sub-Committee for euro-deutschemark bonds was formed with representatives of six leading German banks meeting together to regulate issues under the auspices of the Bundesbank. The Sub-Committee decided on the total new issue amount and the allocation of places in the new issue queue, normally on a monthly basis. They also set issuance guidelines with regard to size, form and maturity. The Sub-Committee reaffirmed the Bundesbank's preference for all deutschemark issues to have a German lead manager. The Bundesbank thereby would have greater control over the German currency and avoid conflicts in the scheduling of such financings in relation to domestic government bond issues. As regards euro-deutschemark bond trading, among the early players, the Deutsche Bank's Wolfgang Kron, assisted by a very young Oswald Gruebel, operated from Frankfurt in cooperation with Albrecht Nicholas and Hartmut Fischer in Mannheim. Other euro-currency sectors emerged: the first euro-guilder bonds appeared in 1965 and the first euro-French franc issues in 1967, although this market dried up with the student protests in May1968.

Just as the issuing houses celebrated more than $1bn of issuance in 1967 the market received a further shot in the arm from the US. On New Year's Day 1968 President Johnson announced a new programme designed to achieve a swift and decisive improvement in the US Balance of Payments. New mandatory restrictions were imposed on US companies' direct overseas investments above set quotas, and the former Voluntary Restraint Programme was abandoned. The quotas varied according to the type of country in which the investment was to be made; developing countries had the highest quotas. Quotas were also linked to a company's past record of investment in the period 1965–66. Any dividends and liquid balances had to be repatriated in amounts in line with historical experience. The new controls would be administered by the newly created Office of Foreign Direct Investment (OFDI).

US multinationals now *had* to borrow overseas.

Accordingly the amount of borrowing by US corporations increased from $527m in 1967 to $1963m in 1968. In fact, during the six years the programme would be in force, US issuers launched 271 issues totalling $6978m or almost a third of the entire new issue market over the period.[51] With a bull market on Wall Street, convertible bonds were particularly popular and almost $1.5bn of convertibles were issued for 70 US companies in 1968. Issue sizes also increased with 13 companies bringing convertible offerings for between $50m and $75m.[52] The largest issue was $75m for Texaco followed by Eastman-Kodak at $70m. Shephard Baker recalls: 'One of the largest of these "hot" convertible issues was $70m of 4.5% due 1988 by Eastman Kodak in May 1968. With universal recognition of Kodak's "little yellow box" trademark, the issue could almost have been sold without any coupon at all – the subscription book amounted to over $500m!'[53] Issues were heavily oversubscribed as the retail investor base had an insatiable appetite for paper of US blue chips, particularly those with well-known consumer products. A number of companies tapped the market again and again: ITT via its offshoot International Standard Electric Company (ISE) launched nine offerings of both straight and convertible issues between February 1966 and March 1970, worth a total of $222m. The number of top quality convertible issues began to decline as share prices began to fall on the US stock market at the end of 1968. The increased US issuance attracted more US houses to London. By 1970, 79 US banks had 536 overseas branches.

Prior to July 1984 there was a US foreign withholding tax of 30% on interest payments made by domestic US firms to foreign investors. There was a tax treaty (US-Netherlands Tax Treaty of 1948), however, that exempted the withholding tax on interest payments from any Netherlands Antilles subsidiary of a US incorporated company to non-US investors. Many US firms therefore took advantage of the treaty, issuing dollar-denominated bonds in the Eurobond market through financing subsidiaries in the Netherlands Antilles. To facilitate sales the US parent corporation could guarantee the bonds. The proceeds from the sale of the Eurobonds were then loaned by the foreign subsidiary to the parent corporation.

Instead of using the services of a foreign finance subsidiary certain US companies issued debt via domestic finance subsidiaries which were known as Delaware subsidiaries, or '80-20' companies. In this case if more 80% of gross income of a domestically incorporated company was from foreign sources, i.e. its income must be derived from outside the US, then interest paid on bonds to non-residents were free of US withholding tax. These companies were normally formed in Delaware because of the relative ease of incorporation in that state.[54]

At the time, bond issues were traded for either New York or Luxembourg delivery, with two distinct methods of settlement. For Luxembourg transactions, payment was made on the settlement date, delivery of the bonds taking place on a free payment basis as soon as possible thereafter. Bonds dealt for settlement in New York were on a cash against delivery basis. Certain problems were common to both New York and Luxembourg deliveries, non-matching instructions being given to their respective banks by the two counterparties to a transaction, or instructions from one counterparty arriving late, or not at all. For Luxembourg delivered bonds the problem was not so acute, since all deliveries were on a free of payment basis, and the receiving bank would always accept any bonds offered to it on behalf of their clients. Whereas in New York non-matching instructions resulted in failed deliveries.[55] New York banks, with their manual settlement processing, were already overwhelmed with the needs of the domestic securities market, let alone having to now cope with an increasing burden of settlement instructions from Europe.

Eurobond trading was proving a tough business to make money in, as financing costs often exceeded the low yields on traders' bond holdings. But from 1967 onwards they also started experiencing a sharp rise in the number of 'DK' or 'Don't know' notices. Their New York correspondent banks were seemingly increasingly unable to match delivery and payment instructions and a backlog of uncleared trades was developing. Failed deliveries inevitably led to a vast increase in trader's positions which had to be financed in a period when Eurodollar interest rates were around 12–13%. Any trading profits were now wiped out as financing costs mounted awaiting deliveries out of the New York clearing houses. When deliveries finally did take place they were often to the wrong counterparty. Dollar bonds intended for the stockbrokers Astaire and Co. in London were delivered to the Astaire Dancing School in New York while bonds intended for the Julius Baer Bank in Zurich were delivered to a Julius Baer, chemist in Geneva – fortunately a cousin of the eminent banker.[56]

In 1967 Stanley Ross moved from Strauss Turnbull to Kidder Peabody. He recalls:

Each day we sent instructions to receive and deliver. Bonds certainly came in and our account debited but nothing went out (and therefore no proceeds were received) and thus, the interest cost to us just went through the roof … So the market seized up, but people found ways to profit from the chaos. One practice was that firms who had been paid for bonds sometimes didn't deliver them for one or two years … and had the use of the money in all the period. Worse still, when the bonds did finally come to them for onward transmission they had cut off all the intervening coupons … I know of one firm who had $5m in its so called unclaimed coupon account … Well I went to New York because Schroders, our agent there, were only taking our bonds in and so they were debiting us, but they weren't delivering anything out … I went down to the vaults in Schroders and I said 'Show me the Kidder Account'. So they brought me out the Kidder account and I lifted it up and all our instructions were cut into little pieces and I just opened them up and they fluttered. I put my head in my hands and I said, 'Oh my God' and then Wolfgang Kron (of Deutsche Bank) put his hand on my shoulder and he said 'Stanley' he said 'I have to say I've been here a week and I've turned a $13m debit into a $8m credit.'[57]

The problems reached such proportions that some firms stopped trading on certain days per week just to chase the settlement backlog. Wood Gundy's Ian Steers was told by his chairman 'You've got all the capital of the firm tied up in late deliveries.'[58] Tom Beacham of Wood Gundy recalls the difficulties experienced by Weedon & Co.:

As successful third market makers in US listed equities, a senior partner (Donald Weedon) came to London and was persuaded to branch out into Eurobonds. They quickly became the most prominent dealers in convertible bonds, employing names such as Walter Imthurn, Viktor Boehler and Norman Lawrence. Quoting the finest prices and writing the largest tickets, they were the undisputed centre of Euro-convertible activity. Having established themselves as major players, they ultimately fell victim to the settlement chaos which inevitably developed from over activity.[59]

By late 1968 Weedon & Co., had in excess of $50m of fails representing three times the firm's entire capital. Weeden had to suspend Eurobond trading for six months and then withdrew again in September 1969 in order to preserve their capital.[60] Other dealers maintained the façade of being market-makers, but kept business to an absolute minimum whilst their back offices tackled the backlog of deliveries.

After Autostrade most Eurobonds were listed on the Luxembourg exchange and the closing of deals often took place in the Grand Duchy. In the best banking traditions closing would normally involve a splendid lunch for all the deal participants. But Luxembourg could be a difficult place to get to, particularly from Paris or Zurich, and its cuisine was not of the highest order for well-travelled investment bankers and lawyers. In 1965 John Cattier from White Weld in Zurich enquired of Morgan Guaranty in Brussels whether it would be possible to have deal closings in Brussels. Morgan Guaranty was the New York paying agent for a large number of dollar bonds (and Belgium cuisine was highly regarded). The Belgium tax authorities took some persuading that a closing was nothing more than the execution of a mandate to deliver securities against payment, and therefore should not attract tax. With no objections finally raised, White Weld arranged the closing of their Cyanamid International bond offering at Morgan Guaranty's Brussels office. Further closings followed.[61]

Bonds were not fungible at this time which meant that individual certificates, with the correct individual serial numbers, had to be prepared at the closing for delivery to the relevant counterparties. A further complication was that each bond had to be signed manually and so if you had a $25m transaction in denominations of $1,000 then someone had to sign 25,000 pieces of paper. Lead managers would appoint bank officers as Directors just so that they could sign the closing documents for a transaction and then they were obliged to resign.[62] After a deal was closed, underwriters were increasingly reluctant to take their allotments of bond certificates back with them as often they had already been sold on to other counterparties. In this case Morgan Guaranty was asked to keep the paper in their vaults and to await notification of new beneficial owners. Before long, James Chandler, head of Morgan Guaranty's securities department, was asked whether they might be prepared to hold on to the securities until maturity. Chandler put the request to New York and assembled a working group to look into the possibility of developing a settlement system for dollar bonds in Europe. His key associates in the task were Charles D'Ursel, who secured the support of the New York head office for the project, and Evan Galbraith, who would be key in selling the service to the market. The project gained urgency as rumours emanated from London that a UK-based Eurobond clearing house was being developed.[63]

A system was launched in July 1967 but it soon ran into numerous teething problems. Much more work needed to be done and further personnel hired. In the following year two key breakthroughs were made: firstly, the process of 'matching' of participants' instructions and then automatically selecting trades chronologically for clearance, which dramatically reduced the number of fails; and secondly, the adoption of fungibility, whereby good delivery did not require certificates with specific serial numbers.[64]

In November 1968 the *Economist* acknowledged 'the latest initiative in this area (delivery and settlement) is by the Morgan interests in forming Euroclear, a European-based equivalent of their pioneer New York based Bondclear.' But they argued '… the best solution, surely, would be for the London Stock Exchange to organise some sort of central clearing house.

This would help enormously to keep the business in London. Already some issues (pioneered by S.G. Warburg with an issue for Mobil) have come out with London type trust deeds, and handled on the London pattern (the documentation required is so much less than under the United States regulations).'[65]

Despite such comments, Euro-clear (as the new service was called for its first 22 years), was launched by Morgan in December 1968 with more than 50 banks and brokers signed up. Anxious to avoid working with New York settlements, Stanley Ross was among the first to sign up to the new service. A further incentive for traders like Ross was the credit lines that Morgan made available, allowing them to gear up their modest trading books. Before long Ross was requiring all Kidder's trading counterparties to become Euroclear members. White Weld's Walter Koller was initially sceptical but would remark later 'Without Euro-clear we would all have gone broke.'[66]

* * *

Walter Imthurn, Koller's former trading assistant, was now a trader at Weedon and Co. in London. Having worked for some time in Canada, he had been taken by the camaraderie of the Montreal Bond Club. He put forward the idea that the bond traders in London might get together to form a similar grouping, and in 1967 a group of six bond traders met at Weedon's offices. 'It was a bit of a social occasion … more of a social club' remarked Ross, an attendee at the first meeting.[67] Nonetheless they planned further meetings and elected a Secretary, Iwan Datwiler of First Boston Corporation. As the settlement problems gained pace throughout 1968 and bond issuance mounted, the realisation grew that the market's ad hoc trading and settlement practices urgently needed to be more formalised. In addition there was an increasing need to stamp out malpractices and adopt some common rules. Accordingly in October 1968 19 senior bond dealers gathered in N.M. Rothschild's Board room in London to form a Steering Committee to establish a new association. The Committee comprised Rolf Hallberg of Stockholm Enskilda Bank, Paul Sherwood of Strauss Turnbull, Richard Weguelin of Eurotrading, Walter Koller of White Weld and Armin Mattle of Bondtrade. The Committee was charged with drafting a set of articles for the new association. The Association of International Bond Dealers (AIBD) was formally founded on 7 February 1969 with 19 members who then invited applications from market participants to join the Association.

The *Economist* heard about this early meeting and commented 'At the moment the objectives of the association seem vague – to keep in touch with one another and with issuing houses. But it will be the first formal recognition of this growing secondary market already the largest non-governmental bond market in the world. No-one even knows who are the biggest dealers in it; and it will impose an obligation on issuing houses to talk to dealers about forthcoming issues.'[68]

The first General Meeting of the Association took place at the Great Eastern Hotel in the City on 18 April 1969. An 11-man Executive Committee was elected who in turn elected Rolf Hallberg as the first Chairman of the Association, Armin Mattle as Secretary and Georges Gason of Samuel Montagu as Treasurer. Ross recalls the inaugural meeting with 90 participants being greeted by Richard Weguelin, Chairman of the Steering Committee: 'the first three words at the opening were "Mademoiselle Courtine, gentlemen", for in the entire assembly there was only one woman.' [69] Robert Genillard, senior partner of White Weld, was the guest speaker at the meeting and observed that the Eurobond market 'offered a vivid demonstration of the capacity of the international private sector to organise, on a complex and multi-national basis, the raising of substantial amounts of capital, both for private and public needs'. He made an impassioned plea for governments to look beyond nationalism in their reactions to the Eurobond market, arguing that it would be 'in the interests of governments to encourage a gradually increasing overlap of the Eurobond market with their national markets ... Surely the future of the Western world in an era of constantly growing economic interdependence and instant communications lies in accepting multinational finance and the development of a truly European and Atlantic financial community.'[70]

The evening before the meeting there was a cocktail party sponsored by the Bank of London and South America (BOLSA) instigating a social side to the General Meeting which would grow to heroic proportions over subsequent decades.

Inevitably the hot topic of discussion at the meeting was the settlement and delivery log-jam. The Executive Committee therefore established a Committee for European and New York Settlements chaired by Walter Koller. Within days Koller flew out to New York to talk to the 16 US clearing houses. The outcome of his negotiations was to get the New York banks to agree to the use of a discrepancy form which he drew up. In this form a bank was obliged to itemise the reasons for non-delivery or failure to make payments, e.g. lack of instructions received, bonds with missing coupons, non-endorsement or mutilated securities. A copy of this discrepancy form would go to the bank, a copy to the beneficiary and one to the order giver. This discrepancy procedure was adopted along with many other new rules at an Extraordinary Meeting of the AIBD which took place in November 1969 at the Intercontinental Hotel, Geneva. Koller and Mattle, in particular, worked tirelessly over that first year to resolve the settlement and delivery issues. Settlement committee meetings would often start on a Friday afternoon and end on Sunday. They drafted regulations covering precision of contract, buy-in rules for delayed deliveries, standardisation of settlement dates (trade date plus five working days) and many other related legal issues.[71]

Two other sub-committees were established at the inaugural General Meeting – the Committee for Liaison with the Issuing Houses chaired by Paul Sherwood, and the Committee for Standard Market Practices chaired by Stanley Ross. The latter Committee drafted the first trading rules and produced the first Members' Register. The Committee decided that the Eurobond market standard yield should be based on annual compounding as opposed to the semi-annual compounding common in most domestic government markets, a decision Ross recalls which led to 'a tremendous fight from the American houses ... I remember "Chuck" Treuhold of Arnold and Bleichroeder was always getting on his feet and complaining about that.'[72]

The Committee for Liaison with the Issuing Houses was important, as in the early days, bond trading and bond issuance were handled by different financial institutions. The former comprised brokers and securities houses while the latter comprised the merchant and investment banks. Neither party had been consulting the other as the nascent market developed, so work was needed to align standards and practices. Progress was made but the divide persisted. The founders of the AIBD were largely diehard traders who felt ill at ease working with corporate financiers and vice versa. Corporate financiers were typically more senior in their banking institutions than bond traders giving rise to a hierarchical divide. Within a decade or so both bond trading and new issuance would reside in the same key investment banking institutions and yet a sense of mutual distrust did not fully disappear.

Armin Mattle, the AIBD's first secretary, made the following, somewhat harsh, judgement on the tenth anniversary of the AIBD:

> *One committee never achieved anything. It should have aimed at improving relations*
> *with Issuing Houses. I share the blame for this failure. While I convinced the Founder*

Members that the AIBD should not be a club of professional dealers but an association comprising the entire community, I failed to realise at that time that the involvement of the issuing houses should have been actively sought prior to the formation of the Association. Through the choice of its name and its declared objective of establishing relations with the primary market, the AIBD identified itself as a secondary market institution, a predicament from which it has never been able to extricate itself.

He concludes: 'Is there anyone courageous enough to set up an International Bond Issuers Association?'[73] Five years later such an association would be formed from amongst the AIBD's own ranks.

Nevertheless the Issuing Houses Sub-Committee began by addressing problems which would often arise over subsequent years. At the first meeting the question was raised 'whether or not it was possible to limit the number of new issues in some way in order to prevent the over-saturation of the market which has in the past taken place from time to time. It was agreed that this suggestion had a certain merit, but in view of the competitive nature of the market, it would not be a possibility in the near future.' The Committee members also observed: 'Recently it has again become more apparent that certain members of the selling groups have been offering bonds with a larger reallowance than is permitted. Although this practice should be eradicated, it was felt that the remedy lay in the hands of the individual Issuing Houses.'[74]

At the EGM in November 1969, two more committees were formed, recounts Mattle:

One was the Committee on Legal Matters whose immediate task was the revision of the Statutes. A firm of English lawyers was engaged. The proposal to make the AIBD a UK incorporated offshore entity, worked out after long meetings, proved unsuitable. Within a few days before the distribution of the documentation for the 1970 AGM, Walter Koller and I, together with Swiss Counsel, rewrote the Statutes on the basis of Swiss Civil Law. Our version was submitted to and approved by the Members and later was polished by Dr Kammerer.[75]

Koller recalls: 'The AIBD's rules at that time were very simple. There were just a few. I had been in New York and because I was a registered member of the NYSE, and had passed the exams, I took the NASD book and took over a lot of that but tailored it to the international market. I did it together with Armin Mattle. His English was better.'[76]

English had been adopted as the official language of the Association. Koller and Mattle, without doubt, made the pivotal contribution to the successful establishment of the AIBD. Rolf Hallberg, Chairman at the time, referred to their work: 'no group of people are quite as organised as the Swiss-Germans, and in the early stages it was organisation the AIBD really needed.'[77] Nonetheless the work was well received with membership of the Association totalling 165 firms from 14 countries by December 1969.

* * *

From the earliest days Luxembourg was at the heart of the developing Eurobond market. Autostrade was listed on the Luxembourg exchange without the need for a prospectus and accompanying bureaucracy experienced when pursuing a London listing. Therefore most subsequent Eurobond issues were listed in Luxembourg. While the Belgian dentist was a familiar figure on the 'Coupon Express' train from Brussels, Luxembourg also became an offshore banking centre for German banks seeking to avoid the Bundesbank's reserve requirements. And to avoid the UK stamp tax requirement London issuing houses would issue temporary scrip certificates which would be exchangeable for bonds in physical form in Luxembourg up to six months after launch. With all these developments Luxembourg became active in the settlement of bearer bonds, albeit by physical delivery, between the banks there.[78]

These Luxembourg banks were particularly unhappy with the launch of the Euroclear service in Brussels which they perceived as a threat to their activities. In response the Luxembourg banks, along with a group of major foreign banks, set up a study group to look into settling dollar bonds in Europe without New York delivery. They drafted in as consultant Professor Georg Brun of the Frankfurt Kassenverein who was keen to adapt German systems and software for the Eurobond market.[79] The AIBD EGM in November 1969, arranged to show members all that had so far been accomplished by the association, 'witnessed the start of the hostility between the newly formed Euro-clear and the Luxembourg bankers who were considering setting up their own system'.[80]

In early 1970 Koller's Settlement Committee recommended that a uniform system of European 'delivery versus payment' (DvP) be adopted and both Euroclear and the Luxembourg banks began working on it. By now the Luxembourg banks' venture was named 'Centrale de Livraison de Valeurs Mobilières' or 'Cedel'. By the 1970 AIBD AGM in Copenhagen 'most of the action was devoted to keeping the clearing systems from each other's throats … In any case, Euro-clear's dapper James Chandler was more than a match for Cedel's Jean Krier who, built like a bulky wardrobe, stood and roared his defiance of Armin Mattle trying to rule him out of order.'[81] The Cedel service was launched with a capital of $1.15m in September 1970 by 71 banks from 11 different countries. This structure allowed it to promote itself as an independent operation run by the market for the market, while Euroclear was portrayed as being run for the benefit of Morgan Guaranty – a US institution. However like Euroclear, Cedel required users to open securities and cash accounts and settle transactions by book entry.

While Euroclear had attracted the trading houses in its initial phase, Cedel attracted the continental banking community and proved a success from the start. So began a fierce rivalry that has persisted for most of the history of the market. Cedel's aggressive first Chairman, Edmond Israel, from Banque Internationale à Luxembourg, soon started undercutting Euroclear's rates – much to the delight of market participants. So the launch of Cedel not only added competition but also put pressure on Morgan to mutualise Euroclear.[82] At the 1971 AIBD AGM in Paris a resolution was proposed calling upon Euroclear and Cedel to negotiate a bridge for the settlement of transactions between participants of the two systems. The rival settlement systems agreed but the project moved painfully slowly: 'It was to turn into the longest bridge building exercise in the history of the world,' quipped Ross.[83]

* * *

However delivery and settlement problems were not the only woes of these early days – there were also defaults. As the 1960s drew to a close the quality of borrowers tapping the Eurobond market dipped from the household name companies – so beloved of the retail client base – to more speculative enterprises. About 2% of issues introduced in 1968 and 1969 totalling $165m got into serious difficulties. Names such as: Famous Artists Schools Inc., ICC International, Levin-Townsend International, Farrington Overseas Corporation, King Resources Capital, Commonwealth Overseas NV, Giffen International NV, Unexcelled International NV, Equity Funding and Granite Overseas would all end up in default within a few years.[84]

Famous Artists Schools was an American company who issued a $10m convertible bond via S.G. Warburg and Bear Stearns. It holds the dubious accolade as being the first Eurobond to default in June 1971. King Resources Capital, Commonwealth Overseas NV, Giffen International NV and Unexcelled International NV were convertible Eurobond issues led by Investors Bank, Luxembourg, a financial institution closely allied to Investors Overseas Services, Ltd (IOS).

IOS was founded in 1956 by Bernie Cornfeld, a former US mutual fund salesman. Cornfield had entered the industry just as mutual funds were experiencing their first strong surge of growth since the stock market crash of 1929. In 1956, he moved to Paris, planning to sell shares of popular American mutual funds, chiefly the Dreyfus Fund, to Americans living abroad. Using his trademark recruiting challenge 'Do you sincerely want to be rich?' he built Investors Overseas Services, pocketing 20% of the money invested and paying 8.5% to its salesmen. At its peak, it was a far-flung organisation that included a vast and intensely loyal sales force, a secretive Swiss bank, an insurance unit, real estate interests and a stable of offshore investment funds operating beyond the reach of any single country's securities laws.

In the 1960s, the company employed 25,000 people who sold 18 different mutual funds on doorsteps across Europe. The company principally targeted American expatriates and US servicemen who sought to avoid paying income tax. IOS became one of the biggest financial organisations in the world. Over 100 IOS salesman had become millionaires by the mid-sixties and the high returns had made legendary a company about which little was known by government regulators or its own investors.[85] By 1970, his company had pumped millions of overseas dollars into the American mutual fund industry, initially through its aggressive sales force and then through Mr Cornfeld's trailblazing Fund of Funds, an offshore fund that invested in other mutual funds' shares. By the end of the 1960s they were managing about $2.5bn of other people's money, and were predicting that by 1975 it would be over $15bn.[86]

Cornfeld's personal fortune was well over $100m and he led a flamboyant life style to match. Cornfeld's fund managers were set high targets for growth which led to ever greater investment in speculative bonds, the phenomenal growth of which was almost entirely caused by IOSs having twice as much money to invest annually as share issues were available in the American market. IOS became *the* major investor in new Eurobond issues, particularly those convertible issues introduced by Investors Bank, Luxembourg, e.g. $3m in Unexcelled, $8m in King Resources, $5m in Giffen and $19m in Commonwealth United. IOS buying would guarantee a rise in the underlying shares and a healthy premium on the new issue.[87]

Bernie Cornfeld and IOS did fine while the American stock market continued to be bullish during the Kennedy and Johnson administrations. Eventually the war in Vietnam took its toll, dampening American economic expansion and triggering what would become known as 'stagflation'. Cornfeld and IOS were brought low by a declining stock market that cut his ability to return dividends to investors and eroded the value of stocks held in the funds. When international markets turned down the promised returns had to be paid straight out of the capital – in effect, making it a pyramid scheme. The actual profits, after all the creaming off by salesmen, managers and the international overheads, were almost non-existent, and that was before making provision for an enormous number of bad investments. By March 1969, IOS was running out of operating cash and so was forced to raise capital via an IPO to meet its liabilities. The bear market in 1970 saw the price of IOS shares drop from $18 to $12, and investors began bailing out. In response Cornfeld formed an investment pool with some other (equally dubious) investors, but the share value continued to plummet to $2 as now all IOS's investors tried to sell off their shares.

Financier Robert Vesco who, at the time, was also in financial difficulties, turned to Cornfeld and offered his help with an injection of $15m. Vesco took control of IOS and proceeded to use more than $200m worth of IOS's money to cover his own investments in his International Controls Corporation. When the scheme was discovered, Vesco fled the United States for the Bahamas, and eventually settled in Cuba. There was no money for IOS to meet debts and the whole structure crashed, ruining investors everywhere and causing bank failures in the US and Europe. In 1973 Mr Cornfeld was charged with defrauding employees of Investors Overseas Services by selling them stock in the faltering company and spent 11 months in a Swiss jail.

NOTES

1. Peter Spira, *Ladders and Snakes: A Twist in the Spiral Staircase* (1997) p. 94, © P J R Spira.
2. Ibid. p. 101.
3. Niall Ferguson, *High Financier: The Lives and Time of Siegmund Warburg* (Penguin Press HC, June 2010) p. 124.
4. Burk, *Witness Seminar* p. 74. Reproduced with permission.
5. SGW to John Schiff, 30 October 1958 cited in 'Siegmund Warburg, the City and the Financial Roots of European Integration' Niall Ferguson, November 2004, p. 17.
6. *The Times*, London, 14 May 1963.
7. Remarks by Martin Gordon, Senior Advisor, UBS, Luxembourg Stock Exchange Dinner, 17 July 2003.
8. Kynaston, *City of London*, Vol. 4, p. 275.
9. Bank of England OV47/6 69, JM Stevens note for record, 21 May 1963, cited in: *Siegmund Warburg*, by Niall Ferguson, p. 29.
10. Ian Fraser, *The High Road to England: An Autobiography* (Michael Russell Publishing Ltd, August 1999) p. 260. Reproduced by permission of Alexander Fraser Esq.
11. Kerr, *A History of the Eurobond Market*, p. 14.
12. Fraser, *The High Road to England*, pp. 260–261. Reproduced by permission of Alexander Fraser Esq.
13. Ibid. pp. 261–262. Reproduced by permission of Alexander Fraser Esq.
14. *Financial Times*, London, 2 July 1963, p. 1.
15. Fraser, *The High Road to England*, p. 261. Reproduced by permission of Alexander Fraser Esq.
16. Kerr, *A History of the Eurobond Market*, p. 14.
17. Ross interview for ICMA's 40th Anniversary Video, 2008.
18. US Treasury Secretary Dillon, Hearings before the Committee Ways and Means of the US House of Representatives, 88th Congress, 1st session on H R 8000, 165 1963, 64; cited by Owen Alan Knopping, Why an Interest Equalisation Tax? (1964) 5(2), Art. 6, *William & Mary Law Review* 242.
19. Ron Chernow, *The House of Morgan: An American Banking Dynasty and the Rise of Modern Finance* (New York: Atlantic Monthly Press, 1990) p. 544.
20. *New York Times*, 9 September 1963, p. 43.
21. Shearlock and Ellington, *The Eurobond Diaries*, p. 4.
22. Recent Innovations in European Capital Markets, *Federal Reserve New York Monthly Review*, January 1965, p. 10.
23. Fraser, *The High Road to England*, p. 262. Reproduced by permission of Alexander Fraser Esq.
24. Recent Innovations in European Capital Markets, *Federal Reserve New York Monthly Review*, January 1965 p. 11.
25. Kerr, *A History of the Eurobond Market*, p. 27.

26. Recent Innovations in European Capital Markets, *Federal Reserve New York Monthly Review*, January 1965, p. 11.
27. Shearlock and Ellington, *The Eurobond Diaries*, p. 13.
28. Burk, *Witness Seminar*, p. 84. Reproduced with permission.
29. F.G. Fisher III, *Eurobonds* (London: Euromoney Publications, 1988) p. 153.
30. Peter Gallant, *The Eurobond Market* (Woodhead Faulkner Ltd, 1988) p. 77.
31. Clifford R. Dammers and Robert N. McCauley, Basket Weaving: The Euromarket Experience with Basket Currency Bonds, *BIS Quarterly Review*, March 2006.
32. Hayes and Hubbard, *Investment Banking*, p. 33.
33. Kerr, *A History of the Eurobond Market*, p. 22.
34. Shearlock and Ellington, *The Eurobond Diaries*, p. 25.
35. Kynaston *City of London,* Vol.4, p. 326.
36. *AIBD Gazette*, Issue 3, April 1979, p. 11.
37. *Euromoney*, Founding Fathers and 35-year-olds, Philip Moore, 1 June 2004.
38. *AIBD Gazette*, Issue 3, April 1979, p. 16.
39. Fraser, *The High Road to England*, p. 262. Reproduced by permission of Alexander Fraser Esq.
40. Burk, *Witness Seminar*, p. 81. Reproduced with permission.
41. Ibid. p. 81. Reproduced with permission.
42. Ibid. p. 81. Reproduced with permission.
43. Fraser, *The High Road to England*, p. 272. Reproduced by permission of Alexander Fraser Esq.
44. *AIBD Gazette*, Issue 3, April 1979, p. 20.
45. Kerr, *A History of the Eurobond Market*, p. 84.
46. Ibid. p. 8. Reproduced with permission.
47. Burk, *Witness Seminar*, p. 78. Reproduced with permission.
48. Ross interview for ICMA's 40th Anniversary Video, 2008.
49. *AIBD Gazette*, Issue 14, December 1984, p. 67.
50. Shearlock and Ellington, *The Eurobond Diaries*, p. 31.
51. Fisher, *Eurobonds,* p. 12.
52. Shearlock and Ellington, *The Eurobond Diaries*, p. 28.
53. *AIBD Gazette*, Issue 3, April 1979, p. 15.
54. Michael Bowe, *Eurobonds* (Dow-Jones-Irwin, 1988) pp. 104–107.
55. *AIBD Gazette*, Issue 3, April 1979, p. 22.
56. Shearlock and Ellington, *The Eurobond Diaries*, p. 43.
57. Ross interview for ICMA's 40th Anniversary Video, 2008.
58. Shearlock and Ellington, *The Eurobond Diaries*, p. 34.
59. *AIBD Gazette*, Issue 14, December 1986, p. 68.
60. Shearlock and Ellington, *The Eurobond Diaries*, p. 35.
61. Ibid. p. 39.
62. Burk, *Witness Seminar*, p. 81. Reproduced with permission.
63. Shearlock and Ellington, *The Eurobond Diaries*, p. 40; Peter Norman: *Plumbers and Visionaries: Securities Settlement and Europe's Financial Market* (John Wiley & Sons Ltd, 2007) pp. 29–30.
64. Ibid. p. 41.
65. © The Economist Newspaper Limited, London, 2 November 1968.
66. Kerr, *A History of the Eurobond Market*, p. 98.
67. Ross interview for ICMA's 40th Anniversary Video, 2008.
68. © The Economist Newspaper Limited, London, 2 November 1968.
69. Ross interview for ICMA's 40th Anniversary Video, 2008.
70. Kynaston *City of London*, Vol.4, p. 402.
71. Shearlock and Ellington, *The Eurobond Diaries*, p. 47.
72. Ross interview for ICMA's 40th Anniversary Video, 2008.
73. *AIBD Gazette*, Issue 3, April 1979, p. 28.

74. Minutes of the Issuing Houses Sub-Committee, AIBD, 2 July 1969.

75. *AIBD Gazette*, Issue 3, April 1979, p. 28.

76. Norman, *Plumbers and Visionaries,* p. 24.

77. Kerr, *A History of the Eurobond Market*, p. 94.

78. Norman, *Plumbers and Visionaries*, pp. 26–27.

79. Shearlock and Ellington, *The Eurobond Diaries*, p. 48.

80. Stanley D.L. Ross, *From Where I Stood: Recollections of Twenty Five AIBD Meetings,* p. 3.

81. Ibid. p. 3.

82. Norman, *Plumbers and Visionaries*, p. 38.

83. Ross, *From Where I Stood*, p. 4.

84. Gallant, *The Eurobond Market*, p. 16.

85. *The Independent*, Obituary: Bernie Cornfeld, 1 March 1995.

86. Kerr, *A History of the Eurobond Market*, pp. 32–33.

87. Ibid. pp. 32–33.

CHAPTER 3

Oil and Turmoil

1970–1979

Minos Zombanakis was born in Crete, the son of a local farmer. In 1943 he set off for Athens University but, it was wartime, and the teaching was sporadic. So the young Zombanakis found casual jobs to survive and made up for the lack of teaching with self-study. In 1949 he was drafted into the Greek army, having still not completed his degree. He returned to Greece a lieutenant, after seeing action in the Greek civil war and the Korean War. On leaving the army he went to Washington where he worked on the implementation of the Marshall Plan for Greece. While in the US, he tried to enter Harvard University but with no degree he was unable to register at the graduate school. Undeterred, he had to pay his own way and follow lectures from the back of the class. Eventually he won a scholarship and emerged with a master's degree in public administration. From Harvard he moved to Lebanon but as civil disturbances increased in Beirut he decided to leave and seek a banking position via his former US contacts. He took up a position with Manufacturers Hanover Trust Company of New York as their Middle East representative. Zombanakis was stationed for 10 years in Rome travelling extensively throughout southern Europe and the Middle East.

By the early 1960s the Eurodollar interbank deposit market was well established. As the Eurocurrency pool grew, the deposits were lent out for longer periods. However there was a resistance to issuing term loans, say, for two up to five years as it was felt such loans must be backed by bank deposits of a similar duration. But bank deposits were rarely for more than three or six months. Zombanakis remembers: 'My idea was that if I could create a system where I could have banks commit themselves for two or three year loans, by giving them the possibility to renew the interest rate of these loans every 3 or 6 months, I could hook them for a 2 or 3 year loan.'[1] In 1968 Zombanakis persuaded his bosses in New York to give him £5m to start a new merchant bank in London, Manufacturers Hanover Limited, to carry out syndicated financing.

Before long Zombanakis was approached by an old contact at the Central Bank of Iran who needed $80m to implement 1969's contribution to the country's five-year plan:

I said, sure, I will raise it for you, but I hadn't the slightest clue how to go about it. I started calling various banks, especially banks that had some interest in Iran and I said can you come in for $5m, to the other can you come in for $10m, and to cut *a long story short, I over subscribed the loan ... The question was at what kind of rate do they renew because there would be a syndicate of 10, 15, 35, 50 banks or whatever, and what was the rate?*[2]

Zombanakis set about talking through his idea of advancing a term loan where the rate payable by the borrower would be re-determined every three or six months. The rate would be based on the participating banks' cost of funds plus a spread or profit; which in the case of the Iran transaction was 1.5 to 2%. Bank of America made the first commitment and others followed.

The Iran loan was followed by a $200m loan for Instituto Mobiliare Italiano (IMI). The 'hot autumn' (*autunno caldo*) of 1969–1970 saw a massive series of strikes in the factories and industrial centres of Northern Italy, during which workers demanded better pay and better conditions. The Banca d'Italia was experiencing a substantial outflow of money from Italy due to the social unrest, so the IMI borrowing was in fact for them. 'I said to Carli [Guido Carli, Governor, Bank of Italy] why don't we try to recycle this outflow of money by just giving me one of the good agencies of Italy to come as a borrower and the money then can come back to the central bank,' says Zombanakis. 'I went out for two hundred million dollars which I succeeded in raising and that gave us also the possibility ... to bring up a loan agreement which is used to this day.'[3]

Again Zombanakis used the formula whereby a select group of 'reference banks' within the syndicate would report their cost of funds to the agent bank shortly before the rollover date, and the weighted average, rounded to the nearest $\frac{1}{8}$% plus a 'spread' for a profit, would become the price of the loan for the next period. This key concept for assessing the bank's cost of funds came to be known as the London Inter-Bank Offered Rate, or Libor, and enabled the syndicated loan market to take off. The IMI loan agreement outlined the rights and responsibilities of both borrower and lenders.[4] Indeed it became the blueprint for all subsequent Euroloans which, in the early days, developed largely as a sovereign business.

Minos Zombanakis has become the stuff of legend in the Euromarkets; he was known simply as 'the Greek banker' during the 1970s. He was highly engaging, an outstanding salesman and a shameless self-promoter. He was the first man to publicise his syndicated credits with 'tombstone' advertisements and overtly cultivated the Euromarket media. While he is lastingly remembered as the inventor of the syndicated loan, an international syndicated credit had been put together for Austria at least a year before the Iran loan.

* * *

In the mid-1960s the post-war boom was maintained by the US administration; pouring money into Johnson's 'Great Society' domestic social welfare policies and increasing expenditure for waging the war in Vietnam. Inevitably inflation jumped from just over 1% early in 1966 to nearly 4% in 1967 and continued to rise, reaching 7% late in 1969. Eurodollar interest rates moved sharply upwards in 1969, way in excess of the Regulation Q rate ceilings in the US domestic market. As a consequence dollar deposits were withdrawn from US domestic banks and the funds placed overseas. Short-term rates rose as banks competed for deposits. With short rates increasing rapidly and exceeding the levels offered on long-term bonds, investors sold their bond holdings to invest their funds short-term. With rising rates, and an inverted yield curve, the issuing volume of the overall Eurobond market recorded a decline in 1969 of 27%, the first decline since the market began.[5]

Against this interest rate scenario, arises one of the most popular and, perhaps, least plausible Euromarket stories. Evan Galbraith, then a director of Bankers Trust International (BTI) in London, was taking a bath at his house in Pelham Crescent, Knightsbridge, London. While contemplating the market situation, or his toy duck according to some versions, he came up with the concept of a floating rate note where the interest rate on a loan might be varied at regular intervals in line with the general movement in interest rates. The idea is heralded as one of the key innovations of the Euromarkets.

Perhaps the floating rate note was not quite such a remarkable innovation as recorded in market literature. It was only a small step on from Zombanakis's floating rate syndicated loans and indeed a small bond issue with a floating rate structure had been placed a year earlier on behalf of Dreyfus Offshore Trust NV. Evan Galbraith admitted 'Euro-dollar syndicated bank loans were taking off, and it was familiarity with the bank market that inspired the idea to take a banking concept (changing the interest rate every six months) and apply it to a negotiable bond, marketing it to both banks and bond dealers.'[6] Nonetheless Yassukovitch defended the ENEL FRN's pivotal role in the market:

ENEL was interesting because it was the first example of an innovation developed on this side of the Atlantic. We used to think of ourselves as great innovators in the Euromarket, but the truth is that most breakthroughs were American techniques and concepts that we had adapted for the growing market in Europe. The FRN did not exist in the US at the time, so it was a genuinely de novo concept in the Euromarket.[7]

Peter Spira of Warburgs takes up the ENEL story:

Van came round to discuss his brainchild with Siegmund who immediately saw its significance, especially as interest rates were then very high and borrowers were reluctant to incur burdensome fixed-rate debt obligations, whereas a floating rate would give them maximum flexibility. It was agreed that we should work together on the first issue in this new form, adding White Weld as a third partner. Siegmund again consulted Guido Carli, Governor of the Banca d'Italia (who had come up with the name of Autostrade in 1963) and this time he suggested ENEL, the Italian Electricity Authority, as the borrower. The loan was to be for $125m and would have a maturity of seven years, with the interest rate being fixed every six months at three quarters of one per cent over the rate at which major banks in London borrowed from one another ('LIBOR').

Siegmund decided that, as we had produced the borrower, we should lead the issue, which was quite unfair as Van had thought of the idea. David Scholey and I were duly charged to do battle with Van on this delicate subject and David wisely kept his mouth shut, whilst I made myself unpopular with Van. The upshot was that Warburgs' name appeared first in the prospectus and in the 'tombstones' in Europe whilst BTI prestigiously 'ran the books' (a technical term meaning that they contacted potential buyers and dealt with the paperwork etc.) and they appeared first in the US 'tombstones'.[8]

When Zombanakis, at Manufacturers Hanover heard about the potential ENEL floating rate issue, he was alarmed and took the first available flight to Rome to speak with his old friend, Guido Carli, at the central bank. 'I told Carli that first of all he was going to be paying something like 2.5% front end fees on the bond issue. And I told him that as these notes were totally negotiable they could be sold by anybody, at any time and at a discount that suited the seller, whereas if he did the loan, the paper could only be sold with the consent of the borrower.' Zombanakis offered to do up to a $500m financing for a fee of 0.5. 'The next thing he calls me up and says "I cancelled the mandate, you are to do the loan". I said "I am not going to do the loan, the other guys will do it on my terms".'[9] Accordingly, the Warburg syndicate, in addition to the floating rate note issue, placed a $300m loan on a private basis principally among the London branches of US banks.

David Clark, a money market dealer at BTI and later Group Treasurer for Midland Bank recalls:

> *I remember being in the dealing room all night with Gordon (Anderson) sending out old fashioned telex tapes with the offering details. At about 02.00 a.m. on the Friday a number of senior BT types poured themselves in from Annabels to see how things were going … The FRN was seen at the time as a sort of bridge with the money markets, because of the 6 months fix, at a time when the CD market was taking off. In fact, when we started trading it we made two prices – one in bond price terms less fees and the other as an interest rate yield for 6 months … In reality, the money markets didn't like the issuer as most CDs were in prime bank names, and we reverted to a bond basis quite quickly.*[10]

He also notes that the ENEL deal was the first time the expression 'Libor' had been used in a bond prospectus.

The ENEL Floating rate note (FRN) issue was followed by a $75m 10-year floating rate issue for Pepsico. The Pepsico coupon was set at 75bps over Libor with a minimum coupon of 6.5% and a maximum of 13%. The Pepsico FRN and then a $25m offering for Insilco were both lead managed by Bankers Trust International who would become the leading market-maker in this new sector. Unfortunately a poorly received floating rate note issue for Argentina in late 1970 effectively closed the market for the next few years. The same cannot be said of the syndicated loan market. It is estimated that the volume of loans arranged in 1971 totalled between $8bn and $9.2bn – well above the more publicised Eurobond market's $3.6bn.[11]

But the ENEL FRN was not the only milestone of note. In 1971 Esso Overseas Finance issued the first $100m straight bond issue comprising 7-year and 15-year tranches.[12]

* * *

By the end of the 1960s, the US balance of payments was deteriorating, inflation was continuing to rise, and the dollar was overvalued. The declining international confidence in the dollar led to the depletion of US government gold reserves, as international holders of dollars demanded redemption of their dollars for gold.

On 15 August 1971, without prior warning to the leaders of the other major economies, US President Nixon announced in a televised address to the nation that the US was removing the gold backing from the dollar. This action, which Nixon presented as part of a plan to combat inflation, effectively ended the commitment by the US to redeem international dollar holdings at the rate of $35 per ounce, which had formed the central foundation of the post-war international financial system set in place at the Bretton Woods conference of 1944.

The growth of the Eurodollar market had clearly contributed to the situation, with growing amounts of finance capital now able to move around the world outside the control of governments. This made the task of maintaining stable exchange rates increasingly difficult. The pound came under pressure in 1967, followed by the dollar in 1968. In 1971 the US, for the first time since before the First World War, experienced a balance of trade deficit, leading to the Nixon announcement. The implications of the 'Nixon shock' for domestic and international affairs were profound.

A revision to the Bretton Woods Agreement was signed at the Smithsonian Institute, Washington DC in December 1971. This agreement aimed to maintain fixed exchange rates, but without using gold, and to allow greater fluctuation between currencies. While Bretton Woods allowed the dollar to float in a range of 1%, the Smithsonian Agreement proposed a range of 2.25% ('the snake'). The deutschemark and Dutch guilder were revalued by 13.6% and 11.5% respectively and the dollar was devalued by 7.9% – the first dollar devaluation. Canny bond investors had switched from the weakening dollar into euro DM bonds and were now rewarded for their foresight. With exchange rate realignments agreed, the Eurobond market boomed in 1972 with the Eurodollar sector 67% ahead of the previous year.[13] Stock markets were also buoyant encouraging strong investor demand for convertibles.

By the early 1970s Cedel's settlement system was putting Euro-Clear under increasing competitive pressure. Also Morgan Guaranty was sensitive to the market's ongoing criticism of the system's US ownership. Accordingly in 1972 Morgan Guaranty bowed to the pressure to mutualise the Euro-Clear service and offered shares in the newly incorporated Euroclear Clearance System Ltd to its bank users.

The improved market conditions in the early 1970s allowed new market sectors to develop. 1972 saw the first Australian dollar issue launched for the Rural & Industries Bank of Western Australia and lead managed by Orion Bank. Also in 1972 the Bank of England permitted the first straight Eurosterling issue for Amoco Corporation, formerly Standard Oil Company (Indiana). Because exchange controls were still in place the front page of the prospectus had to carry the rather bizarre legend '£10 million sterling, this is not a sterling security under the meanings of the Exchange Control Act'. It was sold entirely outside the UK.[14] Unfortunately the increasing economic and political uncertainties in the UK at that time contributed to sterling's weakness which impeded the development of the sector. The first Canadian dollar bond issue appeared in 1974. This was a C$15m issue for the British Columbia Municipal Finance Authority led by Crédit Commercial de France.

Orion Bank was a prime example of the new group of consortium banks that had been established in the late 1960s and early 1970s. At that time even large commercial banks had little experience in international banking. For many banks taking a shareholding in a consortium bank was a way of learning the international banking business and of servicing major international clients more effectively. The consortium bank could provide financing on a scale beyond that of individual banks. And indeed most consortium banks were formed to undertake medium-term euro-currency lending. A small number of these banks offered a wider set of investment banking services, most notably Orion Bank and European Banking Company (EBC). These new consortium banks attracted talent from the established players in the market. Ronald Grierson, formerly of Warburgs, became the first Chief Executive of Orion and he, in turn, hired William De Gelsey from M. Samuel (forerunner of Hill Samuel) who would lead their Eurobond activities. Stanislas Yassukovitch, then head of White Weld's London office, which he had established in 1969, was coaxed away to become CEO of

European Banking Company. Eventually Orion would be sold to Royal Bank of Canada and EBC bought by ABN Amro.

* * *

The Euromarkets were growing exponentially, attracting many new entrants into the industry. Walter Koller proposed to the AIBD Board that the Association should undertake a professional education programme. Koller suggested two education programmes, one for junior and one for senior traders. However at the AGM in 1973 the senior trader programme was rejected but Koller was asked to develop the junior programme and appointed Director of Professional Education:

> *During my search for appropriate material … I was able to obtain the help of Professor Michael von Clemm as education consultant … We went through the reading material already collected and the questions put together in numerous hours and Professor von Clemm undertook the task of composing the curriculum. It was designed to give a thorough understanding of the political, economic, legal and monetary context in which Euro-capital markets function and, more importantly, a strong grasp of the workings of the markets in all aspects such as the creation and syndication of new issues, secondary market practices and settlement procedures.*[15]

Koller then set about recruiting 'expert' lecturers. Happily these were found close to home among the AIBD Board members. These senior practitioners proved more than willing to set aside time to educate new entrants to the market. The first one-week residential seminar took place in Montreux in November 1973. 106 students signed up for the course which proved a considerable success. Highlights of the first seminar were Professor von Clemm covering topics from 'Macroeconomics and the Euromarket' to trading in short and medium-term paper. Stanislas Yassukovitch made a presentation on 'New Issues – How to get them', Walter Koller on 'Making a Secondary Market' and Armin Mattle discussing 'Support Operations – Clearing and Settlement'. This was a remarkable line-up of speakers in a market where little had been written down or recorded. The AIBD Diploma course would become a regular annual feature at the Montreux Palace Hotel in Montreux, Switzerland.

Stanley Ross recalls his involvement:

> *I must give credit to Walter Koller because Walter took on education – in fact I think there's still now even a prize given, the Walter Koller Prize in Montreux. But I went there for 10 straight years and I spoke and talked about trading. I once said to somebody, 'I'm going to Montreux again to make a speech' and he said 'What is it this time?' and I said 'Ethics in bond trading' and he said 'Well that's going to be one hell of a short speech'. But it wasn't because there was a bit to say about that.*[16]

A permanent Education Committee was eventually formed in 1977; the same year the AIBD established a permanent Secretar iat in Zurich.

* * *

As the Eurobond market's tenth anniversary approached, dark storm clouds were looming. In 1973 the volume of new Eurobond issues fell from the record $5.3bn in 1972 to $3.5bn and bond prices declined across the board.

Keynesian economic theory suggested that the economy could enjoy permanently lower levels of unemployment, if only it were to tolerate moderately higher levels of inflation. The economists at the US Federal Reserve were diehard Keynesians and the Fed decided to use its monetary policy to increase overall demand for goods and services and keep unemployment low. The only trade-off, these economists believed, would be a safely rising rate of inflation.

Unfortunately, they were proved wrong. The result of unnaturally low unemployment in the 1960s was a 'wage-price spiral'. The government poured money into the economy to increase demand, making prices rise. Workers, noting the rise in prices (inflation), demanded their wages rise accordingly. For a while, employers were willing to raise wages, but then inflation began to rise faster than wages, so unemployment increased even as inflation continued to rise. This situation where the inflation rate is high, the economic growth rate slows down, and unemployment remains steadily high became known as 'stagflation'. It makes life tricky for economic policymakers since measures designed to lower inflation may make unemployment worse, and vice versa.

So on the same date that President Nixon suspended the convertibility of the dollar into gold, he imposed wage and price controls to address these issues. But the wage-price spiral alone wasn't enough to trigger stagflation. The real kicker was the OPEC oil embargo of 1973, which brought oil prices to record new levels. Prices skyrocketed, not only at petrol stations – where long queues and shortages were common – but across all US industries. In 1970, US inflation was 5.5%, by 1974, it was 12.2%, and then it peaked at a crippling 13.3% in 1979. The US was by no means alone; in Britain the annual increase in the retail price index (RPI) peaked at 27% in August 1975.

Despite the Smithsonian currency realignment, the US continued to experience payments deficits throughout 1972, which forced the second dollar devaluation by the beginning of 1973. In February 1973 the dollar's official value was reduced by 10% and the currency was free to float in accordance with market pressures. In the ensuing currency volatility the pound sterling and Italian lira both depreciated relative to the dollar while other European currencies led by the deutschemark and the Swiss franc grew markedly stronger. Between May 1970 and January 1974 most major currencies were floated.

From 1947–1967, the price of oil in US dollars had risen by less than 2% per year. President Nixon's decision to take the US off the gold standard in 1971 had reduced oil exporting countries' earnings and led Organization of Petroleum Exporting Countries (OPEC) members to consider alternative options, such as pricing oil in gold rather than dollars. In October 1973, OPEC ministers were meeting in Vienna when Egypt and Syria launched a joint attack on Israel. After initial losses in the so-called 'Yom Kippur War', Israel with military assistance from the US, Netherlands and Denmark began reversing the Arab gains. By 17 October, the tide had turned decisively against Egypt and Syria, and OPEC decided to use oil price increases in retaliation against Israel and its allies. Israel, as expected, refused to withdraw from the occupied territories, and the price of oil increased by 70% to $5.11 a barrel (from $1.80 in 1970). The following day, oil ministers agreed to an embargo, a cut in production by 5% from September's output, and to continue to cut production in 5% increments until their economic and political objectives were met. Although the fighting ended in late October, OPEC continued to raise the oil price. At OPEC's conference in December, oil prices were raised another 130%, and a total oil embargo was imposed on the United States, the

Netherlands and Denmark. Eventually, the price of oil quadrupled, causing a major energy crisis in the United States and Europe that included fuel shortages and rationing. In March 1974, the embargo against the US was finally lifted after Secretary of State Henry Kissinger succeeded in negotiating a ceasefire agreement between Syria and Israel.

Although prices stabilised, the oil crisis had a profound impact on the global economy. The sharp oil price rise generated unprecedented current account surpluses for oil exporting nations such as Saudi Arabia, Kuwait and the United Arab Emirates (principally Abu Dhabi). Saudi Arabia's revenues ballooned from $7.8bn in 1973 to $35.6bn in 1974, Kuwait's from $3.8bn to $11bn and Abu Dhabi's from $1.8bn to $6.4bn.[17] These 'petrodollar' surpluses, that is, US dollars of oil exporting nations which were in excess of their internal development needs, largely ended up being deposited in US banks. Through a system that came to be known as 'petrodollar recycling' many of these funds were, in turn, lent to oil-importing developing nations to help them finance their energy imports. Nearly $500bn petrodollars were recycled from oil producers with a capital surplus to countries with trade deficits. The foreign debts of 100 developing nations (excluding oil exporters) increased 150% between 1974 and 1977.

Zombanakis recalls:

> *Then came the first oil crisis, we had huge surpluses in the oil producing countries and tremendous deficits in the consuming countries ... I went down to Saudi Arabia ... I knew the Minister of Finance very well, and we started recycling money through this mechanism. This went on and on and the surpluses were becoming bigger, the demands of the various countries were bigger and obviously other banks followed us ... and other syndicated banks opened up.[18]*

Some of those banks were based in the Middle East, most notably the two consortium banks Arab Banking Corporation (ABC) and Gulf International Bank (GIB). Their shareholders were Middle Eastern governments and they became big recyclers of petrodollars through syndicated lending to the developing world. The loans market was the principal beneficiary of the OPEC surpluses, with major syndicated loans to the likes of Mexico, Brazil, Italy, Nigeria and Turkey.

The oil crisis exacerbated the economic difficulties then facing the industrialised nations of the West; increased energy prices dampened economic growth and fuelled inflation. Stock markets everywhere plummeted. Between January 1973 and December 1974, the New York Stock Exchange's Dow Industrial Average benchmark lost over 45% of its value. Worse was the effect in the United Kingdom, and particularly on the London Stock Exchange's FT 30 Index which lost 73% of its value during the crash. From a position of 5.1% real GDP growth in 1972, the UK went into recession in 1974, with GDP falling by 1.1%. Strike action by trade unions led to a three-day week in 1973–74 to conserve power. In addition, the UK's property market was going through a major crisis, and a secondary banking crisis forced the Bank of England to bail out a number of lenders via their 'lifeboat' operation.

Short-term dollar rates hit 13% in 1974 but with the increasing international turmoil investors preferred to focus on safe haven investments such as US Treasury bills. 1974 was a difficult year for all bond markets but particularly the Eurobond market. In February the rate of US Interest Equalisation Tax was reduced to zero and repealed entirely two months later. Many bankers predicted that with the fragile state of the Euromarkets, bond issuance would move back to New York. The *Financial Times* commented:

> *It is clear the promised removal of the US investment restrictions – the Interest Equalisation Tax, the guidelines on US bank lending abroad and the controls over*

direct overseas investment – could imply the disappearance of one of the main foundations of the City's pre-eminence as a world financial centre. It is these controls which have allowed London to flourish and made it a magnet for American and other international banks. In the absence of these artificial restrictions, there is no technical obstacle to stop the market moving back to New York.[19]

Yankee bond issuance increased from approximately $1bn in 1974 to $3.3bn in 1974, to $6.5bn in 1975 and $10.5bn in 1976 reflecting a period of dollar strength. From 1974 to 1978 the volume of US dollar issues by foreign borrowers offered in the US market exceeded the amount of US dollar Eurobond issues.[20] However Yankee issuance tailed off in subsequent years as the low costs and lack of regulation managed to keep the Euromarkets competitive for dollar issuers.

Difficult conditions led to financial crises. In May huge losses were announced at the New York-based Franklin National Bank, which resulted chiefly from their currency trading activities and fraud. A month later Bankhaus I.D. Herstatt, a German private bank, failed resulting in substantial settlement losses. Some of Herstatt Bank's trading counterparties had paid deutschemarks to the bank during the day before its banking licence was withdrawn, believing they would receive US dollars later in the same day in New York. But it was only 10:30am in New York when Herstatt's banking business was terminated. Herstatt's New York correspondent bank suspended all outgoing US dollar payments from Herstatt's account, leaving its counterparties fully exposed to the value of the deutschemarks they had paid the German bank earlier on in the day.

The Herstatt collapse in 1974 had a more lasting legacy as the incident prompted the G-10 nations to form the Basel Committee on Banking Regulations and Supervisory Practices, under the auspices of the Bank of International Settlements (BIS) located in Basel, Switzerland. The BIS itself was established in 1930 to deal with reparation payments imposed on Germany by the Treaty of Versailles following the First World War. Over time the BIS activities changed to concentrate 'on cooperation among central banks and increasingly, other agencies in pursuit of monetary and financial stability'.

It was also a time of political turmoil. In August the long-running Watergate scandal in the US came to a head and President Richard Nixon resigned in the face of almost certain impeachment and removal from office.

All these events took their toll on Eurodollar new issue activity which was down almost 48% in 1974, with just 76 new issues totalling $2bn. The 10 to 20-year maturities common in the first decade of Eurobond issuance were now replaced by issues of 5 to 7 years and issue sizes were cut back.[21] Some lead managers permanently lost their traditional standing in the league tables, for example Hill Samuel, Kredietbank, Kuhn Loeb, Lehman Brothers and Rothschilds.[22]

The high short-term dollar rates meant dealers were reluctant to carry bonds on their books because of the 'negative carry', i.e. short-term financing costs exceeding bond returns. Secondary market turnover slumped – Euroclear's transactions fell from around 4,000 a day to just 1500.[23] Many market participants were unhappy with the reduction in market-making and the consequent reduced liquidity and pressed the AIBD to regulate traders. But the AIBD responded at their AGM in 1975:

In order to crystallise the situation your Board took the initiative to invite a representative group of market-makers to join them in Paris on October 18th (1974), and give their views. As a result it soon became apparent that it would be pointless to continue to try to obtain an agreed definition or lay down measures to regulate the function of a market-maker. There was ample evidence that our community knew their market-makers and what they expected of them, and that during the near twelve years of existence of our market no-one had trouble in contacting those they chose to give business to.[24]

* * *

Times would have been more difficult if not for the developing bond market activity in the Middle East. Middle Eastern Central Bank reserves ballooned after the oil price hike. From 1974 to 1977 oil exporters' surpluses amounted to $172bn of which $67bn was placed on short-term deposit with a group of major commercial banks and so available for recycling in the loan market. However a sum of $76bn was invested in bonds, stocks and real estate.[25] Flights to the Middle East were now booked out by hungry investment bankers.

With the oil price hike, Saudi Arabia, as the dominant oil producer, was accumulating the largest reserves. The Saudi Arabian Monetary Agency (SAMA), the central bank, had appointed 'three wise men' as financial advisors; John Meyer, Chairman, J.P. Morgan, Alfred Schafer, Chairman, UBS, and Robert Fleming, Chairman of the British merchant bank which bore his name. David Potter, who joined White Weld in 1969 as a money market trader and later became Managing Director of Crédit Suisse White Weld, was despatched to Jeddah, where SAMA was then based, to try and acquire deposits. He remembers:

These ['three wise men'] advisors had told SAMA that the only safe place to put your money was on deposit with these five major banks – one of which did not know they were on the list. Over the next few years I sold SAMA several hundred million dollars of CDs (on behalf of this bank) – SAMA used to love CDs because it kept them anonymous – the bank could not believe where this demand was coming from.[26]

Potter recalls visiting Jeddah post the oil price rise:

The Kandara Palace was the only hotel and they would double, or treble book people to stay but, when you arrived, there was 'no room', so I would offer [an incentive of] $10, – 'no room', $20, – 'no room'. A guy gave me a tip; they had Cadillac taxis outside and the guy said go to the front of the queue and say 'Look here's $20 dollars can I sleep in the back seat? The minute you see somebody go, I am going in there to get his room'... I did that several times in 73, 74, 75.[27]

With the rapidly increasing reserves the 'three wise men' advised SAMA to hire experienced investment bankers to manage the rapidly rising cash mountain. Potter recalls that the father of an executive at White Weld in the US had been a doctor to the Saudi royal family and the Saudis felt in his debt. Accordingly when looking for investment advisors White Weld was chosen alongside Barings. Initially two advisors from each bank were selected, David Mulford and David Reid-Scott from White Weld, and Leonard Ingrams and Michael Baring from Barings. Mulford, as Senior Advisor, undertook the investments in as conservative and low key a way as possible in order not to destabilise markets: 'We created a huge portfolio of private placements,' says Mulford. 'SAMA was the biggest operator in the government bond markets, and the biggest holder of US Government bonds. It had a portfolio of private placements and equity in AA and AAA corporate names. We negotiated with governments to smooth out tax barriers and the like, on the understanding we wouldn't disrupt the local market.'[28] 'SAMA's tax-free status and its ability to negotiate special arrangements allowed us to buy assets from Japanese government bonds to German Schuldscheine. We pushed open many doors.'[29]

Potter recalls: 'They started doing private placements for AAA government borrowers and I acted for Warburgs a number of times. Warburgs were on the blacklist.'[30] This was a blacklist of global firms that engaged in business with Israel maintained by the Central Boycott Office of the Arab League. Dr Wilfried Guth, spokesman for the Board of the Deutsche Bank, recollected:

The channelling of funds from surplus to deficit countries took dimensions without precedent in the aftermath of the oil crisis. The recycling process via the Eurobond market started through mid-1974 through unpublicised private placements for various governments and international organisations and continued in 1975 with large sized public issues of $100 million or more – amounts which had formerly been unknown on the Eurobond market.[31]

As Saudi Arabia's reserves grew so did the fortunes of the Kingdom of Bahrain. While Bahrain's oil reserves were modest it was situated close to the sources of petrodollars and had close ties with Saudi Arabia and Kuwait. The Kingdom's importance as a financial centre grew with the Lebanese civil war in 1975. Beirut had long been the financial centre of the Arab world, but the outbreak of hostilities in the country had an immediate impact on the banking industry. Bahrain offered a new location at the centre of the booming Persian Gulf with a large educated indigenous workforce and sound fiscal regulations. In 1975 the Bahrain Monetary Agency (BMA) under the Governor, Alan Moore, initiated a policy of licensing offshore banking units (OBUs) and within months 32 international banks had successfully applied for licences to share in the region's prosperity. In the following five years Bahrain pioneered the growth of a distinct financial market, trading in offshore US dollars.

Kuwait rapidly became the most attractive prospect for aspiring bond salesmen. As their reserves grew, the story circulated that the Kuwait authorities approached the Crown Agents in London to manage the reserves on their behalf but were turned down. The Crown Agents, already managing around $1bn on behalf of foreign government entities and an active investor in the Euromarkets since 1967, were not convinced they wished to substantially build that side of their activities. In subsequent years the story was repeated as the investment banking equivalent of a record company turning down the Beatles. The Crown Agents fell victim to the secondary banking crisis in 1974 and had to be bailed out by the UK government.

Kuwait's investment activities were more diverse and open than those of Saudi Arabia. The Kuwait Investment Office in London was active in the London Stock Exchange and by 1976 owned 5–10% stakes in an array of British companies.[32] At home, Kuwait competed with Bahrain to become the principal financial centre in the Gulf establishing new banks covering traditional and investment banking. Before long every Middle East bond salesmen would be familiar with the three 'Ks', The Kuwait Investment Company (KIC), the Kuwait Foreign Trading Contracting and Investment Company (KFTCIC) and the Kuwait International Investment Company (KIIC). While these investment banks attracted what experienced Kuwaiti bankers there were, most banks, as elsewhere in the Gulf, were managed by US or

European 'ex pats'. As the pool of bond investors proliferated so did the number of visiting bond salesmen in search of business.

The Sheraton hotel in Kuwait City was the staging post for most bankers. Because of the constant flow of bank visitors and the lack of a public transport system, the hotel drivers were constantly busy. Wise sales people would book their driver before their arrival – and the drivers took advantage of the bounty. They would pass on to visiting salesman details of bankers that had recently visited and the different offices they visited. The author acquired a number of new Kuwaiti clients on this basis.

Overseas client visits were important because international communications were at an elementary stage in the mid-1970s. Intercontinental phone lines from Europe were not available on demand. If you wished to speak to your client in the Middle East an international call would have to be booked for a specific time and at least a day in advance with the international operator. At the appointed time the following day the operator would call back and put your call through. If your client was away from his desk then the call was wasted and a new call would have to be booked.

Brian Scott Quinn describes a dealing room in 1975:

> *A dealer's trading office comprises simply a room with a telephone for each trader, which generally has private lines to other traders in the same city. In addition there are telex machines, which allow surer communication with foreign countries than the telephone. Communication in the market, whether by phone or telex is in English. Dealers will also normally have the Reuters Information System, and if they deal in convertibles, will have Videomaster screens for instant access to world stock prices.*[33]

The aspiring Eurobond trader or salesman could not rely on much technological support. Computer technology was confined to 'mainframe' computers where the end-user's requests were filtered through operating staff, or a time-sharing system in which one large processor was shared by many individuals. The personal computer or PC would not appear until the wide availability of microprocessors towards the end of the 1970s. The only technology for calculating bond yields, apart from a slide rule, was a cumbersome 'hand-cranked' mechanical calculator.

The most important long-term effect of the oil crisis on the Euromarkets was to hasten the change from a predominantly retail-dominated investor base to a largely institutional investor base. Large, liquid sovereign and agency issues were increasingly taken up by institutional investors in the Gulf, attracted by the anonymity the bearer bonds provided.

*   *   *

Stanilas Yassukovitch set up White, Weld and Co. Ltd's London office in 1969, and Walter Koller and his team 'rented houses in Wimbledon and got trading' says Yassukovitch.[34] 'They were very cosmopolitan – a lot of Americans, Germans, Swiss and French – a little more flamboyant than the traditional, bowler-hatted London banker.'[35] White Weld's London operation became heavily involved in Eurobond underwriting and trading. By 1972 White Weld would be in second place in the new issue league tables, helped by its relationship with Crédit Suisse. By 1974 Crédit Suisse increased its interest in White Weld and formed the joint venture Crédit Suisse White Weld (CSWW).

In 1963 the First National City Bank of New York (later known as Citibank) had hired Dr Michael von Clemm, a bright, innovative young banker. Von Clemm was born in New York into privileged circumstances: his father was a Bavarian aristocrat, his mother an English one, and he was educated at Exeter, the American equivalent of Winchester.[36] In time he would obtain an anthropology degree from Harvard and a doctorate from Oxford and then spend time as a reporter on the *Boston Globe*. In 1961, First National had launched a new product in the US to its domestic clients, the negotiable certificate of deposit (CD). The CD was a negotiable claim issued by a bank in return for fixed term deposits. The term could vary from one month to five years and because the investor had a fixed term, the instrument paid a higher return than regular bank accounts. Von Clemm was sent to London where he set to work with Yassukovich of White Weld in creating a Eurodollar-denominated CD market. He launched the first issue for First National City Bank in 1966. The market, after a slow start, grew rapidly and CDs became an important cash management tool for banks and corporate treasurers, bridging the gap between term deposits and Eurobonds. However von Clemm himself left First National City Bank in 1966 to lecture at Harvard Business School.

In 1971 Yassukovich coaxed Michael von Clemm back from academia to work for the firm; initially as a consultant on the feasibility of a euro-commercial paper market. A few issues were launched with Schroders but the idea did not catch on.[37] The following year Yassukovitch left White Weld for the European Banking Company (EBC) and, much to von Clemm's annoyance, the CEO role went to John Craven. With the first oil shock, von Clemm focused on developing Euromarket clients in the Middle East. David Potter recalls that von Clemm had T-shirts printed up with a picture of a hand sticking out of the waves and bearing the plea 'Buy Bonds'.

Von Clemm would prove a legendary product champion: he had developed the CD market, particularly as a product for Japanese banks, but more notably he championed the Floating Rate Note (FRN) market. The FRN market had lain dormant since the first issues in the early '70s. 'One day in 1975 we were sitting around doing nothing because the fixed rate market was dead,' remembers a CSWW colleague. 'Suddenly Michael said that it would have to be the private banks which intermediated between OPEC and the deficit nations. But the banks were funding all the new lending with short-term deposits. Michael saw that FRN's could provide them with a more stable liability base.'[38]

Between 1970 and 1975 only 20 FRNs or 'floaters' had been issued, mainly for industrial borrowers and government agencies, with only two bank issues launched, both for Spanish banks. The breakthrough came with a BNP 6-year issue in 1975 that carried a margin of only $\frac{1}{4}$% over Limean, much lower than on previous issues. It was a success and established what was quickly to become the classic bank FRN formula. Other issues quickly followed for the likes of Midland Bank, Bank of Tokyo, C.C.F., Crédit Lyonnais and Banque de Paris et des Pays Bas. Banks became both the main issuers and main investors for floating rate notes. Due to their success in the FRN sector CSWW held on to third place in the league tables from 1976 to 1978. However Japanese city banks were denied access to the floating rate note market by their Ministry of Finance. In response in 1977 CSWW combined their favoured products, with the launch of the Floating Rate Certificate of Deposit (FRCD). The FRCD concept circumvented the restrictions on the FRN market but could provide the required medium term funding.

* * *

In 1978 Merrill Lynch announced its intention to purchase White Weld; driven principally by an interest in their US operations rather than any joint venture in Europe. After extensive negotiations Crédit Suisse sold White Weld but purchased back the minority share in CSWW. This left CSWW with cash but no US partner, and as there was no appetite to build a US business from scratch, then a new partner had to be found.

CEO of CSWW, John Craven, favoured a tie-up with a small firm such as Dillon Read, whereas von Clemm, now Vice Chairman of CSWW and Rainer Gut, Crédit Suisse Chairman, favoured linking with a more significant US firm, preferably a special-bracket firm. (Gut had taken over as Chairman of the Swiss parent bank after the Crédit Suisse, Chiasso scandal.) Discussions veered towards a possible link with First Boston, probably the most lacklustre of the special-bracket firms, whose ranks included Merrill Lynch, Goldman Sachs, Salomon Brothers and Morgan Stanley. First Boston's Jack Hennessy responded positively to the approach as First Boston International had been looking to develop an international presence for some time. A cross-shareholding agreement was reached in July 1978 and company's name changed soon afterwards to Crédit Suisse First Boston (CSFB).[39]

Craven claimed that the agreement between Crédit Suisse and First Boston was reached in secret between von Clemm, Gut and George Shinn of First Boston: 'the terms of the agreement were not disclosed to me, the chief executive, until three hours before the deal was signed. It was a shocking performance and it caused a number of us to say "a plague on both your houses".'[40] A disgruntled John Craven resigned, together with White Weld veterans John Sanders and John Stancliffe, in November 1978. Michael von Clemm became chairman and chief executive of the new bank. 'I remember the day after Craven left, Michael said that we needed such a big market share that we could influence pricing. That was a breathtakingly simple strategy, and it succeeded in FRNs – we won mandate after mandate against other houses bidding cheaper.' recalls David Potter.

With interest rates turning down in 1975 the Eurobond market returned to some semblance of normality and heralded a period of strong growth. New issuance reached $8.3bn that year, $15.2bn in 1976 and $18bn in 1977 and competition among underwriters was hotting up.[41] The first $100m offering came with a two-tranche issue for New Zealand from Kidder Peabody in 1975. Later in the year a further offering by Kidder Peabody for New Zealand was notable as the first 'pre-priced' transaction. This was an 'underwritten placement' where the issuing banks committed to the price up-front thereby adopting increased underwriting risk. The idea was the brainchild of Kidder's Managing Director, Hans-Joerg Rudloff.

Rudloff, often considered as the architect of the modern Euromarkets, was born in Cologne in 1940. Rudloff, whose family business was in the leather trade, studied economics at the University of Bern, where he graduated cum laude, before undertaking further studies at Grenoble. He began his career as a trainee at Crédit Suisse in Geneva. 'It was horribly boring, but later on very useful,' he remembers. After two years he moved to Kidder Peabody: 'A lot of people told me I should have pursued a classic career in banking, and that only bad boys who had failed to make it elsewhere, went to work for American brokers.'[42] After a year at Kidder's New York office he returned to Switzerland and worked his way up to Managing Director of the US firm's Geneva office, dividing his time between Geneva and London.

The New Zealand transaction in October 1975 was managed by a group of seven banks who committed to underwriting the whole issue. There were no sub-underwriting or selling groups, just 20% offered to a select group of selling group members. The invitation telexes stated: 'The issue is being entirely underwritten by a limited number of banks, including the undersigned (Kidder) and will for the most part be placed by them.'[43] Pre-pricing was particularly attractive to borrowers and it did not take long for them to realise that they could invite competing bids from any new issue houses eagerly searching for a mandate.

With continued dollar weakness the deutschemark sector was the principal beneficiary. Euro deutschemark activity grew from DM1.34bn in 1974 to DM7.54bn in 1975. The primary market was still controlled by the German Capital Market Subcommittee established in 1968, comprising the six leading German banks, together with representatives of the Bundesbank and the German Bankers Association. By 1977 primary issuance was being limited to DM1bn to DM1.2bn per month. With increased investor demand for deutschemark investments the sector represented 40% of total issuance in 1978 and strains were appearing within the queue system. A DM500m issue for Canada in 1978 from the Deutsche Bank appeared clearly in excess of the limit.

1977 saw a revival in the Eurosterling market with an offering by the European Coal and Steel Community followed by a further five offerings. The activity was stimulated by sterling's new (North Sea) oil-backed economy and the narrowing differential between sterling interest rates and those prevailing in certain other currency sectors. The Bank of England required that all borrowings over £3m be subject to their timing and consent procedures under the Control of Borrowing Order 1958. The sterling sector subsequently experienced regular stop-start conditions. In 1980 there were 17 new Eurosterling issues – three times the principal amount of the previous year. Now the Bank would allow foreign banks to co-lead manage a Eurosterling offering as long as there were reciprocal arrangements in the foreign bank's market.[44]

The Euroyen market was opened in 1977 with an immensely popular ¥10bn issue for the European Investment Bank. Until this time yen financing had only been available through the foreign bond, or 'Samurai' market. The liberalisation of both markets was aimed at reducing pressure for the appreciation of the yen. Both markets started off under strict government control with detailed guidelines on issuer eligibility, bond structure and issue amounts. Borrowers that were allowed to use the Euroyen market had to be triple-A rated supranationals and sovereigns. Supranationals had to have issued in the Samurai market at least once and sovereign issuers at least three times before they could qualify for the Euroyen market and in any event issue size was limited to ¥15bn.[45] Euroyen bonds would become more common after 1984, when Japan extended the type of borrowers who could access the market, as long as they could meet strict criteria with regard to their financial condition.

Eurodollar issue sizes were growing rapidly. By early 1976 the EEC would launch a $500m issue through Deutsche Bank, and by December 1977 a single tranche $500m 12-year offering for Shell International Finance was launched by UBS. This was again a 'pre-priced deal' with the three major Swiss banks making a joint proposal to Shell and then forming a syndicate once the proposal was accepted.[46] It would stand as a corporate issuance record for the next six years.

In order to circumvent the Swiss law preventing Swiss banks from underwriting Eurobonds the major Swiss banks set up overseas underwriting subsidiaries. Armin Mattle was appointed Managing Director of UBS (Securities) which opened for business on 1 January 1975. Mattle shunned the traditional practice of allowing Eurobond underwriters who couldn't place paper to return their unplaced bonds to the lead manager. He now insisted that underwriters *must* honour their underwriting commitment regardless of whether they had placed their paper. He stated publicly that 'syndication was a business not a charity'.[47] Other houses would follow his example in the increasingly competitive new issue markets.

From the earliest days cut-throat competition had characterised the new issues market. Banks were desperate to feature in as senior a position as possible on 'Tombstones'– a transaction advertisement ranking the syndicate banks' roles – and thereby gain valuable league table status. In practice many syndicates degenerated into various degrees of indiscipline and covert practice.

Houses in the market wanted to become big new issue players quickly, and they assumed if they could lead manage a high profile deal they might attract other, similar prestigious mandates. Increasingly, banks were prepared to do loss-leading deals, and they would look to pass those losses to the syndicate and/or dump the excess paper on the syndicate. There was no obligation on the lead manager in the early days to supply a supporting bid when launching an offering.

Surely with such mispriced deals other banks would be unwilling to join the syndicate?

But co-managers felt pressured to accept invitations into deals that they were unlikely to sell at a profit. A refusal to the lead manager could risk exclusion from future deals. So finely priced transactions prompted a race by co-managers to dispose of their bonds as quickly as possible – whether to investors or intermediaries it didn't matter. While Eurobonds at the time carried fees amounting typically to 2% on a 10-year offering, these fees were seldom earned, as initial offering prices of new issues typically fell to, at least, full fee levels. This was especially the case once Ross and Partners were posting 'grey market' new issue prices.

By the mid-70s central banks and large investing institutions were probably taking around half of all new issues and they soon realised they could demand big discounts on new issues from underwriters. In addition 'junior league underwriters were often happy to cut a deal in order to be able to inflate their indications of interest to the lead manager – something that might let them in the next hot issue.'[48] No amount of losses or failed offerings seemed to dampen the banks' competitive appetite to lead new issues. Eugene Rotberg, former Treasurer of the World Bank recollects:

> [S]preads got extremely tight, and it was clear underwriters just wanted to grab league table credit because few of these issues could be sold at two, three or five basis points over Treasuries. Indeed, that was one of the reasons why an institution like the World Bank was rather late entering the Euromarket because we realised that the bonds would often be held within the underwriting syndicate for a long period of time because they were so tightly priced … The expression that I some-times used was the underwriting firms were delighted to be buried under their own tombstone ads.[49]

Tombstones were a US import. In a 'tongue-in-cheek' article in the *AIBD Gazette* entitled: 'Sense and Nonsense of Tombstones' Stanislas Yassukovich explained that:

> the phrase 'This announcement appears as a matter of record only' started life as an untruth. It should read 'This announcement is made to show existing and potential clients that we have bagged another mandate, against stiff competition, particularly against the firm whose name appears after ours, and we invite inquiries for operations

of a similar nature as well as any other business that a reminder of our name and prestige may occasion.'… As tombstones proliferated, to the delight of the financial publications and the yawns of their readers, banks not in the business grew restive at their conspicuous absence from these mysterious boxes with names of banks neatly listed.[50]

The launch of financial publications such as *EuroWeek* and *International Financing Review* (IFR) kept participants up to date with developments in the new issue market, and fuelled the competitive appetite of the banks.

The surge in new issuance activity prompted the Board of the AIBD, under the Chairmanship of Yassukovich, to form a Primary Market Committee. 'Even though the AIBD has no specific jurisdiction over primary market matters, it would be regrettable if government initiatives were taken which could interfere with the presently smooth functioning of the Eurobond market without some advance consultation … The existence of a Primary Market Committee will encourage the authorities to undertake such consultation.'[51]

A further initiative had been taken to support primary issuance. The *AIBD International Bond Manual* was launched in 1977. This gave all the relevant details on every new issue as it came to market, from the commercial terms to the members of the syndicate. On its first printing 800 copies were sold.

The *Bond Manual* complemented the invaluable *Quotations and Yields* book for the secondary market. Initially this was produced monthly with quotations and yields on every extant Eurobond and a list of the relevant market-makers. In May 1976 the *Financial Times* began publishing the market quotations and yields on a monthly basis so raising awareness of the expanding market.

* * *

The secondary market remained the key area of focus for the AIBD. In the Eurobond market's early days, traders were expected to make two-way prices to their investing clients regardless of whether they knew the investor's intention to buy or sell. This largely followed traditional London Stock Exchange trading practice. In active or large issues there could be more than 20 market-makers per issue. A price would be quoted, normally with a half point spread in amounts varying from $100,000 to $1,000,000 by individual market-makers who would look to make an $\frac{1}{8}$% on average market size transactions. Investors would check various two-way quotations and then deal with the market-maker with the most attractive price. Such 'blind' dealing practices gradually fell out of favour as traders found it increasingly difficult to avoid losses from unscrupulous traders and, occasionally, unscrupulous clients. Increasingly market-makers, particularly with the influx of the US trading houses, would request that investors declare their dealing intentions before making a price.

Market-makers themselves could ask two-way prices of other market-makers, often conditional on supplying requested two-way prices in return. Both trading parties were at liberty to deal with each other on this 'knock-for-knock' basis. The AIBD expected a Eurobond market-maker to provide a two-way price to any AIBD-recognised (i.e. 'reporting') dealer in all those issues in which he was listed as a market-maker in the monthly *Quotations and Yields* publication. As of 1979 there were 92 market-makers registered with the AIBD, of whom 41 conducted their business from London.

Brian Scott Quinn describes Eurobond trading in 1975:

Although the market has been in existence for only ten years, already there are hundreds of securities available. It is noticeable that dealers do not trade actively in all of these ... The greatest activity usually follows the new issue when the so-called backing and filling process takes place. This is the time when bonds not in firm hands come back on to the market and are resold ... Secondary market activity then tends to decline as an issue becomes seasoned and floating supply diminishes. After this time activity in the secondary market will tend to fluctuate according to the structure of the sinking fund. Since interest rates have shown a secular rise for many years, a great many bonds are now trading below par. It is thus advantageous for issuers to fulfill their sinking fund obligations by purchasing bonds in the market. One dealer has said that sinking fund activity represents the single most consistent and powerful source of volume and support of the secondary market. Investment buying in the secondary market on the other hand is erratic and influenced by the level of new issue activity.[52]

It was usual at the time for Eurobond issues to include sinking funds. The borrower agreed to redeem a portion of the bonds each year until final maturity, beginning a number of years after issue:

The reasons why investors require a sinking fund differ from those associated with sinking funds on domestic bonds or on Eurocurrency credits, namely applying discipline to the borrower. The primary reason seems to be to give support to the secondary market ... Eurobond secondary markets are generally held to be weak with selling predominant: and without a sinking fund to take up such sales, prices in the secondary market would tend to be depressed.[53]

So how did traders manage their trading risk? Iain Baillie, formerly of Strauss Turnbull and Salomon Brothers, comments: 'My guess is it was the late 1970s before the average Eurobond desk discovered that they could hedge out interest rate risk by selling US Treasuries. Until then the major price determinant was interest rates, not credit. It was from the late 1970s, early 1980s when most Eurobond books started to be fully hedged. That was a very simple limiter of risk.'[54]

A recurrent topic at the time for the AIBD Board was the development of automated trading systems. Stanley Ross bemoaned the AIBD AGM in Paris in 1977 for the 'curiously negative attitude adopted by the assembly generally (the Board included) towards the debate on automated systems in our marketplace. I think they will come. Whether we like it or not automation is here to thrive.'[55]

In 1978 Stanley Ross was ousted from the management of Kidder's London desk by the rapidly rising Hans-Joerg Rudloff. Ross picks up the story:

So then I set up a small firm called Ross and Partners, the activities of which made me famous, or should I say infamous in the eyes of the global new issue community. It was the so-called 'grey market'. This was to change forever the way the new issue market operated. In those days, managers competed so fiercely for issues and in order to win them they often bid over the odds. Thus, deals came to market over-priced in relation to the same name or similar issues.

The idea of the opportunity to position our little company came when a Japanese house offered me some (Nitto) convertibles less 5.5%. This was amazing, I had never heard of such a discount. But nobody wanted to buy them. It came at par, but there was no after-market. The first trade took place 10 days later at 88.5. I thought to myself there is a turn to be made here somewhere. But for us to capitalise on that, we first had to make the market transparent.

Now using the word transparency to the early Eurobond managers had the same effect as holding up a cross to Dracula. My firm was the very first to use the new Reuter communication screen facility to display to the world my own take on the new issue prices, on the very first screen RAPC ... Reuters told me gleefully that they had so much demand to get my screen, particularly from the Swiss banks, they simply could not install the sets fast enough ... All the Swiss banks had begun to wonder why they were paying issue price net when offers on my screen showed at less 1 % or even lower. At one time I feared that groups of the new issue managers were going to come round to my office, break down the doors, and string me up ... They didn't like what I was doing and they would try to act upon my prices in order to make me change them to a level at which the new issue house wanted them to appear.[56]

The AIBD 10th Anniversary AGM took place in London. Ross regarded it as the most important:

The Board had been persuaded by the new issue firms to try to stamp out grey market trading, or, as I preferred to call it, pre-market trading, in new issues. In our Rulebook was a recommendation which they insisted now be turned into a Rule. It basically forbade the trading of an issue until the deal had been signed. I had felt it absurd ...There must have been enormous pressure on (Yassukovich) from the great band of powerful issuing institutions to put a stop to an activity which dared to challenge their collective judgements of how a deal was to be priced and traded. Amazingly enough however, they all totally misjudged the mood of the times ... When it came to a vote, after long and heated exchanges from the floor, the assembly, virtually, unanimously threw out the Board's proposal ...

Although I lived to fight again, suddenly I no longer had a monopoly, since all those firms which had formerly stood aloof from 'grey market' business, now after such support, considered it to be a perfectly legitimate activity and trading boomed.[57]

Indeed the acceptance of the 'grey market' contributed in attracting inter-dealer broker (IDB) firms from New York. The inter-dealer broker is a brokerage firm that acts as an intermediary between major market-makers to facilitate inter-dealer trades. The broker normally only deals with market-makers, seeking to match buy and sell orders. He works for a very small fee payable by the initiator of an order and not by the counterparty. The broker provides anonymity to traders' activities – particularly valuable in the primary market as Ross & Partners had demonstrated. In time traditional trader-to-trader dealing fell away. With the arrival of the brokers, market-makers would increasingly look to unwind or 'lay off' their trades with the broker rather than ring up another market-maker directly.

The first IDB to arrive was Purcell Graham in 1978, but within a few years, despite pockets of opposition from the traditional trading community, five inter-dealer brokerages were operating in London. The development of a US-style broking system in Europe had been particularly promoted by Salomon Brothers. Ian Baillie recalls:

> *It was the American investment banks that really encouraged the introduction of inter-dealer brokers. They were not enthusiastic about the amount of time that dealers all spent dealing with each other – and out drinking with each other, it has to be added … That was the driving force behind bringing in interdealer brokers, because the view was that it freed up the trader's time so they could focus a) on value, and b) providing liquidity to clients, which was becoming the primary goal.*[58]

Charles McVeigh had relocated from Salomons' famed New York trading floor in 1975 and set about establishing a trading franchise in Europe. Salomons started trading Eurobonds out of their London office in 1976 and were prepared to deal in larger size than the market norm and on narrower spreads – narrowing the bid-to-offer spreads from the standard half point to a quarter point. In time the core of the secondary market was formed by those houses acting as reporting dealers and a small number of inter-dealer brokers.

The development of the grey market enabled unscrupulous issuing houses, who competed with each other in trying to win mandates, to sell competitors' issues short and look to spoil their transaction, while themselves remaining anonymous. Increasingly lead managers would need to stabilise transactions by keeping a bid in the market to maintain the performance of the issue.

Stabilisation is a procedure designed to prevent volatility in the price of the bonds caused by the actions of intermediaries or short-term investors. The process of selling a new issue to 'end' investors can take time and, to prevent downward price volatility, the managers may offer for sale more bonds than the issuer is in fact going to issue (for example selling of $105 million bonds on a $100 million issue) and then purchase the over-allotted bonds ($5 million in our example) in the market, thus supporting the price of the issue. On the closing of the transaction, the managers would set off the bonds they were entitled to receive (e.g. $5 million) against the bonds they were obliged to deliver to the investors (e.g. $105 million), eliminating the excess.

Since stabilisation effectively involves market manipulation or creating an artificial market, it is permitted only under prescribed conditions in today's regulated markets. Previously, as new issues tended to be priced too tightly, then the stabilisation of new issues was commonplace. Of course stabilisation activities could result in a profit or a loss for the underwriting syndicate. Robert Gray, formerly of J.P. Morgan, remembers: 'there was not much science as to which of the bonds the lead manager had bought back should be deemed stabilisation bonds, and for which the syndicate would be charged accordingly'.[59] In the early days stabilisation losses were charged in a cavalier fashion to all syndicate members, often wiping out their fees. For example, when UBS (Securities) launched a convertible issue for Ciba Geigy in July 1979, they charged the underwriting syndicate more for stabilisation costs than they received in fees. The underwriting fees were 0.5% while the expenses cap was 1% of commitments. 'In all probability, the underwriters had probably sold their allotments back to the lead.'[60] In time the rules were changed limiting the underwriters' liability for stabilisation claw-backs to the level of gross commissions.

However one had to be careful when selling bonds back to the lead manager through the inter-dealer broker, particularly if some traders might be selling short. Gray adds: 'syndicate members did not know until very late in the day sometimes as to what their allotment was.

This created an extraordinary game of bluff with the lead manager, with the implicit threat of a (bear) squeeze by under-allotting the syndicate if the thing went extremely badly, which it did on several occasions.'[61]

If the international bond market was growing apace then the syndicated loan market was exploding, fuelled by petrodollars. In 1977 there were 460 loans amounting to $34,859m, in 1978 there were 1019 loans totalling $81,763m and in 1979 1077 loans for a total of $101,612m. Over $43bn of this 1979 figure was going to non-OPEC emerging markets. Concern was growing at the ballooning debts of developing countries, with Zaire defaulting in 1976 and Turkey in 1977.[62] A 1977 report from the US Senate Subcommittee on Foreign Relations noted: 'The most immediate worry is that the stability of the US banking system and by extension the international financial system may be jeopardised by the massive balance of payments lending that has been done by commercial banks since the oil price hike.'[63]

$*$　$*$　$*$

With the collapse of the Bretton Woods system, European leaders had been keen to maintain the principle of stable exchange rates rather than moving to the policy of floating exchange rates that was gaining popularity in the USA. In March 1972, the EU Member States created the 'snake in the tunnel'. This was a mechanism for managing fluctuations of European currencies (the snake) within narrow limits against the dollar (the tunnel). The tunnel collapsed in 1973 when the US dollar floated freely leaving a modest deutschemark zone comprising Germany, Denmark and the Benelux countries. However the early demise of the snake did not diminish interest in trying to create an area of currency stability.

A new proposal for European Monetary Union (EMU) was put forward in 1977 by the then President of the European Commission, Roy Jenkins. It was taken up in a more limited form and launched as the European Monetary System (EMS) in March 1979, with the participation of all Member State currencies except the UK and sterling (which joined in 1990). The idea was to establish stable but adjustable exchange rates in relation to the newly created European Currency Unit (Ecu) – a currency basket based on a weighted average of EMS currencies. The Ecu became the basis of the idea of creating a single currency in Europe. Within the EMS, currency fluctuations were controlled through the Exchange Rate Mechanism (ERM) and kept within 2.25% band either side of the central rates, with the exception of the Italian lira, the Spanish peseta, the Portuguese escudo and the pound sterling, which were allowed to fluctuate in a 6% band.[64]

While continental European governments feared the de-stabilising effect of hot money flows and created the European Monetary System, the UK and US were looking to abolish controls.

In May 1979 a new Conservative government led by Margaret Thatcher was elected in the UK. This government was committed to lifting the controls and regulations that they believed were stifling enterprise and distorting markets. In October Chancellor Geoffrey Howe announced the abolition of UK exchange controls to a stunned financial community, saying they 'had outlived their usefulness'. The *Financial Times'* Lex column remarked: 'After 40 years – longer than the working lifetimes of most people in banking and the stock market – exchange controls have gone.'[65] Though abolition was undertaken mainly for ideological reasons, it was also driven in part by the fact that Britain had become a major oil producer for the first time. North Sea oil was earning generous dollar revenues which, if not offset by an outflow of capital, would have led to a significant balance of payments surplus, an over-valued pound and a consequent deterioration in the competitiveness of British exports. Indeed, the initial effect of abolition was a sharp appreciation of the pound causing problems for UK exporters and exacerbating the recession of the early 1980s.

But the result was that institutions, such as insurance companies and pension funds, could now move money across borders. In Britain that presented a challenge to the stockbrokers and market-makers (known as 'jobbers') who had controlled share trading. Big investors complained that the brokers charged too much under an anti-competitive system of fixed commissions. Thus began the inevitable move towards deregulation and 'Big Bang' in the City.

Prior to the abolition of exchange controls, currency swaps were developed to get around UK foreign exchange controls. At that time, UK companies had to pay a premium to borrow in US dollars. To avoid this, UK companies set up 'parallel' or 'back-to-back' loan agreements with US companies wishing to borrow sterling. For example, two companies, one based in the UK with a subsidiary in the US and one in US with a subsidiary in the UK, might decide to conduct a parallel loan arrangement to avoid exchange controls. The UK company would loan out a fixed amount of sterling to the US subsidiary in the UK. In turn, the US company would extend a specified amount of dollars to the UK-based subsidiary in the US, with the exchange rate being based on the current daily exchange rate. The two companies would agree on a term for the loans, usually five to ten years, at which time they would exchange currencies once again, completing the cycle. The loan agreement often included some form of forward contract, so that if one currency depreciates, the party lending that currency will increase total payments in order to offset changes in the loan's value arising from the change in the exchange rate. Both subsidiaries get the currency required without needing to go via the forex market. A 'back-to-back' loan differs from a parallel loan only in that the parent companies lend funds to each other directly.[66]

In September 1979 a subsidiary of Royal Bank of Canada, Roylease, sought to raise Canadian $38 million. The Treasurer of Roylease instructed his lead manager, Orion Bank, that he required funding below 11% equivalent in Canadian dollar terms but without exposing Roylease to foreign exchange risk. Phillip Hubbard, Managing Director of Orion Bank at the time, devised a novel solution. Roylease would issue a DM60 million private placement, deutschemarks being the currency particularly favoured by investors at the time. The deutschemark proceeds were then converted into Canadian dollars and the deutschemark exposure hedged forward for the full five-year maturity. Clearly there was a cost to the hedge but taking this into account Orion managed to provide their borrower with funding at an all-in cost of 10.95% in Canadian dollars. Bonds with currency swaps attached now opened up a much wider potential range of funding options for international borrowers, although the concept didn't gather pace until the World Bank, IBM full liability swap in 1981.[67]

Inflation was running out of control on both sides of the Atlantic. The new Thatcher government in the UK, unlike their Labour predecessors, strongly supported monetarist economic theory. Monetarism placed a priority on controlling inflation rather than controlling unemployment.

The US Administration had been holding on to the Keynesian view that inflation could 'prime the pump' of the economy and be self-correcting, and so had resisted raising interest rates. The outcome of this policy was a collapsing dollar. In the year to November 1978 the dollar had fallen nearly 34% against the German mark and almost 42% against the Japanese yen, prompting the Carter administration to launch a 'dollar rescue package' including emergency sales from the US gold stock, borrowing from the International Monetary Fund, auctions of Treasury securities denominated in foreign currencies and raising the discount rate to a then historic high of 9.5%.

The bond markets had to adapt to a new high interest rate environment and a consequent drop in new issue volumes. Six-month Libor moved from 12.43% on 31 December 1978 to a high of 16.06% on 20 October 1979.[68] As rates kept rising, floating rate notes were the product of choice. In March 1979 Citicorp issued the first 3-monthly-refix FRN which enabled the bearish investor to remain in the market but minimise risk to the 3-month interest rate. A further variant, attractive in the rising rate environment, was the Citicorp Rolling Rate Note. This fixed monthly at 3-month Limean, thus allowing the investor to receive a 3-month return while only exposed to a 1-month risk. A less successful innovation was the 'drop-lock' FRN. TVO Power issued an FRN which converted automatically into a fixed rate bond with a coupon of 9% if 6-month Libor fell below 8.75%. Finally FRNs convertible at the lender's option were experimented with. As a result, in 1979 35% of dollar issuance was accounted for by FRNs.[69]

The second oil shock would add to the US administration's inflationary woes. After the first oil price hike, the rapid rise in oil revenues transformed the economic fortunes of the Middle East oil exporting countries. However in Iran, a mood of resentment was building, particularly with regard to the Shah and his family, with accusations of corruption and extravagance rife. Opponents of the Shah's regime called for a return to traditional Islamic values. As social and political tensions increased, support was building for Ayatollah Khomeini, a conservative Islamic cleric who was exiled in Iraq. Strikes, demonstrations and riots grew to such an extent that the Shah was forced to flee Iran in January 1979 and Ayatollah Khomeini became the country's new leader.

The Islamic revolution severely disrupted the Iranian oil sector, with production greatly reduced and exports suspended. When oil exports were later resumed under the new regime, they were intermittent and at a lower volume, which pushed prices up. The US administration under President Jimmy Carter began a phased deregulation of oil prices in April 1979, and within 12 months the oil price more than doubled, adding to the already high US inflation rate. As oil prices doubled the OPEC surpluses soared yet again to $62bn in 1979 and $115bn in 1980.

Inflation and interest rates in the US soon reached their highest levels since the Second World War. In August 1979 a beleaguered President Carter appointed the economist Paul Volcker as Chairman of the Federal Reserve. The bond market rallied briefly on the news but the dollar continued to deteriorate. Volcker persuaded the Federal Reserve Board that they should target monetary reserves rather than the federal funds rate, effectively allowing interest rates to rise to unforeseen levels. By November, with inflation at 13% and the oil price trading at $40, Volker was forced to raise interest rates again, increasing the US prime rate to an alarming 15.75%.

The second oil shock intensified the debt-service problems of less developed countries (LDCs). In 1979 debt-service ratios of Latin American economies averaged more than 30% of export earnings, with Brazil's debt-service ratio near to 60%. The higher interest rate environment in 1980 led to an appreciation of the dollar exchange rate, increasing the difficulty of meeting these, largely dollar-based, debt burdens.

NOTES

1. Minos Zombanakis interview for ICMA's 40th Anniversary Video, 2008.
2. Ibid.
3. Ibid.
4. Kynaston, *City of London*, Vol. 4, pp. 445–446.

5. Fisher, *Eurobonds*, p. 13.
6. Kerr, *A History of the Eurobond Market*, p. 38.
7. *EuroWeek*, Issue: 1970s – 'Blazing a Trail', 20 June 2003.
8. Spira: *Ladders and Snakes* (1997) pp. 164–165.
9. Zombanakis interview for ICMA's 40th Anniversary Video, 2008.
10. Note to the author, 1 November 2012.
11. Kynaston, *City of London*, Vol. 4, p. 445.
12. Gallant: *The Eurobond Market*, p. 20.
13. Fisher, *Eurobonds*, p. 14.
14. Burk, *Witness Seminar* p. 75. Reproduced with permission.
15. *AIBD Gazette*, Issue 3, April 1979, p. 45.
16. Ross interview for ICMA's 40th Anniversary Video, 2008.
17. Richard Roberts, *Take Your Partners: Orion, the Consortium Banks and the Transformation of the Euromarkets* (Palgrave, 2001) p. 93.
18. Zombanakis interview for ICMA's 40th Anniversary Video, 2008.
19. *Financial Times*, London, 19th February 1973, p. 26.
20. Hayes and Hubbard, *Investment Banking*, p. 50.
21. Gallant, *The Eurobond Market*, p. 20.
22. Hayes and Hubbard, *Investment Banking*, p. 49.
23. Shearlock and Ellington, *The Eurobond Diaries*, p. 75.
24. AIBD AGM 1975, Report of the Market Practices Committee.
25. Roberts, *Take Your Partners*, p. 94.
26. Conversation with the author, 5 November 2012.
27. Ibid.
28. *Euromoney*, Heroes and Villains, June 1999.
29. IFR, 25th Anniversary, 1974 to 1999, August 1999, p. 32.
30. Conversation with the author, 5 November 2012.
31. *The Eurobond Market: 10 years of Development*, A Conference sponsored by the AIBD, London, 30 May 1979, p. 28.
32. Roberts, *Take Your Partners*, p. 98.
33. Brian Scott Quinn, *The New Euromarkets: A Theoretical and Practical Study of International Financing in the Eurobond, Eurocurrency and Related Financial Markets* (London: Macmillan Press Ltd, 1975) p. 78.
34. *Euromoney*, Heroes and Villains, June 1999, p. 34.
35. *Bloomberg*, Gruebel, Crédit Suisse Survivor, 27 June 2008, quoting S. Yassukovich.
36. ©The Economist Newspaper Limited, London, *Michael von Clemm*, 20 November 1997.
37. *Euromoney*, Michael von Clemm; End of a Legend, January 1986.
38. Ibid.
39. Hayes and Hubbard, *Investment Banking*, pp. 299–302.
40. *EuroWeek*, Taming the Wild West, 20 June 2003.
41. Kynaston, *City of London*, Vol. 4, p. 568.
42. *EuroWeek*, Blazing a Trail, 20 June 2003.
43. Kerr, *A History of the Eurobond Market*, p. 105.
44. Hayes and Hubbard, *Investment Banking*, p. 197.
45. Gallant, *The Eurobond Market*, p. 91.
46. Kerr, *A History of the Eurobond Market*, p. 53.
47. Shearlock and Ellington, *The Eurobond Diaries*, pp. 55, 62.
48. Ibid. p. 55.
49. IFR, 2,000th Issue, *Eurobond Retrospective Roundtable*, September 2013.
50. *AIBD Gazette*, Issue 5, April 1980, pp. 13–14.
51. *AIBD Gazette*, Issue 1, January 1978, p. 12.

52. Scott Quinn, *The New Euromarkets*, pp. 79–80.
53. Ibid. pp. 53–54.
54. IFR, 2,000th Issue, Eurobond Retrospective Roundtable, September 2013.
55. Ross, *From Where I Stood,* p. 6.
56. Ross interview for ICMA's 40th Anniversary Video, 2008.
57. Ross, *From Where I Stood,* p. 7.
58. IFR, 2,000th Issue, Eurobond Retrospective Roundtable, 12 September 2013.
59. Ibid.
60. Shearlock and Ellington, *The Eurobond Diaries*, p. 62.
61. IFR, 2,000th Issue, Eurobond Retrospective Roundtable, September 2013.
62. Kynaston, *City of London*, Vol. 4, p. 568.
63. US Senate Subcommittee on Foreign Relations, International Debt, the Banks, and US Foreign Policy, 95th Congress. 1st Session, 1977.
64. EU Commission website (www.ec.europa.eu) *Economic and Financial Affairs: The Road to EMU, Phase 2. From the Werner Report to the European Monetary System, 1970 to 1979.*
65. *Financial Times,* London, 24 October 1979; Kynaston, *City of London*, Vol. 4, p. 585.
66. Bowe, *Eurobonds*, p. 212.
67. Kerr, *A History of the Eurobond Market*, p. 56.
68. Ibid. p. 55.
69. Fisher, *Eurobonds*, p. 16.

CHAPTER 4

Masters of the Market

1979–1984

The subject of Michael von Clemm has always evoked mixed responses. 'A visionary of the Euromarkets … he built (the FRN) into the largest single component of the international bond markets. He did so almost single-handedly, and, in von Clemm fashion, totally single-mindedly. Banks, power companies, governments: all received the famous von Clemm visit: the compelling sales talk, the piercing eyes, transfixing issuers in the remotest parts of the world.'[1] 'He impressed most of the bankers and borrowers he encountered, with his intellect, his powerful personality and the breadth of his interests.'[2] Others describe him as 'vain, aggressive, arrogant and autocratic', browbeating borrowers into awarding CSFB mandates.[3] His three-year tenure as Chairman and Chief Executive of CSFB was characterised by great creativity, considerable risk-taking and continuous internal strife. One of his managing directors at the time felt 'Von Clemm's management style changed the character of the bank. In the 1970s we'd had a good team spirit, but it stopped being an enjoyable place to work. You had to fight to get things done, and he liked to unsettle people.'[4]

If von Clemm felt people needed to be unsettled, then the hiring of Hans-Joerg Rudloff in early 1980 to run CSFB's syndicate department, would certainly do the trick.

With his new hire Von Clemm would revive the pre-priced issue concept that Rudloff had pioneered at Kidder Peabody and take it a step further into the 'bought deal'. Oswald Gruebel, who had joined CSWW in 1970 from Deutsche Bank, Mannheim, was now heading the Eurobond trading desk at White Weld Securities *(despite the First Boston merger their old identity was retained until becoming CSFB Securities in 1984)*. Not long after Rudloff's arrival, Gruebel observed at a morning meeting that there was very good demand for triple A rated paper and questioned 'why don't we go to an issuer and offer to buy the paper direct?' Von Clemm immediately telexed IBM in the US, proposing fixed terms for a bought deal. IBM declined the offer and a similar proposal to buy $100m of five-year bonds at a rate at 13.125% was made to Thomas Patton, GMAC's Executive Vice President. The rate looked very competitive to Patton but he was required to respond rapidly. Patton awarded CSFB the mandate 30 minutes later, but too late in the day to launch in Europe. CSFB carried the risk of the entire transaction overnight until a successful launch the following morning. It was notable that GMAC had been a long-standing customer of Morgan Stanley. The bought deal gave underwriters the ability to break traditional corporate finance relationships.

Von Clemm and Rudloff followed this successful bought deal with a similar offering for J.C. Penney and a host of others:

> *I realised very rapidly that borrowers could not live with the interest rate volatility we were seeing in the early 1980s. You would start out negotiations for an issue priced at 8.25% and by the time you had been through all the preparation and documentation, which would take four weeks, the market would have moved against you and the borrower was looking at higher rates. We said 'Let's remove that risk by taking the exposure ourselves', which is obviously the role a bank should be playing. It was a question of judgement on how a name would be accepted by investors.*[5]

A colleague, Michael Dobbs-Higginson, observed: 'Von Clemm saw that bought deals were a way we could differentiate ourselves from other houses. Large banks could not compete with us in making semi-instantaneous decisions.'[6]

It was all about winning deals from the competition. Now, the lead manager or managers would buy the whole of a new issue on predetermined terms and price prior to announcement rather than waiting until the formal offering day, some two weeks later, when such terms were normally set in the light of then prevailing market conditions. It was about financial muscle, balance sheet capacity and risk appetite. Furthermore, transactions were protected from possible losses arising from uncontrolled selling by syndicate members. 'We weren't prepared to go out and discuss with the issuer which banks should be included in the management group. We eliminated the whole syndicate discussion which normally takes place with the borrower.'[7] Over time the bought deal was a significant influence in pushing peripheral players out of the market and promoting a 'bulge bracket' of new issue players with large balance sheets. But it was a high-risk strategy.

Rudloff's understanding of the investment preferences of the core Swiss investor base was without parallel. He remembers bringing a $100m 10-year deal with Morgan Guaranty for triple-A rated Campbell Soup. 'We did the deal at 12.25% about two minutes after Morgan Stanley came with a triple-A insurance company at 13%. A 0.75% difference! Why? Because I knew everybody in Europe would buy Campbell Soup regardless of whether it was priced at 11%, 12% or 13%.'[8]

Unfortunately for non-corporate borrowers, Rudloff's instincts were less well-honed. Although the bought deal transaction that almost sank the bank, it appears, was the responsibility of Michael von Clemm rather than Rudloff. Dollar interest rates had been moving down between March and June 1980 but just as the decline was running out of steam von Clemm bid on a bought deal for the triple-A rated Export Development Corporation of Canada (EDC). 'Michael felt the big break in rates had come, others were more cautious,' recalls one CSFB executive. The bank was in competition for the mandate and bid a rate of 9.5% for the $150m offering (compared to 15.25% the Kingdom of Sweden had paid less than three months earlier). 'Normally at the daily directors' meeting we were told details of all deals. But none of us were told anything about the EDC deal. Only Michael and Gut knew how and who took the decision to buy it.'[9]

Having bought the issue, rates moved up sharply. Not only would no investor buy the paper but most banks declined their invitation into the syndicate, which was an unprecedented state of affairs in a CSFB transaction. CSFB was left with an estimated $127m of bonds that had to be financed on the Crédit Suisse balance sheet. Rates continued to rise sharply and the position haemorrhaged losses, which accrued to the account of CSFB. Neither von Clemm nor Rudloff could persuade Crédit Suisse to cut the position. It was finally unwound later in the year for a cumulative loss of, some believe, $40m. Some contemporaries claim Crédit Suisse absorbed the loss via a revaluation of the heavily written-down value of the bank's headquarters in Paradeplatz, Zurich.

Rudloff's reputation suffered no lasting damage from the EDC fiasco and many more bought deals were successfully competed for. Increasingly Rudloff took over the driving seat of the new issue business from von Clemm, who went on the road visiting clients. Von Clemm, ever the salesman, had a pair of cufflinks made with the EDC initials engraved upon them; 'Look at these,' he would say 'isn't it a sign of a firm committed to its client that I wear these?'[10]

With von Clemm on the road, Hans-Joerg Rudloff consolidated his position and influence among the senior hierarchy of CSFB in London. Rudloff's style, however, was different from the traditional corporate financier as he explained: 'The theory changed from getting a mandate through your personal relationships, the services you offered your client. You now had to get a mandate at a price, which someone else had been fixing. That was a totally new experience for the old type of banker. And that doesn't go without any change in mentality. It does create frictions. Some people adopt it very easily. Some don't.'[11] Friction soon developed between the market-orientated Rudloff and some of his senior relationship-orientated corporate finance colleagues.

The bought deal became commonplace in subsequent years with mandates often awarded after a telephone auction. Such auctions could comprise up to a dozen issuing houses competing; with the inevitable result that the winner would often have overpriced the deal. In 1983 Joan Beck was hired from Morgan Stanley to be Rudloff's deputy on the CSFB syndicate desk, a move people felt at the time to be as much about removing a key competitor from the marketplace as any urgent need of the syndicate area. Beck remembers: 'There were days when we would be glued to the screens for the money supply figures or whatever coming out of the US. We'd buy a deal overnight and hope that New York would close up so we had something that was sellable the following day. If the New York market didn't go our way we had a problem.'[12] As risks increased, timetables were accelerated to avoid any sudden changes in market conditions and invitations to syndicate now required a response within a few hours at most. Capital market borrowers also had to respond to bids speedily, but of course they were delighted with the new bought deal process as they were no longer subject to market volatility as they had been in open-priced issues.

* * *

In 1980, Fed Chairman Volcker tightened the US money supply, which halted job growth in the economy. In response businesses began cutting their prices, and workers their wage demands, to stay in business. Volcker argued that eventually this would wring inflationary expectations out of the system.

The effect on the markets was an interest rate rollercoaster. The US prime rate ranged from 20% in March 1980, then fell sharply to 10.75% in the summer (when CSFB launched EDC). Volcker then orchestrated a series of interest rate hikes that took the federal funds target from around 10% to near 20% by year-end, creating a painful recession. In 1980, the 'misery index' – unemployment plus inflation – touched 20% for the first time since the Second World War. US Presidential candidate Ronald Reagan blamed this on Jimmy Carter, and went on to win the Presidency.

These extraordinarily volatile conditions in the markets called for innovative thinking; new issues either had to be defensive or offer opportunities not previously available.

On the defensive side, oil and energy-related companies were popular issuers with investors; particularly in convertible form. By year-end $2.5bn in convertible bonds had been issued. The inflationary environment was also conducive to experimentation with defensive 'asset-backed' bonds linked to gold or silver prices.

An innovation from CSFB was the 'partly paid' or 'deferred purchase' bond. Hans-Joerg Rudloff who worked with David Potter on the issue, explained 'We were attempting to emulate the London Gilt-Edged market by introducing a bond which would provide leverage.' Rudloff felt it would suit investors who were 'unsettled at the moment but optimistic in the longer term'.[13] The bond for Alcoa of Australia carried a coupon of 12% for eight years. Investors interested in paper had to pay 25% of the issue price on 4 September 1980 and the balance of 75% on 15 January 1981. If interest rates fell then investors would benefit from the leverage. However if interest rates rose the leverage would work the opposite way. Unfortunately the latter happened and a week after launch the price was 21.5 bid, representing a 14% loss on the issue for investors. But what would happen to the borrower if the price fell to zero before the second payment was due? This eventuality was covered by a clause in the terms and conditions that holders who did not take up their residual payment would forfeit the interest and principal on their 25% initial payment. Rudloff concluded 'the borrower's objectives were achieved and we pioneered a broad move into leveraged investments, which Salomon Brothers developed into the debt warrant concept'.[14]

In the tough but highly innovative environment, issuing houses experimented with attaching various 'bells and whistles' to 'vanilla' bond issues to increase their attraction. Bonds were launched with debt warrants attached. The brainchild of Salomon Brothers in the US, these were first launched in the Yankee market for the Kingdom of Sweden. The warrants gave the investor an option to buy additional bonds over a specified period. Their attraction was based on the opportunity for capital gains on the warrants should interest rates fall. The first Eurobond offering was for Crédit National who issued $50m 13.75% five-year notes with six-month warrants to purchase the same principal amount of 13.75% ten-year bonds. The cum-warrant price of the note quickly rose to 105.5% in a rising market, yet the warrants alone were quoted at $15. Arbitrageurs spotted the anomaly and the warrants quickly rose to $50.[15] The issue price of these early warrants was largely guesswork, set at what the lead manager thought investors might pay for them, rather than on any mathematical option pricing methodology. Such issues became a regular feature over the following years.

With coupons on dollar Eurobonds reaching towards 17% in summer 1981, CSFB issued the first syndicated zero coupon bond issue. Zero coupon bonds are bonds that do not pay interest coupons during the life of the bonds. Instead, investors buy the bonds at a deep discount from their face value, which is the amount the bond will be worth at final redemption. When a zero coupon bond matures, the investor receives a lump sum equal to the initial investment plus the imputed interest. This first euro-issue was a $75m three-year offering for Pepsico Overseas with an issue price of 67.25% giving a yield of 14.14%. It raised three-year money at 100 basis points below the yield on the US Treasury. Rudloff was unsure of its success: 'It will never play a major role in the market because the tax treatment varies so much.'[16] Indeed Pepsico themselves had been encouraged to make the issue due to domestic tax benefits for the company. After Pepsico, General Motors Acceptance Corporation (GMAC) took the next logical step with a 10-year zero coupon bond priced at 25.25 to give a yield of 14.76%. In the initial instance investors focused on the possible tax benefits of zeros or 'streaker' bonds as they were sometimes called. In certain jurisdictions, particularly Japan, the tax advantages of zero coupon bonds proved very popular as capital gains on securities did not attract tax. Japanese investors flocked to zero coupon bonds as all income could be declared as a capital gain and zero coupon bond issuance totalled $3bn in January 1982 alone. In March 1982, fearing mass tax evasion, the Japanese Ministry of Finance prohibited its citizens from further purchases of zero coupon bonds.

Some issues would be for much longer maturities, offering greater leverage in a rising market. The enduring characteristic of zero coupon bonds is the absence of reinvestment risk arising from interim coupon payments. They would prove to be valuable investments for insurance companies and pension funds which were required to match long-term point liabilities. An unexpected interest in zero coupon issues came from bond forgers. With no coupons to be clipped, a forged bond would lay undiscovered for years but still be used as collateral for a loan. In 1983 forged J.C. Penney zero coupon bonds were discovered by Morgan Guaranty Trust.

In the difficult market conditions all types of combinations and permutations were experimented with. For example, Morgan Guaranty issued $100m zero coupon bonds for Citicorp with warrants to buy 14.5% straight bonds, and subsequently a $75m issue for Wells Fargo of 15% seven-year notes with warrants attached into a zero coupon issue.[17]

But such product innovation did not spread to the deutschemark market. 'The Bundesbank was mistrustful of certain short-term instruments, such as CDs, FRNs or anything linked to commodity prices or inflation. That is why Germany always lagged behind in areas like swaps or derivatives. There was always this strange subtle link between the Bundesbank and the German banking industry which did not help to promote the development of a financial centre in Frankfurt,' explains Rainer Stephan formerly of Deutsche Bank and Barclays, Frankfurt.[18]

*   *   *

While many of the innovative structures had a short shelf life in the history of the Euromarket, one innovation in 1981 was to change the nature of the capital markets forever. This was the first liability swap transaction where two parties would exchange liabilities with each other for mutual advantage. The swap can involve currencies or interest rates or both.

The International Bank for Reconstruction and Development (IBRD) or World Bank charges its developing country borrowers an interest rate based upon the rate the Bank itself has to pay for the funds. It is naturally motivated, therefore, to always seek out the lowest cost of borrowing.

Eugene Rotberg, then Vice President and Treasurer of the World Bank, takes up the story:

The World Bank at the time was borrowing about $8bn a year through about 50 bond issues in 20 currencies … At the time interest rates were quite high. Costs for dollars were approaching 17%; deutschemarks 12% and Swiss francs 8%. Governments had restricted access to their markets, particularly for non-resident borrowers, in order to reduce competition for domestic financing. Nonetheless the Bank was beginning to saturate the Swiss franc and, to a lesser extent, the deutschemark markets.

The Bank was reluctant:

to pass on 17% borrowings in dollars at a fixed rate to some of the poorest countries in the world.

    Salomon Brothers, through John Rosenstreich and Peter Gottesgan, approached the bank with a proposal from IBM to swap its Swiss franc and deutschemark borrowings for dollars … It turned out that IBM had, sometime before, borrowed both deutschemarks and Swiss francs. Because of the devaluation of those currencies, IBM could show a substantial profit if it could remove from its books its deutschemark and Swiss franc obligations. The swap provided a vehicle to meet IBM's needs.

World Bank issued Eurodollar bonds of the appropriate maturity and exchanged the proceeds immediately for deutschemarks and Swiss francs. World Bank agreed to pay all the future interest and principal repayments of IBM's deutschemark and Swiss franc borrowings. In return:

IBM was willing to take on, given its very large cash position, an obligation to service dollars at 17% … The spot conversion which would occur simultaneously with the Bank borrowing US dollars would supply the Bank with the Swiss franc and deutschemark needed to service IBM's debt. IBM on its part would schedule its payment of interest and principal precisely to match the debt service on the Bank's dollar bond issue.[19]

As Rotberg stresses:

It took the World Bank two months to do the first swap transaction with IBM. Every government in the world, believe it or not, had to approve the transaction. And even after it was done, what is generally not known, is that the counterparty risk, IBM, was insured by Aetna Life Insurance Company. Governments of the world insisted that we get an insurer against the corporate obligation.

    We did not think it was going to be a precedent … the circumstances, we thought, were too unique to be replicated. We were wrong.[20]

The swap transaction created the potential for arbitrage, issuing bonds in one currency and swapping them for another, creating lower interest rates for both borrowers. It was a short step from currency swaps to interest-rate swaps. Borrowers on floating rates could swap with those on a fixed rate. This allowed company finance directors, and speculators, to change their risk exposure depending on their view of where rates would go. Rather than pay each other's interest costs directly, the payments would be netted out:

The market exploded in a way that you didn't have to do a bond issue contemporaneous with a swap. You just could swap obligations which were already on your books. It formed the basis for interest rate swaps, currency swaps, credit swaps … not just swaps for hedging, but swaps for speculation. When it was superimposed, therefore, on a whole range of different kinds of securities transactions on both the liability and the asset side, it meant that for the first time managers or chief financial officers could change the mix of what they had done, currency or interest rate or type of asset, immediately or six months later. It meant liability management could become a profit centre, which it had never become before, from the corporate side. From an asset manager's side, it permitted a turnover and complexity which was quite remarkable.[21]

In the early days swap deals were bespoke, there was no secondary market and substantial gains could be made by borrowers. But Rotberg cautions: 'It however was an example of when a transaction went faster than the accounting system could cope with. That is to say, the accounting system did not know how to handle over-the-counter, off balance-sheet transactions.'[22] This didn't appear to deter the World Bank who became prolific swappers. In its fiscal year 1982–83 it executed 49 swaps totalling $1.7bn.[23]

By 1984 swap-driven new issues were claimed to account for as much as two-thirds of Eurobond primary market activity, and in 1985 the International Swaps and Derivatives Association (ISDA) was founded to standardise contracts and procedures in the market.

* * *

With such tempestuous markets and sky-high interest rates how was the AIBD managing? The *AIBD Gazette* reported in November: '1981 has been a very straining year for those concerned with running the Association. The largest single factor in terms of strain was the calculator.'[24] In summer 1980 the AIBD Executive Committee had commissioned a prototype electronic bond calculator from a small UK electronic instruments manufacturer. Their requirements were 'a machine that was small enough to be carried conveniently in a briefcase and big enough to allow easy and speedy operation of the buttons. Furthermore the machine had to be capable of doing yield calculations in less than 2 seconds (most available calculators are very much slower) and had to be very simple to operate.'[25] The Association knew its trader community well. 'This speed requires a chip with a very large capacity, which in turn consumes a great deal of power, meaning powerful batteries … The size of the chips and hence the circuits and the batteries has also of course influenced the price … Indications at present are that the cost to members would be around £200.'[26] Conservatively at today's prices this would be £700. Nonetheless 800 calculators were delivered to AIBD member firms in late 1981. 'An almost total majority of those we have consulted feel that the machine provides the required combination of speed and flexibility at a reasonable price considering the high level of technology employed in its manufacture.'[27]

The AIBD was only just in time; the AIBD calculator would have a limited life as a technical revolution was gathering momentum.

Hewlett Packard in California had started manufacturing calculators in 1972. In 1981 they launched the HP-12C financial calculator, low in price (less than £100 equivalent at launch) but high in functionality. The 12C was adept at bond calculations and calculating mortgage payments, even for odd time periods, in a truly pocket-sized configuration. The HP-12C quickly became the de facto standard among finance professionals, becoming Hewlett Packard's longest and best-selling product. Remarkably, despite all the advances in technology, and subsequent faster models with more functions, the HP 12C is still in production today.

Then in 1983, Lotus Software launched their spreadsheet application, Lotus 1-2-3. This rapidly became the essential application for the 1980s personal computer (PC) revolution. The speedy spreadsheet programme, developed specifically for the PC, facilitated the breakdown of any financial instrument into its basic cash flows, opening up the possibility to structure a wide range of new products. Lotus 1-2-3 rapidly became the standard spreadsheet programme and enjoyed a near monopoly position for most of the next decade until overtaken by Microsoft's Excel.

Along with developing their calculator, the volatile market conditions led the AIBD in April 1982 to announce: 'We are putting the last touches to the new 0 and 3–18% yield book, which has been thoroughly reviewed because of drastic changes in the market and for which we wrote an entirely new programme. The zero issues have been added as well as the 15–18% range, although I hope that the latter will only be of the briefest use to you.'[28]

With continued interest rate volatility there was an increasing need for hedging instruments. The 1970s saw the development of the financial futures contracts, which allowed trading in the future value of interest rates. In 1973 Fisher Black and Myron Scholes published their option pricing model, perhaps the most famous formula in financial markets. The Black-Scholes model, as it came to be known, set up a mathematical framework that formed the basis for an explosive revolution in the use of derivatives. It revolutionised the investment world and by the 1980s ushered in the age of derivatives. Although the OTC options and forwards had previously existed, the generation of financial managers of that decade was the first to come out of business schools with exposure to derivatives. Soon most large corporations were using derivatives to hedge, and in some cases, speculate on interest rate, exchange rate and commodity risk. In response, banks established derivatives desks to develop new products to hedge the now increasingly recognised wide variety of risks for their customers and for their own account. Throughout the decade, traditional style head traders in the Euromarkets would be increasingly replaced by those with a grasp of derivatives.

An important development was the use of exchange-traded contracts as opposed to OTC transactions. These contracts had the advantage that their associated secondary markets were far more liquid. The Chicago Mercantile Exchange (CME) introduced 90-day Eurodollar interest rate future contracts in 1981. CME Eurodollar futures prices are determined by the market's forecast of the three-month US$ Libor interest rate expected to prevail on the settlement date. So Eurodollar futures provided a way for companies and banks to lock in an interest rate today, for money it intends to borrow or lend in the future. This had an enormous impact on the development of the interest rate swap market.

*   *   *

When the world economy went into recession in the 1970s and 80s, and oil prices took off, developing countries found themselves in need of funds. Oil exporting countries had invested their money with international banks, which recycled a major portion of those funds as loans to Latin American governments. The sharp increase in oil prices caused many countries to seek out ever more loans to cover the high prices. Deterioration in the exchange rate with the US dollar meant that Latin American governments ended up owning huge quantities of their national currencies. Outstanding debt grew from $29bn at the end of 1970 to $159bn at the end of 1978, of which about 80% was sovereign debt. As interest rates increased in the US and in Europe through 1979 and 1980, debt payments increased in line, making it harder for borrowing countries to pay back their debts.

Mexico's total debt increased in 1981 alone from $55bn to $80bn and it owed almost $34bn (60%) to US banks.[29] Foreign debt had grown to more the 50% of GDP and foreign debt service in 1982 represented almost half the value of total exports – and Mexico was an oil exporter. What specifically triggered the Mexican crisis was a combination of high interest rates, falling oil prices, rising inflation, an overvalued peso and a deteriorating balance of payments that prompted capital flight. The government devalued the peso three times during 1982 and in August the Mexican Finance Minister indicated that his nation could no longer meet interest payments.

Minos Zombanakis remembers:

> *By October 1982 Mexico appears to the IMF and says that they are going to declare a unilateral moratorium which means they cannot service their debt … On my visits to the IMF, just by coincidence on a Friday afternoon, I went there to see Mr Jacques de Larosière and he said to me the Mexicans have just left and on Monday they are going to declare a unilateral moratorium. I said 'Don't let them do that' and he asked 'How can I stop them.' 'Well I said I am the one who created the loan agreements, and I have a cross default clause that if one is going to default every other thing becomes immediately defaulted and payable. So it is just going to be the collapse of the whole system.' He said to me 'What am I going to do, I cannot stop them?' I said of course you can stop them, just tell them to go and ask for a rescheduling of their loans, not a unilateral moratorium … Call Paul Volcker and ask him to get in touch with the major banks. Bring them in at the weekend to Washington and try more or less to convince them that they have to reschedule the loans because if they are going to allow them to do a moratorium they are going to lose the money anyway.*
>
> *To cut a long story short, after great resistance, the banks gave into this suggestion and on Monday morning the Mexicans asked for a rescheduling instead of a unilateral moratorium.*[30]

Mexico declared that it couldn't meet its payment due dates, and while announcing a moratorium of 90 days, it also requested a renegotiation of payment periods and new loans in order to fulfil its prior obligations. The US government, alarmed by the implications of Mexico's debt crisis, arranged a package in August 1982 in which the United States agreed to buy $1bn of Mexican oil for its strategic reserve at prices well below market value, and to pay in advance. Subsequently negotiations between the IMF, Mexico, the United States, and the banking community developed an austerity programme for Mexico.

In the wake of Mexico's default, most commercial banks reduced significantly, or halted, new lending to Latin America. As much of Latin America's loans were short-term, a crisis ensued when their refinancing was refused. Billions of dollars of loans that previously would have been refinanced, were now due immediately.

By October 1983, 27 countries owing $239bn had rescheduled their debts to banks or were in the process of doing so. Sixteen of the nations were from Latin America, and the four largest, Mexico, Brazil, Venezuela and Argentina, owed commercial banks $176bn, or approximately 74% of the total LDC outstanding.[31] The primary US concern was the risks to the major US commercial banks, whose exposure to the developing countries significantly exceeded total bank capital. The ratings of the money centre banks started to deteriorate in 1982 and continued to deteriorate for the remainder of the decade as LDC losses mounted.

A month before the meeting of Mexican creditors in Washington, Merrill Lynch launched a $100m retractable or 'put' Eurobond issue for Mexico carrying a record coupon of 18.5%. The issue proved difficult to place. With the news a month later the notes would trade at a yield of 22%.

In the high interest rate environment floating rate note issues proved particularly popular. Latin American borrowers had been a feature of this market. With the Mexican crisis, investors started to demand higher quality borrowers and the profile of issuers changed completely.

The summer of 1982 was a turning point in the dollar bond market. There was growing concern over the solvency of the US money centre banks with looming Latin American debt defaults and over the effects of high interest rates on other countries. The domestic US economy was proving weaker than expected, with worrisome declines in production and increases in unemployment. The Federal Reserve was facing increasing pressure from Congress and the Administration to loosen policy. On 20 July the Federal Reserve lowered the discount rate from 12% to 11.5%.[32] It went on to cut the discount rate seven times in the second half of 1982 heralding an historic bond market rally.

US issuers were quick to take advantage of the highly competitive Eurobond market. Coca Cola led the way with a seven-year offering priced 80 basis points below the equivalent US Treasury yield. With rates in free fall, partly-paid issues came back into vogue. To maximise the leverage effect in a rising market, issues were launched with increasingly modest initial down payments. In November 1982 CSFB and Morgan Stanley launched a deal for Dupont that required no down payment until January 1983. By the end of the year coupons on triple-A bonds had fallen from 16.5% to 10%. Despite the volatile conditions over $43bn equivalent of new offerings had been brought to market in 1982: more than 20 times greater than in 1974.[33] In the first few weeks of 1983 there were 28 partly paid issues totalling some $3bn. Soon however interest rates would rise rather than fall and, as losses mounted, investors questioned whether or not to make the final instalment payments on their partly paid holdings.

As a refuge from the volatile dollar markets the continental banks reverted to the basket currency concept where they had developed expertise and a loyal retail investor base. The European Currency Unit (Ecu) had been established as the cornerstone of the European Monetary System (EMS) in 1979. Eurobonds denominated in Ecu first appeared in 1981. By 1983 the Ecu became the third most popular issuing currency after dollars and deutschemarks. After totalling some Ecu200m in 1981, their yearly volume increased very rapidly, climbing to Ecu9.4bn in 1985. If, in the first years, European issuers were the main driving force, in 1985, issues by non-Europeans represented a third of the total amount issued. As a result of this expansion, the Ecu that year became the fifth most widely used currency for the denomination of international bond issues, far behind the dollar, but at a level quite close to the deutschemark, yen or sterling.

International borrowers were learning lessons from the volatile conditions. Second-guessing interest rate movements was a thankless task and fraught with danger. Floating rate funding was the safer alternative. The use of swaps with fixed rate deals was now widespread and floating rate note issues themselves were popular. However the major international banks whose capital raising exercises had previously formed the staple diet of the FRN market were less conspicuous as the swap market provided them with significantly cheaper financing. The scene was now set for an explosion of activity by sovereign borrowers.[34]

The New Year opened with the first $1bn bond issue, a floating rate note offering, for the Kingdom of Sweden. This 10-year issue, priced at Libor plus 25 basis points was subsequently increased to $1.2bn. 'At one stroke the issue succeeded in establishing a credible alternative to the syndicated loan market, the collapse of which was starving banks of suitable assets and through its sheer size changed the conditions in which FRNs were traded in the market.'[35] By June the EEC broke the record again with an FRN issue for $1.5m. These were seven-year notes with a 'put' after five years. The size of the issue attracted large-scale investors and was quickly increased to $1.8bn. There followed a $850m issue for Malaysia in July and a further $1bn issue for Sweden in November. This new 'jumbo' market brought with it a decline in issue spreads for borrowers and a sharp narrowing in dealing spreads in the secondary market. Crédit Suisse First Boston led the way with these jumbo offerings and they had now built an unassailable position in the primary market league tables.

* * *

After continuous internal strife at CSFB, Hans-Joerg Rudloff was now in the driving seat and courting controversy. Not long after Rudloff's arrival, allegations had flown back and forth between rival management factions about improper behaviour in the management of the bank, and in particular syndicate. A series of internal inquiries culminated in von Clemm being replaced as CEO by Hans Ulrich Doerig of Crédit Suisse and Rudloff being promoted to the Board of Financière CSFB. In 1982 Doerig was replaced by Jack Hennessy, Vice Chairman of First Boston. Hennessy was a graduate of Harvard College and MIT's Sloan School of Management and had been an Assistant Secretary at the US Treasury. He now had the unenviable task of managing the powerful egos at the top of the bank.

Before long a team comprising Jacques Gelardin, Peter Luthy and Peregrine Moncreiffe left CSFB for Lehman and then in 1984, Stephen Licht, Michael Dobbs-Higginson and Caleb Watts led a team of disgruntled colleagues to Merrill Lynch. On the day of the announcement of the mass defection to Merrill Lynch, von Clemm, now Chairman, made a rare appearance at the Directors' morning meeting in London. (He had become known as the 'dinosaur' among CSFB staff as he was now so rarely seen.) Arriving late, he marched confidently into the Board room and swung his chair about to mount it cowboy style. The discussion focused on fire-fighting measures to minimise the effect of the departures on the bank's business. Von Clemm was principally concerned whether any deals in the pipeline might be prejudiced by the defections. On learning that Caleb Watts, who had been responsible for originating transactions in Scandinavia, was in advanced negotiations with Statoil in Norway, von Clemm announced that he would immediately go and visit Statoil.

The story goes that a few days later von Clemm arranged to join up with Watt's young assistant for an early morning flight to Stavanger to visit Statoil. Unfortunately the young assistant was delayed and arrived at Heathrow after the departure of the flight. Von Clemm was enraged and told him to book them the next flight immediately. Unfortunately the assistant was informed that there was no further flight to Stavanger that day. By now von Clemm was apoplectic and explained to the airport authorities that he must get to Stavanger that day. They obliged by offering a bespoke private jet flight from London Luton airport and provided a limousine to get him there.

Von Clemm and the young assistant arrived later in Stavanger to find that it was a public holiday in Norway and all offices were shut. Von Clemm's expense account was as legendary as the man himself, although he repeatedly denied the accusation of breaking the $1m expenses barrier in a single year.

Not all Rudloff's landmark transactions were successes. In early 1982 Merrill Lynch had introduced Tigers (Treasury Investment Growth Receipts) into the US domestic market. These were effectively stripped versions of US Treasury bonds, that is, separating the coupon payments and the principal payment. Each coupon payment could then be traded as a zero coupon bond. Rudloff responded with a $450m serial zero coupon issue for Chemical Bank with separate maturities from two to 20 years – the notorious 'Chemical zeroes'. These would prove attractive financing for the borrower but investors showed no interest in the paper other than for the very short maturities. Most tranches remained stubbornly on CSFB's own books. Over time Rudloff himself found takers for the paper, principally in Switzerland, through whatever means he could.

Mr Rudloff defended his view of the market in an interview for *Euromoney*, along with von Clemm and Hennessy: 'I'm known for having very strong opinions. And I have very strong opinions about the market. That market is my life. Other people show up in that market for two years, and go back to other markets, or get rotated into it. Their identification with this market is not the same as mine. I have spent all my professional life in the market. That's where the strong opinion comes from …'[36]

The years 1982 to 1986 were halcyon days for the Eurobond market. The old controls and restrictions on international financial flows had been largely dismantled. Financial liberalisation continued, particularly in Japan and the UK, and the swap market was booming. Declining rates fuelled the primary markets as borrowers chose to issue new lower coupon bonds and pre-pay older more expensive financings.

The new Chairman of the AIBD, Damien Wigny of Kredietbank Luxembourgeoise, set the tone in late 1982:

The growing importance of the Euromarket vis-à-vis most other capital markets is due, to a large extent, to the freedom and creativity it has always enjoyed. New ideas can easily be introduced to the Euromarket, tested in various forms, then adopted or abandoned. It is, of course, difficult to determine where new ideas originate but, whether first implemented in the Euromarket or in the domestic market, they are very often more successful in the Eurobond market.[37]

* * *

Nowhere was the gung-ho spirit of the times more in evidence than at the AIBD Annual General Meetings. This two-day event was held in late May in a different international city each year. The event involved a short conference on the first morning, followed by the Annual General Meeting of the Association on the second morning. Despite the best attempts of the AIBD Board to portray the meeting as principally a work event, it was very much more the market at play. Bond dealers from all around the world would gather to test their generous expense accounts to the limit at the bars and nightclubs of the host city. The first AGM of the Association in 1969 had 90 participants. By 1975, in Berlin, the number of participants had grown to 450 and by 1979 in London there were 950 attendees.

The event began the evening before the conference with a cocktail party organised by the Association. This would typically be followed later by further parties arranged by individual firms to entertain their clients and counterparties. 'In those days major companies vied with each other to give the most memorable parties,' recalls Stanley Ross.[38] The following evening the AIBD would host its extensive gala party. On the tenth anniversary of the Association the AGM was held in London with the gala party at the Royal Academy during the Summer Exhibition. In 1980 the bond dealers decamped to New York to enjoy a party at the Tavern on the Green in Central Park. The following year, with Hamburg being the host city, the party was rather poorly attended as delegates were drawn away by the bawdy temptations of the Reeperbahn. However, most fondly remembered amongst older market participants is the conference in Venice in 1982 – gondolas to a garden party on the Lido. After the gala party, late night receptions would be hosted by Euroclear and Cedel.

John Wolters, AIBD Secretary General, responded to critics of the AGM: 'The social aspect is an extremely important function. It helps the traders get together face-to-face, not just to drink, but to see each other and exchange views.'[39] As the partying increased, the AIBD faced a problem as evidenced by a note from the Chairman after The Hague meeting in 1983. 'I am sure that all of you who attended this year's general meeting in The Hague were equally surprised at how close we came to not having a quorum for the meeting and how low voting participation was on particularly important issues.' Could the bond dealers be persuaded to party less? Probably not. 'The board came to the conclusion that, as a preventative measure, it should propose to the general meeting in Nice that the quorum be lowered from 50 per cent to one third of the total membership.'[40] Perhaps the bond dealers at The Hague were celebrating the first year when the secondary market volume exceeded $1trn equivalent.[41]

One notable feature of the annual AGM jamboree was the executive search consultants, or 'headhunters' that would appear at the various get-togethers. Having so many aspiring young bond dealers in one place was too great an opportunity to ignore. The months following the AGM were often a time of great activity in the jobs market with the headhunters collecting their typical 30% of the candidate's first year's earnings. A tongue-in-cheek article in the *AIBD Gazette* in May 1986 featured a fictional headhunter coining the term 'body arbitraging' which it defined as 'the simultaneous sale and purchase of an approximately similar body between two different companies at a 30% profit margin on both bodies for us'. The AIBD Register of Members was an invaluable document for the headhunter, and while not available to the headhunting community they found ways and means of obtaining copies. This register was updated annually with the names and contact details of most bank personnel operating in the Euromarket.

With the Euromarket expanding by more than 20% a year in the mid-1980s and barriers to entry comparatively low, setting up a Eurobond affiliate in London with a reasonable staff complement seemed an attractive prospect for an increasing number of banks looking to boost their international credentials. This just exacerbated the jobs merry-go-round for experienced personnel and remuneration packages on offer grew accordingly. The structure of remuneration packages and respective employment conditions varied along broad types.

At the most aggressive end of the spectrum were the US 'hard' commission houses such as Prudential Bache and Bear Stearns. Here, front office employees received a small nominal salary and then took a percentage of hard cash of the profits they generated for the firm. Repeated underperformance however would quickly lead to dismissal.

The major US investment banks and securities houses preferred a package comprising an average salary with a strong incentive bonus. The bonus would not be purely profit related but could be dependent on achieving other objectives either individually or as a team. In a good year the employee would expect his bonus payment to be a multiple of his base salary. The typical minimum expectation was for a bonus equal to 100% of base salary. Yet again, performance is what mattered, and staff turnover was high. In 1984 the author attended a gathering to celebrate CSFB's first retiring employee, where Dr von Clemm bemoaned the fact that the average life of a CSFB employee at the time was only 1.9 years.

European banks found it difficult to compete with the US houses. The UK merchant banks generally followed the US lead, but salaries were likely to be higher with bonus multiples lower. This was even more the case with clearing banks and European universal banks where a bonus of 100% of salary might be the remuneration for good performers. Finally came the

Japanese banks who would pay reasonable salaries with very modest bonuses but with the prospect of 'a job for life'.

As competition in the markets grew, banks searched for other ways to compete on remuneration, some of which brought them under the scrutiny of the tax authorities. A few firms experimented with offshore payments, which proved a costly error, while other firms experimented with paying bonuses in the form of government bonds, to delay the tax burden.

In time, if a bank wished to entice a key market participant to join them then they would have to pay a 'golden handshake' or 'golden hello'. These started out as payments to the candidate for any bonus payment he would have to forego if he moved to a new firm. As competition increased they would grow to include a substantial up-front payment to incentivise the candidate to change jobs.

Peter Gallant observed, somewhat sweepingly, in 1988:

Given the high salaries earned the level of professionalism is low, as are levels of experience … Eurobond specialists do not feel that they will be in their jobs forever; they expect to be replaced by younger and quicker technicians by the time they reach 40. As a result they are highly strung and determined to maximise their personal rewards; their spending patterns are extravagant, and it is a moot point as to whether it is the stress of their jobs or the strains of their private lives that causes their premature burnout.[42]

* * *

As new instruments multiplied, the need for improved financial data and analytics became apparent. Reuters had established the Reuter Monitor Bond Service back in 1973 with contributed data pages providing quotations direct from the market place (e.g. Ross & Partners in 1979) as well as information pages supplied by Reuters' news desk. By 1983 Reuters had over 2,000 subscribers including 75% of AIBD members. By 1980 the 'Telerate' electronic screen service became available in Europe with improved real-time data regarding the US bond markets and the foreign exchange markets.

Datastream, a UK-based company, had provided an early electronic database going back to the late 1960s which was targeted at analysts rather than traders. Datastream was accessed through special Datastream terminals or through a personal computer. The information was sold in a series of packages covering, for example, equities, company accounts, options, fixed interest, exchange rates and financial futures. Eurobonds were part of the financial futures package.[43] The AIBD entered into a partnership with Datastream to produce the monthly AIBD *Quotations and Yields* book.

The need to produce more real-time data prompted the AIBD in 1983 to agree with Datastream to make the *Quotations and Yields* book a weekly publication, the *Eurobond Guide*, and to include deutschemark bonds. Reporting dealers would now supply their prices to the AIBD on a Friday night with closing prices available to most subscribers on Monday morning. By July 1984 the AIBD had established a London office to concentrate on satisfying the growing need for real-time data. Now a Daily Eurobond listing was printed and mailed the following day – effectively an 'official list' of AIBD average prices. This data could be also transmitted electronically and was available through various commercial vendors such as Datastream, Extel, Bondspec and Telekurs. By late 1985 the AIBD database previously managed by Datastream was brought in-house to the AIBD's expanded London premises.

However it was developments over the other side of the Atlantic that would herald a data and analytics revolution.

After his MBA at Harvard University, Michael Bloomberg joined Salomon Brothers. By the late 1970s he had been placed in charge of developing the firm's in-house computer system. John Gutfreund, Managing Partner of Salomon Brothers, felt however that the company needed more capital to compete in the top echelons of the capital markets and in 1981 he sold the firm to Philipp Brothers ('Phibro' Corporation), a major, if not particularly well known, commodity trading company. Bloomberg was effectively fired, but as a partner, could sell his shares back to the company and received severance of more than $10m. Bloomberg decided to set up a business to develop a computerised information system that would allow Wall Street firms to have access to real time data as well as an advanced analytics capability via a computer terminal on their desks. Bloomberg got together a group of six computer programmers and in 1982 formed Innovative Marketing Systems (IMS).

The only Wall Street firm that showed any interest in his project turned out to be Merrill Lynch. Merrill needed a system that could be used by its army of traders and salesmen and a wide array of bond investors. In 1983, 22 machines were installed in Merrill Lynch, but with one condition: Bloomberg must not market the platform to Merrill Lynch's competitors for five years. To help finance Bloomberg's development of the platform, Merrill Lynch bought a 30% stake in IMS for $30 million. By late 1984 IMS was selling Merrill's proprietary financial platform, 'MarketMaster' to Merrill Lynch's clients and launching a portable version of the system.

By the mid-1980s at least 20 companies were offering screen-based news, market data, and research to investment banks and brokers. But Bloomberg's constantly evolving platform stole a march. Besides providing bond and stock prices and volume and other basic data, the 'Bloomberg' (as the terminal soon came to be called) offered a range of complex analytical calculations for determining the relative value of securities.

It was not long before Merrill's competitors found that their investing clients had access to data and analytics superior to their own. But despite their approaches, Merrill rejected all requests from rivals for subscriptions to the service. Bloomberg himself of course was keen to market his service to other market players and approached Merrill to see if they would relent on the five-year moratorium on sales to competitors. Eventually, because Merrill Lynch's 30% stake in Bloomberg's product meant it would benefit from IMS's expansion, it agreed to allow Bloomberg to sell the terminal to any market participants that were interested.

Now free, Bloomberg and his IMS partners aggressively marketed their terminal to the financial markets at large. IMS was soon leasing Bloombergs (at $1,000 a month) to many major international investing clients. In 1986 Bloomberg changed the company's name from IMS to Bloomberg L.P. and expanded his customer base from 'buy side' firms, that is, the investing community: to 'sell-side' firms – investment banks and securities houses. Bloomberg opened a London office in early 1987 and four months later launched an office in Tokyo. By then, 5,000 Bloomberg terminals had been installed and the Bloomberg Trading System had been launched. A Bloomberg screen on every trading desk became pretty much standard by the end of the decade.[44]

* * *

In March 1984 Crédit Suisse First Boston announced a hugely ambitious 10-year convertible issue for Texaco Capital. Texaco was looking to restructure its debt following its $10.1bn takeover of the Getty Oil Company in the previous month. Originally announced as an $800m offering it was increased to $1bn making it twice as large as any previous corporate bond issue. To encourage global distribution, the lead manager organised a number of management groups each responsible for distributing the issue in a specific geographical region. Indeed so successful was this distribution technique that a month later CSFB would launch a further $500m issue for Texaco on largely similar terms. Texaco's President Alfred De Crane claimed that 'a convertible issue of this size and kind just would not have been done in the States'.[45] So began a process which would eventually culminate in the concept of a 'global' bond, where new bond issues could be sold in multiple jurisdictions both in the domestic and Euromarkets.

With these successes, Rudloff was in buoyant mood and wanted to make a splash at the upcoming AIBD AGM in Nice. Firstly he chartered a substantial yacht where the CSFB team visiting the conference would be based. This would offer hospitality to CSFB's guests 24 hours a day. Stanley Ross recollects that 'Rudloff (or should I say Crédit Suisse) hired a massive yacht and the cognoscenti were whisked out to sea for a few hours on a most enjoyable trip; saw the Onassis yacht, which made Hans-Joerg's look like a row boat'.[46] Rudloff also enquired of a senior CSFB salesman if he could arrange to hire two elephants, one for him and one for Stanley Ross so that they could make a grand entrance at the AIBD gala party in the Cimiez Garden. Unfortunately no zoo or circus company in the region seemed prepared to loan their elephants, which was just as well, as the party was moved into the Acropolis conference centre in the middle of town due to the appalling weather.

Ahead of the Nice AGM the AIBD Chairman, Damien Wigny, expressed concern: 'The Association seems to be susceptible to separatist tendencies in its members. Some would be happier in a more specialized Association – be it that of market-makers, issuing houses, or why not one day? – brokers!' While the broker debate had dominated AIBD discussions for some considerable time, these comments were specifically directed at the increasing discussion among the issuing houses in setting up a specialist primary market association. 'I cannot see how the organisation of our industry is advanced if everyone goes off to sulk in his own tent. The AIBD is, and wants to remain, a forum for discussion for *all* the participants in the market.'[47] Despite the Chairman's comments there was a strong feeling amongst the members of the Primary Market Committee and beyond that the Association was not focusing sufficiently on that area of the market which was making by far the largest contribution to their profit and loss. Accordingly at the Nice AGM it was decided (not without acrimony) that the primary market deserved its own independent representation.

In October 1984 the Primary Market Committee of the AIBD decided at their Geneva meeting to create a new association focusing on the primary markets and in December the 'International Primary Market Association' was formed.

For banks to be considered for membership they had to have 'run the books' on syndicated Eurobond issues at least nine times over the three years or at least six times over the two years preceding 31 December 1984. Fifteen banks immediately signed up to the new association with 29 other banks following closely behind (all, of course, AIBD members). The objectives of the new Association were:

> *To make recommendations to its members in respect of the conduct of issues of international securities in the primary Eurobond market; to monitor standards of documentation; to promote cooperation between practitioners in the primary market and also between those in the primary and secondary market; to make recommendations to liaise with governments, government departments, agencies or other bodies, organisations and associations concerned with the market in international securities.*[48]

Two committees were formed, the Legal and Documentation Committee chaired by Theo Max van der Beugel and the Market Practices Committee jointly chaired by John A. Mayer and Hans-Joerg Rudloff.

Robert Gray, a former Chairman of IPMA stresses:

IPMA was formed at a time of significant market disarray. In particular the level of discipline within syndicates at the time really was quite poor. IPMA was created in large part to address some of those weaknesses, and mechanisms that obstructed the transparent and cooperative relationship between the major firms. We had phenomena like stabilisation costs being charged back to syndicates … and the practice of shorting other people's issues. Because the competition was so intense, the pricing on new issues frequently was excessively tight and it resulted in parties taking advantage of shorting issues on the assumption they could buy bonds at a particular price at a later date. And there were some memorable transactions, where the lead manager in fact ended up owning more than the entire issue.[49]

John Wolters, the AIBD Secretary General, would comment in 1985:

The perception of AIBD as representing the Eurobond market has changed completely. An entirely "free" market sees the need for some limitations in the interests of all participants. The creation of IPMA is a recognition of the fact that the free-wheeling primary sector will have to do some self regulating after all. At a time when industry deregulation is the order of the day, regulators start taking an interest in investor protection.[50]

Within a year of IPMA's formation, dealers responded: 'after a long period of indecision, market makers have decided that their particular area of the capital markets needs a platform …' and so the Secondary Market Makers Association (SMMA) was formed. However this grouping did not separate from the AIBD but would metamorphose into the Council of Reporting Dealers of the Association under its first Chairman, Tom Beacham of Wood Gundy.

*   *   *

Deregulation was on the political agenda on both sides of the Atlantic. In the US, the Reagan administration was advocating a reduction in taxes, a reduction in government spending and the reduction in regulation. In July 1984 President Reagan signed a tax bill, the Deficit Reduction Act 1984 (DEFRA), that removed the existing 30% withholding tax on interest and dividend payments to non-residents of the US. Previously this tax had to be paid by nearly all foreign investors in US securities. US companies could only avoid withholding if at least 80% of their gross income was from foreign sources (an '80-20 company': see above) or they had established Netherlands Antilles finance subsidiaries. The repeal of the withholding tax allowed US companies to now issue debt directly from the US to Europe or simultaneously in the United States and Europe.

This raised a number of issues. Would the Wall Street banks now enjoy the lion's share of dollar issuance? What of the yield differential that existed between the Eurobond market and the US domestic market? Prime US corporate names tended to command a lower yield in the Eurobond market, sometimes issuing below the rate on US Treasuries. Would yield levels now realign?

With a huge domestic deficit, the US Treasury itself was becoming increasingly interested in tapping the relatively cheap Eurobond market. Treasury officials understood that the Eurobond investor had a clear preference for bearer bonds. However the US Internal Revenue Service was alarmed at the possibility of the US government issuing bearer bonds, believing that US citizens might buy the paper to avoid paying domestic taxes. They therefore insisted any issue must be in registered form.

The Tax Equity and Fiscal Responsibility Act of 1982 (TEFRA) required that the majority of debt obligations in the US must be issued in registered rather than bearer form. Financial sanctions were imposed on issuers (both resident and non-resident) and holders of 'registration required' obligations in bearer form. There was an exemption available for US borrowers in the Eurobond market. The exemption allowed bearer form debt to be issued if there were 'arrangements reasonably designed' to ensure the paper was only sold in the primary market to non-US residents, that interest was only payable on the obligation outside the US, and that the obligation carried a legend as to the TEFRA sanctions.

As an added protection in the private sector, Eurobond investors in US corporate issues required that, should withholding tax be subsequently imposed, then the issuer would gross-up any payments due, to take account of the tax, or would redeem the issue at par. But if the US Treasury was the potential issuer it would be bizarre to offer an indemnity to investors to protect them from the US government's own action. While the Treasury was deliberating with the Internal Revenue in autumn 1984, a rush of US corporates took advantage of the tax repeal and the attractive rates available in the Euromarkets. Most notably, IBM launched an issue 50 basis points below the equivalent US Treasury yield.

Eventually a compromise was reached whereby the US Treasury Euromarket issues would be registered, however the registered party would be the institution purchasing bonds on behalf of clients, rather than the end clients themselves. On initial purchase and on each coupon date, the institution had to provide 'negative certification' that the final beneficial owners of the bonds were not otherwise liable for the payment of US tax. In addition the US Treasury bonds to be auctioned would have coupons payable annually as was customary in the Euromarkets as opposed to the semi-annual coupons normal in the domestic market.[51]

The US Treasury decided to auction their first $1bn issue of four-year 'Specially Targeted Treasury Notes' or 'Foreign Targeted Treasury Notes' in October 1984. The foreign investor had to certify that, on the day of issuance, they would place these notes only with non-US citizens. After a 45-day period, foreign investors could then exchange these notes for comparable domestic issues, or sell them to US citizens. The Treasury would set the interest rate according to the results of an auction and would provide book-entry form during the 45-day waiting period. Afterwards, the Treasury made registered notes available.

It didn't get much bigger than being the lead manager to the first ever Eurobond issue for the US Treasury and the leading Euromarket issuing houses pulled out all the stops. The US Treasury required all bids for the auction to be submitted by 5pm New York time or 10pm in London. Each house participating in the auction coralled institutional investors to join their team to present an aggressive bid to the Treasury. As head of sales at CSFB, the author had to invite in key investing institutions to join the CSFB bid in direct competition with Salomon Brothers and Morgan Stanley. The institutional investors came into the bidding banks' offices in the evening to finalise the bid behind closed doors. On returning to the office at 10pm the author arrived just as the CSFB meeting ended and our bid had been submitted.

When Rudloff emerged from the meeting he seemed to be in a particularly buoyant mood. (I had feared the opposite, in case my clients had proved unwilling to bid aggressively for the paper.) I asked Hans-Joerg how he felt it had gone and he replied triumphantly 'It's ours!' I said that I was surprised he was so confident as the market had been saying Salomon were likely to make the most aggressive bid. He simply replied 'No, it's ours.' I concluded, well, we would see when the results would be announced at the opening the following day. Rudloff responded there was no need to wait, as he had had information from the other meetings, and he knew he had won!

Sure enough, when the auction results were announced the following day, CSFB had the winning bid. Total bids amounted to $4bn and the price was set 31 basis points below where very similar notes were offered in the domestic market. A further auction of $1bn five-year and two-month Treasury bonds were issued before the end of the year.[52]

Taking a lead from the US and encouraged by a substantial surplus in their current account, West Germany tentatively began a liberalisation of the deutschemark market. In 1984 the authorities lifted the 25% coupon tax on foreign holdings of domestic issues that had been imposed in 1965. As a consequence foreign investors increased their exposure to the market. German government bond sales rose from DM36.7bn in 1984 to DM57.8bn in 1986 principally through purchases by foreign residents.[53]

A particular irritant of the deutschemark market was the queuing system for new issues managed by the Bundesbank. The queue slowed down the issuing process and banks, in response, adopted the practice of booking several dates for the same issue in the calendar, in case the market conditions or swap levels were not suitable when the first date came up. In 1985 the Central Capital Market Committee was abolished together with its Sub-Committee for Foreign Issues. The old queuing system was replaced by a simple notification procedure between the lead manager and the Bundesbank, typically two weeks before issuance, outlining the issue, amount, terms and placing method. As part of the liberalisation, West German authorities also permitted the issuance of zero coupon bonds, dual currency bonds and floating rate notes.[54]

When late in 1984 Deutsche Bank decided to move its non-deutschemark bond issuing business to London, the Bundesbank was prompted to allow foreign banks, through their German subsidiaries, to lead manage euro-deutschemark issues. From 1984 onwards the deutschemark foreign bond market was largely absorbed by deutschemark Eurobonds. By 1987 this was further promoted by the German authorities' decision to re-impose a withholding tax of 10% applying to German domiciled borrowers.

Liberalisation of the Japanese market began in earnest in 1984 when restrictions on the convertibility of foreign currency into yen were abolished and dealing by banks in public bonds took off. In December the guidelines on the issue of yen-denominated bonds by non-residents were relaxed. This triggered a surge of new Euroyen bond issues. First out of the blocks was an issue of ¥50bn for Dow Chemical, the first ever corporate Euroyen offering. In the same month CSFB organised a Y20bn transaction for Pacific Gas and Electric Co. thereby becoming the first non-Japanese lead manager of a Euroyen issue. The following year liberalising measures came thick and fast. In April the eligibility requirements for Euroyen issues were eased, opening up access to the Eurobond market for almost 150 Japanese corporations. In addition the 20% withholding tax formerly imposed on non-resident investors in issues by Japanese borrowers was repealed. Later in the year the government bond market was opened up to foreign banks and these banks were allowed to establish 50% owned subsidiaries in Japan.

In 1983 yen-denominated Eurobond issues accounted for 0.5% of the market. By 1985 this had reached 5% and would reach 13.5% in 1987. Japanese securities houses competed fiercely to become major underwriters of these issues. Some issues were termed 'Hara-Kiri' bonds, reflecting the willingness of Japanese underwriters to lose money to win mandates.

The abolition of UK exchange controls in 1979 kick-started deregulation in London. City institutions and the Stock Exchange now had to consider overseas markets and the challenges they presented. On the same day as the abolition of UK exchange controls was announced, the London Stock Exchange Rulebook was referred to the Restrictive Practices Court. In July 1983 the UK government and the Stock Exchange agreed that the case before the Restricted Practices Court would be dropped if the Stock Exchange agreed to certain terms and conditions: that minimum commissions be abolished by end-1986, an independent appeals tribunal be appointed, outside firms to be permitted to become members of the exchange, and the single function restriction on member firms that is, broker or jobber, be relaxed.

Along with the planned deregulation of the Stock Exchange, in 1981 the Thatcher government appointed Professor Jim Gower, an acknowledged expert in securities law, to report on the adequacy of the statutory regulation framework for the financial markets.

With impending liberalisation came the possibility of mergers and link-ups between market players to form – using a favourite term at the time – 'financial supermarkets'. Could there be first-mover advantages? Cultures clashed, as the banks considered possible partners, while stock exchange firms accepted the inevitability of takeover and looked to exact the highest possible prices from suitors. The Bank of England looked to encourage unions between UK institutions.

The Independent newspaper reported: 'After years of being kept at bay by an anachronistic old boys' network, foreign interlopers, armed with sacks of cash, were now free to take over some of the most hallowed of City institutions. UK retail banks, meanwhile, were free to set up integrated investment banking operations for the first time. Face-to-face trading was rendered obsolete with the switch to dealing-rooms filled with electronic screens, which greatly increased the efficiency of the market.'[55]

Two approaches were taken in the years running up to 'Big Bang'. In the first, and most popular case, banks and investment houses bought up to 29.9% of the equity in a UK jobbing or broking house (the maximum permitted at the time under London Stock Exchange rules) with the ultimate aim of acquiring the rest after 'Big Bang'. The *AIBD Gazette* noted: 'This method of gaining a foothold in the UK securities industry has turned many partners in broking or jobbing houses into overnight millionaires and triggered off an explosion in salaries the like of which can be found in the Eurobond market.' But, it cautioned:

> *With partners and key staff usually tied to the buyer via 'golden handcuffs', other personnel, basically representing the real value in a broking or jobbing unit, have been lured away by big money … Because of this, some financial institutions have chosen to build from within their own organisation a securities trading unit and frequently have recruited some of the brains that have made many of the old established jobbing and brokerage houses such successes.*[56]

An early mover was S.G. Warburg who purchased a stake of 29.9% in jobber Ackroyd and Smithers in 1983. This grouping would expand with the acquisition of Rowe and Pitman and government gilt broker, Mullens and Co. Kleinwort Benson bought Grieveson Grant, and N.M. Rothschild, Smith Brothers. In 1984 Midland Bank's merchant banking subsidiary Samuel Montagu bought into broker W. Greenwell. Barclays went a step further with a very expensive three-way merger of a broker, De Zoete and Bevan, and a jobber, Wedd Durlacher, to form

BZW. The US banks were not to be left out with Citicorp taking a 29.9% stake in Vickers Da Costa and Scrimgeour Kemp Gee, Security Pacific Bank investing in Hoare Govett, and Chase Manhattan acquiring Laurie Milbank and Simon and Coates. By the time UBS announced its deal with Phillips and Drew in late 1984 most mergers had been arranged.

By the time of 'Big Bang' in October 1986 19 of the 20 largest brokerage firms had disappeared. Of the larger merchant banks in London only Schroders and Lazards declined to take part. A few stockbroking firms like Cazenove, with its blue-blooded reputation as broker to the Queen, decided to remain as an old-fashioned partnership - but they too would succumb some two decades later.

Twenty-five years later the *Observer* newspaper would look back on Big Bang as 'that radical Thatcherite reshaping of the City, a period in which the Americans arrived to snap up ancient City institutions for huge premiums, leading to the clubby atmosphere of the Square Mile being replaced with the rapacious, bonus-grabbing culture of the investment bank'.[57]

As Yassukovitch points out:

London got most of the publicity because the changes known as Big Bang were perhaps the most dramatic. But there were many Big Bangs going off in all the other European markets – in France, in Germany etc. Suddenly these were no longer markets that were heavily protected and entirely dominated by domestic players. So it really led to a final breakdown of the barriers that had separated national markets from the international marketplace. There was no longer anything to stop a UK bank operating in the German capital market and vice versa.[58]

More harshly Yassukovitch wrote in November 2008 in the light of the financial crisis: 'Big Bang in the City was supposed to ensure its competitive place in the new global order in the face of post-Glass-Steagall conglomerates. It stripped the City of its remaining wisdom, destroyed the distinction between agency and principal functions and introduced an extreme compensation culture.'[59]

One fallout from the link-ups between banks and brokers was on the London property market. If synergies were to be extracted from the newly merged conglomerates then larger dealing rooms were required. Traditional offices in the heart of the City were no longer fit for purpose as banking groups searched for hangar-like premises that featured under-floor cavities to take the miles of cabling for the latest dealing room technology. Such premises were in short supply within the City confines, so sights had to be set further afield.

In early 1985 Padraic Fallon, editor of *Euromoney*, took a call from Michael von Clemm on his car phone, 'Fallon, guess where I'm calling from'. Some wild guesses ensued until von Clemm replied, 'The Isle of Dogs. You think I'm looking at a bunch of derelict warehouses. I know I'm looking at the world's next financial centre.'[60]

As well as being a renowned investment banker and academic, von Clemm was also a redoubtable gourmet, being an early financial backer of the Roux brothers and their restaurant, Le Gavroche, the first in the UK to be awarded three Michelin stars. Von Clemm was visiting the vast rundown 'Docklands' area in East London to search for a site for a processing plant for the restaurant business. Surveying the eight and a half square miles of disused docks, derelict land and redundant buildings he also considered the commercial potential of redeveloping the inexpensive space to house the operations of securities firms like CSFB. That incident proved the beginnings of Canary Wharf. Of course Canary Wharf went on to rival the City as a financial centre and contains many of the UK's tallest buildings. There is a relief sculpture of von Clemm in Cabot Square at Canary Wharf, to commemorate his involvement in the scheme.

*   *   *

In the high interest rate environment of the 1970s certain US banks and 'thrift' institutions (Savings and Loan institutions, similar to UK Building Societies) had started selling off some of their mortgage loans to outside investors. These residential mortgages were earning less than what the banks were paying for deposits. Investors were interested in the returns available on such loans while not needing to originate them. However they had to choose their loans wisely to protect against possible default. Consequently the 'whole-loan' market was relatively illiquid.

If, however, one invested in bundles of loans then hopefully any particular defaulting loan losses would be more than covered by the profits on other loans in the bundle. A US federal housing agency, the Government National Mortgage Association (GNMA) or 'Ginnie Mae' was established in 1968 to promote affordable housing in the US by channelling capital into the nation's housing finance markets. By combining similar loans into pools, the agency was able to pass the mortgage payments through to the investors, i.e. a 'pass-through' of principal and interest payments. This change made the secondary mortgage market more attractive to investors and lenders alike. Investors now had a liquid instrument and lenders had the option to move any interest rate risk associated with mortgages off their balance sheet. The Ginnie Mae guarantee allowed mortgage lenders to obtain a better price for their loans in the capital markets.

Ginnie Mae was followed by the Federal National Mortgage Association (FNMA), 'Fannie Mae', a private corporation that had been chartered by the federal government during the Great Depression, and later in 1970 by the Federal Home Loan Mortgage Corporation (FHLMC), 'Freddie Mac', to promote home ownership by fostering and expanding a secondary market in home mortgages.

One feature limiting the growth of 'pass-through' issuance was pre-payment risk. When interest rates are falling, homeowners look to refinance fixed rate mortgages. Investors therefore receive an unexpected return of principal that they are then forced to reinvest at a lower return. This problem was first addressed in a \$100m mortgage-backed deal brought by Bank of America in 1977 by dividing the offering into 'tranches' of different maturities. In 1983 Salomon Brothers and First Boston developed this idea further with the collateralised mortgage obligation (CMO).

A CMO is essentially a way to create many different kinds of bonds from the same mortgage loan so as to satisfy different kinds of investors. For example, a group of mortgages could create four different classes of bonds, or 'tranches'. The first group would receive any prepayments before the second group would, and so on. Thus the first group of bonds would be expected to pay off sooner, but would also have a lower interest rate. So a 30-year mortgage is transformed into bonds of various lengths suitable for various investors with differing goals.

Legally, a CMO is a debt security issued by a 'special purpose entity' or 'special purpose vehicle' (SPV) – and is not a debt owed by the institution creating and operating the entity. The SPV is the legal owner of a set of mortgages, i.e. the 'pool'. Investors in a CMO buy bonds issued by the SPV, and they receive payments from the income generated by the mortgages according to a defined set of rules.

In the late 1970s Salomon Brothers in New York established a leading position in this burgeoning 'mortgage-backed' market. This area was headed by Lewis ('Lou') Ranieri, a former mailroom clerk, who realised that maturing baby boomers were about to create demand for housing which would way exceed the capability of the US thrift industry. Ranieri realised mortgage loans could be packaged into bonds to create an alternative liquid investment market.[61] Salomon led the market with most of the important innovations: pass-throughs, GNMAs and CMOs. In the three years up to 1981, Ranieri provided more than half of the firm's profits.[62]

In September 1984 Salomon Brothers launched a $125m issue for the American Savings and Loan Association in the Euromarket. As collateral for the issue, American Savings and Loan placed in escrow $187.5m in AAA rated debt of the Government National Mortgage Association, or 'Ginny Mae'. While being one of the first examples of a mortgage-backed security (MBS) in the Euromarkets it also represented a back door offering of US government debt. The Eurobonds themselves were straight Eurodollar bonds with a fixed coupon of 12%.[63]

This opened up a new world of collateralised or asset-backed bonds where weaker credit risks could issue paper at levels only previously available to higher rated entities. The UK pioneered the use of mortgage securitisation in Europe with the first MBS issued in January 1985. British building societies became regular issuers of variants of CMOs. In 1985 they together raised around £1.25bn almost entirely in floating rate Eurosterling offerings.[64]

Before the end of 1984 the Federal National Mortgage Association (FNMA) had followed the US Treasury's lead and issued $300m of three-year 11-month notes directly into the Euromarket. The FNMA issue was yet another scalp for Mr Rudloff who introduced this domestic US borrower and its Chairman, David Maxwell, to his standard European deal roadshows with their 'eclectic' entertainment options.

Rudloff was a party animal at heart and believed in working hard and playing hard. His lack of apparent need for sleep matched that of the UK Prime Minister at the time, Margaret Thatcher. Often leaving CSFB's Bishopsgate offices in the late evening he might dine at Mr Chows in Mayfair then go on to Annabel's night club in Berkeley Square to meet with other eminent Euromarketeers. Alternatively he might seek out more colourful late night entertainment at Miranda's, off Regent Street, where he was more likely to mix with the Euromarket's trading and sales fraternity.

With deregulation, new financial conglomerates, new deal structures and new borrowers, 1984 proved a record year in the primary markets with 726 issues raising the equivalent of $71.5bn. For comparison, total issuance in the US corporate bond market was $49bn that year.[65] The liberalisation of national or foreign bond markets encouraged their absorption by the Eurobond sector. Overall international bond issuance reached $106bn equivalent, the first time breaching the $100bn mark.

At the year-end Rudloff threw a celebratory party.

Peter Montagnon in the *Financial Times* hit the nail on the head:

> *A quiet but profound revolution has occurred in the $100bn a year international bond market. Almost imperceptibly to all but the most specialist insiders, the market has gone global. The rigid demarcations that once separated, say, the Eurodollar bond market from its counterparts in West Germany and Japan have been broken down. Now, more than ever, practitioners are used to the idea of talking in terms of one market place, covering effectively the whole of the industrialised world … Suddenly borrowers are no longer restricted only to that particular market which offers the currency and type of debt they require. Instead they can pick and choose, launching*

issues in markets where they will get the best receptions or where funds are most readily available and then switching the debt into another currency, or from fixed to floating rate or vice-versa ...[66]

Twenty-one years after Autostrade, the Eurobond market had come of age.

NOTES

1. *Euromoney,* Michael von Clemm, 1 December 1997.
2. *Euromoney,* Michael Von Clemm; End of a Legend, 3 January 1986.
3. ©The Economist Newspaper Limited, London, *Michael von Clemm*, 20 November 1997.
4. *Euromoney*, Michael Von Clemm; End of a Legend, 3 January 1986.
5. *EuroWeek*, Taming the Wild West, 20 June 2003.
6. *Euromoney*, Michael Von Clemm; End of a Legend, 3 January 1986.
7. *Euromoney*, Behind the Bravado of the Bought Deal, August 1980.
8. *EuroWeek*, Taming the Wild West, 20 June 2003.
9. *Euromoney*, Michael Von Clemm; End of a Legend, 3 January 1986.
10. *Euromoney*, Michael von Clemm, 1 December 1997.
11. *Euromoney*, The CSFB Interview, March 1984, pp. 46–69.
12. *EuroWeek*, Taming the Wild West, 20 June 2003.
13. *Financial Times*, Deferred Purchase Eurobond Debut, 14 August 1980, p. 20.
14. Kerr, *A History of the Eurobond Market*, p. 64.
15. Ibid. p. 69.
16. Ibid. p. 70.
17. Ibid. p. 71.
18. *Euromoney*, Founding Fathers and 35 year olds, 1 June 2004.
19. IFR 1,000th Issue, The Currency Swap: In the Beginning, 9 October 1993.
20. Rotberg interview for ICMA's 40th Anniversary Video, 2008.
21. Ibid.
22. Ibid.
23. Shearlock and Ellington, *The Eurobond Diaries*, p. 102.
24. *AIBD Gazette*, Issue 8, November 1981, p. 4.
25. *AIBD Gazette*, Issue 6, November 1980, p. 6.
26. Ibid. p. 7.
27. *AIBD Gazette*, Issue 8, November 1981, p. 21.
28. *AIBD Gazette*, Issue 9, April 1982, p. 5.
29. *The New York Times*, 17 August 1982.
30. Zombanakis interview for ICMA's 40th Anniversary Video, 2008.
31. Philip A. Wellons, *Passing the Buck: Governments and Third World Debt* (Harvard Business School Press, January 1987) p. 225.
32. *Federal Reserve Bank of New York Quarterly Review*, Autumn 1982, p. 55.
33. Kerr, *A History of the Eurobond Market*, p. 75.
34. *AIBD Gazette*, Issue 13, May 1984, p. 20.
35. Ibid.
36. *Euromoney,* The CSFB Interview, March 1984, pp. 46–69.
37. *AIBD Gazette*, Issue 10, October 1982, p. 5.
38. Ross, *From Where I Stood*, p. 9.
39. *Financial Times*, Eurobond Dealers Prefer a Club to a Policeman, 5 November 1981, p. 26.
40. *AIBD Gazette*, Issue 12, November 1983, p. 4.

41. *AIBD Gazette*, Issue 14, December 1984, p. 66.
42. Gallant, *The Eurobond Market*, pp. 169, 251.
43. Ibid. p. 241.
44. www.fundinguniverse.com: *Bloomberg L P History:* Source: International Directory of Company Histories, Vol. 21. St. James Press, 1998.
45. Kerr, *A History of the Eurobond Market*, p. 83.
46. Ross, *From Where I Stood*, p. 8.
47. *AIBD Gazette*, Issue 13, May 1984, p. 7.
48. International Primary Market, Press Release, 25 January 1985.
49. IPMA 20th Anniversary Booklet, 2005, p. 5.
50. *AIBD Gazette*, Issue 15, May 1985, p. 8.
51. Fisher, *Eurobonds,* p. 21.
52. Ibid. p. 22.
53. Ibid. p. 133.
54. Gallant, *The Eurobond Market*, pp. 85–86.
55. *The Independent*, The day Big Bang blasted the old boys into oblivion, 29 October 2006.
56. *AIBD Gazette*, Issue 16, December 1985, p. 41.
57. *The Observer*, 9 October 2012, reproduced with the consent of Guardian News and Media Ltd, London.
58. Yassukovich interview for ICMA's 40th Anniversary Video, 2008.
59. S. Yassukovich, Accidents Happen, *Financial World*, a publication of *ifs University College*, in association with the CSFI, November 2008.
60. *Euromoney*, Michael von Clemm, 1 December 1997.
61. IFR Special Report, The IFR 30: Lou Ranieri, 2004.
62. Hayes and Hubbard, *Investment Banking*, p. 240.
63. Bowe, *Eurobonds*, p. 35.
64. Ibid. p. 34.
65. IPMA 20th Anniversary Booklet, 2005, p. 5.
66. *Financial Times*, 9 July 1985.

CHAPTER 5

Going Global
1985–1989

From the mid-1980s floating rate notes (FRNs) tended to replace bank loans as a major form of borrowing. In 1984 and 1985 FRNs were the fastest growing area of the Eurobond market. They accounted for 55% of issuing activity in the dollar Eurobond market in 1984 and in 1985 the FRN sector accounted for 23% of *all* borrowing activity in the Eurobond market. The development of the interest rate swap market in the early 1980s clearly contributed to demand. Banks looking to raise floating rate funding, their natural liability, could now access sub-Libor funding through the swap market. Some of these funds found their way into the FRN market where banks could invest and make a clear margin. As banks left the FRN market as issuers, the slack was taken up by increasing sovereign issuance. The FRN market offered a number of benefits over the traditional syndicated loan market and new sovereign issuance replaced maturing syndicated loans.

Inevitably with this massive growth in the FRN sector came a rapid decline in the spreads paid by borrowers. When Sweden launched its first jumbo issue in 1982 the margin over Libor was 45 basis points. Its second jumbo issue in November the same year was priced at 33 basis points over. By early 1984 the effective spread over Libor for Sweden was around 15 basis points. In August 1986 a £1bn FRN offering by the Kingdom of Denmark was issued at a yield of 10 basis points under Libid.

New issue fees were also squeezed, falling by two-thirds between the early and mid-1980s. Approximately half of the issues were bought by commercial, mainly Japanese banks, who made a small profit by funding them with interbank money. Richard Briance of CSFB complained of the increasing competitive pressures in May 1984, 'The downward spiral in front-end fees has had the undesirable result of squeezing out the sub-underwriting group from the majority of FRN issues today. Furthermore, the pressure exerted on major firms jockeying for position and consequently bringing mispriced clients to the market has meant that often only the lead manager will make a profit.'[1]

In April 1984 the first FRN issue without a fixed maturity, a 'perpetual FRN' or 'perp', was launched by County Bank for its parent, National Westminster Bank. The transaction was for $300m and carried a margin of $\frac{3}{8}$% over Libor. This margin looked attractive to investors who had experienced continuous spread compression on regular FRNs. They were not unduly disturbed by the lack of a maturity as they reasoned the FRN market was so liquid, with around 40 market-makers quoting 10 basis point bid-to-offer spreads, they could always exit if need be.[2]

For the issuer, the driver behind the perpetual FRN was a powerful one. If structured correctly with strong equity-type features, the regulator could treat them, in part or whole, as capital on the banks' balance sheet. Such treatment required that failure to make timely interest payments should not be considered an event of default, as long as the bank declined to pay a dividend at the same time on their common shares. The FRNs' subordination to the claims of depositors allowed NatWest to account for the financing as though it were primary capital for Bank of England ratio purposes.[3]

The floodgates opened, particularly for UK clearing banks looking to strengthen their balance sheets with multiple 'perp' issuances. Japanese banks became the principal investors, in time holding between 50 and 70% of the total market. The Japanese Ministry of Finance exempted perpetual FRNs from the deposit requirements for Japanese banks holding less liquid assets.[4] Large issues would be launched overnight, during Tokyo hours, to first attract the key Japanese demand, and then finalised in the morning in Europe.

Gradually certain other central banks would accord equity capital treatment for perpetual FRN issues made by their banks. Perpetuals totalling $18bn were issued in 1985 and 1986 with the main issuers being British, Canadian and Australian commercial banks (as well as an issue for Citicorp in 1986). Investors built up portfolios of perpetual issues totalling hundreds of millions of dollars. By early 1986 the bid-to-offer spread on prime name perpetuals was 10 basis points, tradable in $5m lots and margins over Libor compressed to a skinny $\frac{3}{16}$.

The natural buyers of bank perpetuals were other banks and there was some concern, with the rising popularity of the instrument, that risks were not being shifted outside the banking sector. Bank of England rules prohibited UK banks from holding other banks' perpetuals and they had warned of the risks of holding perpetuals as early as 1984.[5]

By summer 1986 the sovereign FRN market was coming under pressure. The huge supply of new issues, culminating in the largest issue to date of $4bn for the United Kingdom in September, exhausted investor demand. Investor confidence waned and prices came under pressure falling by approximately 150 basis points. New sovereign issues now required a small margin over Libor rather than Libid.[6] In addition there were a growing number of CMO deals (US government-backed FRNs collateralised by mortgage obligations) in Europe which offered higher yields for those investors looking for floating rate assets.

Once investor confidence in the price stability of regular FRNs deteriorated it was only a matter of time until the perpetual sector would be affected. Here, however, the reaction was much more severe, as secondary market liquidity was a fundamental requirement when investing in a perpetual instrument. The trigger came with a $200m issue for Standard Chartered in December 1986. It was nothing about the issue itself that caused the crash, but it brought to a head a number of deep concerns with the sector and an investor reassessment of the value of these hybrid securities. Investor interest had been waning for some months but new issues kept coming to market and traders' inventories were building up. With the year-end approaching, market-makers looked to cut their positions but could find no buyers. Panic spread and prices fell as much as 6% in a few days. Losses in December alone were estimated at $400m with many dealers refusing to pick up their phones and make markets.[7] Meetings were organised among the FRN traders to try and establish renewed dealing guidelines.

A key contributor to the collapse of the 'perp' market was a rumour which began circulating in December of an impending change in international banking regulations. The rumour was that the Basel Committee on Banking Regulation and Supervisory Practices would require that banks deduct holdings of perpetuals issued by other banks in computing their capital for regulatory purposes. Japanese banks in particular became concerned that their Ministry of Finance might adopt such measures. Some Japanese banks were alleged to have bought more than $1bn in perpetuals by the end of November, in expectation of lower rates and price appreciation. In fact interest rates rose, wiping out their margins and forcing them to try and liquidate their holdings.

Thankfully the market closed for the Christmas break but on reopening in January most prices fell a further two to five points – overall losses now totalling $600m, the majority accruing to Japanese banks. Between December 1986 and May 1987 perpetual prices fell by up to 15% and bid-ask spreads rose from 10 basis points in July 1986 to 50 basis points in August 1987. The secondary market in perpetual FRNs virtually disappeared. The perpetual debacle left a bitter taste in the formerly highly liquid FRN market.

After the crash in the perpetual market a series of repackagings appeared. These would typically involve adding a high quality zero coupon bond to a perpetual FRN to create an asset with the characteristics of a dated FRN.

* * *

Although there had been $1bn plus sized floating rate and zero coupon issues for some years; in February 1986 Deutsche Bank Capital Markets issued the first single tranche $1bn fixed rate transaction for Canada – acclaimed as the first 'jumbo' straight bond issue. It was a 10-year offering with a coupon of 9% and was warmly welcomed by investors, having been increased from a proposed $750m offering. For most of its life it represented a liquid trading benchmark and Treasury proxy in the dollar market and was known simply as the 'Canada Nines'. The Nines soon narrowed to a 10 cent bid/offer spread in $5m a side in the secondary market and remained so for years, recalls Kevin O'Neill, Executive Director, Daiwa Securities and former primary trader at CSFB, a co-lead on the transaction. The issue played a significant part in encouraging the market to think in terms of spreads to a benchmark rather than simply outright yields.

Another landmark was the first Eurobond issued via a medium-term note (MTN) pro-gramme for First Interstate Bancorp. This was the eighth largest bank in the US at the time, headquartered in Los Angeles (and taken over by Wells Fargo in 1996).

The medium-term note concept was a US import. General Motors Acceptance Corporation (GMAC) created the MTN market in the early 1970s in the US. The market was established as an alternative to short-term financing in the commercial paper market and long-term borrowing in the bond market; hence the name 'medium term'. Most MTN activity actually started as an adjunct to the ECP desk in the investment banks active in this area. To improve their asset and liability management, GMAC and the other auto finance companies needed to issue debt with a maturity that matched that of the auto loans they offered to dealers and consumers. However, underwriting costs made bond offerings with short maturities impractical, and maturities on commercial paper could not exceed 270 days. The auto finance companies therefore began to sell MTNs directly to investors. But this proved expensive because borrowers had to obtain the approval of the SEC each time they changed the posted coupon rates on their MTN offering schedule.[8]

In March 1982 the SEC approved Rule 415, which allowed US firms to register securities and gradually sell them to the public for two years following the initial registration. Because the securities were already registered, they could be sold on short notice with relatively little additional paperwork. Moreover, they could be sold in small amounts without incurring substantial issuance costs. The securities were 'on the shelf,' ready to be issued, which gave rise to the term 'shelf registration'. The US market evolved from a relatively niche market for auto finance companies into a major source of financing for large corporations.

In the early years the EMTN was perceived as a new 'type' of bond rather than a format for more cost efficient issuance of regular bonds. Issues were not syndicated and consequently often proved illiquid in the secondary market, which deterred Euromarket investors. EMTN issuance only totalled $3bn by March 1988 with the *Financial Times* observing, 'The growth of this younger market, which saw its first issues only in 1986, has disappointed many of its proponents.' Substantial growth would only come in the 1990s as the distinction between EMTNs and straight Eurobond issues became blurred. In 1991 14% of Eurobond issuance would be off EMTN programmes; by 1996 this had grown to 45%.[9]

Bonds and FRNs were traditionally issued as a 'one-off' issue (or 'stand-alone' issue). EMTNs, however, are issued in several series (i.e. separate sets of issues) through a 'programme'. The programme involves the issuer and arranger agreeing to a set of legal documentation under which the issuer can issue notes of varying currencies, maturities and formats on a continuous basis. The agreed documentation specifies the terms and conditions of any series of notes which are issued. The programme will also appoint a number of 'dealers', one or more of whom may act as a lead manager to each issue (or 'drawdown') of notes. By having the programme in place prior to issuance, it allows a borrower to issue a wide variety of notes at short notice and save the costs of individual one-off issuance.

EMTN programmes also facilitate 'reverse enquiry'. An investor, or group of investors, may request a type of investment and a particular return they are looking for from a borrower. If it meets the borrower's funding target under the programme the bespoke security will be issued. Private placements in the Euromarkets are commonly reverse enquiry MTNs. So, rather than denoting a narrow security with an intermediate maturity, an EMTN is a highly flexible debt format that can easily be designed to respond to market opportunities and investor preferences. The emergence of the EMTN market has transformed the way that corporations raise capital and that institutions invest.

* * *

In the UK preparations were underway for the deregulation of the markets, or 'Big Bang', scheduled for 27 October 1986. Nigel Lawson, who introduced the reforms as Margaret Thatcher's Chancellor, insists they were as much about strengthening the London Stock Exchange as slashing red tape; as much about regulation as deregulation.[10] The Gower Report commissioned by the first Thatcher administration in 1981 became the basis for a government White Paper in 1985 entitled: 'Financial Services in the United Kingdom: A New Framework for Investor Protection'. While reviewing the financial services landscape in the UK the White Paper had largely managed to ignore the existence of the Eurobond market. After considerable debate and amendments the subsequent Financial Services Act became law in November 1986. The Financial Services Act 1986 introduced the concept of self-regulation within a statutory framework. At the top of the tiered structure a cabinet minister (the Secretary of State for Trade and Industry) was vested with full oversight powers. The minister delegated regulatory responsibility to a 'designated agency', the Securities and Investment Board (SIB). The SIB had the power to regulate financial and investment businesses in the UK and regulate persons permitted to conduct investment business. Authorisation depended on individuals or organisations being deemed to be fit and proper to run investment businesses and those conducting investment business without authorisation would be subject to criminal sanctions.

When the SIB published its draft rules in February 1986 the *Financial Times* commented:

For even the most sympathetic and conformist investment firm this SIB rule book will give a chilling impression of the sheer bureaucratic cost of the new regulatory regime. Customer agreement letters will have to spell out information under 14 different headings, and will have to be renewed each year. Comprehensive information on every transaction will have to be recorded and kept for at least three years …[11]

Below the SIB in the regulatory structure came the various 'Self Regulatory Organisations' (SROs). SROs were responsible for regulating the relationships between their members and their customers; however SRO rules should not impede competition or go beyond restrictions needed to protect investors. Initially five SROs were established covering different sectors of the market: The Securities Association (TSA) regulating securities trading; the Association of Futures Brokers and Dealers regulating commodities and futures trading; the Financial Intermediaries, Managers, and Brokers Regulatory Association (FIMBRA) regulating smaller firms and independent brokers; the Investment Managment Regulatory Organisation (IMRO) regulating investment management firms; and the Life Assurance and Unit Trust Regulatory Organisation, (LAUTRO) regulating insurance companies and unit trusts.

The London Stock Exchange's largely disdainful attitude to the Euromarket prompted those firms in the international securities community, led by the AIBD and IPMA, to seek support for the formation of an international SRO, the International Securities Regulatory Organisation (ISRO).

A fourth tier of the regulatory structure was made up by 'recognised investment exchanges' (RIE). As with SROs, these exchanges were authorised by and reported to the SIB. It was expected the Stock Exchange was likely to be an RIE but what of the Eurobond market? ISRO formed a working party with the Stock Exchange to discuss whether they would jointly create a designated investment exchange for bonds and equities. The Stock Exchange had been worried after the formation of ISRO that it might lose oversight of the rapidly growing market in international equities.

The Lex column in the *Financial Times* commented forcefully on the debate:

The Stock Exchange has always had a haughty view of the Eurobond market and it is unlikely that either the AIBD or IPMA can be persuaded at this stage that the Exchange loves them after all. The Exchange's concern is of course not with Eurobonds but with international equities. But to distinguish as it does, so clearly between the two again suggests that the point has been missed. Not only is London experiencing a convergence between equity and debt instruments with the growing popularity of warrants and other whistles; the likelihood must be that, for wholesale customers, it is the Euromarket and not the London Stock Exchange which will provide the trading model … Over the last twenty years London has developed as the leading market in international debt in spite of the Stock Exchange. If London has the opportunity to establish the same pivotal role in equities, it should not be inhibited by the Stock Exchange …[12]

Eventually after extensive, and at times acrimonious, negotiations, the Stock Exchange was designated as a recognised investment exchange, being now called the 'International Stock Exchange', and appointed the eminent Euromarketeer, Stanilas Yassukovich as its deputy chairman. The AIBD also acquired investment exchange status. However to operate as an RIE the AIBD would need to move its head office to London and to fulfil certain reporting requirements. Wood Gundy's Tom Beacham, Chairman of the AIBD Council of Reporting Dealers, observed at the time 'We're very willing to become an RIE but if the reporting requirements are too onerous, we won't be able to carry the membership ... There's no way a Swiss Bank would let auditors pry into its business.'[13]

The AIBD, being a Zurich-based association, was regulated only in principle under the SIB rules and was finally deemed 'an overseas investment exchange' (OIE) under the Financial Services Act. This understanding entailed that the association receive an expression of satisfaction from the SIB stating that the self-engendered trading rules of the association broadly met the investor protection provisions of the SIB in the UK. Furthermore, this understanding would not permit individual members of the association to trade Eurobonds in the UK unless authorised by the TSA, which, as an SRO, would oversee the business practices and financial resources of the association's members. AIBD rules applied to authorised UK firms doing business with persons overseas. However an overseas-based firm authorised to do business in the UK would not be subject to rules on business undertaken overseas.

'The designation of AIBD as an overseas exchange appears eminently sensible to me – it is a recognition of the role the Association plays in the market,' remarked Damien Wigny, AIBD Chairman.[14] The AIBD was updating its own structure to prepare for life in the new environment. An Extraordinary General Meeting of the Association took place in December 1985 transferring power to make rules away from the AIBD membership to the AIBD Board, introducing a new approach to the selection and composition of the Board and to strengthen the power of the regions.

The AIBD Chairman reflected on the changes in the *AIBD Gazette* in May 1986:

> *AIBD started as a pure trade association. It has now already changed radically. Where will it be going? With the growing international market in fixed income securities; with the budding international equities market; with the increasing securitisation of debt we will inevitably see a greater demand for effective rule making – self regulation – in what was once a completely free and unregulated market ... We will have to break new ground in becoming an International Exchange; the first and only one of its kind, with no real fixed abode but with rules that will give it a structure of rights and obligations for its members. Rules that are so formulated that they will function, within a completely international atmosphere, by the interest that* all *professional participants in the Market will have in seeing them work, in seeing them respected, in seeing them recognised by all.*[15]

As questions of oversight of the Eurobond market were settled in the UK, Europe was now stirring. By the mid-1980s the European Community had grown to 12 members: France, West Germany, Italy, the Netherlands, Belgium, Luxemburg, Great Britain, Ireland, Denmark, Greece, Spain and Portugal. Although the European Community had been in operation for nearly 30 years, it had not achieved its aim of establishing a genuine common market. While it had produced a large number of directives and regulations, it was having problems in implementing them because the need for consensus made it difficult to move forward with the single market project. The Single European Act (SEA) was signed in February 1986 and became effective in July 1987. It was the first major revision of the 1957 Treaty of Rome. The SEA's main purpose was to set a deadline for the creation of a full single market by 1992, with a key part of this integration process being economic and monetary union (EMU).

A number of measures forming the basis for the integration of securities markets at the European level were already underway. In 1980 the Commission submitted preliminary drafts for a Public Offer Prospectus Directive. These drafts were revised in 1986. Former IPMA Chairman Michael von Brentano noted at the Association's 5th AGM:

> *As the stream of Directives flowing out of Brussels becomes a flood of national laws in each Member State throughout the Community this will affect transactions inside national borders as much as cross-border deals. IPMA's job is to do what it can to try to encourage this legislation to run in a positive direction, running with the flow of the industry. As an industry, we want to avoid having to swim constantly upstream against a tide of unsuitable regulation.*[16]

IPMA's focus was on gaining exceptions from rules that governed Europe's domestic capital markets. The association became engaged at an early stage in the discussions leading up to the publication of the Prospectus Directive in 1988. The proposals required that any prospectus for a new issue would require regulatory approval before any issue could be launched. In addition such a prospectus would have to be written in every language of the EU where the issue was to be offered for sale. In the fast moving Eurobond primary markets these requirements would be untenable as long delays before launch could prejudice the success of an offering. Chairman of IPMA's Legal and Documentation Committee (LDC), Jean Pierre Wellens (of Banque Bruxelles Lambert) along with LDC colleagues lobbied the mandarins in Brussels to try and gain an exemption for Eurobonds (or 'Eurosecurities' in Brussels-speak) from the main thrust of the Directive. Eighteen months of negotiations followed, focusing on trying to define a 'Eurosecurity'.

Eventually the following definition was agreed:

> *Eurosecurities shall mean transferable securities which: are to be underwritten and distributed by a syndicate at least two members of which have their registered offices in different states; are offered on a significant scale in one or more states other than that of the issuer's registered office; and may be subscribed for or initially acquired only through a credit institution or other financial institution.*

As a result of IPMA's efforts, Eurosecurities that met the above criteria were exempted from the Prospectus Directive.

* * *

Eurosecurities covered both bonds and equities. The challenge of developing a Euroequity market along the lines of the Eurobond market had been exercising the industry for some time. Yassukovich recalls:

> *I gave a speech in 1979 announcing the immediate arrival of the Euroequity market, and suggesting that the little problem of flow back (of shares to the domestic market) would be easily overcome. Of course, it took another 15 or 20 years before that actually happened, but there were already some attempts to create a market for primary issues of equity, syndicated and distributed on an international basis.*[17]

With deregulation in the mid-1980s the Euroequity debate became particularly pertinent. The first international equity offerings appeared in late 1983, when Nomura brought an issue for Murata Manufacturing, and UBS and Swiss Bank Corporation led European tranches for secondary offerings for two Canadian companies, Bell Canada and Alcan. International equity offerings received a significant boost the following year with the Thatcher government's privatisation of British Telecom (BT). As the UK market was felt to be too small to absorb such a large issue on its own, shares were offered in simultaneous public offers in the UK, Canada and the USA. BT shares were also distributed in Europe and the Middle East. Such internationally distributed deals were still considered the exception and were only contemplated for large offerings. Nor were they always successful as evidenced by the rapid flowback to London of the British Telecom shares placed in New York. In 1985 CSFB launched three Euroequity deals for Nestlé using an international syndicate of underwriters for international distribution. The new or primary international equity issues, other than equity-linked bonds, grew from $300m in 1984 to $18bn in 1987.[18]

While Euroequity deals were in their infancy, equity-linked transactions had been a prominent feature of the Eurobond market from its earliest days. In the late 1970s Japanese companies became active in the convertible market. However unlike their US counterparts, whose convertibles featured modest coupons and high conversion premiums, the Japanese convertibles were typically long-dated and offered both low coupons and low conversion premiums. While initially attracting investor demand, in time they began to perform poorly with issues trading down to substantial discounts. One such issue was the Nitto convertible that had caught Stanley Ross's attention when contemplating establishing a 'grey market'. The market then tested out the concept of bonds carrying higher coupons but with a shorter life and with equity warrants attached. The Ministry of Finance's initial response to the new instrument was one of caution, and they refused to allow such warrants to be detachable.[19]

After considerable lobbying with the Ministry in Tokyo, they relented and allowed the warrants to be detachable as long as they were not sold to Japanese investors. This constraint limited the flow of new issues. Yamaichi brought the first issue with Morgan Stanley for Mitsubishi Chemical, guaranteed by Mitsubishi Bank. This was a $50m issue with a coupon of 11%. Investors received one warrant per $5,000 bond that was detachable on delivery. The warrant gave the right to purchase Mitsubishi Chemical's shares at 2.5% premium to the current market price for a period of five years; effectively a call option on the shares. The warrants began trading in the grey market at $17 suggesting a yield of almost 16% on the ex-warrant bonds. A few further issues followed but the market suffered from liquidity problems as, away from the lead manager, only Cresvale International would make a market. Cresvale was a trading firm established in 1979 by a team of former Dillon Read traders led by Steve Burnham.

When the Tokyo stock market turned down in late 1982 many investors panicked and looked to dispose of their warrants at any level. Canny traders picked up the warrants, in many cases for next to nothing and, with a five-year life, some of these issues would later make them a fortune. An issue for Nomura would go from a low of $12 to eventually $5,000.[20]

The US Federal Reserve under Paul Volcker had halted the stagflation crisis of the 1970s by raising interest rates, but this resulted in the dollar becoming overvalued to the extent that it made industry in the US (particularly the automobile industry) uncompetitive in the global market. In September 1985 the governments of France, West Germany, Japan, the US and the UK signed the 'Plaza Accord' in New York. This was an agreement to depreciate the US dollar in relation to the Japanese yen and German deutschemark by intervening in currency markets. It prompted a sharp yen appreciation; 46% against the US dollar by end-1986. As a result,

Japan's export and GDP growth essentially ground to a halt in the first half of 1986. With the economy in recession and the exchange rate appreciating rapidly, the authorities responded by providing a sizeable economic stimulus. The Bank of Japan lowered short-term interest rates by 3% and allowed the Japanese money stock to expand by an average of 10.5% per year from 1986 until 1990.

The asset price bubble was exacerbated by financial deregulation in the early 1980s. This allowed large Japanese companies to access capital markets rather than rely on bank financing, prompting banks instead to lend to real estate developers and households seeking mortgages. As a result bank credit to these two sectors grew by about 150% in the period 1985–1990, roughly twice as fast as the 77% increase in overall bank credit to the private sector. The average land price doubled in the same period.

The Nikkei stock price index began to rise in the early 1980s and by 1989 had risen to five times its 1980s level – the biggest asset bubble in history.

Against this background, it is not surprising that the market for Japanese equity warrants took off, aided in January 1986 by the Ministry of Finance deciding to allow Japanese investors, the natural buyers, to purchase Eurobond equity-linked issues. By attaching warrants to their bonds Japanese companies now paid a significantly lower interest rate for their borrowings. Investors liked the warrants because in a rising market they rose much faster than the underlying stocks. Also as the warrants could be detached from the underlying bond they had the advantage over convertibles that conversion could not be forced by having the bond called.

The total value of bonds issued with warrants attached grew from $2.7bn in 1985 to $15.3bn in 1986 taking their market share of all Eurobond offerings from 1.9% to 7.7%. Issuance amounted to $10bn in the first half of 1987 making the market by then almost as large as the FRN market prior to its collapse in late 1986.[21] In total, during the stock market bubble years of 1986 through to 1990, Japanese companies issued a massive $435bn in Eurobonds with warrants or convertibles.[22] Coupons fell and conversion premiums widened from the early days. In the summer of 1987 Yamaichi launched a deal for Tokyu Corp with a coupon of 0.875%. As coupons fell the proportion of the cum-warrant price ascribed to the warrant rose.[23]

With the sharp appreciation of the yen, Japanese companies started to use 'zaiteku' or financial engineering to cover up the declining profitability of their core businesses. They issued bonds with equity warrants at ever-lower coupons. The proceeds from these issues were converted into yen sometimes providing negative coupon yields. They would look to reinvest the proceeds from their issues into other financial securities, bonds or futures, and report the difference between the coupon paid and the coupon received as a profit. New issues came thick and fast with companies issuing warrants in quantities that added up to a larger proportion of an issuing company's capital than would be the norm in any other market. At the height of 'zaiteku', two thirds of listed Japanese industrial companies were making 20–50% of their profits this way. A joke at the time went: 'How many workers does it take Toyota to build a car? Four. One to design it, one to build it and two to trade the long bond.'

As the warrants were issued offshore in London by Japanese firms they were not listed on an exchange or traded through a dealing platform and so were not open to scrutiny. Market-makers' quotes could, and did, differ widely. Prices were volatile, being very sensitive to corrections in the Nikkei index, with huge bid-to-offer spreads. Various trading firms, such as Kleinwort Benson and Shearson, had come in and then left the market. Many careers and a few fortunes were made on the back of equity warrant trading.[24]

Among them was Terry Ramsden, the son of a post office engineer and office cleaner from Romford, Essex. He left school at 16 for a succession of jobs in various City brokerage firms. After years in back offices, in 1975 he became a trader specialising in Japanese warrant issues. By the early 1980s he was working for Cresvale International. There, he aggressively traded the Japanese warrant market both on behalf of the company and for his own account. In 1984 he bought an Edinburgh-based company called Glen International that at the time had a turnover of £18,000. At Glen International Financial Service Co. he continued to trade Japanese warrant issues. He gambled heavily on a rising market in Tokyo, taking substantial proprietary positions, and he got it right. In late 1985 he bought up most of a warrant issue for Minebea Co., a ball-bearing maker. Topping up his holding with convertible bonds he eventually controlled 37% of the company and, with partners, made an audacious hostile bid to buy the company for $1.4bn. Hostile takeovers were anathema in Japan and the bid was promptly rejected. By 1987 Glen International's turnover had risen to £3.5bn pounds and Ramsden was said to be the UK's 57th richest man. He lived the lifestyle to match. At his peak the bond trader reportedly owned two helicopters, a Gulfstream jet, 27 cars, a dozen houses, 120 racehorses, a 30% share of Chelsea Football Club and the whole of Walsall Football Club. But when the markets collapsed in late 1987 hundreds of millions were knocked off his and Glen International's holdings. Within a year Glen International crashed owing £98m. In addition Ramsden lost £58m on the racetrack. He was declared bankrupt in 1992 with debts of £100m and was given a two-year suspended sentence for fraud.[25]

The volume of with-warrant issues, by the summer of 1987, was straining the absorptive capacity of the market. Investors became nervous that if all the warrants were exercised, earnings per share of the borrower would be significantly diluted. In fact, it is believed that few warrants were ever exercised.

* * *

Stories of excessive investment returns always excited the markets. In May 1986 an article in *Institutional Investor* caused a stir among the investment community when it reported that, since 1980, Julian Robertson's 'Tiger Fund', a hedge fund, had earned its investors a 43% average annual return. Robertson, a stockbroker and former US Navy officer, had started Tiger Management in 1980 with $8 million in capital.

Hedge funds were not new. Alfred W. Jones, an academic and journalist, started an investment partnership in the US in 1949. Jones adopted a novel approach to investment, hedging his long stock positions by selling short other stocks to protect against market risk. Jones invested his own money in the partnership and took a 20% share of any profits. Now the spectacular profitability of the Tiger Fund captured the market's imagination and prompted many imitators.

With lots of new hedging tools available in the mid-1980s and favourable publicity, the hedge fund business took off, offering an increasing array of products, using more sophisticated strategies. Many talented money managers and traders left their traditional institutional and retail investment firms attracted by the high fees and potential to take a share of a fund's high returns. By 1990, there were over 500 hedge funds worldwide with assets of about $38bn.

The key characteristics of hedge funds were that, unlike mutual funds, they were not collective investment vehicles and their shares were not normally available for purchase by the public. They consequently had less transparent financial reporting than other collective investment vehicles. Typically they only solicited and accepted funds from investors who could demonstrate a sufficient level of net worth. Large initial investment amounts were required and investors' funds were tied up for some minimum lock-up period. Most importantly they could use leverage to enhance their returns.

The investment banks and securities houses welcomed the arrival of the hedge funds as they were active dealers and, thanks to leverage, often traded in substantial size. Securities sales people favoured building relationships with hedge funds rather than the traditional staid 'buy and hold' or 'long only' investors, such as insurance companies and pension funds. Indeed to help build their relationships with such funds the banks would offer generous credit lines to support their leveraged activities. Before long, hedge fund activities were moving markets.

After record new bond issuance of $182bn in 1986, the demise of the perpetual FRN market contributed to a decline in 1987 to $143bn. The year was notable, however, for yen and sterling issuance. The growth of yen issuance, in addition to the surge in Japanese equity warrant issues, enabled Nomura to knock CSFB off the top of the league table for 1987. Nikko and Yamaichi also managed to break into the higher echelons of the league table for the first time. In the sterling sector there was a modest, yet landmark, £50m issue for National Home Loans, from Salomon Brothers: the first sterling mortgage-backed security (MBS). By the end of the year around £1bn of MBS had been issued. In 1988 sterling issuance would treble, with the largest corporate issue to date, a £200m offering for Sears, followed by a £150m five-year deal for Marks and Spencer, which was soon trading below the yield on Gilts.

In 1987 the UK Building Societies Act allowed societies to raise debt in foreign currencies and swap the proceeds back into sterling. Halifax was first mover with a $150m five-year issue, followed almost immediately by Abbey National with a $200m offering.

But 1987 will be best lastingly remembered for the stock market crash. On 19 October 1987, a day that became known as 'Black Monday', stock markets around the world plummeted. The crash began in Hong Kong and spread west to Europe, then hitting the United States after other markets had fallen significantly. People feared this might be a repeat of the events of October 1929 when the market crashed, leading to the Great Depression of the 1930s. In the US the Dow Jones Industrial Average plunged 508 points, or 22.6% in value, its largest single-day percentage drop.

With the expansion in trade in international equities and equity-linked issues, international stock markets had grown more interdependent. What was unique about the 1987 decline was not so much the scale of the decline but the speed with which it happened and then spread from one market to another. Countries with short settlement periods reported exceptional pressure from foreign market participants looking to use the liquidity of their markets to meet obligations elsewhere. The declines were particularly sharp in Euroequity issues and issues related to privatisations. The day after the crash, equity-linked Eurobond prices collapsed while trading in straight bonds virtually came to a standstill.

Numerous reasons have been put forward for the crash. The lack of liquidity in markets was a major factor. The markets failed to manage the sudden and extremely high volume of sell orders. As computer technology had become more available, the use of 'programme-trading' had grown significantly, particularly on Wall Street, and many blamed programme-trading strategies for blindly selling stocks as prices declined. Others have focused on the interplay between stock markets and index options and futures markets as on 19 October, the stock index futures market was flooded with billions of dollars' worth of sell orders within minutes, causing both the futures and stock markets to crash.

The overvaluation of stocks also played a role. From 1982 onward, stock markets around the world had advanced almost without interruption until August 1987, by which time the

S&P had gained 138% from its November 1982 high. By September 1987 US price/earnings ratios (P/Es) were at historic highs. In the UK the stock market had risen by 47% from the beginning of the year to mid-July, and this strong performance had followed gains in each of the previous five years.

While the crash didn't herald another Great Depression, as had been feared, it did alert investors to a new era of stock market volatility. Following the 1987 crash the New York Stock Exchange (NYSE) and the Chicago Mercantile Exchange (CME) together introduced the 'circuit breaker' mechanism. The circuit breaker halts trading if the Dow Jones Industrial Average declines a prescribed number of points in a prescribed amount of time. In addition the SEC modified the margin requirements in an attempt to lower the volatility of common stocks, stock options and the futures market.

The market rebounded remarkably following the 1987 stock market crash. The market began a slow and steady climb almost immediately. In fact, before the end of 1989, the Dow Jones Industrials would once again be setting new record highs. History would show that 'Black Monday' was a minor blip in a 30-year bull market for equities.

*　*　*

Until the 1970s, few companies issued bonds rated below investment grade. The only paper available was from established companies whose credit had subsequently deteriorated, i.e. 'fallen angels'. That changed in the late 1970s when young companies with no credit standing approached the bond markets for finance and issued bonds that were rated as speculative grade or 'junk'. Some investors felt the high returns these bonds offered outweighed the default probabilities, and 'junk bonds' became a popular investment by the early 1980s. An ambitious trader, Michael Milken, who worked for the investment bank Drexel Burnham Lambert, recognised the considerable financial opportunities that came with the emergence of junk bonds and encouraged both bond issuers and investors to take full advantage of them.

Milken convinced hungry entrepreneurs of the idea of issuing high-yield securities to raise money to take over a company. With junk bonds, the acquiring company could borrow serious cash with little or no assets and use it to bid for another unwilling company, or target. This was termed a 'leveraged buy out' or LBO. Junk-bond LBOs were often accompanied by some form of 'asset stripping' of the acquired entity as a way to finance the payments on the debt. Not all market participants felt this was fair business practice and animosity grew towards Milken. By the end of the decade corporate default rates rose significantly, and investors stopped buying junk paper. Issuance collapsed from $25bn in 1989 to $1bn in 1990. Milken's successful financial trading career ended on a sour note when he was accused of insider trading and securities fraud. Drexel Burnham Lambert was forced into bankruptcy in early 1990, largely due to its heavy involvement in junk bonds. Some years later the, now termed, 'high yield' market would revive in the US and be exported to Europe.

While junk bonds took a back seat, leveraged buy outs did not. In October 1988, RJR Nabisco, the tobacco and food conglomerate, announced the largest ever leveraged buy out, with the company looking to raise $17bn to buy out its shareholders. Kohlberg Kravis Roberts (KKR), a private equity firm, responded with an LBO proposal of their own and acquired the company in April 1989 for a staggering $25bn. As RJR Nabisco's share price rocketed from $21.25 to $77 their bond spreads ballooned from 100 basis points over US Treasuries to an unprecedented, for an investment grade credit, 350 basis points. Other major companies that might be subject to acquisition also saw their spreads widening. International bond investors, previously only exposed to default or insolvency risk, now needed to factor in 'event risk'. This was the risk that some unexpected event will cause a substantial decline in the market value of a security, for example, a leveraged buy out that entails huge amounts of new debt causing a decline in the market value of the target company's outstanding debt. By 1989 US LBOs led to 77 credit downgrades due to event risk affecting $50bn of debt. The LBO would become another US export.

Euromoney's lead article in June 1989 was entitled 'The Joy of Corporate Restructuring'. It noted that:

> *Many Americans are convinced Europe is where the action will be in the next five years. In the US, LBOs have already unearthed many undervalued (and mismanaged) corporations. 'The smart money around the world is looking at Europe because there is a substantial number of undervalued companies', says Tom Swayne, head of capital markets products at Chase Manhattan in London.*[26]

*   *   *

On 19 May 1987 Citicorp announced a $2.5bn loss for the second quarter and a $3bn provision against its third world debt. The news served as a sobering reminder that the problem of financing heavily indebted countries had not gone away. Despite various rounds of rescheduling and restructuring sovereign and private sector debt since the Mexican crisis, by the late 1980s, it was widely believed that most debtor nations were no closer to a financial recovery. Bilateral negotiations with LDCs from 1983 onwards suggested that many loans would never be repaid. This raised two major challenges. Firstly, significant debt relief was going to be required to turn around the LDC economies and to enable them to regain access to the international capital markets. And second the deterioration in the capital ratios of the large international banks needed to be halted.

Citicorp's unilateral debt write-down forced other major US banks to follow suit. David Mulford, then US Treasury Under Secretary pushed for write-offs to reduce the overall debt of the LDCs. When Nicholas Brady became US Treasury Secretary the following year, he pressed for future refinancings to provide some debt relief to the borrower.

In September 1987 *Euromoney* speculated:

> *Why not take the $300bn of Latin American debt, convert it into junk bonds and sell it to junk bond investors? … No-one is saying that it will be a big market, at least not in the beginning, but together with debt-for-equity swaps and the secondary market in Third World loans it will be a significant move towards removing the wet blanket that has covered Latin America and the world economy since Mexico hit the wall in 1982. Salomon Brothers, Merrill Lynch, Citibank and Shearson Lehman are searching for a magic formula that will induce insurance companies and pension funds to take Third World obligations off the hands of commercial banks.*[27]

The Brady Plan, announced in March 1989, called for the US, the IMF and the World Bank to cooperate with commercial bank creditors in restructuring and reducing the debt of developing countries. There were three key elements to the Brady Plan: firstly, bank creditors would grant debt relief in exchange for a greater assurance of payments being made; secondly, debt relief needed to be linked to some commitment to structural and economic reforms; and third, the resulting debt should be tradable, to diversify the indebtedness away from the banks.

The indebted nation and the banks would enter negotiations to exchange defaulted loans for a package of newly issued Brady bonds. Most Brady restructurings included at least two basic options for debt holders: the exchange of loans for either 'Par Bonds' or 'Discount Bonds'. Par Bonds involved an exchange of loans for bonds of equal face amount, with a fixed, below-market rate of interest, allowing for long-term debt service reduction by means of the concessionary interest rate. Discount Bonds resulted from an exchange of loans for a lesser amount of face value in bonds (generally a 30–50% discount or 'haircut'), allowing for immediate debt reduction, with a market-based floating rate of interest.

The Brady bond's principal was collateralised by US Treasury zero coupon bonds, with cash collateral covering a set number of future interest payments. Collateralisation was achieved by the issuing country purchasing US Treasury zero coupon bonds with the same maturity as the individual Brady bond and placing these zeros in escrow at the Federal Reserve for the benefit of the investor. The cash collateral component was usually equal to 6, 12 or 18 months' interest invested in money market instruments, rated double-A or better, and similarly lodged with the Federal Reserve.

Later Brady plans included a wider array of options, fixed, floating rate, bullet or amortising principals with collateralised and non-collateralised principal and interest payments. No Brady bond was US government guaranteed.

Mexico was the first nation to restructure under the Brady Plan. In addition to Mexico, Brady bonds were eventually issued (in an aggregate face amount of over US$ 160bn) by Argentina, Brazil, Bulgaria, Costa Rica, the Dominican Republic, Ecuador, Ivory Coast (Côte d'Ivoire), Jordan, Nigeria, Panama, Peru, the Philippines, Poland, Russia, Uruguay, Venezuela and Vietnam. The large issue size of many Brady bond issuances helped promote a liquid market in the paper. Brady bond prices were quoted in both London and New York but it was normally off a New York-based trading book.[28]

The Brady Plan enabled many LDCs to regain access to the international capital markets for their financing needs. The enduring legacy of the Brady plan for the cross-border markets resulted from the many significant debt exchanges (Eurobond for Brady) in the second half of the 1990s as the LDC economies recovered.

But what of the question of banking standards? The Basel Committee on Banking Regulations and Supervisory Practices sought to uphold capital standards in the banking system and to agree on a system to measure whether international banks had adequate capital for the risks they were undertaking. The Committee was additionally concerned about the Japanese banking sector, which had grown rapidly in the previous decade. In 1974 when the Basel Committee was created, only one of the ten largest banks in the world was Japanese; by 1988 nine of the ten largest banks in the world were Japanese. This rise of Japanese banks was mirrored by a decline in the position of US banks. But worryingly, the capital ratios of both Japanese and US banks had moved inversely to their market shares.[29]

A major sticking point on the way to an agreement concerned what items could be included in the definition of 'capital' for regulatory purposes. This was driven more by whether individual national banking interests would be competitively disadvantaged rather than whether any proposal was adequate to protect the financial system. The Basel Capital Accord was finally approved by the G10 Governors and released to banks in July 1988. The Accord confined itself to credit risks, while acknowledging that banks must guard against other risks as well.

The basic approach was to assign each asset or off-balance-sheet item held by a bank to one of five risk categories, calculate the capital required for each asset or item based on the risk weighting, and then add all these amounts together to produce the total minimum capital required to be held by the bank. The Accord created two minimum capital ratios to be achieved by the end of 1992. A bank's core capital, called 'Tier 1' capital by the Committee, was to be at least 4% of risk-weighted assets, and a bank's Total Capital, which included so-called 'Tier 2' components, was to be at least 8% of risk-weighted assets.

Core or Tier 1 capital principally comprised shareholders' equity and retained earnings. Other elements – such as revaluation reserves, subordinated debt, general loan-loss reserves and certain hybrid capital instruments – were designated as Tier 2 capital, that is, they only absorb losses after Tier 1 capital has been lost. Overall Tier 2 capital could not exceed 100% of Tier 1 capital. The use of two separate capital ratios maintained a focus on core capital while accommodating national differences.

In June 1988, IBCA released a report showing that only three of the 11 largest banks in the US would have met the Basel standards. In the same report, IBCA calculated that Japanese banks would require $50bn of additional capital to comply with the minimum Basel requirements.[30]

As the new capital standards were adopted by banking regimes in different jurisdictions, bond originators set to work to adapt funding practices to take advantage of the new rules. Innovative subordinated and hybrid capital structures were devised, particularly in the FRN sector, designed to meet the new requirements for Tier 1 or Tier 2 capital. Hybrid capital desks sprang up in investment banks and securitisation structures adapted to enable the growth of off-balance-sheet activities. So the whole panoply of a regulatory arbitrage industry developed.

* * *

For almost a decade the AIBD had debated the question of introducing automated systems into the Eurobond market. In the mid-80s a study was commissioned by the Board to consider developing a system for bond trading based on the US NASD system and the project was called AIBDQ. However AIBDQ was not welcomed by all parties; some felt they would be disadvantaged by such a system, while others felt its development was beyond the AIBD's remit. As early as May 1986 a prominent German member expressed concern in the *AIBD Gazette* about:

The strong expansion in the creation of new products on a commercial basis and correspondingly, a strong expansion of the number of employees of the AIBD. AIBD – Quo Vadis? In the direction of the 'Association of International Dealers and Market Participants' or 'AIBD Incorporated'? … I am afraid that a combination of the two, without sooner or later having identification problems, is impossible.

He questions:

whether commercial products must be managed responsibly by an organization such as AIBD or can this be achieved by other professional companies? Could an organization like AIBD then concentrate on the important activities at the beginning of its career: with fundamental problems that are of concern and should be of concern to its members.[31]

At the Oslo AGM in 1987 the AIBDQ project was shelved but a part of the proposal, the 'Trax' system, was accepted. Stanley Ross, a long-standing advocate of dealing technology, commented 'I believe the turn down of AIBDQ somehow made acceptance of the Trax component that much easier. It was the most important thing achieved in new technology for years, saving huge amounts of time, money and people-intensive jobs.'[32] Other commentators saw it somewhat differently, 'it is obvious from the row about Trax that many dealers did not know what they were voting for in Oslo. A vote for Trax was considered a vote against AIBDQ … AIBD members did not have a second chance to vote on Trax.'[33] Trax was a proposal for a real-time trade matching mechanism. Until the late 1980s trade agreement took place by the issuance of trade confirmations, normally in the form of telexes which were not necessarily picked up in an efficient manner by the other counterparty. The Trax system would require both counterparties to a transaction to input the details of the trade within stipulated times of the trade being agreed. The Trax computer would then search for a matching instruction from the counterparty. The status of advised trades could be monitored in real time.

A year after the project's acceptance it was still meeting hurdles. Ross remembers the Dallas AGM in 1988: 'In the weeks prior to the meeting there had been a massive build up of opposition to Trax by Euroclear and Cedel who saw their interests threatened.' In order to quell the concerns of the clearing systems, the AIBD had been working on a project with them to create a system for confirming and matching trades, known as ACE (for AIBD, Cedel and Euroclear). The clearing systems maintained that Trax duplicated the functions of ACE and would put an unacceptable financial burden on AIBD members. 'In all events the attempt to torpedo the project or to engineer another vote on the subject was swiftly disposed of by a René Jacquet in fighting mood, who must have been greatly cheered by the SIB's Richard Britton, being so eloquently supportive of the AIBD's work in this direction.'[34]

Britton of the SIB had argued that ACE did not meet the requirement of the UK regulators that trades must be reported in real time. 'Despite the apparent benefits of Trax, many Eurobond dealers outside the UK remain opposed to the system. Even though the AIBD has said that Trax will pay for itself in three years, many non-UK dealers remain convinced they are bearing the cost of British regulation.'[35]

Nevertheless by the Vienna AGM in 1989 Trax was up and running and 90% of London reporting dealers were on live or active testing. The key to the adoption of Trax was that all UK members of the AIBD, together with all reporting dealers of the Association, irrespective of their domicile, were obliged to use the system. A joint link-up with Telekurs was undertaken to enable the Swiss region and others to use Trax via Telekurs.

Members of Trax were required to issue a trade message to Trax within 30 minutes of trade execution; if not, a fine was imposed. This was on an escalating scale, so the later the message was received, the larger the fine. In addition fines could be imposed for other non-compliance reasons, such as failure to provide all necessary trade details and failure to act upon a non-matching advice within a reasonable time frame. But Trax, from its earliest days, was not just a trade matching but also a trade reporting platform. In the newly emerging regulatory environment Trax reports were available to the regulatory authorities, particularly in the UK – although counterparty names were not revealed.

The Trax project involved the AIBD in significant expenditure; estimated to be in the region of $8.9m. By the time of the Vienna meeting in 1989 the AIBD's service company in London had grown to 67 employees with 36 working on Trax. In fact it was not many years before costs were covered and Trax was making a healthy profit; not so much as a result of higher fees but due more to the incidence of fines which remained 'surpisingly high', generating income of more than Sfr1.5m in 1991 alone.[36]

Trax set the AIBD on a different trajectory from hitherto. The financial success of the Trax project moved the Association's centre of gravity from focusing principally on members' needs to building a commercial IT business to compete in the post-trade matching and reporting space. As the debt capital markets expanded exponentially in the following decade with new instruments and new structures, the AIBD retained a somewhat insular view, focusing on the secondary Eurobond business and enjoying the success of their unique IT franchise.

To support such a product-focused structure, executive responsibilities were transferred from the AIBD Board to the management of the Association. The previous role of Secretary to the Association was upgraded to Secretary General and Chief Executive, in charge of the day-to-day management of the Association. In 1990 John Langton, a long-time Eurobond trading head (with Bondtrade and Orion Bank) and Board member, was appointed to this position. He would remain in it for 15 years.

* * *

Meanwhile when IPMA members gathered for their annual meeting in April 1989 their chairman, Michael von Brentano of Deutsche Bank, raised the key issue: 'The deteriorating profitability of the Eurobond business is a cause for serious concern in our industry.' A former syndicate head of Salomon and Citigroup, Mark Watson, recalls: 'People would underwrite deals without distribution and take a market view. We played all sorts of shenanigans to persuade the market that deals were in good shape when they weren't necessarily.'[37]

Watson adds: 'You would often end up with underwriting positions and you had to figure your way out of them, which wasn't easy because, if a new issue was incorrectly priced, and lots of them were, you were trading from an underwater position. The syndicate desk was a big focal point on the trading floor. It was where a lot of the big risk decisions were taken and a lot of capital deployed.'[38]

In addition, aspiring new issue houses would buy their way into the market to gain league table status with deals often subsidised by the attached swap. In the case of Japanese banks some of the more aggressive swap arrangements were termed 'kamikaze swaps' for obvious reasons. The major issuing houses became increasingly alarmed with the rising overcapacity and the progressive erosion of profitability in the Eurobond market.

Frequent issuers, in particular, were frustrated that their offerings often traded poorly in the secondary market despite an assurance from their lead manager or managers that the paper had been well distributed in the primary phase. Increasingly they would press for more details on where the bonds had actually been placed. Protected by investor anonymity the managers would suggest broad areas of distribution, by investor type and geography, often based on what they thought the borrower would like to hear, rather than the hard facts of the placement.

In 1989 Toyota Motor Credit Corporation issued an Ecu100m bond into a depressed sector and on terms that looked unattractive against other current Ecu offerings. Before long the lead manager owned Ecu120m as co-managers and traders shorted the issue. The lead manager as a result withdrew any indicative prices and insisted on only dealing by telephone so that any short sellers would have to identify themselves if they wished to buy back paper. The short sellers complained that the lead manager was in breach of the IPMA Recommendation to make two-way prices in their own issue. The lead manager pointed out in response his obligation to make prices was only to 'reporting dealers' and that there was only one reporting dealer for the bond in question.

This was yet another of the many examples of the practice of 'dumping' tightly priced issues by co-managers and traders.

In mid-August 1989 Morgan Stanley convened a meeting at its offices with six other new issue houses to notify them of the terms on which it would be syndicating a new five-year issue for New Zealand. It was a system already in use in the New York market. The 'Fixed Price Re-offer' system would require that all banks accepting an invitation to underwrite the transaction would undertake only to place bonds at a price set by the lead manager, until syndicate was 'broken'. The rationale was to give all parties a level playing field, as all bonds must be offered at the same price with no party offering discounts. So investors are assured that they cannot get the securities more cheaply from another dealer while the issue is in syndication. It was designed to prevent underwriters from selling bonds back to the lead manager (i.e. 'dumping') at a discount to the re-offer price.

In addition, the syndicate for the New Zealand transaction would comprise fewer banks than the conventional Euromarket syndicate and all underwriters would receive the same, reduced (from traditional Euromarket levels) fee. Co-lead managers for the $500m New Zealand offering would be required to offer the bonds at the issue price of 99.75 or better for a fixed underwriting fee of 0.375% until the breaking of syndicate when bonds would be allowed to trade freely.

As the New Zealand transaction was priced reasonably generously at 73 basis points over US Treasuries, the new method of syndication had a positive initial reception. Bob Scott, head of worldwide underwriting at Morgan Stanley, said: 'We think this is an important first step towards a new method of managing international bond issues that satisfies issuers and investors and allows underwriters a reasonable prospect of earning compensation for their role. We hope it challenges other managers to consider their approaches to underwriting.'[39] Morgan Stanley followed up their success with a $1.5bn transaction for Italy which was also well received. Deutsche Bank took up the challenge with a fixed price re-offer of $300m for KfW. But not everyone was happy, as smaller banks with retail networks felt the fixed price would make it more difficult to distribute bonds to those networks and saw it as another attempt by the 'bulge bracket' houses to push them out of the primary market.

Gradually the fixed price re-offer method of syndication gained traction with the main issuing houses and brought with it improved syndicate discipline. John Walsh, head of syndicate at CSFB in 1989 recalls: 'During the 1980s the Euromarkets went through a transformation from the old cowboy markets of less $\frac{7}{8}$ offered immediately a deal was announced, to the introduction of the fixed price reoffer system.' New issue fees had proved largely meaningless for years, as syndicate members in large syndicates of 50 or more would simply sell tightly priced offerings at full fees to the interdealer broker who would sell them back to the lead manager. Walsh continues:

The fixed re-offer changed the way it worked. You couldn't take a flyer in the same way. Before its introduction, you knew what borrowers' targets were and you could pick a deal off the shelf, not hedge it and make a lot of money. If you were bound by the fixed price re-offer, you had to offer securities at the stipulated price and this took a large part of the risk factor away from the syndicate desk.

Simon Meadows, a member of Salomon's syndicate desk at the time adds: 'As soon as the mindset started to change, the whole idea of massive syndicates looked ridiculous and started to fade out. Issuers also started to understand that …their securities had to be distributed into firm hands so they would trade better and the price would improve.'[40]

Did the fixed price re-offer resolve the indiscipline of the primary markets? Not entirely. Reduced reallowances and more realistic fees certainly helped. However the practice relied heavily on syndicate participants working honestly with each other – a big ask when investment banks are competing tooth and nail. It was not long before the naturally competitive nature of the market forced tighter new issue spreads and deals that proved more difficult to place.

Mis-priced deals threw up dilemmas for syndicate participants in a fixed price re-offer. If a transaction was selling well, the lead manager would 'break' syndicate within a reasonable time after launch. If the deal was moving slowly then according to the fixed price agreement he could not break syndicate. If there were delays in breaking syndicate then the signal to other managers, and of course investors, was that the deal was not being well received. In this case participants might decline or reduce their demand for the transaction. In time, to avoid this outcome, the unscrupulous lead manager might notify participants that syndicate was broken when in fact only a minority of bonds had been distributed. Accusations might fly back and forth about unseemly syndicate practices but as always in an opaque bearer bond market such accusations were difficult to substantiate.

Paul Hearn, syndicate veteran from BNP Paribas, pointed out: 'Yes, in theory you were not meant to sell bonds below the fixed price re-offer until the deal broke syndicate – but deals would tend to hold at the fixed price re-offer for about an hour and then syndicate would break and the thing would trade down again, so it was abused fairly quickly as a result of competition.'[41] By 1992 *Euromoney* concluded: 'what everyone expected was shown to be true; no syndication mechanism, fixed price reoffering or other, could guarantee either sensible pricing or responsible syndicate behavior.'[42]

Despite the problems the fixed price re-offer was introduced into the Japanese market in the early 1990s in a transaction for NTT, the Japanese telecoms company. By 1992 the Kingdom of Sweden would launch the first fixed price re-offer in the deutschemark market with DM2.5bn offering. One week later Deutsche Bank led a DM5bn five-year fixed price re-offer transaction for the United Kingdom.

*   *   *

It had been widely expected that the first borrower to bring a fixed price re-offer issue to the Euromarket would be the World Bank. They had been focused for some time on the differential financing costs they experienced when issuing in the Yankee or the Eurobond markets. The Bank had been raising most of its dollar funding in the Euromarkets as its paper traded significantly wider in the Yankee market. Kenneth Lay, head of dollar funding at the World Bank, observed: 'We had become convinced by 1985 or 1986 that we were paying too much to do Yankees and still not getting broad US placement.'[43] 'There were occasions on which we would issue a Yankee bond and then within a month or two either side we would issue a Eurobond, with the same maturity and the coupons very close, but the two deals would trade on a 50bp spread, even having adjusted for the coupon payment frequency.'[44]

Lay and his team started to examine the barriers that prevented dealers from taking advantage of the obvious arbitrage. Lay began to investigate the possibility of structuring a bond offering which could be distributed in both the Eurobond and domestic bond markets on identical terms. He and Jan Wright put forward a paper in the *Journal of International Securities Markets* in autumn 1988, which outlined ideas on how to overcome the markets' inefficiencies. It stated: 'Looking out over the next several years, we envision a product mix that would have as its centerpiece a globally syndicated 'institutional offering', issued in size and saleable at issue (i.e. no 'lock-up') in each of the three major centres.' Lay and his team canvassed a total of 125 institutional investors in 16 countries on his 'Global' bond concept. Investor feedback supported the pursuit of more liquid issuance and a reduction in cross-border investment barriers.

But the major issuing houses, particularly those in the US, were more apprehensive about the new 'Global' bond concept. At the heart of Lay's proposal was the adoption of the fixed price re-offer method of syndication. Lay points out:

> *In the US, there were much richer fees – a ten-year Yankee cost 0.50% or 0.60%, and the fixed price re-offer meant that dealers kept the full gross spread. This was sustained by a virtual cartel that the five 'bulge bracket' firms enjoyed. So there was a lot of concern among the US houses that a Global deal could import into the US the remarkably skinny fee structure in London that resulted from the combination of unfettered competition and the practice of re-allowing fees to investors.*[45]

European issuing houses were initially wary of the global bond idea believing it was a ruse by US houses to increase their market share.

But, as Lay stressed, 'The idea wasn't going to work unless the paper traded with little or no friction across borders. There was therefore a lot of work that went into what you could call the plumbing.'[46] Since US domestic bonds are registered and Eurobonds bearer instruments, there needed to be special settlement arrangements to transfer ownership between markets. Since part of a Global bond issue would be placed in the US then such Global bond offerings (or at least that portion placed in the US) must be registered with the SEC.

Extended negotiations took place between the World Bank's lawyers and the New York Fed to hammer out cross-border settlement procedures. 'A major problem was that the infrastructure was not integrated. It revolved around two systems: in the US, the Fedwire: and in Europe, Euroclear and Cedel (now Clearstream). The links between the two systems were slow and cumbersome, took two to three days and needed manual intervention,' said Lay.[47] The Fedwire Securities Services is a book-entry securities issuance and transfer system provided to US banks and US branches of foreign banks by the Federal Reserve banks. The Fedwire Securities Services supported the 'omnibus' account structure, i.e. accounts representing multiple investors. The World Bank eventually persuaded the Fed to allow the Euroclear and Cedel portions of the deal to be traded on the Fedwire in omnibus accounts. The key technical innovation came when connecting Fedwire with the Euromarket clearing systems with newly automated links. This breakthrough reduced the time it took for euro and Yankee bonds to trade across borders from two to three days to a day or less.

After two years' preparation the World Bank launched its long heralded 'Global' bond issue in September 1989, a $1.5bn offering for 10 years with an 8.75% coupon. This landmark transaction, twice as big as any previous World Bank issue, was launched via the fixed price re-offer method of syndication with lead managers Deutsche Bank and Salomon Brothers. Investors on both sides of the Atlantic showed enthusiastic support for the new transaction which was heavily oversubscribed. Lay declared: 'Funding cost savings on our first Global were around $15m in NPV terms: development costs were around $300,000. We assumed that the Yankee market was a non-starter for pricing, so we priced off Eurobonds. And after the issue, our Yankees began to tighten as well.'[48] In the secondary market the new Global bond tightened from 37.5bps spread over US Treasuries at the time of launch, to 24bps within a few days.

The bond was listed in the US, Europe and Asia and clearing and settlement was available through a choice of national or international settlement systems: Euroclear, Cedel, the Deutscher Kassenverein and either the Federal Reserve Book Entry system (FRB) or DTC in the US.

The pattern developed that each Global bond would be deposited with the Deposit Trust Company (DTC) and registered in the name of DTC or DTC's nominee. Purchasers of Global bonds in the US would do so only through DTC, while purchasers of Global bonds in Europe could do so through Cedel (now Clearstream) or Euroclear. Because DTC was the only registered owner of the bonds, Cedel and Euroclear would buy and sell Global bonds through their DTC depositories, such as J.P. Morgan Chase. So Euromarket investors could trade and settle Global bonds like they would Eurobonds, while US investors could trade and settle Globals as they would US domestic bonds using their existing accounts in the relevant settlement systems.

However because of the need for registration a Global offering was more expensive to structure than a standard Eurobond offering. The trade-off was between this extra cost versus the reduction in re-offer spread that might be obtained by an issue which would be distributed and traded in multiple markets. This trade-off gave rise to two characteristics of Global bonds: they were typically large issues to encourage liquidity, and as supranational and sovereign issuers were subject to lighter registration requirements with the SEC, these borrowers predominated.

Lay was keen to develop the Global bond concept further: 'After the initial US dollar global, we did a New Zealand dollar global, which was also very successful: then a first yen global in 1992 and after that a first deutschemark global.'[49] Others were not slow to follow. In November 1989 Ontario Hydro issued the first Global in Canadian dollars with an unprecedented C$1.25bn issue. The Republic of Finland was the first sovereign to issue a Global in 1992 with a $2bn five-year transaction. In the same year the first corporate Global bond was issued by Matsushita Electric with a $1bn offering for 10 years. By September 1993, Goldman Sachs, Merrill Lynch and Salomon Brothers accounted for almost 50% of all Global lead management positions.[50] The first multicurrency global bond issue was launched in July 1994 for the Republic of Italy. This was a five-year floating rate offering amounting to $4bn equivalent with simultaneous issuance of yen, US$ and DM, all with the same margin.

By 1994 the ISMA Quarterly Comment observed:

There are now at least five distinct categories of global bonds: the World Bank-style issue that essentially offers investors an alternative to government bonds; dollar offerings from major European issuers (largely sovereigns) which use the US market as their back-stop bid; 'quick and dirty' non-dollar Yankees which target US demand for foreign currency debt and make smaller sales offshore; and so-called 'super Eurobonds' or the contradictory sounding, domestic globals. The latter have been seen in New Zealand and Australian dollars and will soon be offered in French francs.

When Mexico's Bancomext issued a $1bn global in 1994 the Comment was moved to note:

As the Global bond format widens and becomes used by a much larger stable of issuers, some argue that the very sound reasons behind using the product have been forgotten in a haze of marketing hype and a scramble for international league tables.

This has meant, in the view of many observers, that the global bond concept has been sold to inappropriate users ...Cynics also argue that the christening of glorified domestic issues as global deals risks deceiving investors with promises of liquidity that will not be fulfilled.[51]

* * *

The gradual erosion of borders between national and international securities markets was increasingly apparent to US regulators. By 1985 the Eurobond market had become the world's largest securities market as measured by new issue volume. At the same time the growth of securities markets in the UK, Japan and Italy was beginning to outpace that in the United States. In 1987 the SEC produced a massive study on the internationalisation of securities markets which ushered in new thinking and a re-evaluation of the SEC's rules and policies.

Until that time, issuers who had some jurisdictional link to the United States and wanted to make a foreign bond offering would approach the SEC for a 'no action' letter. This stated that the SEC would take no action if the issuer did not register the securities under the 1933 Act, as the offering would take place abroad rather than in the US. Of equal concern was whether such issues could be resold into the US without registration. By 1986 an SEC executive observed there were 'three feet' of no-action letters 'and it was just getting ridiculous – using far too many resources'. The Commission concluded that a new rule needed to be created and Regulation S was introduced in 1990.[52]

'We wanted to say, if you're selling outside the United States, you don't have to register with the SEC, period,'[53] says Sara Hanks one of the primary drafters. Regulation S was adopted in 1990 (and amended in 1999) to ensure that securities sold outside the US 'come to rest abroad' and do not flow back into the US domestic market. The rules are divided into three categories primarily based on the type of borrower and the likely interest in the issue by US domestic investors. The concern is to prevent bearer securities entering the US public market. Category 1 securities are the least restrictive category where no real flow back risk exists. Category 2 is more restrictive depending on the likely level of interest by US investors (i.e. dependent on 'SUSMI' – 'substantial US market interest'). Category 3 is the most restrictive category where the risk of flow back of the securities into the domestic market is high. Categories 2 and 3 require that there be no offers or sales *to a US person* during a 40-day distribution compliance period, i.e. the 'lock up', in order to prevent flow back into the US market. In all cases the regulation requires that offers and sales of the securities must be made outside the United States and that no offering participant engage in 'directed selling efforts'(targeted at the US).

The SEC was further concerned how large US institutional investors, such as mutual funds, banks and insurance companies, might be able to participate in the international cross-border bond market, specifically in securities which were not registered under the 1933 Act. Rule 144A was passed in 1990 as part of an amendment to the Securities Act of 1933 providing an efficient, low-cost way for borrowers to access US institutional investors. It allowed for the sale of private placement securities by underwriters among qualified institutional buyers (i.e. QIBs – institutions that manage at least \$100m in securities) without requiring public registration. Now foreign issuers of securities could raise capital in the US without submitting to the SEC's accounting and disclosure requirements if they were to sell only to qualifying 'sophisticated' institutions, and not to retail investors.

When an underwriter is selling securities in reliance on Rule 144A, it must be clearly stated, and the underwriter must reasonably establish, that the buyer is a QIB. As the offering is a private placement it must not be the subject of 'general solicitation or advertising' in the US. In addition, underwriters must ensure that 144A securities are not sold back to the public market and so 144A securities are 'restricted securities' and subject to resale restrictions. This restricted period is between six months and two years. Rule 144A doesn't avoid the anti-fraud provisions of US law so such issues normally require a 10b-5 letter or opinion from US Counsel to confirm satisfactory due diligence has been undertaken.

Rule 144A was a significant breakthrough and provided efficient access to US capital at a lower cost than traditional public US offerings. The *Financial Times*, in December 1989, described the introduction of Rule 144A as 'just one of the plans designed to make the US an attractive stopping place for global capital flows'. Since 1990, issuers from all over the world have used Rule 144A to raise capital and increase their profile with US institutional investors.

Although the drafters of Rule 144A and Regulation S did not originally focus on how the two rules might function together in the international markets, it soon became clear. Regulation S would govern when an issuer was selling outside the US, and Rule 144A would then allow institutional investors to trade such bearer securities in the US.[54]

Because of the extra-territorial nature of US laws, IPMA required that US selling restrictions, that is, Regulation S and Rule 144A, should be disclosed in all primary bond offerings. Typically, Regulation S bonds are generally accepted for clearance through (Cedel) Clearstream and Euroclear while 144A bonds are generally accepted for clearance through the DTC system.

British Aerospace was the first borrower to take advantage of the new regime, with a $100m transaction led by Goldman Sachs. CSFB brought the first equity transaction under the new rules for Atlas Copco.

The development of Global bonds along with the amendments to US securities regulation made a significant contribution to the elimination of barriers between financial markets. The globalisation of capital markets was now becoming a reality.

Political developments in 1989 and 1990 also made a massive contribution towards globalisation. The collapse of the Berlin Wall was a major turning point in the long struggle between the Soviet Union and Eastern Bloc countries, and western European nations in alliance with the United States. Improvements in communications helped make people behind the 'Iron Curtain' increasingly aware of the different living standards and freedoms enjoyed in the West. The newly elected President of the Soviet Union, Mikhail Gorbachev, announced plans to accelerate economic reform and he did not interfere as Eastern Bloc countries like Poland and Hungary became independent democracies. This movement towards democracy and change also took place in East Germany. It was only a matter of time before unification between East and West Germany would take place, ending 45 years of partition.

In February 1990 Nelson Mandela was freed after 27 years of incarceration in a South African jail, ending another long-standing repressive regime and isolation from the principal democracies.

The free markets had triumphed and benefits of globalisation were at hand.

NOTES

1. *AIBD Gazette*, Issue 13, May 1984, p. 24.
2. Gallant, *The Eurobond Market*, p. 169.
3. Fisher, *Eurobonds*, p. 23.
4. Bowe, *Eurobonds*, p. 22.

5. Ibid.
6. Ibid. p. 23.
7. *New York Times*, Undated notes post a record decline in Europe, 8 January 1987.
8. *Federal Reserve Bulletin*, The Anatomy of the Medium-Term Note Market, August 1993, pp.751–752.
9. Philip Moore, *Autostrade to the Superhighway: The Future of the Global Debt Markets* (published by Euromoney Books and ISMA, London 2001) p. 71.
10. *The Observer*, Big Bang's shockwaves left us with today's big bust, 9 October 2011.
11. *Financial Times*, 27 February 1986; Kynaston, *City of London,* Vol. 4, p. 684.
12. *Financial Times*, My Word is my Eurobond, 17 October 1985, p. 48.
13. *Euromoney*, Is the party over for the AIBD?, May 1986.
14. *AIBD Gazette*, Issue 16, December 1985, p. 7.
15. *AIBD Gazette*, Issue 17, May 1986, p. 6.
16. IPMA 20th Anniversary Booklet, 2005, p. 9.
17. Yassukovich interview for ICMA's 40th Anniversary Video, 2008.
18. Dilip Das, *International Finance: Contemporary Issues* (Routledge, May 1993) p. 18.
19. Shearlock and Ellington, *The Eurobond Diaries*, p. 105.
20. Ibid. pp.107–108.
21. Bowe, *Eurobonds*, p. 30.
22. IFR, 2,000th Issue, Warrants and stock bubbles: when Japan ruled the world, September 2013.
23. Shearlock and Ellington, *The Eurobond Diaries*, p. 108.
24. Ibid. p. 109.
25. *Daily Telegraph*, Ramsden faces yet another legal hurdle, 23 December 2007.
26. *Euromoney*, The Joy of Corporate Restructuring, June 1989.
27. *Euromoney*, September 1987.
28. EMTA website: www.emta.org, *EM Background: The Brady Plan.*
29. Daniel K. Tarullo, *Banking on Basel: The Future of International Financial Regulation,* (Peterson Institute for International Economics, December 2008).
30. *EuroWeek*, 20th Anniversary Edition, April 2007, *Turning point*, p. 39.
31. *AIBD Gazette*, Issue 17, May 1986, p. 30.
32. Ross, *From Where I Stood,* p. 10.
33. WatersTechnology, *AIBD, Eurobond clearing Houses take feud over Trade Matching Systems to Dallas*, 20 June 1988.
34. Ross, *From Where I Stood*, p. 10.
35. WatersTechnology, *AIBD, Eurobond clearing Houses take feud over Trade Matching Systems to Dallas*, 20 June 1988.
36. Minutes of the Annual General Meeting of the AIBD, 1992, p. 47.
37. *EuroWeek*, 20th Anniversary Edition, April 2007, *The changing art of the bond syndicate*, p. 20.
38. Ibid.
39. Moore, *Autostrade to the Superhighway*, p. 48.
40. *EuroWeek*, 20th Anniversary Edition, April 2007, *The changing art of the bond syndicate*, pp. 20–21
41. *EuroWeek*, 1990s: Believe the hype, 20 June 2003.
42. *Euromoney*, March 1992.
43. IFR 30th Anniversary Report: *The World that changed the Bond*, July 2004.
44. *EuroWeek*, 1990s: Believe the hype, 20 June 2003.
45. IFR 30th Anniversary Report: *The World that changed the Bond*, July 2004.
46. *EuroWeek*, 1990s: Believe the hype, 20 June 2003.
47. IFR 30th Anniversary Report: *The World that changed the Bond*, July 2004.
48. Ibid.
49. Ibid.
50. Moore, *Autostrade to the Superhighway*, p. 26.

51. *ISMA Quarterly Comment*, Vol. 18, July 1994, p. 12.
52. 4 February 2008 interview with Sara Hanks, reproduced by permission of the virtual museum and archive of the history of financial regulation at www.sechistorical.org.
53. Ibid.
54. Website: www.sechistorical.org: *The Imperial SEC? – Foreign Policy and the Internationalization of the Securities Markets, 1934–1990: The Harmonization of Securities Laws: Regulation S and Rule 144A.*

CHAPTER 6

The Derivatives Dash

1990–1995

Allen D. Wheat was born in New Mexico, the son of a career military officer, who had lost money speculating on Wall Street. After graduation Wheat started as a trainee with Chemical Bank in its US retail division. Three years later he took a job at the treasury department of General Foods, in White Plains, New York. At General Foods Wheat worked on hedging the company's interest rate exposures, his first derivatives experience. During an eight-year tenure at the company, he rose to head the group's international treasury before being lured to Bankers Trust in 1982 by a college friend turned headhunter, to build the bank's US swaps business.

'The money was good and it was an interesting business. We'd done a couple of swaps at General Foods, but the truth is I had not the slightest idea what the other side of the transaction was. Pricing was something I had to learn,' he remembers. 'If we wanted to price a swap in the early 1980s, we'd use the "Wall Street Journal" as the main point of reference.' He adds: 'I thought I was going to work with a whole bunch of people in swaps. When I got there I found that the guy who'd been running the swap business was moving over to real estate and I was on my own.'[1]

During the 1970s and 1980s Bankers Trust had become an acknowledged leader in risk management under Charles Sanford, later to become Chairman and CEO. Sanford developed a methodology for allocating capital to individual transactions in a manner to reflect their risk. By comparing the return generated by a transaction to the amount of risk capital that it required, he was able to calculate the 'risk-adjusted return on capital' or RAROC for that deal. RAROC subsequently came to be used as the basis for setting banks' capital adequacy levels. A further refinement was the use of probability of loss or a standard deviation-based measure to measure risk. Bankers Trust adopted the standard deviation of market value as a measure of risk in 1977–78. By the early 1990s, this application of probability theory to risk measurement was commonly referred to as value-at-risk (VaR).[2]

Sanford was determined to make banking more dynamic and innovative, so Bankers Trust became a leader in the rapidly growing derivatives business. Wheat recalls:

At the start, the swaps business was a very customised drawn out process. You'd find a customer, say, the World Bank. Then you'd have to wait a month to find a counterparty for the swap. Then another month while you sorted out the pricing to suit both sides. We became the first bank to stand in the middle and warehouse the deals so you didn't have to wait for a counterparty. And the margins were very good. Because we had deep books we found we could do more and more structured deals.[3]

After a period running Bankers Trust's global capital markets business in Tokyo, Wheat moved to London. There Wheat and his deputy, Chris Goekjian, set up an equity derivatives desk to use the engineering skills they had developed in the fixed income and currency derivatives markets to manufacture bespoke equity products. By the end of the 1980s derivatives were making approximately a quarter of Bankers Trust's global net profits.

Over at CSFB the late 1980s proved a tumultuous period. In 1988 First Boston lost more than \$1bn on bridge loans it had made to finance mergers and acquisitions in the hot takeover market of the time. Crédit Suisse injected equity into the bank in exchange for control, becoming the first foreign owner of a major Wall Street investment bank. Crédit Suisse renamed itself CS Holdings and became a parent company/shareholder of a newly renamed CS First Boston. Power struggles continued among the turf conscious CS holdings subsidiaries.

As Hans-Joerg Rudloff confronted the new decade he knew that derivatives and structuring would likely dominate the business going forward. He was not fully at ease with the rapidly developing derivatives markets and certainly did not have the natural feel for them which he undoubtedly had in bonds and equities. A derivatives desk had been established in the early 1980s with a young Marcus Everard as the rising star. Products were created which supported CSFB's presence in the primary markets. However by the end of the 1980s the generous profit margins were declining as many of these products had become 'commoditised'.

Now the need for new enhanced sources of revenue was driving financial institutions originating products to create new derivative structures and strategies to provide more customised types of risk protection and investment opportunity. These 'second generation' derivative products, while based on the fundamental derivative instruments, were enhanced to provide participants with even more bespoke pay-off or protection profiles. The range of asset classes was expanded and derivatives, vanilla or complex, used new 'references' e.g. property, tax, inflation, electricity and natural catastrophes. This structured business was highly profitable as it involved creativity, financial engineering expertise and a risk management capability.[4]

Knowing that CSFB would have to up their game in derivatives and financial engineering, Rudloff and Hennessy lured Allen Wheat, by then chairman of Bankers Trust International, away from Bankers with a large team of colleagues from their London and Tokyo offices. Poaching the 41-year-old Wheat came at a price. While Wheat saw the opportunity to build a business with Crédit Suisse's triple-A rating behind it, and access to First Boston's US sales team, Rudloff persuaded the Crédit Suisse Board to allow Wheat to set up an independently managed business, Crédit Suisse Financial Products (CSFP) with \$150m of capital and complete freedom to establish his own global derivatives business. Wheat, in turn, managed to negotiate an unprecedented slice of the revenues for the people who would run CSFP under his command. Fortunately he enjoyed the support of CEO Jack Hennessy, whose position in the overall group had been much enhanced after the takeover of First Boston. 'CSFP felt like Bankers Trust did at the beginning,' said Wheat:

Jack Hennessy kept the establishment away from us. That was crucial because derivatives touch everything; government bond trading, foreign exchange, equities. When all these groups are allowed to impact on how a new business is organised and operates, you end up killing it because they say 'You can't do that this way, you have to do it that way'. We were fortunate to be able to operate at CSFP without a lot of external politics to deal with.[5]

Crédit Suisse Financial Products hit the ground running and became both a highly creative operation and hugely profitable. Wheat remembers an early deal: 'We were working on a deal involving a Japanese securities house, a Mexican company, a US corporation, and investors. There was a bond deal, two currencies, and a swap. The profit we made on the deal took us over our target for the year.' By the late 1990s 'that deal would barely be significant enough to be reported on our major deal sheet'.[6] CSFP's rapid success was recognised when Wheat was appointed Chairman and Chief Operating Officer of CSFB in September 1993. When he addressed the firm's management committee in London on his appointment, a colleague reported: 'He told us that he had accepted the job, because he saw it as a great way to vastly increase his personal wealth and that he would make us all incredibly rich. He never once mentioned the clients.'[7] In 1994 CSFP profits alone totalled $240m; all of First Boston could only muster $155m.

But Wheat was not the only prominent name in the rapidly developing derivatives world. After the launch of the swaps market, J.P. Morgan quickly took a leading role in developing swap-related business. In 1984 Conrad or 'Connie' Volstad, with a degree in mathematics, an MBA and a law degree, was put in charge of the newly created global swaps group based in London. Volstad happily admitted 'I'm much more of a numbers guy than a lawyer.' Over the next three to four years he developed Morgan's derivatives business. 'I was always involved with products that had the same sort of approach – swaps, then options, then the concept of managing risk on a portfolio basis; it was a fascinating and energetic time.' When asked by Morgan to return to the US in 1988, Volstad preferred to remain in London and moved to Merrill Lynch. The problem with working on derivatives at Merrill was that their credit rating was only single-A, whereas at J.P. Morgan Volstad had enjoyed a triple-A rating. Volstad set about solving this problem by synthetically creating a triple-A balance sheet by the use of heavy over-collateralisation, so forming a triple-A swap subsidiary, Merrill Lynch Derivatives Products. After months of work with the rating agencies the subsidiary's triple-A status was confirmed.[8] The development of triple-A derivatives conduits was copied by other lower rated financial institutions.

At Merrill, Volstad now worked with Edson Mitchell who headed the syndicate and capital markets group. Mitchell understood the value of using derivatives 'It was our specific strategy to weave derivatives instruments into the capital markets as a way to catch up and overtake others in the market, such as Salomon Brothers, Morgan Stanley or Goldman Sachs, that were more established capital market players.' The team Mitchell built around him in trading and sales all had strong derivatives backgrounds. In 1995, after 15 years at Merrill Lynch, Mitchell moved to become head of global markets at Deutsche Bank's newly launched investment bank, Deutsche Morgan Grenfell (DMG). Mitchell set to work on integrating Deutsche's disparate European divisions and created a central risk book. Before long Mitchell was recruiting former colleagues from Merrill Lynch. Mitchell emphasised: 'It's still the same ideas as it was at Merrill: using the derivatives thought process, employing smart people, focusing on relative value and integrating the group.' Looking back some years later Mitchell observed, 'It was a phenomenal challenge. When I joined we weren't even in the top 15 derivatives firms globally. Now we're in the top five, and in some products we're number one or two. All the polls are showing that now. It is probably the biggest improvement in the shortest period of time, with the exception of Crédit Suisse Financial Products.'[9] In 1998 Deutsche Bank bought Bankers Trust, which was merged with DMG.

Bankers Trust had never fully recovered from the departure of Wheat and his team. In the 1990s under Sanford's leadership there was an increasing shift in the bank's culture, emphasising profit over client relationships, and in 1994 both Procter & Gamble and Gibson Greetings sued the bank for mis-selling them derivatives.

*   *   *

The over-enthusiastic marketing of derivatives had already created problems in Europe. In June 1988, the UK Audit Commission was alerted by a lady working on the Goldman Sachs swaps desk, that the London Borough of Hammersmith and Fulham had a massive exposure to interest rate swaps. When the Commission contacted the council, they discovered that the council had built up a major position betting on interest rates declining. Hammersmith & Fulham's transactions, which had taken place without the knowledge of the councillors, featured a range of highly speculative instruments including interest rate swaps, swap options, caps, floors, collars and forward rate agreements (FRAs). A total of 592 transactions had been executed, mostly between 1987 and 1989, with a notional value of over £6bn. The council was dealing in notional sums that reached 20 times its total debts and more than 100 times its annual turnover. Unfortunately for Hammersmith, interest rates had gone up from 8% to 15%.

By January 1989 the Commission obtained legal opinions from two Queen's Counsel. Although they did not agree, the Commission preferred the opinion which made it generally beyond the powers ('*ultra vires*') for local authorities to trade in derivatives. The auditor and the Commission then went to court and had the contracts declared illegal; the five banks involved lost millions of pounds. With 78 local councils involved in some form of interest rate management, the many banks involved faced potential losses of between £300 million and £400 million, with the prospect that interest rate hedging deals, going back years, would need to be unravelled.

An appeal by the banks was heard in the Court of Appeal in February 1990. The appeal judges ruled, in effect, that wherever they enabled a council to manage the interest rate risk on its loan portfolio, swaps were facilitating a function and were therefore legitimate. Where they were traded in pursuit of a profit, they were not. In the case of Hammersmith and Fulham specifically, the trades were therefore speculative and unlawful. In January 1991, however, the House of Lords overturned the Court of Appeal's decision, ruling that local authorities had no power to enter into swap contracts. Counterparty losses arising from the Hammersmith and Fulham case amounted to approximately $178m, according to a 1992 ISDA report.

In February 1992 Gerald Corrigan, then president of the Federal Reserve Bank of New York, delivered a speech that contained a warning to the over-the-counter derivatives industry:

> *... the interest rate swap market now totals several trillion dollars. Given the sheer size of the market, I have to ask myself how it is possible that so many holders of fixed or variable rate obligations want to shift those obligations from one form to the other. Since I have a great deal of difficulty in answering that question, I then have to ask myself whether some of the specific purposes for which swaps are now being used may be quite at odds with an appropriately conservative view of the purpose of a swap, thereby introducing new elements of risk or distortion into the*

*marketplace – including possible distortions to the balance sheets and income state-
ments of financial and nonfinancial institutions alike. I hope this sounds like a warning, because it is. Off-balance sheet activities have a role, but they must be managed
and controlled carefully, and they must be understood by top management as well as
by traders and rocket scientists.*

The Group of Thirty (G-30) is an international body of financiers, academics and regulators
formed in 1978 to increase understanding of economic and financial issues in the global
markets. A few months after Corrigan's speech, with concerns about derivatives growing,
G-30 undertook a study of the derivatives market. Dennis Weatherstone, Chairman of J.P.
Morgan, was charged with forming a steering committee and a working group of senior
managers from derivatives dealers, end-users, and related legal, accounting and academic
disciplines. Weatherstone, a former trader himself, was clear about their purpose: 'This should
not be a study that gathers dust on the shelf. I want to produce a guide by practitioners for
practitioners that has so much useful advice that it will be referred to for years to come.'

The end result was a 68-page report, which the G-30 published in July 1993. Entitled
Derivatives: Practices and Principles, it came to be known as the 'G-30 Report'. The report
concluded that no new regulations were required to manage the derivatives markets. The
core of the study was a set of 20 recommendations to help dealers and end-users manage
their derivatives activities. The report emphasised the importance of daily mark-to-market
procedures for dealers as a way of tracking their positions and quantifying risk. It promoted
value-at-risk (VaR) using statistical analysis to assess potential changes in value by risk type.
It described how to measure credit exposure, using market value plus a measure of exposure
reflecting a potential shift in market value. The authors recommended the establishment of
independent market risk and credit risk management functions. They promoted the use of Master Agreements and urged that netting be enforceable by law. Finally the report recommended
that derivatives should be accounted for in the same way as the risks they are used to manage.

Euromoney picked up the theme in September:

*The regulators are expressing concern just as the derivatives market is facing a
number of tests. First more and more banks and securities firms are trying to build up
or expand derivatives operations, creating the danger that mediocre individuals under
pressure to produce revenues to justify their salaries will take excessive risks. Second
firms that have grown their derivatives operations in recent years are struggling to
keep technology and management systems developing apace. Leslie Rahl, a consultant
who worked 20 years at Citibank says: 'I wonder how many senior managers can
actually read the reports their derivatives teams give them.' Third, some established
dealers have written so much business with each other they are straining credit
limits.*[10]

The G-30 Report was heartily welcomed by William McDonough, Corrigan's successor
as President of the Federal Reserve Bank of New York: 'I believe that the adoption of the
full set of recommendations in the report by all major users of derivatives would significantly
reduce the chance that a major financial disruption will originate in any one firm's derivative
activities.'[11]

*   *   *

From November 1982 to July 1990 the US economy had experienced the 'Reagan boom' with robust growth, modest unemployment and low inflation. But as the 1980s progressed, problems were developing. The stock exchange crash in October 1987 revealed investors' concerns about the inflationary impact of large US budget deficits. The Fed's decision in 1989 to raise interest rates to combat inflation also slowed the economy down. The American housing market was very weak, as large numbers of Savings and Loan associations went bankrupt. The large government bailout of the S&L industry placed further strain on the budget.

Another cause of the early 1990s recession was Iraq's invasion of Kuwait in the summer of 1990. This drove up the world price of oil, decreased consumer confidence, and exacerbated the downturn that was already underway. It was a period of rising inflation and rising interest rates along with high unemployment and massive budget deficits. The largest number of corporate downgrades occurred since the Great Depression of the 1930s. The recession spread outside the US through financial contagion, hitting hardest those countries closely linked to the US, including Canada, Australia and the UK.

In February 1990 Goldman Sachs and Morgan Stanley launched the World Bank's second global bond issue but it received a muted response. In August, Iraq's sudden invasion of Kuwait led to a flight to cash among international investors. All in all it would prove a difficult year in the Euromarkets with new issues only reaching $161bn, down from $210bn in 1989.

When the Iraqis ignored the coalition deadline to withdraw from Kuwait in January 1991, Operation Desert Storm was launched. The short war that followed unnerved the financial markets. Underwriting members of IPMA were concerned about possible severe disruption to the primary markets and the pressure from borrowers to go ahead with issues regardless. The debate focused on the need for well-drafted and effective 'force majeure' clauses in bond contracts. Under IPMA auspices after some months of negotiations, underwriters and lawyers agreed two force majeure clauses that are in use to this day.

The early 1990s also marked a spectacular collapse in the Tokyo stock market as the Japanese asset price bubble eventually burst. The Nikkei index, which at one point had reached 39,000, crashed down to 10,000 for most of 1992 – and a 14-year bear market was underway. When the stock market collapsed, Japanese banks had difficulty maintaining the BIS required 8% capital ratio. During the 'bubble economy' Japanese banks had borrowed extensively in the Euromarkets: ¥186 trn by June of 1990. Despite being the largest banks in the world, these Japanese banks were having to pay a premium for their borrowing, the so-called 'Japanese rate'. From the borrowed funds Japanese banks lent extensively, including $30 to $40bn to finance American leveraged buy outs. The Japanese banks were also adversely affected by the decline of property values in Japan, having set up 'jusen', or home mortgage lending companies. Seven of these 'jusen' became insolvent, leaving banks with around $60bn of bad loans.

The *ISMA Quarterly Comment* observed 'The Bank for International Settlements capital adequacy requirements could limit Japanese banks' growth in the Eurobond market by forcing them to play a zero sum game between their securities subsidiaries in London and Tokyo. They just can't spare the capital to maintain big securities operations in both markets, bankers say … The shift from the Euromarket back to Tokyo will be a future scenario.'[12]

In 1991 international banks began cutting their credit lines to one another as well as to their corporate customers. This lack of lines should have limited bond market activity, but in fact, new issuance in the Eurobond market would reach a new record of $230bn in 1991. This was largely due to the expansion in the 'repo' market.

'Repo' is short for a 'sale and repurchase agreement'. A repo is defined as an initial sale of securities followed by a subsequent repurchase. A 'reverse repo' is the opposite – an initial purchase of securities followed by a subsequent resale. The repo is structured so that the economic benefit of owning the securities – income and capital gains/losses – remains with their original owner. All repos are driven by either the need to lend or borrow cash, which is collateralised by securities, or the need to borrow specific securities. The prices for the original sale and the subsequent repurchase are agreed at the outset, the cost difference being the implicit interest rate, called the 'repo rate'. Repos are typically short term, often just overnight but can extend to as much as two years.

For traders the advantage is that they can make use of a bond position or positions in their book to borrow funds either more cheaply, or which they might not otherwise be able to borrow at all. Where a repo is driven by the buyer's need to invest cash the exact nature of the collateral is not so important as long as it is of adequate quality. Occasionally a repo is driven on the buyer's side by the need to borrow a particular bond as a result of being short of that bond. In this case the collateral delivered must be that particular bond rather than any other and is called 'special' as opposed to 'general' collateral. The extent to which any security becomes special depends on the supply of, and demand for, that bond in the market generally.

In the US, repos had been used from as early as 1917, initially by the Federal Reserve to lend to other banks, but the practice soon spread to other market participants. The use of repos expanded in the 1920s, fell away through the Great Depression and Second World War, then expanded once again in the 1950s, enjoying rapid growth in the 1970s and 1980s. After 'Big Bang' a handful of the top London-based American investment banks established dedicated repo trading desks to finance their sizeable bond inventories and generate additional revenue via 'matched book' trading. By the early 1990s repo trading had spread to other London-based US banks as well many European and Japanese banks.

In 1992 a group of 27 major bond houses active in the repo market formed a repo sub-committee under the umbrella of ISMA's Council of Reporting Dealers. The classic repo transaction, as opposed to a traditional buy/sell back, is transacted under one agreement. Work was soon underway with a leading law firm to formulate a standard agreement for repo transactions under the auspices of the Public Securities Association (PSA). By November, ISMA members were provided with the Global Master Repurchase Agreement (GMRA) to be used for repos or reverse repos of non-equity securities. The master agreement designated what types of securities were acceptable to the buyer. These could be governments, supranationals or investment grade Eurobonds. As the repo market expanded, so the list of eligible securities expanded; from commercial paper to emerging market debt. Traders had the right to substitute one eligible security for another, which was invaluable for managing trading books.

According to a market survey of 600 European and Middle Eastern investors by Greenwich Research Associates, total multicurrency repo volume for 1993 expressed in US dollars exceeded $3.5trn up from $1.2trn in 1992. Instruments in 15 different currencies were being used for multicurrency repos. By far the largest users of repos were the central banks, followed by commercial banks, institutional funds, corporations and insurance companies.

A 'tri-party repo' is a transaction for which the post-trade processing – collateral selection, payment and settlement, custody and management during the life of the transaction – is outsourced by the parties to a third-party agent. Tri-party agents are custodian banks. Because a tri-party agent is just an agent, use of a tri-party service does not change the relationship between the parties, as the agent does not participate in the risk of transactions. The European Bank for Reconstruction and Development (EBRD) introduced tri-party repo in Europe in 1992 when it conducted a programme with Swiss Bank Corporation (SBC), acting as dealer, and Cedel, acting as custodian. But the concept was slow to take off and the initial users were mainly central banks who had sufficient volumes to justify the set-up time and who appreciated the security and ease of substitution.

Ellington and Shearlock sum up the value of repo:

> *Repo monetised most of the instruments the market traded. It turned bonds into cash. It provided instant liquidity to the international bond market and financed much of the growth in bond futures trading in Europe – allowing constant arbitrage with the cash market. It also helped international traders operate in domestic government bond markets. Dealers could now arbitrage bonds in different currencies by using short-term currency swaps connected to a repo or reverse repo.*[13]

*   *   *

More than anything else, the 1990s was the decade of Europe and European convergence. It began with the reunification of Germany in 1990. As the deadline for reunification approached the German government bond market came under considerable pressure sending 10-year Bund yields to their highest level for five years. 'The main fear for the fixed income markets has been that the high speed of reunification could lead to a huge public sector deficit which could re-ignite inflation, boost interest rates and undermine the deutschemark, the anchor of the European Monetary System.'[14] A particular concern was that East German marks might be exchanged for West German deutschemarks at a rate of one-for-one. This had been a pre-election pledge of ex-Chancellor Helmut Kohl, despite the fact that inflation, at the time, was running at 20% in East Germany and only 2.6% in the West, and the Ostmark was trading at a rate of between five and ten to one deutschemark on the black market. The conservative Bundesbank advocated a 2-to-1 exchange rate. However, fearing a mass exodus from East Germany if the German government didn't give the East the deutschemark, the political and social arguments won the day. Investor fears were realised when currency union, largely at a one-for-one rate, was officially announced in April 1990 and took effect in July.

Suddenly, East German firms had to compete with western firms at the same level of prices, wages and costs – despite a much lower level of productivity. Industrial output dropped by 35% in one month, July 1990, and in the next month by another 15%. Unemployment soared and migration west continued. Unemployment and falling tax income led to mounting budget deficits: from 5% to 13.2%. By 1991 the Bundesbank was becoming very nervous about the prospects of high inflation and so started pursuing a contractionary monetary policy.

The combination of expansionary fiscal and contractionary monetary policy caused German rates to rise dramatically – about 3% in 1991 and 1992. The high German rates made a difficult situation for the UK, France, Italy and other European countries worse as they were restrained from taking corrective monetary policy actions. The outcome would be the crises of the European Monetary System (EMS) in autumn 1992 and July 1993.

Der Spiegel commented: 'Before the fall of the Berlin wall, European monetary union had been an ambitious EEC project like so many others. Afterward it was the central political tool with which to bind the expanded Germany to the European community.'[15]

Maastricht is the best known and perhaps the most controversial of the European treaties. Signed in the Dutch town of Maastricht on 7 February 1992, it became renowned not only for difficult negotiations in drafting it, but also for the difficulties many Member States had in approving it. It significantly advanced the agenda set out under the Single European Act

(SEA). Maastricht is officially known as the Treaty of the European Union and with it the EU came into existence for the first time. By adding two new areas – justice and home affairs and a common foreign and security policy – to the existing European Community, the so-called three pillars of the Union were established.

Maastricht was also the blueprint for what was to be Europe's biggest project for the next decade, Economic and Monetary Union (EMU) leading to the creation of the euro. This move to monetary union was scheduled to occur no later than 1 January 1999. The Treaty defined the three stages of EMU which would eventually lead to the single currency. By the end of 1993, capital flows were to be completely freed within the EU. By 1999 Member States looking to adopt the euro had to satisfy a set of convergence criteria by which economic policies were co-ordinated across Member States. At the beginning of 1999 the European Central Bank would be established, along with the official euro currency for which member-country conversion rates were irrevocably set.

The convergence criteria imposed control over inflation, public debt and the public deficit, exchange rate stability and the convergence of interest rates. Firstly inflation – inflation rates were to be no more than 1.5 percentage points higher than the average of the three best performing (lowest inflation) Member States of the EU. The ratio of the annual government deficit to gross domestic product (GDP) must not exceed 3% at the end of the preceding fiscal year. If not, it was at least required to reach a level close to 3%. In addition the ratio of gross government debt to GDP must not exceed 60% at the end of the preceding fiscal year. Exchange rate stability required that applicant countries should have joined the exchange rate mechanism under the EMS for two consecutive years and should not have devalued their currency during the period. Finally as regards convergence on interest rates, the nominal long-term interest rate must not be more than 2 percentage points higher than in the three lowest inflation Member States.

The purpose of setting the criteria was to maintain the price stability within the Eurozone even with the inclusion of new Member States. But the treaty had a tough time coming into force. It was first rejected by a Danish referendum, and then after some alterations scraped through. France showed little enthusiasm for the proposals – its referendum approved the treaty by a tiny margin. In Germany it was sent to the constitutional court, which in the end voted for it. In the UK, it squeezed through Parliament after immense pressure. It finally came into force in November 1993.

While European politicians argued over monetary union the Ecu bond market experienced a significant revival. A noteworthy issue was the Ecu1bn offering for France in April 1989. This eight-year benchmark targeted small investors and was launched as a sign of France's commitment to the concept of a single currency in Europe. In October the London International Financial Futures and Options Exchange (LIFFE) launched the first Ecu three-month futures contract. Spain issued a sellout Ecu500m bond offering in the first half of 1990 while Italy followed with an Ecu1bn 10-year transaction. By the end of the year Ecu14.1bn of Ecu bonds had been issued making the Ecu the fourth most popular issuance currency.[16]

In April 1991 the UK government surprised the markets with a substantial Ecu2bn 10-year benchmark issue. As UK reserves were strong, the issue was principally a show of London's support for the evolution of a single European currency and an attempt to attract more of the developing market to London. The offering showed 'the importance we attach to the strengthening of London's position in a growing market and demonstrates our commitment to the development of the Ecu,' explained the UK Chancellor, Norman Lamont.

Surprisingly the UK awarded the landmark mandate to Morgan Stanley rather than a prominent European house. *Euromoney* remarked:

> *The Bank of England is to be congratulated for choosing Morgan Stanley to lead its first Ecu bond. Which other central bank in a financial centre would have picked a foreign institution to bring to market such a headline making deal? If the Germans decide to follow the example of the other large EC countries and issue Ecu bonds, it is unthinkable that a non-German bank (indeed any bank but Deutsche) would be lead manager.*

Euromoney went on to confirm London 'as the only truly international financial centre, where foreign banks know they will receive fair and equal treatment'.[17] Despite an aggressive pricing of 4bps through French government issues, UK institutions were keen buyers and the transaction was increased to Ecu2.5bn.

Other sovereigns followed the UK's example, again driven more by the urge to make political statements rather than a pressing requirement for funding. By end 1991 Ecu issuance had overtaken all other European currency issuance at \$30.6bn equivalent against dollar issuance of \$78.7bn.[18] The Ecu new issue market continued to grow in 1992, particularly in the months following the Maastricht Agreement, with amounts issued in the first half of the year exceeding all other currencies bar the US dollar.

However in January 1992 Peter Krijgsman cautioned:

> *It will certainly take more than the Maastricht summit to convince the investment community of the Ecu's worth. The Ecu bond market to date has suffered from occasional bouts of excruciating illiquidity, partly because the currency is a confection with few real end-users … Therefore today's Ecu market is even more subject to sentiment than any other market. With no underlying real demand for the currency, demand for the Ecu itself is liable to whip in the wind with every newspaper headline that appears.[19]*

As if on cue, when Denmark gave a 'no' vote in the referendum on EMU membership in June 1992 the market shuddered to a halt.

A deal for Paribas in July effectively closed the Ecu market as exchange rate pressures simmered in Europe. Paribas Capital Markets (PBCM) had been the specialist Ecu house from the time a single European currency was first discussed. They headed the league tables for Ecu bonds from 1985 to the early 1990s with a market share of 20 to 30%. Paribas led the first Ecu1bn issue for Italy in 1990 and led a 20-year Ecu2.5bn issue for the same borrower the following year. In 1991 74% of all the deals they underwrote were in Ecu.

The exit of major currencies from the ERM later in 1992 forced losses on holders of Ecu bonds, resulting in a contraction in the primary market with only \$7bn equivalent being issued in 1993. The stock of Ecu bonds shrank for the next five years. Only on the eve of the introduction of the euro in 1999 would Ecu bond issuance recover and then as pseudo euro-denominated bonds. A BIS paper cautions: 'It is more correct to say that the prospect of the euro revived the Ecu bond market than that the Eurobond market grew out of the Ecu bond market.'[20]

From the beginning of the 1990s, the high German interest rates, set by the Bundesbank to counteract the inflationary effects of German reunification, caused significant strains across the whole of the ERM. In the wake of the Danish rejection of the Maastricht Treaty, and then the announcement that there would be a referendum in France as well, the ERM currencies that were trading close to the bottom of their ERM bands came under pressure from foreign exchange traders and speculators. When in September 1992 it became evident that the existing parities could not be maintained, most European countries tried to 'save' their own currencies from devaluation while failing to co-ordinate their exchange rate policies with others. The resultant currency crisis forced Finland, the UK, Italy, Sweden and Norway to float their currencies.

On 16 September 1992, 'Black Wednesday', the pound sterling came under sustained pressure from currency speculators. George Soros's Quantum Fund, a global macro hedge fund like Robertson's Tiger Fund, notoriously made over a billion dollars from shorting sterling. Soros was labelled 'the man who broke the Bank of England'. In desperation the UK government raised the base interest rate from 10% to 12% and eventually promised 15% rates in an attempt to halt the sinking pound. But after spending billions to protect the currency, Britain was unable to keep sterling above its agreed lower limit and, rather than deplete its reserves further, was forced to withdraw from the ERM. The Italian government pulled the lira out of the ERM a few hours later, and Spain devalued the peseta by 5%. Now traders sold other currencies perceived to be likely candidates for devaluation such as the Danish Krone and the Irish punt.

However, unlike Britain, other ERM countries such as Italy, whose currencies had breached their bands during the day, would return to the system with broadened bands or with adjusted central parities.

Were the Euromarkets in favour of European monetary integration? At the bond association's AGM in Munich that year the keynote speaker was Margaret Thatcher. Thatcher had been ousted by her own party in November 1990 after 11 years as British Prime Minister, largely due to her rejection of closer economic integration with Europe. Her speech attacked the Maastricht Treaty and gave impassioned support for 'the nation state'. Stanley Ross recalls: 'After she spoke I looked around to see the entire audience from some forty countries, giving her a tremendous standing ovation. I have never seen, in a quarter century of our meetings, any speaker receive such rapturous applause.'[21] The Munich meeting was notable for one other reason: it was the first meeting of the association under its new name, the 'International Securities Market Association', ISMA. The name change from the old AIBD had been approved at the previous year's AGM in Hong Kong.

The short time frame for monetary union set out in the Maastricht Treaty had significant implications for international investors going forward. They were used to choosing investments after taking into account exchange rate risk. So they would require a higher yield on securities denominated in currencies that might be devalued. With the agreement of EMS members to move towards monetary union it was expected that devaluations would not occur. Yet interest rates were considerably higher in some EMS countries than others. Investors therefore thought they could earn high returns on high-yield currencies, such as the Italian lira and the Spanish peseta, without incurring exchange rate risk. Such 'convergence plays' relied on the convergence of economic performance among EMS countries. It is estimated that such convergence plays totalled $200–300bn during the 1990s. In 1995, the gap between Italian and German sovereign debt was more than 600 basis points.

The Independent commented:

> *Of the many bizarre trends in capital markets right now the strangest of all is the dramatic narrowing of the premium on Italian and Spanish bonds over those of Germany. To put it simply, what has been happening is that the cost of Italian and*

Spanish government debt has fallen to the extent that for the first time it has moved to within 2 percentage points of Germany's. Peripheral bond markets are rising strongly in anticipation of monetary union. If markets believe a country will join EMU, it seems reasonable to align their long-term bond yields with those of the lowest denominator – Germany – since after EMU their inflation and currency rates should be the same. In markets, this is known as 'the convergence play'. The dangers for those who adopt this as an investment strategy are only too apparent. Even Deutsche Bank, which is about as strongly pro-EMU as they come, is warning that any setback in monetary union 'could result in the undoing of recent market trends towards convergence and instead set off a flight to quality'. For the moment, however, these dangers are being ignored.[22]

European Monetary Union was not the only focus for the mandarins in Brussels. The Single European Act had proposed the goal for a single market 'without internal frontiers in which the free movement of goods, persons and services is ensured …' by 31 December 1992. Despite efforts since the 1960s to create a single unified market in Europe with a common regulatory regime, still by the 1980s, seven of the 12 EU countries did not require prospectus disclosure to investors in public offerings, and none had a securities regulatory agency to enforce the laws that did exist. Until 1989, nine of the 12 Member States failed to impose any criminal penalties for insider trading of securities. Coupled with this were a lack of free access to national markets and a preference for concentration rules, i.e. requiring all trade orders to be routed to a particular stock exchange. A key milestone in the creation of a single market for financial services came with the adoption of the Investment Services Directive (ISD) on 10 May 1993.[23]

The ISD established common minimum authorisation or licensing requirements for investment firms and 'investment services' among Member States. The ISD introduced the concept of the 'passport'; firms authorised to conduct business in one EU Member State could then provide their products and services in all others ('host states') without further scrutiny. The European passport meant that restrictive legislation in Member States preventing cross-frontier branches and freedom of services would have to be dismantled. Common minimum financial standards were established among Member States and common conduct of business rules were introduced. This conduct of business regulation faced two ways: between the investment firm and the client, and between the investment firm and the market. The ISD adopted the 'concentration rule', i.e. that Member States require investment firms to route orders only to stock exchanges. Such stock exchanges, referred to as 'regulated markets', were required to adopt minimum transparency rules. Member States had to have the ISD implementing legislation in place by 1 July 1995.

The ISD raised a number of issues for the Euromarkets. ISMA advised members that the ISD required that:

transactions must be carried out on a 'regulated market', where broadly, they are transactions involving securities listed on the regulated market between investors of the member state and a firm or branch located in the Member state, or a firm which is providing investment services in the Member State. Clearly this would have an adverse effect upon the off-exchange markets within the EU. ISMA cannot be a 'regulated market' within the meaning of the ISD, as it is based in Switzerland …

Also the ISD requires:

transactions to be reported to the relevant authority 'at the earliest opportunity'. This may give rise to requirements in some Member States which are stricter than those currently in force, and thus ISMA has been monitoring the position in each country ... The transparency provisions require the publication of various data relating to the prices and volumes of securities traded on the previous day ... Although it is unlikely that these provisions will affect the Euromarkets as they only relate to transactions on a regulated market, ISMA has nevertheless been monitoring these provisions carefully.[24]

This Investment Services Directive was accompanied in 1993 by the Capital Adequacy Directive (CAD). The CAD was largely bringing Basel I rules into the European Directive framework establishing minimum capital requirements for banks. These Directives, along with the Prospectus Directive and the Insider Trading Directive, both adopted in 1989, now formed the cornerstones of the Single European Market going forward.

* * *

Alan Greenspan was first appointed Chairman of the Federal Reserve by President Ronald Reagan in 1987 and then reappointed by President George H.W. Bush. The Fed's prescription for the recession of the early 1990s had been a long period of low interest rates, designed to enable a recovery for the banking system and the housing market. The Federal Reserve had reduced the Federal Funds rate from 8.25% to 3% between 1990 and 1992 where they then remained for the whole of 1993. Meanwhile US Treasury long bonds were still yielding more than 7.5%. This gaping spread created an easy opportunity for banks, securities dealers, hedge funds and speculators to profit by borrowing short-term funds and buying longer-term securities. This practice became known as the 'carry' trade. Traders loaded up on long-term bonds and took on ever more leverage. (See below the discussion of the Orange County bankruptcy.) By late 1993 primary dealers in US Treasuries had borrowed a record $200bn to finance their bond holdings, equivalent to roughly a year's worth of the federal budget deficit. Some hedge funds were buying bonds on margin for a little as 1 or 2 cents in the dollar, with banks and securities dealers putting up the balance.

Against this background 1993 proved to be a bumper year for the international bond markets. The *ISMA Quarterly Comment* noted:

In the last three years, the world's bond markets have enjoyed an unprecedented bull run ... Once bond yields became positive, it was possible to fund these positions economically, so that catching the exact moment of the rally was no longer essential ... The rally has also helped maintain the impetus for new issue activity in the Eurobond market ... Some analysts believe that European markets will continue to offer higher yields than the US market, and that there has been a fundamental shift of asset allocation towards the European markets, which have become more liquid in recent years.[25]

The astute reader will have noted that from the Euromarket's earliest beginnings keynote developments in international debt issuance have often originated in Italy. Having accumulated the world's third largest sovereign debt, the 1979 EMS requirements caused Italian public debt to explode, rising from under 60% of gross domestic product in 1980 to around 120% of GDP in 1994. Interest payments rose from less than 4% of GDP to around 12% of GDP over the same time period. The Italian Treasury developed considerable expertise in managing their debt burden and successfully pioneered the concept of 'benchmark issues', that is, the concentration of funding in large liquid issues at the key maturities on the yield curve which best suited institutional investors. In 1993 this policy reached its apotheosis. The headline deal of the year, indeed many dubbed it the 'deal of the decade', was the Republic of Italy's global deal launched that summer by Goldman Sachs and Salomon Brothers. After months of preparation, Alberto Giovannini, head of international borrowing at the Italian Treasury, successfully launched a benchmark $2bn 10-year and a particularly ambitious £3.5bn 30-year offering, breaking all previous issuance records. This was a remarkable achievement given the country's problems with the ERM experienced less than a year earlier. Giovannini followed up in January 1994 with a ¥300bn global offering taking advantage of the Ministry of Finance's abolition of the 90-day lock-up rule on purchases of bonds issued by non-resident entities.

A sign of the market's confidence was also evident in March 1993 when Goldman Sachs and Lehman Brothers launched an unprecedented $500m 30-year offering for the African Development Bank (AfDB). Latin American issuance bounced back in the bull markets, with the first $1bn five-year issue for Cementos Mexicanos (Cemex) in May 1993 led by Citibank and J.P. Morgan. This was shortly followed by a $1bn 10-year issue for Argentina from Merrill and Salomon.

In the Far East, the growing Asian 'tiger economies' were attracting increasing attention. 'Dragon bonds', that is bonds targeted towards investors in the South East Asian markets outside Japan, saw $3.6bn of issuance. General Electric Capital Corporation (GECC) launched the first corporate US dollar Dragon bond early in the year. In October the first sovereign issue was launched by Lehman Brothers; a $300m offering for the People's Republic of China (PRC), only their second international bond issue. This Dragon bond was the first single-A credit in the market, the first 10-year maturity and the first Asian issuer since the Asian Development Bank (ADB) had opened the market in 1991.[26] In fact the PRC Dragon bond was an idea put to the borrower by the author who had developed a close relationship with the State Debt Administration of the PRC. Unfortunately the mandate was awarded away from HSBC at the eleventh hour, as a sign of the Chinese government's displeasure at Hong Kong bank's decision to move their group headquarters from Hong Kong to London ahead of 'the Handover'.

Securitisation was also developing beyond the mortgage market in Europe. In 1992 there had been an issue for the Shannon-based GPA Group, backed by aircraft leases and in October 1993 Barclays Bank became the first clearing bank to issue a £280m bond backed by personal loans.[27]

By the end of 1993 bond issuance would reach $400bn equivalent, a 40% increase on the previous year's $270bn. But one syndicate manager added a note of caution: 'When people see the record profits of securities firms this year, they are going to rush into the market again. Salaries will accelerate, creating unsustainable cost bases and that will hurt profits.'[28]

*   *   *

But not everyone was happy with the US economy as 1994 dawned. Alan Greenspan saw evidence of the economy picking up and decided to take action to prevent inflationary pressures, 'taking air out of the bubble,' he argued. On 4 February 1994, Greenspan unexpectedly raised US rates prompting a 'gigantic roar' of disbelief across Salomons' famed New York trading floor. The initial increase in the overnight federal funds rate from 3% to 3.25% prompted an immediate 40 basis point increase in the long bond as leveraged bondholders looked to liquidate their holdings.[29] Derivative positions exacerbated the effect of the rate rise. Margin calls drove prices lower and yields higher. This prompted more margin calls and more selling. The Fed hiked the rates again in March, by 0.5% in May and August, and a further 0.25% in November. The Treasury market collapsed dragging the mortgage market down with it. When rates rise, the term of fixed-rate mortgages typically lengthens, as refinancing is unattractive, and in 1994 portfolio managers tried to hedge that by selling long-dated Treasuries, fuelling the panic. Rates rose in both Europe and Japan. In Europe rates had been at 30-year lows in every major economy. A US bond market veteran recalls: 'There was total dislocation. No-one in '94 was prepared for the rate hikes and a lot of people got exposed by the severity of the Fed's tightening that year.'[30]

Those big hedge funds who had gambled on further declines in European rates were particularly badly hit. For example, the hedge fund Steinhardt Partners had built a $30bn position in Eurobonds before the market turned. Each basis point fall in European rates cost the fund $4m, eventually wiping out a third of funds under management. The losses were exacerbated by the new complexity of financial instruments. Investors could now take market views not just by going long or short bonds but via structured notes which contained various formulae allowing leveraged bets on the direction of interest rates.

A few weeks after Greenspan's initial rate hike, the chairman of Procter & Gamble disclosed that liquidating two contracts for interest rate swaps had cost the company $157million. The two losing contracts, which were for floating rate notes in dollars and deutschemarks, were exotic swaps undertaken by Procter and Gamble (P&G) with Bankers Trust on the assumption that US and German interest rates would continue to fall. One of the trades was snappily termed a 'quanto-ed constant maturity swap yield curve flattening trade'. The net result of their swaps was that if the P&G view was right it would be locking in borrowing at a rate 40 basis points below the commercial paper rate. If it were wrong P&G would be forced to borrow way above market rates and suffer substantial losses. By the time P&G covered their derivative exposures, and after further rate rises, the company owed Bankers Trust $195.5 million more than expected.

A US newspaper questioned 'What is a soap company doing in the swap market speculating with hundreds of millions of dollars?' Procter & Gamble, like many multinationals, had been protecting itself against swings in international interest and currency rates for some years, but increasingly they were seduced by derivative structures that would give them more geared returns if their market view was right. The distraught chairman, Edwin L. Artzt, declared: 'Derivatives like these are dangerous and we were badly burned. We won't let that happen again.'[31]

Lawrence Malkin, the award-winning journalist, reveals a different angle to the P&G losses. He recalls back in 1994, when he was New York Bureau Chief for the *International Herald Tribune*, being invited along with other financial journalists to meet the visiting financial team of Procter and Gamble:

> *They had come to New York to sue Bankers' Trust for supposedly misleading a great American company in a way that made it lose money on swaps & derivatives. There was some kind of hearing the next day … Anyway, it transpired that a deal had been*

arranged by Bankers Trust to offer P&G lower rates on its credit lines – and that the P&G treasurer was no Ohio hick and used to work on Wall Street, maybe even at Bankers Trust. It soon became obvious that the deal had been worked out between P&G's treasurer and the bank, and that everyone understood what the deal was. But no one was prepared when the Fed blindsided the markets in 1994 by suddenly changing course. Both sides got swamped, and they now were flinging mud at each other in court.

So I asked the P&G team why they thought they were entitled to lower rates when they were already paying prime or even better. 'Why, we're Procter & Gamble!' said the Treasurer, shocked, shocked that I should even raise such a question. I replied that he was still not answering my question and continued: 'We have already established that there was a shell game going on here; I merely wanted to find out who was the dealer and who was the player.' I got a very dirty look and needless to say was not invited back.[32]

Procter & Gamble took Bankers Trust to court alleging that the bank had convinced the company to purchase complex derivatives, misrepresented the value of these products and, when Procter & Gamble suffered losses or gains, pushed the company to purchase more derivatives in order to continue or reverse the given trend. As part of the lawsuit, it was alleged that Bankers Trust employees were heard talking about derivatives as 'a massive, huge future gravy train'. In addition, there was talk about a 'rip-off factor' and that Bankers Trust 'set 'em (various clients) up'. Bankers Trust denied that this behaviour was widespread and disciplined the parties involved, but the accusations were widely aired in the media and influenced public opinion.

The continuing rate hikes in 1994 revealed further victims of interest rate gambles – gambles that were leveraged with derivatives. In April 1994 Gibson Greetings Inc. lost over $20 million in swaps with Bankers Trust taking the view that interest rates would fall. The company sued the bank and in a settlement later that year, Gibson Greetings paid Bankers Trust $6.2 million, roughly 30% of what it owed the investment bank.

In 1996, Bankers Trust settled with Procter & Gamble, forgiving most of the $200m P&G owed the bank. The Bankers Trust chief executive stepped down and the bank reduced its participation in derivatives. It was eventually sold to Deutsche Bank in 1998.

On 6 December Orange County, a suburban area south of Los Angeles, became the largest municipality in US history ever to file for bankruptcy. Orange County announced that its investment fund of $7.4bn, belonging to county schools, cities, special districts and the county itself, faced losses of $1.5bn. The various participants in the investment pool had hoped to get better returns for their idle cash which they could deploy later for public works. The losses were the result of sharply higher interest rates and an investment strategy that relied primarily on derivatives and leverage. As controller of the various Orange County funds, County Treasurer Robert L. Citron had taken a highly leveraged position using repos and floating rate notes. Citron's aim was to increase current income by exploiting the fact that medium-term maturities had higher yields than short-term investments (see the discussion on the 'carry trade' above). On December 1993, for instance, short-term yields were less than 3%, while five-year yields were around 5.2%. Citron looked to increase the duration of the investment to pick up an extra yield. Through reverse repurchase agreements, Citron pledged securities bought by the pool as collateral and reinvested the cash in new securities, mostly five-year notes issued by government-sponsored agencies such as Fannie Mae. Citron leveraged the County (Investment) Pools to amounts ranging from 158% to over 292%. He also invested in derivatives such as inverse floaters, index amortising notes and collateralised mortgage obligations to the tune of $2.8bn, in order to increase his bet on the yield curve structure.

The County's finances were not suspect until February 1994 when the Fed started raising rates. As the value of securities in Orange County's investment pools fell in value, dealers requested extra margin payments from Orange County. These extra margin payments were funded in part by a $600m bond issue for Orange County. However, this fix proved to be only temporary. In December 1994, Crédit Suisse First Boston (CSFB) realised what was going on and blocked the 'rolling over' of $1.25bn in repos (rolling over means issuing another repo when the previous one ends, but at the new prevailing interest rate). At that point Orange County was left with no recourse other than to file for bankruptcy.

The effects of the Fed's rate rises spread beyond the US borders. The dollar rate hikes generated downward pressure on the Mexican peso. The Mexican Central Bank intervened in the foreign exchange markets to protect the peso but all they succeeded in doing was running their reserves down to zero. The so-called 'Tequila Crisis' was caused by the sudden devaluation of the Mexican peso in December 1994 when the fixed exchange rate to the dollar was abandoned. The current-account deficit of Mexico had reached a perilous 7% of GDP and to help finance the deficit the government had been issuing 'Tesobonos', bonds denominated in pesos but indexed to the US dollar. The currency plunged by around 50% within six months, causing the local currency value of the government's large dollar-linked debts to balloon. Governments and businesses in the region had high levels of US dollar debt, so the devaluation meant that it would be increasingly difficult to pay back these debts. The devaluation ignited inflation that peaked at 52% and sparked capital outflows across the region. In 1995 Mexico's GDP shrank by 6.2%. Mexico dragged down other Latin American markets with corporate spreads widening to 2500bps over US Treasuries.[33]

Mexico was saved thanks to its recent admission to the North American Free Trade Agreement (NAFTA), which had come into effect on 1 January 1994. President Bill Clinton was of the opinion that Mexico, then America's third largest trading partner, must be given a helping hand because of its importance to American jobs and investment. Therefore, his administration along with the IMF, BIS and Bank of Canada set up a $50bn line of credit to help restore confidence in the Mexican economy. Mexico's return from the brink of disaster was swift enabling them to raise almost $2bn international debt in a day in November 1995.[34]

*   *   *

With increased competition and higher cost bases, trading positions had grown and fraudulent behaviour by 'rogue traders' was a growing risk. Not because of the greater likelihood of fraud at the time, but because the use of derivatives and leverage now meant such behaviour could bring a company to its knees.

On the weekend of 25 February 1995 the news broke that the UK merchant bank, Barings was in severe financial difficulties due to the actions of a trader in its Singapore office. Barings was Britain's oldest merchant bank; it had helped finance the Napoleonic wars, the Louisiana Purchase, and was banker to the Queen. Surely the bank would be rescued? Over the weekend the scale of the bank's losses grew to an untenable level and despite attempts, a suitable buyer could not be found, so the bank was put into administration. When it went into administration Barings had outstanding notional futures positions on Japanese equities and interest rates of

US$27bn: US$7bn on the Nikkei 225 equity contract and US$20bn on Japanese government bond (JGB) and Euroyen contracts. Barings had sold 70,892 Nikkei put and call options with a nominal value of $6.68bn. The nominal size of these positions is staggering when compared with the bank's reported capital of about $900 million.

The trader who brought about the demise of Barings was Nick Leeson. Leeson, a young accounts clerk, worked initially in the back office, but by 1993 he had become general manager of Barings Futures (Singapore), running the bank's SIMEX (Singapore International Monetary Exchange) activities. His £10m contribution to profits accounted for about 10% of Barings' profits in 1993. He was general manager, head trader and, due to his experience in operations, de facto head of the back office – a dangerous mix of responsibilities.

Leeson was supposed to be arbitraging price differences in similar equity derivatives on SIMEX and the Osaka Exchange in Japan – a 'straddle' trade. In fact he took on riskier positions by buying and selling different amounts of the contracts on the two exchanges or buying and selling contracts of different types, with any premiums or losses that he made paid into an error account number 88888. By the end of 1994, Leeson's 88888 account had lost a total of £208m. He risked huge amounts of money, betting that the Japanese stock market would go up. By mid-February 1995 he had accumulated an enormous position – half the open interest in the Nikkei future and 85% of the open interest in the JGB future. The market became aware of this and almost certainly traded against him.

Unfortunately for Leeson, the Nikkei index crashed by 1,000 points on 17 January 1995 after an earthquake hit Japan's industrial heartland around the City of Kobe. As Leeson's losses mounted, he had to meet the SIMEX margin requirements. By falsifying accounts and making various misrepresentations, Leeson was able to secure the funding. In January and February 1995, Barings Tokyo and London transferred $835m to their Singapore office to meet the margin obligations. It was astonishing that Leeson was able to accumulate such staggering losses without Barings' management being alerted.

On 3 March 1995 Barings was bought by the Dutch financial company ING for one pound sterling so bringing to a close its illustrious 223-year history. Leeson fled but was extradited to Singapore where he served six and a half years for fraud.

In April the *ISMA Quarterly Comment* was moved to remark:

Financial liberalisation in the past decade has seen an explosion in the development of exciting and innovative tools for risk management. Using derivatives, instruments which derive their value from some underlying security or market, it has been possible to offset some of the risks inherent in globalisation … Derivatives are the private sector's solution to finding protection against the waves of money sloshing around the globe … The demise of Barings and the negative perception of derivatives arising from Gibson Greeting, Metallgesellschaft, Procter & Gamble, Orange County and other stories should not, and probably will not, deflect the growth of these valuable risk management tools.

It is argued by defenders of derivatives that where things have gone wrong, as in the much publicised cases, it had little to do with the inherent risk of derivatives. There is no doubt merit in this claim as the lines of control and reporting and failure to appreciate and monitor the risks seems to be a more obvious and pertinent cause of the problems than the instruments themselves.

… But things are changing. A recent report by the Washington DC based financial industry think-tank, The Group of Thirty (G-30), shows that some 93% of boards of

directors approve their firms' risk management policies compared with a mere 28% in 1993 ... the 'rocket scientists' at the leading edge of derivative innovation have little to fear. Banks will continue to devote large sums to design more complex derivatives as they need them to maintain their competitive edge. What is rocket science today is horse and buggy tomorrow.[35]

ISMA's major contribution to the market in 1995 was the changeover of the standard international settlement arrangements for Eurobonds from seven=day settlement (T + 7 calendar days) to T + 3 business days – 'T' being trade date. The move to T + 3 had been announced at ISMA's 1994 AGM in New Orleans. ISMA commented: 'The change in the settlement cycle promises the prospect of reducing market risk and systemic risk in addition to matching in the same time cycle as domestic bonds, all of which are positive aspects of the ever growing international domestic bond, Eurobond and international securities market.'[36]

NOTES

1. *Risk Magazine*, The Risk Awards 2000, Lifetime Achievement Award: Allen Wheat.
2. Gene D. Guill, *Bankers Trust and the Birth of Modern Risk Management* (The Wharton School of the University of Pennsylvania, 2009).
3. *Risk Magazine*, The Risk Awards 2000, Lifetime Achievement Award: Allen Wheat.
4. Erik Banks, *The Credit Risk of Complex Derivatives; Third Edition* (Palgrave Macmillan, December 2003) Part 1, Derivatives, Credit and Risk Management, p. 5.
5. *Risk Magazine*, The Risk Awards 2000, Lifetime Achievement Award: Allen Wheat.
6. *Euromoney*, Allen Wheat, June 1999.
7. *Daily Telegraph*, Wheat's promise of a rich harvest, 6 June 1998, p. 32.
8. Website: derivativesstrategy.com: *Hall of Fame 1998: Conrad Volstad.*
9. Website: derivativesstrategy.com: *Hall of Fame 1998: Edson Mitchell.*
10. *Euromoney*, September 1992.
11. William J. McDonough, *Federal Reserve Bank of New York Quarterly Review*, Autumn 1993, The Global Derivatives Market, p. 1.
12. *ISMA Quarterly Comment*, Vol. 6, July 1991.
13. Shearlock and Ellington, *The Eurobond Diaries*, p. 119.
14. *AIBD Quarterly Comment*, Vol. 2, August 1990, p. 8.
15. Spiegel Online International, *The Price of Unity: Was the Deutsche Mark Sacrificed for Reunification? Michael Sauga, Stefan Simons and Klaus Wiegrefe*, 30 September 2010.
16. *EuroWeek* 20th Anniversary Issue, April 2007, February 1991: the Ecu has landed, p. 57.
17. *Euromoney*, Editorial, March 1991.
18. Moore, *Autostrade to the Superhighway*, p. 38.
19. *ISMA Quarterly Comment*, Vol. 8, January 1992, p. 15.
20. Clifford Dammers and Robert McCauley, Basket Weaving: The Euromarket Experience with Basket Currency Bonds (March 2006) *BIS Quarterly Review*, 90.
21. Ross, *From Where I Stood*, p. 12.
22. *The Independent*, Convergence Play Leaves Britain out in the Cold, 12 November 1996.
23. Manning Gilbert Warren III, The European Union's Investment Services Directive (1994) 15 *University of Pennsylvania Journal of International Law* 185–186.
24. *ISMA Quarterly Comment*, Vol. 21 April 1995, p. 6.
25. *ISMA Quarterly Comment*, Vol. 15 October 1993, p. 8.
26. Moore, *Autostrade to the Superhighway*, p. 31.

27. Ibid. p. 79.
28. *ISMA Quarterly Comment*, Vol. 15, October 1993, p. 14.
29. *Fortune Magazine*, The Great Bond Market Massacre, Al Ehrbar, 17 October 1994.
30. *Financial Times*, The Ghosts of '94, 20 March 2013, p. 9.
31. Lawrence Malkin, Procter and Gamble's Tale of Derivatives Woe, *The New York Times*, 14 April 1994.
32. Letter to the author from Lawrence Malkin.
33. *EuroWeek* 20th Anniversary Issue, April 2007, Tequila Time: the great bounce back from the crisis, p. 81.
34. Ibid.
35. *ISMA Quarterly Comment*, Vol. 21, April 1995, pp. 14–15, 26.
36. *ISMA Quarterly Comment*, Vol. 19, October 1994, p. 9.

CHAPTER 7

Convergence and Credit

1995–1999

G uy Hands was born in South Africa but moved at an early age to England, where he studied at Judd School, Tonbridge, Kent. He went on to read Politics, Philosophy and Economics (PPE) at Mansfield College, Oxford. Hands' career began as a Eurobond trader at Goldman Sachs. He was promoted to Head of Eurobond trading in 1986 and later rose to become head of global asset structuring worldwide for Goldman's European division in 1990. Hands was keen to make the move from agent to principal on transactions and came up with a proposal for his Goldman management: 'By the mid-nineties most people felt the UK pub business was dead. I went to Goldman and told them I wanted to buy £1bn of pubs and restructure the industry. I needed around £250m of equity, which, considering my trading book had been up to £4bn, I didn't think was a particularly large amount. Goldman looked at the £250m and suggested, maybe if I wanted to do that, I should find somewhere else to get the money from.'[1] Two other banks turned down his investment plan but Nomura in London saw the potential and Hands joined Nomura in 1994 and set up its Principal Finance Group (PFG) with 13 employees.

'On my first day I told my team we would invest £1bn of the bank's capital over the next two years in asset-based businesses such as pubs, trains and houses.'[2]

True to his word, Hands and his PFG team's first purchase was a pub portfolio. Phoenix Inns was a portfolio of tenanted, untied pubs across the UK acquired in 1995 from Grand Metropolitan plc and Fosters. Hands believed that pub prices had been depressed by the conventional view that the UK pub sector was in decline. He argued that the value of the portfolio of pubs would be in analysing it pub by pub to understand how the value of each pub could be maximised, whether as part of other pub portfolios or in alternative use. Operational costs were then streamlined.

Extra upside was created for the portfolio by lowering the cost of finance. Phoenix Inns owned around 1800 pubs across the UK, the vast majority of which were freehold properties. Phoenix's cash flow was predictable and reliable, comprising rental income from the independently operated and managed pubs; a structure that would lend itself to financing via securitisation. The yield on tenanted pubs exceeded the cost of bond finance so the Phoenix Inns acquisition was financed via a Eurosterling bond issue securitising the pub portfolio.[3]

After the initial success with the Phoenix Inns portfolio, Hands stepped up his activity in 1996. He focused on the possible securitisation of the highly reliable contractual cash flows which arose in businesses for sale under the UK government's privatisation plans. Nomura acquired the UK government's Ministry of Defense (MoD) Married Quarters Estate, which was then made up of over 57,400 residential properties for British army personnel. Annington, the acquisition vehicle, became one of the largest owners of residential property in the UK. The estate was sold and leased back to the MoD with properties being released for sale by Annington as they became surplus to the MoD's requirements. The stable government-backed rental cash flow from the leased estate, along with the proceeds from the sale of properties released according to the guaranteed release schedule, was again securitised to reduce the initial investment required to acquire the portfolio. Annington Finance No. 1, a three-tranche deal, was collateralised by the MoD guaranteed rental stream associated with the acquired portfolio of housing. A further securitisation, Annington No. 4, also a three-tranche transaction, was supported by the non-guaranteed portion of the rental stream and proceeds from the disposal of homes.

Since 1996, when the Ministry of Defence sold the 'lease and leaseback' assets for just £1.66bn, Nomura is thought to have made almost £2bn in profit. The original deal gave the MoD a 58% rental discount, but has been criticised because it was fixed to house prices that have risen many times since 1996.

Angel Trains was the largest of three UK passenger rolling stock leasing companies created on the privatisation of the UK railways. Angel Trains owned around 3600 electric and diesel railway engines and carriages, making it the largest passenger fleet in the UK at that time. The fleet of rolling stock was leased to 25 companies operating train services on the public network. As a substantial portion of the future lease payments were government-guaranteed they were immediately securitised to reduce the required investment. The remaining lease payments were considered very reliable and so a second securitisation soon followed. GRS Holding Co., the vehicle used to buy Angel Trains for £696m in January, almost immediately got the bulk of its money back through the two securitisations in January and March 1996 which raised £725m and were the first 'whole business' securitisations. This was the first time securitisation had been used to finance (rather than refinance) an acquisition in the UK.[4]

Eighteen months later, Nomura made a successful exit by selling the holding company to the Royal Bank of Scotland for £395m, of which Nomura took £334m for its stake in GRS. Nomura's PFG showed yet again that they could turn assets into cash flows and then profits.

These various deals by Nomura triggered a principal finance frenzy. Hands reckoned that over the following year his activities spawned some 35 copycat banking outfits trying to replicate his team's success. Perhaps more important is the impact principal finance activity had on raising the profile of the securitisation market.

Asset-backed bond issues, which first appeared in the Euromarkets in the mid-1980s, had grown only modestly as a sector. Residential mortgages (RMBS) were the first asset class to be securitised in Europe. In the UK the National Home Loans Corporation and particularly The Mortgage Corporation, a subsidiary of Salomon Brothers, were the largest originators. In 1987 £1bn of RMBS was issued increasing to £3.2bn in 1988. By 1990 there were a total of over 50 deals amounting to £9bn outstanding. Commercial banks began securitising their loan books shortly after the Basel 1 Rules were introduced, as securitisation provided a means of removing assets from a lender's balance sheet. Barclays Bank issued a £280m bond backed by personal loans via their special purpose vehicle (SPV) Gracechurch Personal Loan Finance in 1993. National Westminster Bank followed with the first major mortgage-backed deal issued by a retail bank via Lothbury Funding No.1. But by 1994 annual asset-backed issuance still only amounted to $10bn equivalent in the Euromarkets before settling back to $8.5bn in 1995.[5] The subdued mortgage securitisation market in the UK resulted from a general downturn in house sales and in new mortgages following a property price decline and economic recession. But this also proved a driver for the market to look to diversify into other asset-backed sectors.[6] In 1995, following successful issuances in the US, MBNA Europe Bank Ltd completed their first European credit card securitisation, i.e. backed by credit card receivables that originated in Europe.

It was 1996 that proved a turning point in the securitisation market with $34.6bn in ABS and MBS Euromarket issuance that year. The principal finance business raised awareness of the value of asset-backed financing for a much broader range of applications than just mortgages. Companies with strong tangible assets generating a predictable cash flow backed by mature demand became candidates for securitisation transactions. Morgan Stanley arranged a $4bn securitisation for the Irish aircraft lessor GPA using future revenue streams for leased aircraft to save the company from collapse. In Spain, three electricity companies securitised some Pta215bn of nuclear moratorium charges. Merrill Lynch bought the first deutschemark ABS issue; a DM1bn credit-card backed bond for Citibank.[7]

Surprisingly, the most notable ABS deal that year was in the French franc sector and was the largest ever non-sovereign bond at the time. The FF40bn Cyber-Val offering formed part of the restructuring of the French state-owned bank, Crédit Lyonnais. The deal repackaged some of the FF145bn loans from Crédit Lyonnais to the Etablissement Public de Financement de Restructuration, a fund set up to manage the sell-down of a pool of bad assets that were acquired from the troubled bank. The *ISMA Quarterly Comment* remarked: 'Selling a plain vanilla Eurobond of more than $1bn equivalent is a task beyond the capabilities of many banks involved in the euro and global markets, so the fact that the Cyber-Val deal, which came in at an equivalent of almost $8bn, was oversubscribed in what many had viewed previously as a marginal market was testament to the growing attraction of the asset-backed market.'[8]

In December 1996 NatWest launched a ground-breaking transaction with its $5bn 'ROSE Funding' issue. This was a securitisation of a portion of its loan book and is notable as the first European collateralised loan obligation (CLO). NatWest transferred 300 revolving corporate loan facilities to ROSE Funding No. 1 Ltd, a SPV, which funded the transfer by issuing floating rate notes and commercial paper to Eurobond investors and US investors under Rule 144A. In fact NatWest retained legal ownership of the loans, but transferred the loan risk in the form of sub-participation interests in the loans. NatWest bank continued to administer the loans as agent for the SPV. The securities issue was divided into a series of FRN tranches with different credit ratings, denominated in both sterling and dollars and a $2.5bn offering of commercial paper. Interest rate and currency risk was removed by the use of swaps. The bank's motivation was to add liquidity to their balance sheet. The assets remained 'on balance sheet' as NatWest retained a 2% equity risk. However by removing loans from its balance sheet for regulatory (if not accounting) purposes, NatWest was able to improve its capital asset ratio and free up approximately £250m of capital.

Profit margins on corporate loans had been shrinking for all banks but until the ROSE Funding transaction, banks had hesitated to securitise corporate loans for fear of an adverse reaction from their corporate customers.

Andy Clapham, previously Managing Director of NatWest, elaborates:

Our Chairman was on record stating that he wanted to free up capital from corporate lending. Something had to happen because our choices were either to not renew loans when they matured or to sell them. Our ambition was to free up capital so we could redeploy it. It so happened that the head of corporate lending, which generated these assets, was also head of structured finance. Maintaining the revenue from the loans was not a reason to hold the loans any more. We had the backing from the top executives.

When you are taking revenue out of a profit centre without really replacing it, you are dealing with a very political issue ... Normally the treasury funds the loan assets, whereas when you securitise, the funding comes from the bond market. So this process cuts across many different areas of the organisation. We had weekly meetings involving all affected departments ... It helped that in our case the head of lending was also responsible for structured finance and was willing to give up earnings in the short-term for long-term flexibility. We wanted to continue to be in the lending market in Europe for our relationships. Now we can.[9]

Now banks could get rid of unprofitable corporate loans, free up capital and improve their return on equity. But was there a willing investor base for investment grade corporate loans? The 11-tranche ROSE Funding deal was three times oversubscribed. Over the next year, $45bn of such CLOs were issued by banks, in over a dozen deals.[10] The *ISMA Quarterly Comment* observed:

European investors starved of yield have been increasingly attracted by the opportunities presented by asset-backed paper. There is little, if any, high quality debt providing yields over Libor, and so far domestic securitisations have in general failed to deliver such paper in any volume. And the increasingly prevalent inclusion of fixed-rate tranches in such deals has also helped to attract a greater number of investors than before.[11]

One notable class of investors in securitisation structures was the aptly titled 'structured investment vehicle' or SIV. A SIV was a pool of investment assets that attempted to profit from credit spreads between short-term debt and long-term structured finance products such as asset-backed securities. Funding for SIVs came from issuing short-term commercial paper that was regularly renewed or rolled over. The proceeds were then invested in longer maturity investment grade assets that had less liquidity but paid higher yields. The SIV earned its profit on the credit spread between short-term debt and its long-term investments. In addition SIVs used leverage to increase the generated returns. The business model (borrow short, lend long) was, of course, similar to that of a bank, but by conducting its business through capital markets and being an offshore entity, it escaped the regulation that banks and finance companies were subject to. They could also typically be kept off balance sheet, thereby avoiding many bank regulatory constraints.

SIVs were originally set up by banks and investment banks as bank capital arbitrage vehicles. The introduction of Basel I regulations made holding bank capital and ABS securities expensive for a bank. A loophole in the Basel Accords meant that banks could provide a liquidity facility to the SIV of up to 360 days without holding capital against it so long as it was undrawn. The liquidity, or 'back-stop' facility, enabled the SIV to issue rated commercial paper.

Citigroup launched the first two SIVs, called Alpha Finance Corp and Beta Finance Corp, in 1988, leveraged five times and ten times respectively. SIVs could be from $1bn to $30bn in size and invested in a range of ABS, as well as some financial corporate bonds. SIVs had an open-ended structure; they continued in business by buying new assets as the old ones matured, much like a bank. The SIV manager was allowed to exchange investments without providing investors asset-by-asset transparency, instead just providing monthly portfolio reports.

Some SIVs were referred to as 'conduits'. The key difference between a conduit and a SIV is that conduits were established and owned by banks while SIVs were not directly owned by banks, although banks had close relations with them as sponsors. SIVs and conduits were generally quite opaque, invested in complex securities, and often did not need to be displayed on a bank's balance sheet.

With a strong investor base now any assets that provided a stream of income were candidates for securitisation. One innovative, although modest, securitisation grabbed the headlines in early 1997. The rock star David Bowie was encouraged by financier David Pullman to issue securities backed by revenues from future sales of his early albums. The $55m issue of so-called 'Bowie Bonds' was backed by the then current and future revenues of the first 25 albums (287 songs) of David Bowie's collection recorded before 1990. Mr Bowie agreed to forfeit approximately 10 years' worth of future royalties from a substantial portion of his music catalogue, including such hits as 'Let's Dance' and 'China Girl'. The bonds had a 15-year final maturity with an average life of approximately 10 years, to yield 7.9%. The 'A' rated issue was bought entirely by the Prudential Insurance Company.

When the bonds matured, the royalties of the songs would return to David Bowie. As extra security, Bowie agreed that if the SPV defaulted on its loan obligation, Prudential would end up owning the catalogue that was sold to the SPV. By forfeiting ten years' worth of royalties, Bowie was able to receive the $55 million up front, which allowed him to buy out the rights to the David Bowie songs owned by a former manager.

The Bowie Bond issuance was the first instance of intellectual property rights securitisation. Following Mr Bowie's success, other artists took advantage of royalty securitisation, including such artists as James Brown, the Isley Brothers, Iron Maiden and Rod Stewart.

In 1997 total European issuance of asset-backed securities reached $41.5bn. UK issuance accounted for 48% of all primary activity, with France contributing 28% and the Netherlands 17%.[12] The securitisation market had moved from a trickle to a flow – but not yet a torrent.

* * *

A key driver of securitisation was the need by banks to free up capital by moving loans off their balance sheet. But what if certain loans could not be removed from a bank's balance sheet? Could a derivative product be structured to protect against the default risk of such exposures?

Blythe Masters, like Guy Hands, was educated in Kent in the UK. Prior to university she undertook an internship with J.P. Morgan in London and was placed with the bank's derivatives team. She entered Cambridge University to read economics but returned to J.P. Morgan each summer and on graduation joined Morgan's derivatives group. Masters became part of a team looking to develop the idea of a credit derivative which might provide protection against default risk on a loan or security. Credit derivative product development was first raised in the financial press in 1993, naming J.P. Morgan, Bankers Trust and Merrill Lynch as pioneers, all working on bespoke products.

In 1994, J.P. Morgan had extended a $4.8bn credit line to Exxon, which faced the threat of $5bn in potential damages for the Exxon Valdez oil tanker spill in Alaska. The credit line tied up significant capital on the bank's balance sheet while only providing a very meagre return by virtue of Exxon's triple-A rating. Ideally Morgan would like to have off-loaded the loan but this risked upsetting a core client relationship. Was there a way of off-loading the credit exposure to a counterparty without actually selling the loan? Masters, now based in New York, contacted the European Bank for Reconstruction and Development (EBRD) in London. The EBRD had been established in haste in 1991 to help rebuild the economies in Central and Eastern Europe after the collapse of communism. EBRD had considerable funds available for investment and they were looking for high quality investment opportunities. Masters proposed to the EBRD that if they were willing to adopt the risk exposure on Morgan's credit line with Exxon, then J.P. Morgan would pay them an annual fee for the life of the transaction. In the extremely unlikely event that Exxon, one of the world's largest and most highly rated companies, defaulted, then EBRD would have to compensate J.P. Morgan for their loss.

As the likelihood of an Exxon default appeared extremely remote, and the income stream offered by Morgan exceeded the returns being offered on other highly rated bonds or loans, Andrew Donaldson, the EBRD director felt 'It seemed like a win-win situation'.[13] After much negotiation and pioneering contract drafting by the respective lawyers the first credit derivative, or Credit Default Swap (CDS) as it was termed, was executed.

The buyer of a credit default swap, or 'protection' buyer, pays a premium for effectively insuring against a debt default, in the Exxon case, J.P. Morgan. He receives a lump sum payment if the debt instrument defaults. The seller of a credit default swap, or seller of 'protection', receives monthly payments from the buyer. If the debt instrument defaults they, in the above case EBRD, have to pay the agreed amount to the buyer of the credit default swap.

However the key to the transaction was whether the banking regulators would acknowledge that such a credit risk transfer would enable a commensurate reduction in a bank's regulatory capital requirement. Masters and colleagues started lobbying the Federal Reserve. Finally in August 1996 the Fed issued a statement suggesting that banks would be allowed to reduce their regulatory capital requirement by using credit derivatives to transfer default risk from their balance sheet. Now banks aggressively looked to participate in the CDS market. In 1996, the Office of the Comptroller of the Currency estimated the size of the single name CDS market was 'tens of billions of dollars'. By March 1998, the global market for CDS was estimated at about $300bn, with J.P. Morgan alone accounting for about $50bn of this.[14] By the age of 28, Masters was made a managing director of J.P. Morgan, the youngest woman to achieve that status in the firm's history.

But having to arrange credit default swaps on an individual credit-by-credit basis proved time consuming and limiting. Could there be a portfolio approach?

It was the confluence of the CDS market and the securitisation market that prompted the breakthrough. More specifically it was combining the collateralised loan obligation (CLO) concept as pioneered in the NatWest ROSE Funding transaction with the J.P. Morgan CDS concept. Banks could now use CDS to transfer the credit risk of a portfolio of various loans to a SPV on a synthetic basis, without a 'true sale' of assets. The first such 'synthetic' securitisation is again attributed to the J.P. Morgan derivatives team with their launch of the BISTRO (Broad Index Secured Trust Offering) transaction in December 1997.

The deal was structured to remove the credit risk on a portfolio of corporate credits acquired by J.P. Morgan. The overall portfolio was made up of 302 corporate credits diversified by geography and industry amounting to $9.7bn. As there was no chance that all the loans would turn sour at the same time, J.P. Morgan managed to persuade Moody's rating agency that the CDO could be just 7% of the size of the underlying loan pool, while hedging all of the credit risk.

Accordingly $697m of five-year notes were issued, in two tranches by the BISTRO SPV: $460m of triple-A rated senior bonds and $237m of Ba2 rated subordinated or 'mezzanine' bonds. J.P. Morgan retained a $32m 'first to default' tranche. The proceeds of the note issue were invested in US Treasury bonds, which in turn were used as collateral for the credit default swap (CDS) undertaken between Morgan and the SPV.

The five-year swap was written on the whole portfolio, with Morgan Guaranty Trust (MGT) as the protection buyer. The pool of reference credits was specified in the offering circular and was static. BISTRO, the protection seller, paid for the coupon on the notes from funds received from the collateral pool and premiums on the CDS. If there was a credit event, payment would be made from the collateral pool.[15] With this structure the first $32m of losses on the loan portfolio would be borne by J.P. Morgan, the next $237m of losses would be borne by the Ba2 bondholders and any losses exceeding $269m would be borne by the triple-A bondholders.

The attraction to the originator of such a synthetic transaction was that it removed the credit risk exposure on a pool of assets without the bank in question having to try and sell the assets; which was often limited by transfer restrictions in the loan documentation. Economically, the originator's exposure to the underlying assets was replaced by exposure to the swap counterparty, and the capital treatment in most jurisdictions came to reflect this. In broad terms under Basel I, if the counterparty is a special purpose vehicle or company, the risk weighting will be 100%; if the counterparty is an OECD bank, 20%; and if the originator is granted a first ranking security interest over cash or OECD government bonds, the risk weighting will be 0%. The BISTRO transaction was the first time a bank had hedged its economic risk while at the same time releasing regulatory capital.

Investors eagerly took up the offering as it provided exposure to particular credits and a risk/return profile, without needing to fund the exposure. J.P. Morgan went on to launch five BISTRO deals in total over the following year amounting to $2.7bn of securities and a risk transfer of $29bn.[16] The BISTRO transaction followed SBC Warburg Dillon Reed's Glacier Finance transaction.

After the Big Bang S.G. Warburg had changed strategic direction, focusing on trading businesses rather than their traditional investment banking activity, and had undertaken an ill-considered and costly expansion into the US. In 1994 the news broke that Warburg was in discussions to merge with US investment bank Morgan Stanley. The fraught discussions were finally abandoned when Morgan Stanley found that Mercury Asset Management (MAM), Warburg's semi-autonomous asset-management arm, required 'unacceptable' conditions. A year later Swiss Bank Corporation acquired, the now somewhat demoralised, Warburg which it merged with Dillon Read & Co. (a firm it had acquired in 1995), to create SBC Warburg Dillon Read. In 1997 SBC Warburg came up with a variant of the collateralised loan obligation (CLO) structure ahead of Morgan's BISTRO transaction.

A 'credit-linked note' (CLN) is a structured note that combines both a debt instrument and a credit derivative. The return from an investor's cash investment in a CLN is dependent on the credit performance of an underlying asset. SBC issued a series of CLNs transferring the risk of exposures in the loan and securities trading books of SBC's New York branch to a special purpose vehicle, Glacier Finance. Glacier received a spread over Libor for taking the credit risk on the exposures. In the case of defaults SBC would pay a principal amount to the SPV derived from the mark-to-market rate for a liquid reference security. Again SBC did not sell the loans but released regulatory capital as the credit-linked notes sold to the SPV provided cash collateral. Euromoney pointed out at the time, 'the subtlety of the deal is that the pool of underlying collateral – the credit-linked notes – may constantly be altered at SBC's discretion. The notes are callable at par on every quarterly interest payment date and the SPV then reinvests the proceeds in new credit-linked notes. The structure reflects that SBC's credit exposure will be ever changing.'[17]

So unlike the BISTRO transaction, the investor has a funded exposure. But more importantly, the SBC Glacier Finance transaction covered a dynamic portfolio of risks and so added a significant degree of opaqueness for investors as to what exactly were their exposures with regard to underlying corporate obligations, or of obligor characteristics – a so-called 'black box' structure. To mitigate possible investor concerns, the rating agencies set down guidelines with respect to average credit rating, issuer, industry and geography for any new credit-linked notes. The S&P 'model' required a minimum of 88% of underlying credit exposures to be rated investment grade according to SBC's own internal rating model. SBC mapped its internal rating system to the ratings of Moody's and S&P so they could continually revolve collateral in the SPV. The rating agencies would not see the individual obligors. Credit enhancement of the structure was through subordination with 8.25% of the whole offering issued as subordinated tranches including a retained equity tranche.

The deal was also notable for using a Master Trust structure. The Master Trust structure was conceived in the 1990s and involved establishing a trust as the securitisation vehicle. The trust issues multiple series of notes, bonds or other debt securities and uses the proceeds from the issue to acquire a revolving pool of assets, particularly prevalent in credit card receivable structures. The main benefit of the trust structure is its flexibility as it allows a revolving pool of assets to be included in one portfolio. The use of the structure by SBC Warburg Dillon Read suggested they were looking to do more transactions of the same type.

The SBC Glacier Finance $1.74bn five-tranche issue was deemed to be generously priced with a spread of 16 basis points over Libor for the senior five-year tranche and 19 basis points on the seven-year Aa1/AA+ rated notes.

Other variants of both the BISTRO and Glacier structures followed. In 1999, 12 European banks raised a total of $11bn in CLOs, with German banks taking a leading role after the German industry regulator (BaKred) amended the rules governing bank securitisations.[18]

Blythe Masters, then global head of credit derivatives marketing at J.P. Morgan in New York, pointed out in their 1999 Guide to Credit Derivatives: 'In bypassing barriers between different classes, maturities, rating categories, debt seniority levels and so on, credit derivatives are creating enormous opportunities to exploit and profit from associated discontinuities in the pricing of credit risk.' The Guide went on to say: 'Five years hence, commentators will look back to the birth of the credit derivative market as a watershed development for bank credit risk management practice. Simply put, credit derivatives are fundamentally changing the way banks price, manage, transact, originate, distribute, and account for credit risk.'

As the credit derivatives market grew, concern arose between issuers and investors as to what type of credit events would trigger the transfer of risk to investors. In response ISDA published its Credit Derivatives Definitions in 1999, listing the six credit events that could be incorporated by contracting parties into credit default swap agreements. With standardised industry terms the market took off. In 2000 the British Bankers' Association (BBA) estimated the credit derivative market had grown to just under $900bn, of which synthetic CLOs made up 20%.

But who were the main investors?

Buying credit protection under a CDS or CLO is similar to buying insurance. It is not surprising therefore that the key investors were insurance companies, export credit agencies and the US monoline insurers, as they received attractive spreads for something very akin to their traditional lines of insurance business.

Monoline insurers guarantee the principal and interest payments on a debt obligation on a timely basis. Such companies charged bond issuers a fee in exchange for a promise to make the bond payments if the issuer defaulted. They are termed 'monoline insurers' because they are regulated to provide only one type, or 'line', of insurance.

While the monolines were regulated in 1989 they had been in existence from the early 1970s providing insurance or 'wraps' for US municipal bond issues. Insuring municipal bonds became increasingly prevalent as a result of the near default of New York in 1975 and the actual default of Washington Public Power Supply System in 1983. The two companies dominating the municipal bond insurance market were Ambac Financial Group (originally the American Municipal Bond Assurance Corporation) formed in 1971 and the Municipal Bond Insurance Association (MBIA) founded two years later. These were later joined by the Financial Guaranty Insurance Company ('FGIC') in 1983, and the Financial Security Assurance Inc. (FSA) in 1985. FSA was the first bond insurer organised to insure non-municipal bonds and established the business of insuring asset-backed securities. The 1990s then saw the combination of the municipal bond insurance business with the ABS insurance business, and also saw the expansion of bond insurance into Europe, Asia, Australia and Latin America.

Bond insurance generally reduces the borrowing costs for an issuer since investors are prepared to accept a lower spread on an offering in exchange for the credit enhancement provided by the bond insurance. The monolines were typically rated triple-A, and would only look to enhance investment grade credits. If the basis points saved exceeded the cost of the monoline 'wrap' then the bond issue would be wrapped.

In the Eurobond markets the monoline insurers frequently insured asset-backed securities where the future flow of receivables was less predictable, such as civil engineering projects, toll roads and football stadiums. They became a well-accepted, and well-respected, part of the asset-backed originator's tool kit.

But with the development of credit derivatives in the late 1990s providing credit protection, the need for insurance wraps declined. As their 'bread and butter' business dwindled the monoline insurers began offering protection in the burgeoning credit derivative market, in particular, in the lucrative CDO space. This market would introduce new risks to the monolines not experienced in their traditional municipal bond market.

$$*\quad*\quad*$$

The *ISMA Quarterly Comment* in October 1996 featured a keynote article entitled '1996 – The Year of the Emerging Market'. The article set the scene:

> *Having shaken off the doom and gloom of 1994 and 1995, bonds issued by borrowers in the world's developing nations have been rallying at breakneck speed, outperforming the bond markets of most developed countries … some $64.5bn in emerging market bonds were issued in the year to late August, compared with $59.5bn in all of 1995. Spread convergence in the secondary market has been reflected in the primary sector, where launch spreads have become increasingly aggressive … Although central and eastern European borrowers grabbed most of the headlines, Latin American issuers have also managed to rack up record volumes of issuance.*

The Latin American totals were boosted by Brady bond exchanges, 'From virtually nothing in the early 1990s, the amount of Latin Eurobonds in issuance has now grown to approximately $80bn. This is still some way short of the total amount of outstanding Brady bonds, which amount to some $125bn. Eurobonds are on a rising trend, however, whereas no more Latin Bradies are likely to be seen after the close of the Panamanian and Peruvian agreements.'[19]

In the Brady and non-performing loan market the strongest performer was Russia. In March 1996 the International Monetary Fund (IMF) approved a $10.2bn loan to Russia for economic reform and in April the Paris Club agreed to restructure $40bn of Soviet-era debt. This helped set the stage for Russia's debut Eurobond offering in November; a $1bn five-year issue via J.P. Morgan and SBC Warburg.

Emerging market bonds remained the focus going into 1997 as European countries reduced their borrowings to meet the Maastricht criteria for joining the euro. Bond issues totalled $743bn in 1997, up from $679bn in 1996 with emerging market borrowers accounting for $105bn 'Amid historically low rates, yield-hungry investors with large sums of cash to invest were hunting for securities offering above-average returns.'[20] But while attention was largely focused on Latin American and Central European markets the emerging market bandwagon would be overturned by the so-called 'tiger' economies of South-east Asia.

Pressures had been building up in Asia for some time. The rapid expansion of South-east Asian economies in the mid-1990s, with growth rates of 6–12% of GDP, attracted substantial speculative inflows. Faced with declining spreads in the developed markets international investors turned to Asia for higher yields and new markets. Annual net capital flows into Asia grew from $50bn in 1993 to over $110bn in 1996.[21] This 'hot' money largely ignored concerns of widening current account deficits, soaring asset prices and rising inflation rates. South-east Asian governments decided to remove financial controls and open up their financial markets because they needed funds in order to cover widening current account deficits. With high domestic interest rates, Asian companies were encouraged to borrow heavily at the lower rates available offshore in order to fund their aggressive expansion. The large current account deficits in countries such as Thailand, Indonesia and South Korea caused their currencies to decline. As speculators moved in, causing more downward pressure, currencies were forced to float. On 2 July 1997 Thailand's central bank floated the baht after spending $33bn to protect it from speculative attack. On 11 July the Philippine peso was devalued and on the 18th the IMF approved an extension of credit to the Philippines of $1.1bn. On 24 July Asian currencies fell sharply. This included the Malaysian ringgit with the Prime Minister Mahathir Mohammad singling out 'rogue speculators' and particularly George Soros as the cause of his problems. Despite an IMF-arranged $17.2bn support package for Thailand in August, Asian stock markets continued to plummet and currencies continued to fall. By October, the process, which became known as Asian 'contagion', i.e. the transmission of market dislocations to other developing and developed financial markets, led to a second round of speculative currency attacks. This time the targets were the Hong Kong dollar and the Korean won.

Excessive foreign borrowing had been a major cause of the crisis. Companies that had taken out large foreign-currency loans, that is, the best rated companies, now faced impossibly high debt repayments in terms of their domestic currency. Capital flight ensued, leaving indebted companies in even direr straits. GDP growth rates contracted sharply, bankrupting companies that had overexposed themselves to foreign-currency risk, and leading to costly and embarrassing IMF bailouts. The IMF structured rescue packages for the most severely affected economies to enable them to avoid default, tying the packages to reforms intended to restore their currency, banking and financial systems. In November the IMF announced a $40bn stabilisation package for Indonesia and in December a $57bn package for Korea. The IMF 'structural adjustment programmes' (SAPs) called on crisis-struck nations to reduce government spending and deficits, allow insolvent financial institutions to fail, and aggressively raise interest rates, strategies that critics say exacerbated the effects of the crisis in some countries rather than alleviating them.

In mid-1997 the Korea Development Bank (KDB), the prime Korean borrower, launched an international bond issue at 115 basis points over US Treasuries; by December KDB failed in its attempt to issue another $2bn bond. *Euromoney* noted that:

> *Following currency devaluations and stock market crashes, Asia now faces its biggest challenge: a full-blown credit crunch. No big bond issues will be done for the rest of the year, spreads on outstanding bonds have gone haywire and trading has ground to a halt. Local sources of credit have also dried up. Corporate borrowers can expect little help from their bankers; devaluation has blasted a hole in many local banks' balance sheets and they have no money to lend even if they wanted to.*[22]

By 1998, with the Malaysian ringit having lost 50% of its value since the beginning of the crisis, the government imposed strict capital controls and pegged the currency to the US dollar. This prompted a fierce backlash from the financial community who warned of the potential collapse of the Malaysian economy and its exclusion from the capital markets in the future. The Indonesian and the Philippine currencies continued to fall in value despite repeated interest rate hikes to avoid default. This contributed to the doubts about the credibility of the IMF and the validity of its high-interest-rate policy to solve the economic crisis.

Another source of contention in the Asian crisis was the performance of the rating agencies. The 1997 KDB bond issue was rated by the principal rating agencies as A+/A1. By the end of the year the issuer was rated B+/Baa1. During the crisis the rating agencies downgraded the sovereign ratings of Thailand, Indonesia and Korea all below investment grade. The agencies came under severe criticism for failing to detect the Asian crisis until it was too late, leading to a series of precipitous downgrades. A group of economists noted:

> *In fact, referring to Moody's only, Malaysia was downgraded by four notches (from A1 to Baa2). Thailand was downgraded five notches (from A2 to Baa3). The largest downgradings (six notches) were for Indonesia and Korea: respectively from Baa3 to Caa3 and from A1 to Ba1. Needless to say, downgradings of this size are extremely unusual, and were decided late in the crisis ... Specifically, they downgraded East Asian crisis countries more than the worsening in these countries' economic fundamentals would justify. Such rating agencies' actions unduly exacerbated, for these countries, the cost of borrowing abroad and caused the supply of international capital to them to evaporate. In turn, lower than deserved ratings contributed – at least for some time – to amplify the East Asian crisis.*[23]

The barrage of criticism that followed led the agencies into publishing defences of their actions. The BIS concluded:

> *While the rating agencies vigorously defend their current ratings, they have identified lessons to be learned from the Asian financial crisis, and have acknowledged, either*

explicitly or implicitly, inadequacies in their rating methodologies prior to the crisis. Risk factors to be weighted more heavily going forward include the burden to the sovereign of the contingent liabilities of a weak banking system, the adequacy of bank supervision, the vulnerability to a liquidity crisis due to concentrations of short-term debt for otherwise creditworthy borrowers, the increased stress in crisis when there are relatively low levels of disclosure and transparency in policy, and the likelihood of contagion from other countries.[24]

Remarkably by the end of the first quarter of 1998 the international mood was lightening. In May, Stanley Fischer, Deputy Director of the IMF declared: 'The worst of the crisis is over.' He was mistaken, the contagion had spread elsewhere.

In 1997, Russia was gaining the confidence of international investors after six years of post-Soviet reform. Inflation had fallen from 131% in 1995 to 22% in 1996 and 11% in 1997 and the rouble was pegged to the dollar. However with the rapidly developing crisis in South-east Asia, commodity prices on which Russia relied began a downward spiral. With collapsing commodity prices, the spreads on Russian and Brazilian bonds widened by around 600 basis points in October alone. In December 1997, the price of oil, the major Russian export, began to drop.

By year-end real wages were less than half of their 1991 level and tax receipts were negligible due to chronic inefficiencies in the tax gathering process. Fears began to arise of a Russian default. Optimistic commentators argued that surely a nuclear super-power could not default. President Yeltsin fired his entire government but this further undermined the confidence of international investors, who sold their Russian government bonds. By late May, demand for bonds had plummeted so much that yields were more than 50% and the government failed to sell enough bonds at its weekly auction to refinance the debt coming due. To add salt to the wounds the oil price collapsed to $11 per barrel.

In late May *EuroWeek* reported: 'Russia replaced Asia as the primary focus of investor concerns this week, with yields on Russian Treasury bills soaring to over 80% and share prices tumbling by 11% on Wednesday. The shakeout was prompted by fears that a devaluation of the rouble could derail the entire economic reform process in Russia.'[25]

In June Goldman Sachs helped the Russian government raise finance by selling $1.25bn in five-year bonds at 650bps over US Treasuries, just days after rating downgrades. A few weeks later, it arranged a deal in which short-term Russian government debt (GKOs) was exchanged for $6.43bn of seven and 12-year dollar bonds at a spread of 940bps over Treasuries. Also the IMF approved a $22.6bn package to help stabilise the country, with $4.8bn of the bailout funds immediately available to the government. Within weeks a significant proportion of these funds had found their way overseas.

On 13 August 1998, the Russian stock, bond and currency markets collapsed as a result of investor fears that the government would devalue the rouble, default on domestic debt, or both. Annual yields on rouble-denominated bonds were more than 200%. Finally on 17 August the government floated the exchange rate, devalued the rouble, defaulted on its domestic debt, halted payment on rouble-denominated debt (primarily GKOs), and declared a 90-day moratorium on payment by commercial banks to foreign creditors.

By the end of August, Russia's benchmark $2.4bn Eurobond was trading at more than 5,000 basis points over US Treasuries.[26]

Many cast a critical eye on the role of investment banks in the Russian crisis. As default seemed increasingly inevitable investment banks plied the authorities with further bond and loan transactions, at ever more costly rates to the borrower. These deals made handsome fees for the banks concerned but did little to solve Russia's predicament. Goldman Sachs was the dominant player as the default approached, yet remarkably admitted to suffering no loss in the crisis.

In October the *ISMA Quarterly Comment* observed: 'currently, the capital market for emerging market debt is more or less dead, awash with awarded mandates for Eurobonds and syndicated loans that are unlikely to see the light for several months.'[27]

There was no let-up in the stream of bad news. Some weeks after the Russian default, news reached financial markets about a financial plan to rescue Long-Term Capital Management (LTCM), one of the largest US hedge funds. LTCM was founded in 1994 by the renowned Salomon Brothers arbitrageur, John Meriwether, in the elegant suburb of Greenwich, Connecticut. Meriwether had attracted funds from some 80 investors who had put up a minimum of $10m each, drawn by the fund's 'rocket scientist' management team, which included Nobel prize-winning economists, Myron Scholes and Robert Merton and former Vice-Chairman of the Federal Reserve, David Mullins.

LTCM's core strategies were 'relative value' and the 'convergence trade': convergence among US, Japanese and European sovereign bonds; convergence among European sovereign bonds in advance of the single currency; and convergence between 'off-the-run' and 'on-the-run' US Treasuries. As yield differences were often modest and the net risks deemed to be small, the fund's strategy was to take large leveraged positions in such convergence plays to make a significant profit. As profits grew, banks were falling over each other to offer funding to LTCM, often without requiring collateral.

After producing annual returns of around 40%, by the beginning of 1998, the fund's equity was almost $5bn and its borrowings exceeded $100bn. *Risk Magazine* valued its swap position at some $1.25trn, amounting to 5% of the entire global market. Alarmingly LTCM was moving from 'playing' the market, to becoming the market. In addition they were a major supplier of index volatility to investment banks, active in the 'interest-only' (IO) mortgage-backed market and an investor in emerging markets such as Russia hedged back into US dollars.

When Russia defaulted on its rouble Treasury bonds LTCM lost money, but the bond losses should have been offset by the devaluation of the rouble currency. Unfortunately for LTCM, the Russian government prohibited trade in the currency so the losses grew. However these Russian losses paled into insignificance against the ensuing effects of the 'flight to quality' or rather 'flight to liquidity' which the Russian default triggered. As the Russian situation was deteriorating, fixed-income investors were moving for protection to the US Treasury market. But even more so, they were seeking out the 'on-the-run' issues that would provide the greatest liquidity. As a result, spreads between 'on-the-run' and off-the-run' Treasuries widened significantly. Unfortunately LTCM was massively positioned the other way, holding that liquidity was not so important and the current yield differentials between 'on-the-run' and 'off-the-run' were too wide. However the size of LTCM's positions meant that exiting their position speedily was impossible.

By 22 September LTCM's equity had collapsed to $600m; yet their overall positions remained largely the same – implying even greater leverage. Banks now doubted that LTCM could meet its margin calls and panic developed. Goldman Sachs, AIG and Warren Buffett opportunistically offered to take over the fund for a knock-down price and provide a capital injection, but the offer was rejected within the hour allowed for their response. Later on the 23rd, the Federal Reserve, fearing a potential systemic meltdown, organised a group of 14 commercial and investment banks, all of whom had extended liquidity to the fund, to take over the fund's management and inject $3.5bn into the fund in exchange for 90% of its equity. The banks then undertook the painful process of unwinding LTCM's positions in the market. By the end of the year many of those banks declared substantial write-offs as a result of their involvement in the LTCM rescue. A systemic collapse of the financial markets had been avoided.

Some commentators criticised the precipitate action of Fed President, Bill McDonough, for setting a 'too big to fail' precedent, i.e. an implicit safety net provided by the Fed, leading to market participants being assured they could not be punished by the market for wrong and unsound decisions. McDonough responded to critics 'I think you have to start with the notion that we were really very convinced that the American people would suffer in a way that is not appropriate for them to suffer if LTCM failed.' Fed Chairman Greenspan added: 'Had the failure of LTCM triggered the seizing up of markets, substantial damage could have been inflicted on many market participants, including some not directly involved with the firm, and could have potentially impaired the economies of many nations, including our own,'[28]

* * *

After Long-Term Capital's fall from grace, many commentators blamed the debacle on a lack of liquidity. *Euromoney* noted in June 1998: 'Suddenly the search for higher yield goes out the window and investors, we are told, are clamouring for greater tradeability. The bond salesman's answer is super-jumbo bonds upward of $4bn and market-maker commitments to dealing spreads of a few basis points. Big tickets, reversible short positions and hefty benchmarks are the result.'[29]

During this period, US government issuance was declining; in response the market started to look at other borrowers as potential government substitutes. The most obvious US candidates were the US agencies, Fannie Mae and Freddie Mac. In January 1998 Fannie Mae established its Benchmark Notes programme with an initial $4bn five-year global bond offering. The deal attracted $8bn in global orders and was hailed as a great success.[30] In February the European Investment Bank (EIB) issued the first jumbo €4bn ten months ahead of the currency's official launch. March saw a $4bn five-year issue from the World Bank and Fannie Mae responded with a $4bn three-year offering. Major investors such as central banks and sovereign wealth funds, who typically bought $100m tickets of government bond issues, could now invest in the Eurobond market without liquidity concerns.

A further development of the growing issuance was the greater usage of Euro-MTN programmes. In 1997 new issuance from MTN programmes amounted to $446bn, according to Capital Net; an increase of 32% on the previous year. While by the end of 1997 total outstandings of MTNs passed the $1trn mark. MTNs were now a mechanism for issuance rather than a defined product. In 1999 new issues via MTN programmes totalled just under $800bn, a 44% increase over the previous year.[31]

Benchmark issuance programmes became the mode for frequent issuers. In addition frequent issuers took to regular 're-opening' of existing issues, whereby new tranches were launched of existing issues thereby making larger more liquid tranches. With the arrival of the euro, Freddie Mac launched a €Reference Note programme in 1999. Under the programme the borrower committed to regular issues of at least €5bn each quarter. The EIB announced the launch of its Euro Area Reference Notes (EARNs) programme whereby they committed to launching issues of a minimum of €2bn per quarter. This was followed by a benchmark issuance programme from KfW, the German government-owned development bank. Major private sector borrowers were not to be left out, with Ford Motor Credit launching its GlobLS (Global Landmark Securities) programme and issuing a $7.5bn transaction in July 1999.[32]

But it was Ford Motor Credit's rival, General Motors Acceptance Corp (GMAC), which caused a revolution in the primary Eurobond market. New jumbo issuance programmes needed more effective syndication to ensure good placement. In January 1998 GMAC launched a $2bn five-year and 10-year dual-tranche issue. Nothing extraordinary about that. The joint lead managers were Bear Stearns, a relatively rare Eurobond lead manager, and Morgan Stanley. However when syndicate invitations went out, invitees were informed that syndication would be organised on a 'pot' basis. The 'pot system' of syndication had developed in the US domestic market in the second half of the 1990s and had been employed on a number of Yankee deals for European borrowers. But its introduction to the Eurobond market caused an uproar.

In a 'pot' distribution all or part of the new issue is set aside to be allocated to investors out of a central order book, the 'pot', run by one or more bookrunning lead managers. Other syndicate members contribute orders to the pot, but they do not control the final allocation or distribution of bonds. This gives bookrunners much more control over how the order book is managed and allocated, and helps protect against the issue underperforming in the secondary market.

Despite the introduction of the fixed price re-offer syndication practice a decade earlier, bond offerings still had a high propensity to underperform in the secondary market. While in general terms this can be put down to syndicate indiscipline, more specifically it was that co-managers were reluctant to honestly report their investor demand for a deal lest they not be invited into future deals. Investor demand was invariably exaggerated to appease both the lead manager and the issuer. This state of affairs exasperated issuers, particularly frequent issuers, who demanded to know where their bonds had been sold and why, as so often was the case, the price had declined. For years the new issue houses assured their issuers of the quality of their placement while excusing their inability to divulge their investors due to various anonymity requirements and the bearer nature of the market. Throughout the 1990s, under pressure from issuers, lead managers would make broad statements about the placement of paper with regard to the percentage of a deal placed with certain categories of investors or in certain geographical regions. These were likely to be biased towards what the lead managers felt the issuer wanted to hear rather than the true details of the distribution.

The seismic change to traditional Eurobond syndication techniques that the pot system introduced was that syndicate members who wished to put orders into the pot were required to disclose the names of their investors – in market parlance, 'name give-up'. This of course flew in the face of the carefully preserved investor anonymity which had been the mainstay of the bearer bond-denominated Eurobond market over 35 years. (It would also mean of course that co-managers would have to reveal their true distribution capability.) European new issue houses, particularly those with a large retail or high-net-worth individual client base, were immediately up in arms at the introduction of this US technique. They rounded on IPMA and demanded that IPMA prevent the introduction of the system. The US banks supported the new system as they were familiar with 'name give-up' in the registered domestic US market. The European banks said the system would mean them breaching their client confidentiality and banking secrecy rules. Others complained that it was just a devious ploy by the US banks to gain access to European banks' client base.

David Walker, Director of Liability Management at GMAC, explained: 'With the pot idea we wanted to give a lot of managers the opportunity to perform, and not just give them all significant tickets and then lose sight of the deal.' He adds: 'A couple of people complained, but interestingly they got over it once they discovered that they could reach investors and perform well. It reflects a bit on the European concern of being overtaken by an American market structure.'[33]

Bookrunning lead manager, Bear Stearns, declared:

> *It is a massive step forward for the market and although not everyone will embrace the concept on day one, based on the reaction we have had from investors and issuers, I certainly believe that you will see it emulated, albeit perhaps in a modified form. Because of the pot system, we have more dealers with information about who bought the deal than in normal globals. They are in a better position to trade it and, for this reason, we expect the GMAC issues to achieve benchmark status and remain liquid.*[34]

Some – presumably European – market practitioners, commented: 'The pot idea bothered European investors a lot and some, who stayed away from the issue, would have bought bonds had there been no name give up.' And 'If GMAC were looking for genuine global distribution, they should not have tested the structure. European investors do not want to have their names revealed either to the borrower or lead managers. And we certainly don't want competitors to know the names of our accounts.'[35]

The battle over the use of the pot system raged for an extended period. When GMAC launched a further issue in August 1998 *EuroWeek* commented: 'Some attributed difficulty in placing the bonds to the fact that GMAC used the pot system in syndicating the deal. The pot has once again highlighted the divide between the US and European banks. One US co-lead in the GMAC issue described the pot system as going some way down the road to fixing the vulgarities of syndicate practices in Europe; [while] a European bank bitterly resented the imposition of this US syndicate practice in the international markets.'[36]

IPMA organised forums to canvass members' views although they resisted taking sides in the debate; thereby infuriating some European banks who threatened to leave the Association. However the banks' attempt to stem the tide of 'pot' syndication was a forlorn one. In a transaction syndicated via the pot system issuers could now see where some or all of their bonds were placed. (Early transactions tended to be hybrids; the pot system used for the lead managers and retention for co-managers.) Frequent issuers had been pressing for such information for years. In time if two issuing houses approached a large frequent issuer with similarly priced transactions, then if one lead manager would suggest pot syndication, and the other retention, then pot would always prevail. Now if the European banks wanted to win the key mandates then they had to use the pot system.

In the 1990s the major issuing houses had developed their own proprietary in-house bookbuilding platforms. These systems would accumulate the 'indications of interest' or orders, received from investors at various price levels and so help 'build the book'. The practice developed that an issuer, mandating a transaction to be syndicated on a pot basis, would be permissioned into a one of the bookrunning lead manager's proprietary bookbuilding systems. There, he could observe, in real time, orders coming into the book. If, as is normal, there was more than one bookrunning lead manager (i.e. cross-market syndication) these other managers would accumulate their orders on their own proprietary systems and then re-key the orders into the principal bookrunning lead manager's system.

While issuers loved the transparency of the new syndication method, the pot system would in time introduce new problems hitherto unconsidered. Securities issues had unique identifiers, such as CUSIP (international numbering system) or ISIN (International Securities Identification Number) numbers to identify them across various IT systems. However no unique identifiers existed for investors. Banks might use various designations or corruptions of a client name in their client relationship management (CRM) and primary bookbuilding systems. So when operating on a cross-market syndication this caused serious client identification problems and a resultant degree of double-counting of client orders.

The pot system introduced a further unanticipated feature: issuing houses could now see key investors' orders being entered into the pot. If a major investor was seen to prefer giving orders to one lead manager rather than another, then, when the unfavoured lead manager was lead managing a subsequent transaction, he might not wish to allot bonds to that investor. Consequently major investors adopted the practice of giving orders to all the bookrunning lead managers. Bookrunners now had to check if orders comprised a single order given a number of times or multiple orders to the lead managers. This again added to the propensity for books under the pot system to be overstated. These problems grew as issue sizes and the number of orders in a deal grew. The market would grapple with these problems for years to come.

Despite these problems, the pot system was revolutionary in transforming syndicate behaviour and efficiency. With name give-up, distribution capacity now became all important. For the first time in almost 40 years, issues were largely placed with investors and the propensity for issues to trade down in the secondary market was no longer the norm. New issue houses could now look to make money on a more consistent basis. New issue fees continued to be squeezed with the ever-increasing competition but new issue sizes were growing accordingly.

NOTES

1. *The View*, Issue 07, Marble Hill Partners, The Accidental Investor: a profile of Guy Hands.
2. Terra Firma, Website: www.terrafirma.com, About Us: Our history.
3. Ibid.
4. Ibid.
5. Moore, *Autostrade to the Superhighway*, pp. 79–80.
6. Hilda Mak and John Deacon, Developments in UK Securitization,;International Securitization & Structured Finance Report.
7. Moore, *Autostrade to the Superhighway*, p. 80.
8. *ISMA Quarterly Comment*, Vol. 28, January 1997, p. 7.
9. John B. Caouette, Edward I. Altman and Paul Narayanan, *Managing Credit Risk: The Next Great Financial Challenge* (John Wiley & Sons, 1998) p. 390.
10. Ibid.
11. *ISMA Quarterly Comment*, Vol. 28, January 1997, p. 7.
12. Moore, *Autostrade to the Superhighway*, p. 80.
13. Gillian Tett, *Fool's Gold: How Unrestrained Greed Corrupted a Dream, Shattered Global Markets and Unleashed a Catastrophe* (Abacus, May 2010) p. 44.
14. Ibid. pp. 48–67.
15. Moorad Choudary, *Structured Credit Products: Credit Derivatives and Synthetic Securitisation* (John Wiley & Sons, July 2004) pp. 476–477.
16. IFR, 2,000th Issue Supplement: JP Morgan's US$700m Bistro bond: the first CDO, September 2013.
17. *Euromoney*, SBC taps it's credit pool for cash, October 1997.
18. Moore, *Autostrade to the Superhighway*, p. 82.
19. *ISMA Quarterly Comment*, Vol. 27, October 1996, p. 14.
20. *ISMA Quarterly Comment*, Vol. 32, January 1998, p. 19.
21. Supervisory Lessons to be drawn from the Asian Crisis, BCBS Working Papers No. 2, June 1999, p. 9.

22. *Euromoney*, Asian financial crisis: When the world started to melt, December 1997.
23. G. Ferri, L.-G. Liu and J.E. Stiglitz, The Procyclical Role of Rating Agencies: Evidence from the East Asian Crisis (1999) 28 *Economic Notes* 336–337.
24. Supervisory Lessons to be drawn from the Asian Crisis, BCBS Working Papers No. 2, June 1999, pp. 21–22.
25. *EuroWeek*, Issue No. 554, 28 May 1998.
26. Moore, *Autostrade to the Superhighway*, p. 35.
27. *ISMA Quarterly Comment*, Vol. 35, October 1998, p. 15.
28. House Committee on Hedge Fund Operations, 1998, p. 38.
29. *Euromoney*, A Mad Rush for Liquidity, June 1998
30. Moore, *Autostrade to the Superhighway*, p. 92.
31. Ibid. p. 71.
32. Ibid. p. 94.
33. *EuroWeek*, 1998 Deals of the Year: Best US Borrower: GMAC.
34. *EuroWeek*, Issue 535, 16 January 1998.
35. Ibid.
36. *EuroWeek*, Issue 565, 14 August 1998.

CHAPTER 8

Of .Com's and Cons

1999–2004

N othing dominated bond market practitioners' minds more in the 1990s than preparations for the Economic and Monetary Union (EMU). The convergence plays put on by investors years earlier largely delivered their returns. By the beginning of 1999 interest rates on Italy's ten-year bonds had fallen to 4.11% compared to Germany's 3.9%, reducing the Italian German yield differential to 21 basis points.

By the late 1990s, the feeling was growing that insufficient work had been done to make the most of the benefits of imminent monetary union. The European authorities felt that an overall framework for the integration of financial services was a prerequisite for the attainment of the EU's economic potential on the introduction of the euro. EU Member States kept adding their own requirements to the centralised requirements and interpreting them in different ways. Brussels termed this behaviour 'super-equivalence' or 'gold-plating', Italy being most culpable. In addition, the integration of financial markets in the EU had progressed much further in wholesale than in retail financial services, with the latter still segmented largely along national lines. To redress these deficiencies, in October 1998 the Commission published a Communication setting out a Framework for Action on Financial Services, followed by the Financial Services Action Plan (FSAP) itself in May 1999.

At the European Council in Lisbon in April 2000, it was agreed that the FSAP should be completed by the end of 2005 with the first stage, the integration of the securities markets, being in place by the end of 2003. The FSAP comprised 42 measures designed to harmonise the Member States' rules on securities, banking, insurance, mortgages, pensions and all other forms of financial transaction. It had three aims: to establish a single market in wholesale financial services, to make retail markets open and secure and to strengthen the rules on financial supervision.

Some FSAP measures took the form of Regulations, which applied directly in all Member States. Most took the form of Directives, which have to be transposed into the law of each Member State. Of these, some replaced earlier Directives (e.g. on investment services), which were felt to be increasingly out-of-date, while others recast earlier proposals (e.g. on takeover bids).

This massive undertaking required a new legislative and regulatory process, the so-called 'Lamfalussy Process'. The Committee of Wise Men, an independent EU committee of experts, chaired by Baron Alexandre Lamfalussy, proposed a four-level approach with regard to the legislative process. Until the Lamfalussy Committee reported, the European Council and the European Parliament needed to agree every detail of financial services legislation – a time consuming process. For example, the EU took seven years to pass the earlier version of the Investment Services Directive. Under the Lamfalussy plan the Council and the Parliament agree only the broad political principles of the proposed legislation. Two new expert committees, the European Securities Committee (ESC), consisting of finance ministry representatives, and the Committee of European Securities Regulators (CESR), were tasked with working along with the Commission to fill in the detailed 'technical' elements of the Directive.[1]

The approach proposed can be summarised briefly as follows: Level 1 measures set out the high level objectives (or 'principles') that the securities legislation must achieve. Level 2 measures set out some of the detailed technical requirements necessary to achieve these objectives (taking advice from CESR). Level 3 measures are intended to ensure uniform implementation of community rules among Member States. The responsibility for uniform implementation falls to regulators in CESR. Level 4 measures relate to the enforcement of the legislation.

In 1995, EU governments had decided that, as of January 1999, all new fungible debt by EMU member states should be issued in euros; however they were undecided whether to redenominate their outstanding bonds into euros. In time the increasing investor desire for liquid government issuance in 'benchmark' issues persuaded EU governments to agree to the redenomination of their outstanding debt. This then required efforts to agree on common bond market conventions across the Eurozone.

ISMA, IPMA and ISDA joined together with other trade bodies as early as 1996 to analyse the practical implications of EMU for market participants. The result of their deliberations was adopted in 1997 as a set of conventions applicable to euro-denominated securities issued on or after the commencement of monetary union.

Bonds denominated in euros would be treated as 'international securities' for the purposes of ISMA's rules and recommendations. Accrued interest on euro-denominated securities would be calculated on an actual/actual day count basis, i.e. 365/365 days. The Associations, with the exception of ISDA, agreed that coupon payments should be made on an annual basis. A 'business day' for euro securities should be a day when Cedel Bank, Euroclear and TARGET (an EU interbank payment system) are open for business and settlement for euro-denominated securities should follow the regular Euromarket convention of taking place three business days following the trade date.

The European Investment Bank (EIB) inaugurated the euro-denominated bond market in January 1997, two years before the single currency's launch date. The transaction led by Paribas, SBC and CDC marches was for €1.3bn, increased from an initial €1bn. Cyrus Ardalan, Chairman of ICMA and formerly syndicate head, BNP Paribas recalls:

> *We were sitting around in Paribas discussing what we were going to do with the European Investment Bank, and the proposal was to go to them with a traditional ECU transaction, but I said 'Why don't we just call it a euro?' People looked at me and said: 'You can't call it a euro, we don't have a euro ... I said so what? Let's just call it a euro, and if it doesn't happen it just converts back into ECU.' So we went to René (Karsenti, EIB Director of Finance at the time), and he thought it was a*

very, very good idea because it avoided re-denomination from ECU into euros, and, secondly it sent a very, very strong signal in official circles that the euro was a reality and was going to happen.[2]

The borrower followed this up with a €2bn global offering, hoping to encourage US participation in the new currency. US investors apparently took up 34% of the offering.[3] After the EIB's lead, European sovereign borrowers quickly followed, led by Italy and Spain with issues of €1bn and €1.5bn respectively. However the transaction which really put the euro-denominated bond market on the map was the €4bn 10-year offering for the Republic of Italy in February 1998 – the largest fixed rate Eurobond to date. One of the attractions of this issue was that it would become fungible with Italian government bonds (BTPs) of the same maturity date after EMU. The head of funding, Vincenzo La Via, at the Italian Treasury stressed 'We have to position ourselves for the single currency market. Capital raising is going to be a very competitive business after EMU. Issuers will have to be in a position to give investors what they want and at the right time.'

That same month *EuroWeek* was prompted to write:

For a currency that does not exist, the euro is showing surprising signs of maturity. Since the launch of the first euro-denominated transaction, a benchmark curve out to 30 years has been built in the Eurobond market; it has attracted a host of leading credits; it has produced some of the most successful deals seen in the markets; and it has lead managers and issuers competing furiously to bring deals.[4]

By the time of EMU, Eurobonds outstanding in EMU currencies totalled €425bn.[5] Before the official introduction of the euro it was used in 'catamaran' or parallel bonds in participating currencies which were designed to convert into euro and become fungible. For example, Siemens brought a three-tranche parallel bond offering denominated in deutschemarks, French francs and guilders. The bonds could be converted into euros and become fungible in 1999. The transaction was the first attempt by a corporate to be positioned for the arrival of the euro.

But what of outstanding bond issues in the 11 legacy currencies? With the launch of EMU, outstanding legacy currency bonds, such as euro-deutschemark or euro-French franc, were redenominated so that payments were made in euros. They were still referred to in their original legacy currency and investors could receive interest in either euros or the original currency up to early 2002 when Member States' currencies disappeared from circulation. Most investors opted for euro payments as the liquidity of these offerings waned. With the launch of the euro in January 1999 the euro-denominated bond market soon became the second largest market in the world after the dollar market.

However the composition of the euro-denominated bond market was very different from its US counterpart. The euro government bond market was comparable in size to the US Treasury market, but the euro area non-government securities market amounted to less than a third of the US market.[6] In the US, 63% of external corporate funds were bonds, whereas in Germany, for example, corporate bonds accounted for only 2% of corporate financing. The under-developed European corporate bond market was partly a result of highly competitive syndicated loan financing and a consequent reliance on bank financing. For example, in Germany 91% of corporate financing was via bank loans. Many European banks had close corporate relationships, with cross shareholdings, overlapping Boards and, as a consequence, they were willing to make below-market loan facilities available.

Banks meanwhile relied on financing themselves in the capital markets and so bonds issued by financial institutions formed a major part of the Eurobond market at the time of EMU. When the euro was launched some 75% of Euromarket issuance consisted of bank paper.[7] With the arrival of the euro, large corporates were keen to diversify their funding away from the banks.

Why had corporate bond issuance lagged behind other market sectors before EMU?

Firstly, the widely adopted 'convergence trade' had served to divert investors' attention from the corporate sector in the second half of the 1990s. Also the decision to invest in a European corporate required credit analysis capabilities and there were simply not enough credit analysts at the banks and investing institutions. It also required a view on the particular currency, limiting investor demand. Currency fluctuations significantly increased the risk of cross-border investments, and many institutional investors, particularly pension funds, were restricted from making these type of investments; for example, prior to the euro, French insurance companies had to invest 80% of their assets in the domestic market.

In April 1999 *Euromoney* trumpeted:

> *Europe's new currency might have had a stinking debut on the foreign exchange markets, falling by nearly 10% against the dollar in the first two months, but participants in the Eurobond market couldn't care less. For Eurobond firms, life has rarely been sweeter. The launch of the euro has brought in its wake a bull market: a boom in new issues and an opening up of the market both to new borrowers and new investors … Last year's favorite bond market theory – that European investors would respond to the single currency by buying credit as never before – has become this year's reality. But the scale and the speed at which institutions, hitherto restricted to buying government debt, have turned to international corporate bonds has surprised even experienced traders and salesmen.*[8]

The decline in government bond yields and government bond issuance, as countries sought to meet their Maastricht borrowing limits, added to the attraction of corporate bond issues.

With the launch of the euro in 1999 corporate debt issuance doubled to $679bn equivalent from $273bn in 1998. European corporates quickly set benchmarks with euro issues and diversified their liabilities away from reliance on bank loans, accessing a wider investor base. The growth of credit derivatives reduced the outright credit risk for investors who could now invest across borders in the single currency. According to Merrill Lynch the credit derivatives market accounted for almost $900bn of notional value in 2000. The first half of the year saw substantial corporate bond issues for the likes of DaimlerChrysler, British American Tobacco (BAT), Elf, Carrefour, Alcatel, Endesa, Deutsche Telecom, KPN, Fiat, Repsol, Telefónica and Tecnost of which many were oversubscribed. (The predominance of telecom issuers reflected the technological changes the industry was undergoing.) The Alcatel €1bn offering was placed 28% in Italy with the Chief Finance Officer remarking: 'The market has really opened up. That a French corporate can sell its bonds primarily to Italy is something new.'[9] The landmark transaction for the new market was the issue for Tecnost. Tecnost was the acquisition vehicle for Olivetti in their hostile bid for Italia Telecom and they boldly raised a €9.4bn floating rate note in the new market. This issue partly refinanced a ground breaking €22.5bn syndicated loan.[10]

In the first six months of 1999, €149bn worth of bonds were issued by corporates in Europe compared with €74bn equivalent in the same period of 1998.

The emergence of the new market fortuitously came at a time when the appetite for Yankee bonds by US investors had declined sharply after the upheavals of 1998.

US borrowers, such as GMAC and Ford Motor Credit, also tested the new European market even though the basis swap from euros to floating rate dollars was only occasionally favourable. The euro market provided US issuers with investor diversification, with most deals, even if designated as globals, going to a European investor base. The inaugural euro issue of Principal Life, the US insurer, was placed 30% in France. 'In the past we might have sold 3% there,' noted the lead manager, CSFB.[11] In addition proposed amendments to US Federal Accounting Standards, FAS 133, threatened to increase the cost for US corporates of using derivatives, in particular, swaps.[12] However for those companies with assets in Europe they could now finance these assets more efficiently in Europe without having to consider the currency swap market, Enron and Phillip Morris launching deals on this basis.

Hutchinson Whampoa, the Hong Kong conglomerate, bought Asia's first euro-denominated corporate issue. The first euro-denominated securitisation issue was for MBNA who issued a floating rate note at 14 basis points over three-month Euribor. Almost all transactions were book-built and issuers accepted market-led pricing in this new sector.

However this flood of corporate issuance in euros brought with it a pricing dilemma. Traditionally corporate credit is priced as a spread against the relevant government benchmark issue. With a multiplicity of government yield curves in Europe, which benchmark government bonds should an issue be priced off? Some issues were priced off German bunds, some off French OATs, others off Italian BTPs or even Belgian OLOs. As issues proliferated, lead managers began to focus more on the swap rate, Euribor, which was a common rate throughout the euro area and highly liquid. Once priced as a floating rate spread it could be translated back into a fixed spread against the desired government benchmark.

New corporate issuance was not only for top rated issuers. Imperial Tobacco, Sprint, Delphi Automotive Systems and Enron Corp issued BBB rated paper. In fact rated high-yield issuance also began to emerge, totalling €9.4bn in 1999.[13] But Cliff Dammers, Secretary General of IPMA, cautioned market participants:

> *The Eurobond market grew up as a market for supranational and sovereign issuers and banks, at a time when most banks which were regular issuers, were rated AA or AAA. As we move to a credit market, issuers, intermediaries, investors and regulators must change their ways of doing business to reflect the new reality. Simple documentation, light prospectus reviewing and cursory due diligence may have been appropriate for issuers like the World Bank and GE Capital but are not sufficient for a BBB corporate, no matter how much of a household name it may be. Investors and intermediaries must acquire credit skills and build up credit departments. Most important and more difficult is that everyone must change their mind-set to reflect the new environment.[14]*

While timely investment in developing credit analysis skills would have benefited institutional investors substantially, many chose the faster and cheaper route of relying on the ratings of external rating agencies. IPMA noted an 'explosive growth in the demand for and acceptance of ratings'.[15] ISMA commissioned a survey on credit research in 2000 finding that:

> *most of the continental European banks appear to lag substantially behind the US banks. In France, for example, some (but not all) of the major banks indicated that*

analysis of corporate bonds falls in principle within the overall responsibility of their equity research departments. This was in sharp contrast to the fixed income research carried out by many banks in London and New York, whose credit research forms a separate area from equity altogether.[16]

Eurobond issuance totalled $1.4trn equivalent in 1999, amounting to more than 4400 deals. Euro-denominated bonds represented a remarkable 43.1% of the market, only slightly less than the US dollar at 45.5%.[17] But the year was not without setbacks. As investment banks competed to get a major foothold in the new market sector, pricing became over aggressive and deals consequently underperformed.

Nonetheless the pipeline of new deals kept filling up, as issuers, driven by interest rate worries and concerns about a possible market collapse due to the 'millennium bug', lined up to get deals done before the fourth quarter. The worry was that computer systems around the world might cease to function on 1 January 2000 (Y2K). Most dates in computers had inevitably been programmed to automatically assume the date began with '19' as in '1963'. So when the date was to turn from 31 December 1999 to 1 January 2000, there was considerable concern that computers would assume the date was '1900' and chaos would follow. By the summer of 1999 swap spreads and credit spreads on bonds began widening as investors sought out the relative safety of the Treasury market. Repo rates rose in anticipation of possible financing problems and the only collateral in demand were government bonds. The influx of funds pushed the yield on the benchmark 30-year Treasury bond to a low of 4.72%.

Leading up to the year-end, a number of central banks, including the Federal Reserve, put in place plans to provide liquidity should investors flee the market. The Federal Reserve auctioned Y2K options to primary dealers. These options gave the dealers the right to borrow from the Fed at a predetermined interest rate. The strong demand from dealers for these instruments confirmed the Fed's concerns and helped ease the liquidity premium of US Treasury securities. In addition, in anticipation of possible problems, the US Treasury Department arranged to have about $80bn in cash on hand at the end of December, about twice the normal amount.

Most investment banks put in place guidelines to reduce all but absolutely essential bond trading activity from mid-December, with no trading due for settlement between 31 December and 7 January. By December the markets were in full defensive mode and an estimated $500bn worldwide had been spent to combat the threat of the millennium bug. As the new century dawned there were sighs of relief in each crisis centre around the globe as the financial markets were given the all clear.

However the abundant credit that had been dispersed to avoid Y2K problems served to further fuel the already soaring stock markets and, in particular, investment in 'dot.com' companies or internet stocks. The NASDAQ composite index moved from 2746 at the end of September 1999 to 5048 on 10 March 2000, an 83% rise in six months.

* * *

The speculative interest in new internet-based, start-up companies can be traced back as far as 1995 as entrepreneurs, both old and new, were attracted by the new business opportunities provided by the worldwide web. They in turn were courted by a growing band of greedy venture capitalists. The sudden low price of reaching millions of customers worldwide instantaneously and the possibility of connectivity with unrelated buyers and sellers promised to overturn established ways of doing business. New software companies were set up daily, sometimes by college students in their garages, and their hastily prepared IPOs were snapped up by hungry investors. Any company related to internet or network development or consumer marketing via the internet saw their stock valuations rocket. Some, very much the minority, would become significant corporations, such as Netscape, Cisco and Amazon. But many did not have well articulated business plans, relying on talk of 'new paradigms', and a new economic order. Nonetheless they succeeded in raising hundreds of millions of dollars of capital. Most business plans did not anticipate robust, if any, earnings in the early years and therefore access to the bond markets was simply not possible.

This was an equity market 'bubble' where equity investors were lured from their traditional reliance on equity analysts' ratios to believe in the miracle of technological advancements and instantaneous access to customers worldwide. From 1996 to 2000 the NASDAQ technology stock index rose from 600 to over 5,000. In 1999 there were 457 IPOs with 117 doubling in price on the first day.[18] Each IPO created new 'dot.com' millionaires.

In early 1999 Federal Reserve Chairman Alan Greenspan, in something of a repeat of his 1996 'irrational exuberance' comments, expressed concern about the high value of US shares. He said high stock prices appeared to be based on expectations that corporate profits would be substantially higher than they had actually been. By March 2000, however, business fundamentals did start to reassert themselves and the 'new economy' began to behave alarmingly like the old economy. Many internet-based companies reported huge losses, others simply failed as investors cut off funding. Panic set in and by the end of 2000, technology stocks had lost about 60% of their value. By the end of 2001 97% of all dot.com IPOs were trading below their original offer price and more than half were delisted or trading at less than $1 per share.[19]

In June 2000 *Euromoney* questioned the role of the investment banks in the dot.com bubble: 'Goldman Sachs, Morgan Stanley and CSFB, the top technology investment banks, were the most prominent arrangers of technology and internet IPOs during the extraordinary bull run that has just come to its inevitable messy end. But the April crash has exposed these three banks to criticism for how they managed their deals. Too many turned sour, others quickly reached stellar valuations way above their IPO price, all rushed out in a frenzy to keep clamouring investors sated. No underwriter escaped this, but the top three fell into the trap more frequently, and more prominently.'[20]

CSFB was investigated by the Securities and Exchange Commission (SEC) and the National Association of Securities Dealers (NASD) for malpractice when allocating shares in initial public offerings at the height of the boom. In January 2002 CSFB agreed to pay a $30m fine and to return to the government and the NASD $70m of their illegal gains. Unfortunately IPO investors received nothing.[21]

The dot.com companies were part of the wider TMT sector, that is, Technology, Media and Telecom, where a wide overlap of products and services existed. Software companies needed the development in telecommunications to reach their customers, be it by mobile telephony, fibre-optic cables, via assymetric digital subscriber lines (ADSL) to provide faster broadband access or developing wireless (wi-fi) technologies. As technological innovation opened up new telecommunications possibilities, in the late 1990s governments looked to deregulate the market and open it up to wider competition. Investors anticipated exponential growth in telecom companies' revenues as a result.

At the beginning of 2000, European telecom companies, most of which were former state monopolies, were invited by various governments to compete in auctions for a third generation

(3G) of radio frequency spectrum to facilitate mobile voice, high-speed data, and internet-accessible wireless capability. These Universal Mobile Telecominications System (UMTS) licence auctions followed the experience in the US telecom sector in the previous year. Only a limited number of 3G licences were on offer, raising the competitive pressure and creating a bidding frenzy. The winning bidders spent huge sums in acquiring the licences, over $100bn in Europe, all the time knowing that they would also have to spend almost as much again on the infrastructure needed to support the services.

In addition there was a craze of M&A activity among the telecommunications companies, or 'telcos', often operating in consortia, in an attempt to carve out a major share of the mobile phone market in Europe, if not worldwide. These transactions set dazzling new records both for the size of the merger or takeover and for the financing packages that accompanied them. Due to their sheer size the majority of transactions involved substantial exchanges of shares rather than cash. The takeover of Telecom Italia by Olivetti in 1999 for $64bn and of Mannesmann by Vodafone for $204bn in 2000 are prime examples of such developments. However the EU competition authorities imposed conditions on most major cross-border mergers, opposing any moves that might reduce competition in the industry. So, for example, the takeover of Italia Telecom by Olivetti prompted the acquisition of Omnitel and Infostrada by Mannesmann, while the takeover of Mannesmann by Vodafone triggered the takeover of Orange by France Telecom.

With the stock market falling due to the dot.com collapse, the telcos looked to finance their activities with debt. The major banks lined up to offer huge short-term loans, the record being the France Telecom €30bn loan financing. Commercial banks with investment banking arms were increasingly willing to use their balance sheet to attract subsequent lucrative corporate bond mandates. The financial regulators, notably the Bank of England, issued warnings to the banks to exercise caution in their lending, but corporate bond financiers took little heed.

Deutsche Telekom stole a march on other operators with a headline grabbing $14.6bn bond offering in June 2000 through Deutsche Bank, Morgan Stanley Dean Witter and Goldman Sachs. The issue, a pot syndication, was increased from an initial launch amount of $8bn and was divided into four currencies, US dollar, euro, sterling and yen, and eight maturities varying from five to 30 years. The dollar portion of the offering totalled $9.5bn.

Deutsche Telekom, like other telcos, found themselves in the awkward position of trying to borrow large sums of money at a time when they were already carrying large debts from their expenditures on 3G mobile licences. Investors were well aware that the market was likely to see a considerable amount of telecom financing so the lead managers offered a new issue premium (a 'NIP'), pricing the deal 15 basis points wider than secondary market levels. In addition rating sensitive coupon step-ups of 50 basis points were incorporated on all tranches. The step-up would be triggered if the company was downgraded below single-A. While the generous terms helped the deal to perform well, they also had the effect of widening the terms of outstanding telecom issues.

Nonetheless the telecom new issues bandwagon rolled on with WorldCom, Vodafone, KPN and France Telecom all raising the equivalent of at least $4bn in individual offerings in the first half of 2000, most with coupon step-ups. And despite a widening in spreads, further issues were launched for the likes of BT and Telefónica. As new disposals and acquisitions took place between the competing telcos, bond investors had to get used to event risk as spreads could suddenly widen on any new announcement.

Deutsche Telekom did not hold the accolade of launching the biggest ever bond offering for very long. In February 2001 France Telecom launched a record $16.4bn bond issue, double its original intention, and attracted $28bn of investor orders aided by a new issue premium of 15 to 20 basis points over similar telco credits. It was a bold move so soon after the poor reception of their Orange IPO and a jittery TMT market. The offering was in three currencies, US dollar, euro and sterling, and incorporated a coupon step-up of 25 basis points for each notch of possible downgrading below the single-A level. The total transaction attracted over 1,000 client orders. Within weeks of the launch, France Telecom had to admit that they would not be able to pay down as much of their €60bn indebtedness as they had hoped and the bond traded down.

Euromoney warned:

> *Time is running out for Europe's telecom companies. Investors don't believe they can meet debt-reduction targets, nor do research analysts or the rating agencies, which are threatening further downgrades. Even the companies' own management teams are starting to have doubts about the tenability of widely publicised restructuring plans, admitting that perhaps they've been a little optimistic. During the past year, telecom companies have slid a long, long way into the red.*[22]

As the overhang of supply depressed the fixed rate sector, telecoms companies looked to the securitisation market to diversify their funding sources.

The massive telecom bond mandates, with their huge order books, exacerbated the problems already being experienced with pot-syndicated transactions. Bookrunning lead managers had to choose one bookrunner as the principal bookbuilder and then re-key all their orders into the principal bookrunner's proprietary bookbuilding system to create the overall book of demand. This was inefficient and the problems associated with the lack of unique investor identifiers, and multiple client orders, mentioned previously, grew, as the size and complexity of deals grew. Syndicate desks were now spending all night in their offices trying to reconcile the new issue book with their syndicate partners. Occasionally, even after this, syndicate participants were unsure if the bookbuild was accurate, and whether the syndicate was still long or short of paper. The issuing houses turned to IPMA for a solution.

IPMA put out a tender for a cross-market bookbuilding system. The large issuing houses had already made substantial investments in building their own proprietary systems and were not ready to abandon them. So the new IPMA system would need to operate between the various proprietary bookbuilding systems without replacing them. A software developer, Marketpipe, was selected and the IPMA member banks were asked to finance this new 'IPMA Match' project. Some investment banks were reluctant as they had been burnt by investing in multibank trading platforms in the tech boom. Eventually 18 banks were persuaded to subscribe to the project for a three-year initial period with their subscription being set against fees due when the full service was up and running. At the core of the system was to be a set of unique investor identifiers and a mechanism to identify and reconcile duplicate orders entered into the book. There began a three-year project to deliver an efficient cross-market bookbuilding system between the aggressively competitive investment banks.

*   *   *

In the secondary markets, electronic communication had long overtaken the telephone as the principal means of communication. Investors, traders and brokers communicated through the ubiquitous Bloomberg messaging screens or via email. Traders' quotes were widely disseminated on screens, either with indicative or actual prices. Investment banks via their sales teams would regularly send messages to institutional investors, typically via the Bloomberg system, indicating trading interest with prices and sizes of bonds and derivatives. But by the late 1990s software developers and investment banks were getting increasingly excited about the opportunities provided by the internet and the establishment of electronic platforms for what was termed 'e-trading'.

Every few months brought announcements of new internet-based bond trading platforms being formed, typically by groups of banks who would share ownership. Banks signed up to new consortia, if for no other reason than to protect against perceived threats to their existing business. Many initiatives were fraught with problems as rival banks struggled to work cooperatively with each other in the highly competitive environment. The earliest platforms were established in the liquid government markets. An early arrival on the scene was TradeWeb, a multi-dealer system launched in 1998 to eight customers to trade US Treasury bonds. Customers signing up to the service and looking to trade would link to the private internet site where they would be confronted by bid and offer prices from the main market-makers. Each market-maker was shown alongside their quotation. The customer could then request firm prices from up to five banks. These banks had 20 seconds to give a firm bid or offer or to decline the customer request. The customer then traded at his preferred price, the whole process taking a few minutes compared to the time it would take manually to check market prices.

In Europe the Italian MTS was the parent of EuroMTS, an interbank platform where benchmark bonds from the 12 Eurozone governments were traded. EuroMTS was launched in 1999 as a pan-European government bond platform with 24 primary market-makers as its shareholders. This service had grown out of the domestic 'Telematico' electronic bond market established by the Italian Treasury and Bank of Italy almost a decade earlier. The EuroMTS service initially offered electronic trading in 27 of the most liquid German, French and Italian government bonds. Bond issues had to have at least €5bn outstanding and at least five market-makers to qualify for inclusion in the MTS system.

Before long, TradeWeb expanded into Europe to trade Eurozone sovereign bonds. In April 2000 MarketAxess was formed as a multi-dealer platform with a view to trading a wider range of credit products than just government bonds. In 2001 they set up a London office and began trading in US dollar and euro-denominated Eurobonds. While these are a few of the names that established credible bond trading platforms and have survived the test of time, 2000–2001 is littered with failed electronic bond trading ventures, among them BondConnect, BondGlobe, BondHub, BondLink, XBond, LimitTrader and Trading Edge. Many platforms, like MarketAxess, had ambitions to expand the product base beyond the government sector and to set up automated corporate bond trading. Predictions were rife that more than half of bond trading activity would take place over electronic trading platforms within just a few years, and banks participated in multiple ventures so as to protect their interests. For example, Deutsche Bank had helped set up BondClick, a European trading platform for government bonds, in January 2000 (later merged with MTS); they then joined the Board of MarketAxess some months later, followed by Board membership of TradeWeb and late in the year became the fifth founding member of BondBook.

To encourage the adoption of their various electronic trading systems, platform vendors added features and services such as straight through processing (STP) connectivity or pre-trade services such as research and analysis software, or primary market applications and prospectus libraries.

In July 2002 the Committee of European Securities Regulators (CESR) extended the Investments Services Directive's (ISD) oversight to the new so-called Alternative Trading Systems (ATS) to ensure the protection of users of these ATSs and the integrity of the market.

ISMA had also been lured into the electronic trading arena. In 1998 it invested $7.5m setting up Core-deal (named after the ISMA Council of Reporting Dealers), an inter-dealer credit trading platform, involving Reporting Dealer member firms. ISMA announced 'We're developing a system which can eliminate telephone trading. A trader types in what he wants to buy and the price, and it sits on the system until ISMA has a matching trade. Orders are placed on the system and, where they match, the trade is executed automatically.' Developing the system cost at least as much again as that initial investment. The platform became a recognised investment exchange (RIE) in May 2000.

But the predictions of the growing market share of electronic trading, proved wildly optimistic. Automated trading systems failed to pick up a significant share of European trading business, particularly in the non-government sector. Why? Some would prove to have inferior technology and software, while others ran out of funding as project costs escalated. Others again failed to attract sufficient users and were taken over by rivals or closed down.

One failed platform was BondBook, a joint venture between a group of major investment banks who invested between $50m to $100m in the project. BondBook was planned as a central marketplace for trading investment grade and high-yield corporate bonds. It had a different model to TradeWeb and MarketAxess where participants were aware of the counterparties they were dealing with. BondBook provided liquidity from its participating members by linking trading counterparties on an anonymous basis, matching live bids and offers in real-time. The idea was to create a liquid marketplace rather than just offering trading from a specific group of dealers. It would, of course, allow institutional investors to deal with each other. But for the system to succeed, it needed a substantial critical mass of participants. This failed to develop quickly enough and after only eight months of operation the project was abandoned. 'The platform's ambitious model required a degree of behavioral change among market participants that BondBook's sponsors concluded was unlikely to be achieved in an acceptable time frame,' the company said.

Investors were frequently not comfortable with this new way of dealing, while for the sell-side participants, their principal concern was with disintermediation by the new platforms.[23] Also traders, who were happy to show their positions in the large liquid markets, were considerably more reluctant to show their hand in the less liquid corporate space. In time the sheer number of competing services was unsustainable. The pace of consolidation amongst online trading systems quickened.

Along with many others, ISMA's Core-deal project also failed to fulfil its potential. ISMA failed to introduce Core-deal by its original January target date. It subsequently agreed with the Bank of New York to use that bank's automated trade matching and order routing system, Bond-Net, and rebrand it as Coredeal. Using licensed third-party software was a less than ideal solution in a rapidly changing environment. Coredeal listed around 5,000 bonds but few ever traded. John Langton ISMA's CEO admitted: 'There is no point saying that Coredeal had good volumes, because it didn't.'[24] Before long those ISMA members who were not participants of Coredeal became disgruntled, as they did not have access to the service and yet were sharing in the funding of the project. To placate members, ISMA sold off 42% of Coredeal to 11 of its broker-dealers. ISMA also managed to sell a 15% equity stake in the company to EuroMTS with an agreement to reduce its holding further by 2004. EuroMTS looked to create a new platform based on their Telematico trading infrastructure. John Langton, probably sighing with relief, added: 'We have made it clear for some time now that there is considerable scope for consolidation amongst the providers of electronic trading services to the international debt markets. This new business model will combine the best attributes and strengths of both systems, bringing significant benefits to the international debt market in the EU.'

The Bond Market Association (TBMA) of the US, started to monitor electronic trading systems in the US and Europe in 1997. They noted there were 11, mostly single-dealer platforms, where bank customers could purchase securities from the individual dealer's book. By 1999 this number had grown to 39 and then in the year 2000 the number ballooned to 80, both single and multi-dealer platforms.[25] By 2003 TBMA listed 21 multi-dealer electronic trading platforms for government bonds in Europe, of which nine were multi-dealer-to-customer, and 12 were multi-dealer-to-dealer. Whereas in the corporate bond sector they listed eight trading platforms, with six being multi-dealer-to-customer and two multi-dealer-to-dealer.[26]

In 2004 EuroMTS's turnover fell 50% from 2003. Some banks argued that they could find better prices over the telephone with dealers, rather than using the MTS electronic platform. In August Citigroup, exploiting the EuroMTS trading rules, outraged other bond traders by selling €11bn of bonds on the platform and then, seconds later, buying back €4bn of it at a lower price, pocketing a handsome profit of €12m and leaving rivals with heavy losses. It was labelled the 'Dr Evil' trade. There was a call to expel them from the platform and investigations were undertaken by the UK's FSA and other European regulators. Citigroup later stated that they should not have undertaken the trade because of its impact 'on our clients and the market'.

* * *

As with the assassination of President Kennedy for an older generation, everyone of the present generation knows where they were when they heard the horrific news, and worse, saw the live pictures, of the terrorist attack on the World Trade Center in New York. Apart from the appalling human tragedy, the attacks hit at the heart of Wall Street and put the financial markets into disarray with declines around the globe. The New York Stock Exchange closed for a week. The US bond market was directly affected as a number of OTC bond trading firms were physically located in or around the World Trade Center. Nonetheless the Treasury bond market resumed limited trading four days after the attacks. When the markets reopened, unsurprisingly, there was a flight to quality to US government bonds.

The Eurobond market remained open, although activity was greatly subdued. Corporate spreads moved 10 to 30 basis points wider as a result of the flight to quality. In the primary sector, banks with new issues in the market had to consider the question of 'force majeure' and whether the disruption to the market was sufficient for lead managers to terminate their offerings. While all acknowledged the exceptional market circumstances, banks did not generally perceive a need to invoke force majeure clauses.

After such a humiliating strike at the heart of American life the US administration went into retaliatory mode. On 20 September President George W. Bush announced his 'war on terror', an international military campaign to eliminate Al Qaeda and other terrorist groups. The markets braced themselves as the international political outlook turned ugly.

Nonetheless, a week after the tragedy, Freddie Mac reopened the international primary market by auctioning a $5bn two-year Reference Note followed closely by a $5bn 10-year issue. The following week the Federal Reserve cut interest rates by 50bps, lowering the Fed Funds rate to 3%. 9/11 contributed materially to the US administration's expansionary monetary policy. Interest rates were lowered and remained low for a long time, fuelling increased leverage and extraordinary credit growth in the US economy.

In December 2001, while the markets were still absorbing the implications of the terrorist attacks in New York, Enron, the major US energy company (and former stock market champion), filed for bankruptcy – the largest in US history. Investigations revealed that its reported financial condition was largely due to inflating profits, hiding debt and generally indulging in fraudulent accounting practices. What is more, the subsequent law suit against Enron directors was notable in that the directors settled the suit by paying significant amounts of money out of their personal wealth. *The Journal of Accountancy* concludes 'the events leading to Enron's eventual downfall appear simple enough: individual and collective greed born in an atmosphere of market euphoria and corporate arrogance.'[27]

In just a little over 15 years Enron had grown into one of the US's largest companies. In 1996 Jeffrey Skilling, ex McKinsey & Co. with a background in banking, became Enron's Chief Operating Officer. Skilling had developed a high profile gas trading business and a unique energy derivatives business for Enron during the 1990s. Skilling took this model and applied it to the market for electrical energy as well. Skilling made full use of the 'three per cent rule' from the Financial Accounting Standards Board (FASB) which implied that companies did not need to record their dealings with a partnership if an outsider owned more than 3%. Accordingly 'partnerships' using 'special purpose entities' (SPEs) were repeatedly created with 3% of the shares owned by an outside party – although just how 'outside' such parties were, was in many cases highly questionable.

With the tech boom underway Enron launched 'EnronOnline', a commodities trading website where Enron was on one side of all trades that took place. However the company booked many of EnronOnline's trades as revenue ignoring the fact that money paid by buyers went directly to sellers. On the basis of these so-called 'revenues' Enron advanced to seventh place in the Fortune 500 list.[28] But Enron's debts were growing. As the company's rating came under pressure Skilling and colleagues stepped up the use of SPEs to increase leverage and the return on assets (ROA) without having to report it on the balance sheet. Chief Financial Officer, Andrew Fastow, took the use of SPEs further, parking all types of troubled assets in these opaque companies.[29]

Fundamentally Enron was a derivatives trading house. The problem was that while espousing a 'mark-to-market' valuation culture, most energy trading contracts or derivatives had no observable quoted contracts. So Enron developed their own evaluation models. Traders would hide profits in 'prudency reserves' or cover up losses by entering false forward curves into their valuation models.The auditors accepted the models as given.

By February 2001 the company's debt levels had risen to $37.3bn, a 91% increase over the previous 12-month period. In time, analysts began to suspect that Enron's financial statements were less than a true reflection of the business. In October Enron posted its first ever quarterly loss after taking charges of $1bn on poorly performing businesses. Enron's stock began to slide, picking up momentum when the SEC in late October announced an 'informal enquiry' into Enron's transactions with various partnerships owned by Fastow. In November Enron announced it had overstated its earnings dating back to 1997 by almost $600m and was quickly downgraded to junk status. The following month it filed for Chapter 11 bankruptcy listing $63.4bn in assets.[30]

The Enron collapse called into question the adequacy of US disclosure and auditing practices. Accounting firms came under the spotlight as never before for cross-selling consulting services to audit clients. Arthur Andersen came under formal investigation by the SEC as well as committees of both houses of Congress, leading to their eventual dissolution. Enron's collapse also encouraged investors to re-examine the financial structure of bond issuers, in case the complexity of corporate balance sheets was masking significant risk exposures.

In December the SEC announced that the annual reports of all Fortune 500 companies were to be scrutinised by its corporate finance division to see if there was any evidence of insufficient disclosure. Subsequently Jeffrey Skilling received a 24-year jail sentence (reduced to 14 years in 2009) while, having deemed to have shown remorse, remarkably, Fastow received a six-year sentence (later reduced to five).

No sooner had the market absorbed the Enron news than the US telecommunications giant, WorldCom, failed and was put into bankruptcy. With $107bn in assets this was a significantly larger default and a significantly larger accounting fraud. WorldCom (a major beneficiary of the dot.com bubble) revealed it had improperly recorded $3.8bn in capital expenditures, which boosted cash flows and profit over all four quarters in 2001 as well as the first quarter of 2002. At the time of the filing WorldCom had $41bn in debt of which $24bn was in bonds. Also, Bernie Ebbers, WorldCom's CEO, had $366m in personal loans from the company.[31] For this reason, he had to show continually growing net worth in order to avoid margin calls on his own WorldCom stock that he had pledged to secure the loans.[32]

Ebbers had pursued a strategy of rapid growth through acquisitions, but rarely made a move without the approval of his CFO, Scott Sullivan. In 1998 WorldCom acquired MCI Communications, the second largest US long-distance telecom provider, and a company with more than two and a half times WorldCom's revenues. The acquisition pushed WorldCom deeper into debt and it was finalised just ahead of a downturn in the telecommunications business. Under pressure to show ever-increasing revenues, Ebbers and Sullivan resorted to financial deception, most notably reporting operating expenses (line costs) as capital expenditures. Subsequent investigations revealed questionable accounting practices had stretched back as far as 1999. In May 2001 WorldCom undertook the largest ever US corporate bond offering for $11.9bn, yet neither the bookrunning lead managers in their due diligence enquiries, nor the rating agencies (nor Arthur Andersen, WorldCom's auditors) picked up on the accounting errors which continued for a further year after the bond issue.[33] The subsequent accounting scandal decimated WorldCom's bondholders as the value of the bonds plummeted by 75%. Experts estimate the total accounting fraud at WorldCom was $79.5bn. As for Ebbers, he later received a 25-year jail sentence, while Scott Sullivan was sentenced to five years as part of a plea agreement in which Sullivan testified against Ebbers.

Both cases raised issues of corporate governance: executives falsifying the books while lining their own pockets, and questions regarding the integrity of analysts, recommending poor stocks in return for business from those same firms. They damaged confidence in the securities markets. In the Eurobond market corporate credits fell out of favour, activity slumped and firms started downsizing.

As accusations flew back and forth in the wake of the corporate scandals, the US Congress hastily passed the Sarbanes-Oxley Act (SOX) in 2002. In July, President George W. Bush signed the Act into law, describing it as 'the most far reaching reform of American business practices since the time of Franklin Delano Roosevelt'.

The Act created new standards for corporate accountability as well as new penalties for wrongdoing. Senior management were now accountable for the accuracy of financial statements. All companies with a listing of their shares in the US must provide a signed certificate to the SEC vouching for the accuracy of their financial statements, signed by CEO and chairman. The Act mandated a variety of internal controls to be signed off by senior executives, who might be criminally liable if controls were inadequate. It described specific criminal penalties for manipulation, destruction or alteration of financial records, or other interference with investigations, while also providing certain protections for whistleblowers.

The Act defined a Code of Conduct for securities analysts and required disclosure of conflicts of interest.

It strengthened the role of auditors. The senior audit partner working on a client's audit must be changed at least every five years. US accounting firms were now effectively prohibited from both auditing and consulting for a given client. An independent five-man board called the Public Company Accounting Oversight Board (PCAOB or 'peekaboo') was established, with responsibilities for enforcing professional standards in accounting and auditing. Corporations were required to test their internal controls regularly, such tests to be carried out by an outside firm other than the external auditor.

While most observers felt regulation to improve both corporate governance and corporate disclosure was necessary, and Sarbanes-Oxley was inevitable, some felt it was an over reaction to events, being 'intrusive, expensive and heavy-handed', encouraging foreign companies to list their shares in London rather than New York.[34] Five years later the *Economist* looked back:

> *Controversial from the start, SOX came to be despised by many businessmen in America (and beyond, where it has touched big foreign firms). Even its authors have reservations, conceding that its hasty passage into law meant it was badly drafted in parts. 'Frankly, I would have written it differently,' Michael Oxley, one of the former congressmen who drafted the act said in March. He added that the same was true of his co-author, Paul Sarbanes. 'But it was not normal times.' The charges levelled against SOX are numerous and serious. Top of the list is the price of compliance … Beyond its immediate price tag, SOX stands accused of undermining America's entrepreneurial spirit.*[35]

The large credit rating agencies (CRAs) came in for another bout of criticism in the wake of the corporate scandals, particularly Enron, with many questioning their competence and the value of their ratings. All SEC-approved rating agencies gave Enron an investment grade rating on its debt up until five days before the company filed for bankruptcy. The Sarbanes-Oxley Act directed the SEC to conduct a comprehensive study on the role of the credit rating agencies in the evaluation of securities issuers and their importance to investors. Specific criticisms raised with regard to Enron were that the CRAs failed to ask sufficiently probing questions of management and did not effectively use their special access to confidential information. The CRAs defended themselves on the basis that they were still reliant on a company's external auditors. If management provided false information and the external auditors did nothing to probe and stop the deceit the CRAs are in an impossible situation. The International Organisation of Securities Commissions (IOSCO), the grouping of the world's securities regulators, also created a task force to examine the credit rating agencies and this resulted in a set of principles for the CRAs to adopt – which they duly did. In Europe the European Parliament called on the European Commission to assess the need for legislation to deal with the CRAs.

In September *Euromoney* observed that:

The trend towards deregulation is most obviously being called into question – after all, most of the recent corporate scandals were in the most deregulated industries. The US financial sector, which has enjoyed 20 years of deregulation culminating in the Gramm-Leach-Bailey Act, has seen some of the most drastic legislation since the 1930s, in the form of the US Patriot Act, which enables much greater government scrutiny of capital mobility, and the Sarbanes-Oxley Act, which beefs up financial disclosure and supervision of auditing.[36]

But not all bondholders' woes were in the corporate space.

*   *   *

When Argentina defaulted on $132bn of debt in January 2002, it was the biggest sovereign default in history. Argentina's public debt had ballooned during the 1990s due to a painful recession and it repeatedly sought help from the IMF. The country's borrowings were growing at an alarming pace and in 1999 its external debt exceeded 50% of GDP. The government looked to ease the problem through a couple of debt exchanges but these just served to exacerbate the already dire situation. The IMF pressed for the implementation of austerity measures in the economy and in December 2001 it refused to release a $1.3bn portion of a loan as the Argentine government had failed to reach agreed budget deficit reduction targets. At the year-end the government suspended payments on its $132bn of debt, including $81bn of bonds.

The possibility of an Argentinian default had been on the cards for some time. A further worry was that was the composition of capital flows into emerging markets had changed with the Brady restructurings from bank loans to negotiable bonds. It would be much harder to contact and co-ordinate bondholders for a restructuring in a future sovereign debt crisis.

Believing that sovereign debt crises were too protracted, the IMF in April 2002 put forward plans for a Sovereign Debt Restructuring Mechanism (SDRM). This was a plan to bring elements of domestic corporate bankruptcy law into international law and make it binding on IMF member states.[37] The markets largely rejected the IMF proposal and responded with their preferred voluntary approach. IPMA along with the Institute of International Finance (IIF) and five emerging market trade associations engaged with the IMF on sovereign debt restructuring burden sharing and the promotion of Collective Action Clauses (CACs). CACs are contractual provisions in bond documentation that facilitate an issuer approaching bondholders with a proposal to modify key terms of the relevant bond or bonds. They enable a majority of those bondholders to agree to the proposed modifications; and, where the requisite majority agrees, provide that the modifications are binding on all bondholders.

The purpose of CACs is to aid the process of restructuring outstanding bonds and avoid 'holdouts' by minority bondholders. Bonds subject to English law had included CACs since the 19th century. Bonds subject to New York law had not included CACs, or certainly not qualified majority voting. New York law required the consent of each bondholder for reductions in amounts due. The IMF believed that CACs were necessary but not sufficient, and the effort to achieve collective action among private sector creditors should be reinforced with a sovereign bankruptcy mechanism. Opponents of CACs argued that if bonds are too easy to restructure, debtor countries may be tempted to treat debt restructuring as an acceptable alternative to debt repayment rather than as a final resort when all else has failed.

IPMA and the group of trade associations put forward a draft set of model CACs developed for bonds governed by New York and English laws including detailed covenants regarding the provision of financial information. After extensive discussions in March 2003, Mexico successfully issued $1bn global notes due in 2015 governed by New York law that included CACs both for majority restructuring (a 75% threshold) and majority enforcement provisions. This took the market by surprise as the Mexican Finance Minister had rejected CACs some months earlier. The issue was priced pretty much in line with its yield curve and was over-subscribed. The Finance Minister declared: 'We wanted to show that collective action clauses were possible and we felt that they are a superior strategy to SDRM.'[38] This offering was followed shortly after by issues for Uruguay, part of a distressed debt exchange to avoid default, that also included CACs. Since that time most internationally targeted sovereign issues have included some form of collective action clauses.

But what of Argentina who had no such clauses in their defaulting debt? There began what the *Economist* refers to as the 'government's bruising campaign to force bondholders to accept a record write-down of their claims'.[39] The process involved a swap of 152 different issues in six different currencies into three new issues representing a write-down of bondholders' claims to approximately 35 cents in the dollar.[40] After almost three years of tortuous wrangling and creditor hold-outs, 70–75% of bondholders reluctantly submitted to the deal. The *Economist* concluded: 'it is wrong to imagine that default has become a painless route to prosperity. It has not.'[41]

* * *

After a bleak year of corporate scandals and a sovereign default the markets started to stage a comeback in November 2002 with $20bn of issuance taking place in a single week. 2003 began nervously as issuers looked to launch deals before the planned invasion of Iraq got underway. An early landmark was a 30-year issue for Olivetti. This part of the curve had become of great interest to institutional investors since the US Treasury had stopped issuing long bonds at the end of 2001. The Olivetti deal was quickly followed by a €1bn similarly long-dated issue for France Telecom which attracted €3bn of orders. This was part of a €15bn refinancing plan for the company to avoid an impending liquidity crisis and extend the average maturity of its debt. Substantial telco issuance remained a feature of the corporate sector. There was a brief market setback in February 2003 when the Dutch supermarket group Ahold confessed to a $880m profit overstatement in its US business, yet overall the corporate sector proved remarkably resilient.

By June the new issue market was deluged with borrowers as swap spreads reached record lows. GMAC re-opened the 30-year sector with a €1.5bn issue that formed part of a record $17.6bn borrowing package. One rare issuer, driven by currency swap opportunities, was the UK Treasury, launching their first dollar issue for seven years. The $3bn 2.25% five-year notes were priced to yield just two basis points over the equivalent Treasury issue yet still attracted $13bn of orders. With spreads on the best credits impossibly thin and interest rates continuing to decline, investors started to move down the credit curve in search of yield.

These conditions proved conducive to the launch of hybrid corporate debt. A €400m undated, subordinated issue for Linde, the German engineering and gases group, was well received by yield-hungry investors, allowing the company to gain equity credit from the rating agencies. Later in the year Michelin launched a 30-year euro-denominated subordinated bond which was increased from €300m to €500m and still oversubscribed. This issue strengthened the company balance sheet without diluting family shareholdings. By December corporate issuance in euros had broken the €150bn barrier.[42]

Against this benign background of low rates and seemingly insatiable investor appetite came a publication that rocked the cross-border bond markets. In October 2003 a group of leading European institutional fixed-income investors published a paper entitled 'Improving Market Standards in the Sterling and Euro Fixed Income Credit Markets'. The paper compiled by a working group of 26 leading investors, popularly labelled the 'Gang of 26', led by Barclays Global Investors, Gartmore Investment Management and Prudential M&G, called for improved documentation standards in the cross-border bond markets.

Among a list of seven proposals, their primary complaint was a lack of adequate protection in standard Eurobond documentation and a call for minimum covenants for investment grade corporate issuers. 'From an investor standpoint, fixed income investors are in the business of evaluating and pricing credit risk, and are generally not paid for being exposed to event risk,' declared the paper.[43] They described event risk as leveraged buy outs or break-up bids, or borrowers undertaking major balance sheet restructuring. There had been numerous high-profile examples of leverage takeovers resulting in considerable losses for bond investors. The group of 26 proposed the inclusion of a particular investor protection that had for a long time been a feature of the UK domestic corporate bond market, the change of control covenant or event risk put option. As they explain, 'The basic principle is that if the borrower is acquired, the deal has to be financed so that it is consistent with the pre-determined ratings level, otherwise existing bonds will have to refinanced as well.'[44] A typical change of control provision would provide that, on the occurrence of a takeover or merger leading to the acquisition of over 50% of the voting share capital, a change of control would be deemed to have occurred. If this is then coupled with a rating downgrade, typically to below investment grade, then the bondholders will have the right to put their bonds back to the issuer, normally at par.

The investor group also articulated a grave concern with negative pledge clauses in bond documentation. As the majority of issues in the cross-border bond markets were issued on a senior, unsecured, unsubordinated basis the key protection for investors is, or should be, the negative pledge clause. The negative pledge clause assures investors that no other similar borrowings will be granted security, and if they are, the same security will be granted to the previously unsecured bondholders. The group of 26 felt that 'The most common negative pledge in the European capital markets is so weak it is virtually meaningless, as it often excludes bank debt'.[45] This was indeed the case, as increasingly negative pledge clauses in international bond issues did not prevent issuers securing bank debt, or domestic debt in loan or bond form. Ever-increasing competition had encouraged increasing carve-outs in bond documentation by investment banks and their lawyers as a further way to win mandates. In fact often the protection was only with regard to 'listed securities denominated in currencies other than the issuer's own'. Nor did the clause protect against structural subordination to borrowings by subsidiaries, unless those subsidiaries were guarantor subsidiaries.

The investor group called for the wider use of credit ratings in bond issuance and enhanced levels of corporate disclosure. They pointed out that in the US companies must file their prospectuses, annual and quarterly reports, current announcements and shareholder circulars with the SEC. This is done via a centralised database (EDGAR) which can be accessed by all through a central website. In addition the DTC provided an issuer with information about the investors holding its securities (debt or equity), whereas in Europe typically issuers were not required to file documents electronically so company information was not freely and easily available to investors. Also the clearing systems through which securities are held do not disclose the identity of accountholders due to the bearer status of cross-border bonds. As a consequence issuers do not have access to the names of the holders or beneficial owners of their securities.

Would the Gang of 26 succeed in getting what they asked for? Well they certainly caused a wave of publicity and provoked debate between various market interests. Within weeks, Fitch Ratings took up the cause in a paper entitled 'Jumping the Queue', identifying examples where negative pledge and structural subordination provisions in European bond documentation proved to be of little value to investors. By July 2004 the Association of British Insurers (ABI) joined the debate supporting the Gang's proposals. The focus fell upon IPMA to debate the issues, via their Market Practices Committee, and respond to the market. Their initial focus was on the negative pledge clause and discussions as to whether it would be feasible to introduce a 'model' negative pledge clause. Despite almost two years of subsequent debate the investment banks rejected the idea of a model clause, with the capital markets' law firms being equally unenthusiastic. The investment banks tended to reject anything that might affect their competitive edge in winning mandates. The lawyers felt that having a 'model' clause could bring with it the likelihood of it being used unduly in the courts in possible disputes. The debate closed with IPMA circulating a rather weak note to its membership suggesting that they should no longer use the term 'senior' with regard to standard Eurobonds, but that investors should ascertain the level of seniority or otherwise, with each individual unsecured issue.

The debate on event risk was ultimately more successful. There had been calls for some time for change of control clauses to be introduced into corporate bond offerings. However with the prevailing condition of hungry investors chasing pretty much every corporate issue that came along, there was little pressure to force such a change. It would take a change in market conditions and some headline transactions to swing the debate toward the investors' case.

In April 2005 ISS Global, the Danish cleaning firm, outraged bond investors when a $3.8bn LBO organised by private equity firms, Goldman Sachs Capital Partners and EQT, loaded the company with debt. As a result €1.35bn of ISS bonds lost 25–30% of their value. Investors increasingly started to demand change of control clauses. A fund manager quoted in *EuroWeek* remarked: 'Throughout the credit rally of 2003, 2004, and early 2005 issuers were on top and they could get away with anything. Now some balance has returned. You have seen specific examples of event risk that have hurt European bondholders, such as LBO risk, and that has highlighted the issue for investors.'[46]

In February 2006 BAA, the UK airports operator, issued €2.85bn of bonds to finance a takeover of Budapest airport. A week later Grupo Ferrovial, the Spanish construction and infrastructure group, announced it was considering a takeover of BAA. The BAA bonds, which had no protective event risk covenant, fell sharply and their five-year CDS widened. Investors were alarmed and, as the new issue had not yet settled, they demanded the inclusion of a change of control clause in the offering, and they succeeded. From that point on, change of control clauses pretty much became the norm in corporate bond issues.

*   *   *

Covered bonds were increasingly making the headlines in the capital markets in the early years following the millennium. Yet the product had a long history dating back to 1769 when the Prussian king Frederick the Great introduced the '*Pfandbriefe*' system to ease credit after the Seven Years' War. A variant of covered bonds emerged in Denmark in 1795. Covered bonds are typically senior, secured obligations of a regulated financial institution. The bonds are secured by a pool of mortgage loans or public sector debt and they offer investors a preferential claim over these assets. (The original *Pfandbriefe* offered a direct claim on the pledged estates of the landowning nobility.) However there are some key differences with the typical asset-backed security. First, and most importantly, recourse on a covered bond is to the issuer; only if the issuer defaults do investors have access to the cover pool. Therefore interest and principal are paid from the general cash flows of the issuer and not from the asset pool, as would be the case with a securitisation. Also covered bonds, unlike many asset-backed securities, are kept *on* balance-sheet by the financial institution. The cover pool itself is dynamic, that is, the borrower can manage the pool as long as the required 'cover' is ensured. Covered bonds are typically subject to 'special' supervision including a special cover pool monitor and periodic audits of the cover pool by the cover pool monitor.

Strictly speaking, covered bonds cannot be considered Eurobonds, as they have domestic market origins and are normally subject to specific local laws. In Germany, the home of the largest covered bond market, the issuance of *Pfandbriefe* is bound by the regulations of the German Pfandbrief Act. These bonds, issued by German mortgage banks, represent the largest segment of the German private debt market, and until the late 1990s were largely the domain of domestic investors. Then international interest in covered bonds picked up due to the high credit quality available, the adoption of credit ratings, the low risk weighting and increasing liquidity provided by large, so-called 'jumbo' offerings. In fact the issuance of covered bonds had been declining until 2001, largely due to the reduction in *Pfandbriefe* issuance; nonetheless Germany had provided the template that other countries followed.

In 1999 France introduced its 'obligations foncières' and upgraded the level of investor protection for covered bond investors. By March 2001 the French market totalled €19.5bn. Spain had had covered bonds, 'cedulas', reaching back to the 1870s, but international interest grew with issuance expanding from €5.5bn in 2001 to €30bn in 2003. As the covered bond markets developed, Eurobond market methods of syndication, distribution and trading became the norm.

The big news in 2003 was the emergence of covered bond markets in Ireland and the UK. After three years' preparation, Ireland introduced its own covered bond legislation in the form of the Asset Covered Securities (ACS) Act. The German borrower, Depfa, opened this new market in February 2003 with a €3bn 3.25% five-year benchmark issue which was increased to €4bn. In the UK there was no covered bond law but growing interest in the product by UK financial institutions looking for alternative funding sources. HBOS tested the market in July with a structured transaction based on contract law. The structure involved Halifax selling its mortgage portfolio to a subsidiary, which then guaranteed the obligations of the issuer. The seven-year bond was awarded a triple A rating from the agencies as opposed to HBOS's own stand-alone AA rating. There was some concern whether traditional covered bond buyers, particularly in Germany, would accept this new contractually based offering. They need not have worried, the deal was healthily oversubscribed with 30% of the paper going to German accounts.[47] HBOS followed this transaction with a similarly structured 10-year issue in October. The door was now open for other UK financial institutions to follow.

Covered bond issuance averaged around €220bn between 2001 and end 2003 with the total volume of covered bonds outstanding in the EU at the end of 2003 surpassing €1.5trn. This had been prompted by a combination of factors: the adoption of new covered bond legislation in some countries along with the modernisation of existing covered bond legislation in certain other jurisdictions.[48] In July 2004 the European Covered Bond Council (ECBC) was launched by the European Mortgage Federation with a 'focus on the developments shaping the economic and regulatory environment at EU level. The goal is to enhance the visibility of covered bonds at the European and global level.'

*   *   *

Spreads on corporate bonds were at very low levels by the end of 2003 after having peaked in late 2001 and early 2002. Yet despite being a bumper year for the international bond markets 2003 would end on a down note.

Parmalat was a leading Italian Group in international dairy and food production famed for the development of UHT long-life milk. The company was founded in 1961 and after its initial success embarked aggressively upon the acquisition trail, starting with an acquisition in Brazil in the mid-1970s. Its most notable acquisition was the US food giant Beatrice Foods in 1997. Acquisitions were financed with debt and Parmalat became a relatively frequent issuer in the Euromarkets. As its debt grew to €6bn, bondholders were comforted by the company's oft repeated assurances of substantial cash reserves. A hiccup occurred in February 2003 when Parmalat was forced to abandon a planned 30-year bond issue when the news of Ahold's over-stated profits shook the market. Investors increased their scrutiny of all corporate deals, particularly those that were road-showing, and Parmalat's shares fell 30% and its CDS spreads ballooned out to 800 basis points as investors began to harbour doubts about the company's financial position. Parmalat gave its explanation for pulling the deal: 'the cost of the operation did not reflect the solidity of the group's fundamental debt position.'[49] In early December the market's concerns grew as Parmalat had difficulty redeeming a modest €150m bond issue. The company clearly had major liquidity issues and yet had reported €4.2bn of cash and liquid investments in September 2003 held in a Bank of America account on behalf of Parmalat's Cayman Island subsidiary, Bonlat. The unsettled bond payment prompted S&P to downgrade Parmalat by eight notches in 24 hours, from BBB- to CC. The market now feared an imminent default. On 23 December Bank of America stated that Parmalat's document showing the bank was holding €3.95bn of assets on behalf of the company was a forgery. On the following day Parmalat filed for bankruptcy. By 2004 Parmalat's debts were discovered to total €14.3bn, eight times what the firm had admitted. For 13 years the company had been overstating revenues and understating debts, creating a global web of over 260 offshore entities in the process. In addition, Calisto Tanzi, the company's founder and CEO, confessed to embezzling €470m personally to cover losses in family companies. Later, Bank of America's head of corporate finance in Italy admitted to participating in a kickback scheme with the company. Parmalat's 40,000 bondholders were wiped out.

The Parmalat debacle, dubbed 'Europe's Enron', alerted the Italian authorities and, more importantly, the European regulators in Brussels, to serious shortcomings in corporate governance and disclosure, auditing standards, bank due diligence processes and investor protection.

NOTES

1. Alasdair Murray, *A half-finished job: the EU's financial services action plan,* Centre for European Reform, Policy Brief, November 2002.

2. IFR, 2,000th Issue, *Eurobond Retrospective Roundtable*, 12 September 2013.
3. Moore, *Autostrade to the Superhighway*, p. 40.
4. *EuroWeek*, Issue 541, The Early Dawn of the Euro Market, 27 February 1998.
5. Frank J. Fabozzi and Moorad Choudary, *The Handbook of European Fixed Income Securities* (John Wiley & Sons, 2004) p. 173.
6. BIS Papers No. 12, *The influence of structural changes on market functioning and its implications for monetary policy: a focus on the Euro area,* Clerc, Drumetz and Haas, p. 47.
7. Fabozzi and Choudary, *The Handbook of European Fixed Income Securities,* p. 173.
8. *Euromoney*, Eurobonds: the joys of the new Euromarket, April 1999.
9. *Euromoney,* Hope, fear and wonder as a new market opens, August 1999.
10. *EuroWeek*, 20th Anniversary Issue, April 2007, p. 101.
11. *Euromoney*, September 1999.
12. Moore, *Autostrade to the Superhighway*, p. 55.
13. Fabozzi and Choudary, *The Handbook of European Fixed Income Securities,* p. 184.
14. IPMA 20th Anniversary Booklet, pp. 27–28.
15. IPMA, *The International Capital Markets 2000*, March 2000, p. 7.
16. Homa Motamen-Scobie, European Economics and Financial Centre, *The Impact of the Euro on the European Fixed Income Market: A Post-launch Appraisal and Outlook* (ISMA, 2000); Moore, *Autostrade to the Superhighway*, p. 65.
17. IPMA, *The International Capital Markets 2000*, March 2000, p. 5.
18. Andrew Beattie, *Market Crashes: The dotcom crash,* Investopedia Website.
19. ©The Economist Newspaper Limited, London, *That was then*, 26 January 2002.
20. *Euromoney*, Did underwriters do a good job?, June 2000.
21. ©The Economist Newspaper Limited, London, *That was then*, 26 January 2002.
22. *Euromoney*, Investors won't pick up cash calls, March 2001.
23. Waters Technology, *The Lost Generation of Corporate Bond Platforms*, 31 May 2013.
24. *Euromoney*, The new Italian connection, November 2001.
25. Moore, *Autostrade to the Superhighway*, p. 164.
26. The Bond Market Association, *European Bond Pricing Sources and Services: Implications for Price Transparency in the European Bond Market*, April 2005.
27. C. William Thomas, The Rise and Fall of Enron, *Journal of Accountancy*, April 2002.
28. Frank Portnoy, *Infectious Greed: How Deceit and Risk Corrupted the Financial Markets* (Profile Books Ltd, 2003) p. 319.
29. C. William Thomas, The Rise and Fall of Enron, *Journal of Accountancy,* April 2002.
30. Ibid.
31. *CNN/Money*, WorldCom files largest bankruptcy ever, 22 July 2002.
32. T.F. Stefano, WorldCom's Failure: Why Did It Happen? *E-Commerce Times*, 18 August 2005.
33. Portnoy, *Infectious Greed,* p. 371.
34. ©The Economist Newspaper Limited, London, *Darned SOX*, 14 September 2006.
35. ©The Economist Newspaper Limited, London, *Five years under the thumb*, 26 July 2007.
36. *Euromoney*, The new New Deal, September 2002.
37. IFLR, How collective action is changing sovereign debt, May 2003, pp. 19–23.
38. *Euromoney*, Blazing a trail down Mexico way, April 2003.
39. ©The Economist Newspaper Limited, London, *Tough Deal*, 3 March 2005.
40. ©The Economist Newspaper Limited, *A Victory by Default?*, 3 March 2005.
41. ©The Economist Newspaper Limited, London, *Tough Deal*, 3 March 2005.
42. *EuroWeek* 20th Anniversary Issue April 2007, p. 119.
43. *Improving Market Standards in the Sterling and Euro Fixed Income Credit Markets,* October 2003 (article put together and printed by a group of institutional investors).
44. Ibid.

45. Ibid.
46. *EuroWeek*, Rapid Recovery masks credit fears, 21 June 2005.
47. *Euromoney*, Covered bonds invade new markets, November 2003.
48. European Central Bank, *The Euro Bond Market Study*, December 2004, p. 38.
49. *EuroWeek*, Issue 792, 28 February 2003.

CHAPTER 9

Mark-to-Model

2004–2007

How long ago is history? The Chinese Premier Zhou Enlai in responding to a question in the early 1970s about the historical importance of the French Revolution famously responded that it was too early to say. On that basis none of our narrative is history. However commentators have subsequently reasoned that the Chinese leader misunderstood the question and believed the questioner was asking about the riots in Paris in 1968 some three years earlier. In 2009 readers of the BBC *History* magazine were polled to discover how long ago events had to be, to be considered history. Roughly 60% answered that it had to be at least a decade ago. Either way our final chapters may not be considered history, as our selection of events may not prove to be the most historically relevant. But to create a story of the market's first half century we must attempt to identify those developments that will prove to be of some historical significance.

As mentioned above, when the euro was launched some 75% of Euromarket issuance was on behalf of banks. Unlike corporates, banks' borrowings are driven by their regulatory capital requirements. The central stipulation of Basel I was that banks should keep a protective minimum capital reserve to asset ratio of 8%. Designed in the first instance for large, international G-10 banks, Basel I was subsequently adopted by banking supervisors in more than 100 countries. The capital markets quickly devised funding structures that would enable banks to receive capital treatment on their borrowings. In 1998 a number of amendments were made to Basel I. The Basel Committee decided to allow 'innovative capital instruments' designed to achieve cost effective Tier 1 capital without diluting common equity, but the use of such instruments was to be limited to 15% of total Tier 1 capital.

Post Basel I the bulk of issuance by banks was in the floating rate note sector as before, but was now structured as subordinated instruments to qualify as Tier 1, or more frequently, Tier 2 capital. However under the Basel rules once a Tier 2 instrument had five years left to run to maturity the capital value had to be amortised on a straight line basis: so with four years left to run only 80% of the borrowing would count as capital, with three years to run only 60% would count, and so on. To avoid this deterioration in its capital treatment the hybrid structurers came up with the idea of adding a borrower call feature when the note had five years left to run. So the typical subordinated issue was for ten years with a borrower's call in year five, i.e. 'ten years non-call five or 10NC5', in market parlance. But how would an investor know the bank would call the note? The structurers also added a punitive step-up in the coupon rate in year five if the borrower did not call the issue. So to avoid having to pay this higher coupon rate the bank would call the issue. The note also included replacement language, which meant if the issuer called the note it would be replaced with a subordinated note offering similar capital treatment. Upper Tier 2 floating rate notes had the same call and step-up features but had to be undated. The whole process offered a type of rolling quasi-equity for the banks.

For years banks issued thousands of such notes with the principal investors being other banks. It was like a term interbank market and these notes were liquid and traded on narrow bid to offer spreads. Banks would typically keep their Tier 1 and Tier 2 issuance towards the maximum allowed limits as it was a significantly cheaper option than having to raise equity.

In time most felt the original Basel Accord of 1988, with its crude single risk weights for a limited number of asset classes, had too little risk sensitivity and needed updating. A new capital framework was first proposed by the Basel Committee on Banking Supervision (BCBS) in June 1999. The most common criticism of Basel I was the undifferentiated pricing for corporate risk, which encouraged higher risk lending to lower quality corporates. Also the original Accord attracted widespread regulatory arbitrage; banks were able to decrease their regulatory capital requirements through securitisation techniques without necessarily lowering the economic risk on their portfolio. The new framework would seek to better align regulatory capital with the real economic risks of a bank's portfolio and provide better incentives for improved risk management.

There had been many industry advances since 1988 that were not reflected in the original Basel I framework. Risk and value-based management had become a core focus for the banking sector. Much work had been done on understanding inter-risk correlation and improving internal processes. The use of credit ratings had now become commonplace. Credit risk transfer technology with the widespread use of credit derivatives needed to be taken into account. Also after crises such as the collapse of Barings, there was an appreciation that other risks, such as operational risks, were also important.

The key principles of Basel II are enshrined in the three 'pillars' of the regime. Pillar One covers the minimum capital requirements which are now a function of credit risk, market risk (introduced in 1998) and operational risk. Required capital can now be calculated in a number of ways. The simplest or 'standardised' approach provides risk weights for a range of asset classes according to the credit ratings assigned by approved external rating agencies, a development not particularly welcomed by the ratings agencies. So, for example, in the case of a corporate exposure the risk weighting under Basel I would always have been 100%. Under Basel II if the company was rated AA- or better then the risk weighting was now 20%. However at the other end of the spectrum, if the company was rated below BB- then the rating was 150%.

Alternatively banks could opt for the 'internal ratings based' (IRB) approach either at a 'foundation' or 'advanced' level. This allowed them to calculate their minimum capital requirement from their own internal risk models. The amount of capital required is based on a statistical distribution of potential losses for a credit portfolio and is measured over a given period and within a specified confidence level. The IRB formula is based on a 99.9% confidence level and a one-year time horizon, that is, there is a 99.9% probability that the minimum amount of regulatory capital held by the bank will cover its economic losses over the next year. Where a bank uses the advanced approach the regulators will ensure its IT systems and loss databases meet stringent quality standards. Banks would expect to see some reduction in required capital using the IRB approach, so it provides an incentive for banks to improve their risk management capability.

Under Pillar Two banks are required to assess risks to their business not captured in Pillar One for which additional capital may be required, e.g. concentration risk, interest rate or liquidity risks. Under Pillar Three, capital adequacy must be reported through semi-annual public disclosures that are designed to provide transparent information on a bank's capital structure, risk exposures, and risk management and internal control processes.

A deadline of March 2000 was set for initial responses to the Basel Committee's proposals. The first consultation paper in 2001 outlined the main building blocks of the framework and set the deadline for implementation as 2004. This timetable proved too demanding and a further consultation paper set the deadline for 2006. But the debate and arguments ran for years. It was all far too complex with the final Basel II text, produced in 2004, running to over 1,000 pages. Many felt that the costs of implementation would outweigh the benefits. Others argued that Basel II would dangerously reinforce business cycles with banks encouraged to lend in good times when ratings were strong, but curtail their lending in a recession as credit ratings fall. SMEs and emerging market borrowers would find it more difficult to borrow under the new arrangements. Critics said Basel II favoured the big IRB banks who would now be incentivised to acquire unsophisticated smaller banks to release capital. There was concern that regulators would be ill-equipped to implement the new rules. Basel II would make securitisation less attractive to banks given the stricter capital requirements. Then again some felt the idea of an operational risk capital charge was wrong headed, arguing that operational risk is not unique to banks. Good management is the answer, not capital charges that might only encourage a false sense of security.

The extraordinary implementation delays for Basel II reflected its complexity and its controversial requirements. In the EU, Basel II was to be introduced via the Capital Requirements Directive (CRD) with implementation to be no later than 1 January 2007 for the standardised and foundation IRB approaches, and 1 January 2008 for the advanced approach – nine years after the original proposal. US banking regulators announced that they would apply Basel II to only 10 or 12 of the very large 'internationally active' US banks, it being optional for others, and implementation would be by 1 January 2009. While final implementation dates suffered considerable delays most major banks were busily preparing for the adoption of Basel II from at least 2004 onwards when the final agreed text 'International Convergence of Capital Measurement and Capital Standards, A Revised Framework' was published. At the same time a number of European countries were introducing new hybrid capital rules for financial institutions.

Against this background the subordinated floating rate note market and hybrid bank issuance saw renewed interest as the low interest rate environment in 2004 drove investors to seek higher returns. Hybrid transactions for insurers and re-insurers were also well received. For example in February a €1.5bn perpetual, non-call 10-year bond for Allianz attracted €6bn in orders and was increased from €1bn.[1] In the first quarter total FRN issuance was up 55%.

Meanwhile the corporate pipeline dried up. The 40% fall in corporate bond issuance was due in part to healthy corporate profits and a consequent reduced need to borrow and partly due to prefunding in the benign markets of 2003. One developing feature of the cross-border bond markets was the emergence of liability management transactions. In the first half of 2004 there were a number of corporate bond buybacks and bond exchanges. The principal driver of the activity was to extend maturities to lock in the low interest rate level. With low rates the high-yield market also saw increased levels of activity. Yet as of end-September 2004 Euroarea high-yield bond spreads averaged 326 basis points, a fifth of their September 2001 peak of 1578 basis points.[2]

* * *

Elsewhere structured transactions proved increasingly attractive to yield-hungry investors. The largest structured asset class was residential mortgage-backed securities which accounted for €133.5bn, or around 50% of the overall European securitisation market in 2003. This trend was most evident with UK and Netherlands-based issuers where the covered bond markets were less developed. Non-mortgage backed securitisations reached €37.9bn in 2003, led by UK credit card transactions.[3]

From 2000 onwards investment banks were distributing 'primers' on structured products to spark investor interest in the possible returns available. There was a developing group of sophisticated institutional investors that understood credit increasingly well, using credit derivatives to hedge their positions or gain exposure to a credit with single name CDS, thus enhancing efficiency and reducing the cost of their portfolio management. In addition the era of low interest rates was beneficial for hedge funds, as the availability of cheap credit made it easier for them to increase their leverage and consequently their investment activity, particularly in structured products. New variations on the basic CDS were being devised by structured product desks and marketed heavily to a growing band of credit market participants.

But the structured sector that dominated the headlines in 2004 was the Collateralised Debt Obligation (CDO) sector. The CDO market had started with balance sheet CDOs driven by bank regulatory capital arbitrage. Now with the expansion of credit derivatives, synthetic CDOs, like J.P. Morgan's BISTRO transaction rapidly came to dominate the sector. Synthetic CDOs substituted credit default swaps for the loans or bonds in a typical cash CDO. The investor in a synthetic CDO gains a credit exposure not by physically holding a bundle of loans or bonds but by selling protection on the assets to one or more counterparties. Synthetic CDOs took off because they were easier, and cheaper to create than traditional CDOs, with no mortgage assets to collect and finance. Consequently creating synthetic CDOs took a fraction of the time of a cash CDO. Moody's estimated that 92% of the European CDO market comprised synthetic issuance in 2003.

Synthetic CDOs of highly rated ABS had been popular for a few years but increasingly issuers experimented with more disparate types of collateral in more complex structures. *EuroWeek* records a typical CDO transaction for Pimco in February 2004:

> *Clarenville CDO pools an extremely broad range of assets including US and European leveraged loans, bonds (with a 10% bucket for high yield), default swaps, catastrophe bonds, ABS and exchangeable equity securities. Like Intercontinental, the group's first European CDO, Clarenville allows the manager to engage in naked short transactions by buying protection subject to interest coverage ratios. The deal also incorporates a natural hedge, by issuing the debt across three currencies, coupled with a portfolio hedge so that never more than £5m or $5m of the assets are unhedged.*[4]

Nor were the investment banks the only originators. Any bank or fund manager that could pool assets and launch a CDO was now doing so. Indeed the challenge increasingly became sourcing the necessary collateral. The booming CDO issuance forced tighter spreads in the European credit default swap market as issuers clamoured to hedge their deals. Before long synthetic CDOs referencing underlying CDOs or 'CDOs-squared' (CDO^2) were tailored to meet investor demand and allow more yield to be accumulated. The appetite for more complex structures such as CDOs-squared grew as spreads on investment grade corporate bonds tightened. According to Standard & Poors, CDO issuance increased by 77% in 2004. Synthetic CDO issuance would peak out at $105bn in 2007.

CDO issuance was not confined to an investment bank's new issue desk. The search for collateral typically involved secondary market trading desks. However by this time to talk in terms of a Eurobond secondary market as a stand-alone business misrepresents the revolution that had taken place in the secondary debt markets. Investment banks no longer talked of a bond trading desk but rather of a 'credit trading' desk.

The total size of the CDS sector had grown from less than $1trn at the start of the decade to $4.5trn notional principal outstanding in 2004 – by 2006 this would balloon to $26trn. Bond traders were now typically designated 'credit traders', and would offer two-way quotes in both bonds and CDS for credits in a particular market sector. Such was the growth of the credit derivatives market that traders reported in 2005 that enquiries in CDS outweighed those in bonds by 5 to 10 times and there was very active inter-dealer broker participation. The standard trading size in a single name CDS would be $5m notional principal but with investment grade names could be $10 to $20m.

According to Fitch Ratings in its 2003 credit derivatives survey, 65% of CDS were used to transfer or trade risk from the corporate sector, 17% from financial institutions and 6% from sovereigns. And 52% of CDS reference entities were rated single-A or higher. In their survey in May 2007, Fitch found that banks were increasingly using credit derivatives as trading tools rather than as hedging instruments.

Another innovation was credit default swaps on credit indices. In this case the reference entity was a diversified index of multiple names. Typically up to a hundred or more investment grade credits with actively traded CDS were selected with liquid debt outstanding. The index is priced at a fixed rate, which is a composite CDS spread agreed between the market-makers at the initiation of the index. The index gives each name equal weight in the index. When the index trades, the quoted price will vary from the fixed rate. A new index is reconstituted periodically, as merged names and downgrades are dropped and new names added. Market-makers will then quote a new fixed rate for the new index and market participants will trade out of the old, and 'roll' into the new liquid index.

Meeting market demand for greater liquidity, transparency and diversification, iTraxx CDS indices were launched in 2004 in conjunction with a group of major investment banks. These rules-based indices comprised the most liquid names in the European and Asian markets. The Benchmark indices in Europe were the iTraxx Europe, the iTraxx Europe Hi Vol and the iTraxx Europe Crossover. The constituents of the iTraxx Europe are the top 125 names with the highest CDS trading volumes selected by dealer poll for the six months prior to the 'roll'. The iTraxx Hi Vol is a subset of the Europe 125; the senior credits with the widest five-year CDS spreads, excluding financials. Finally the iTraxx Europe Crossover gives exposure to 50 European sub-investment grade reference entities.

The tradable iTraxx indices could be used by investors to hedge entire or partial portfolios in one simple transaction, rather than needing numerous single name CDS transactions. Positions could easily be rolled forward or closed as required in only one transaction. These indices were efficient to trade with the typical transaction size being €50- 100m. The liquidity of the product attracted new investors, particularly hedge funds. Investors could express their bullish or bearish views on credit as an asset class, while having the low costs associated with static portfolios and the flexibility to actively manage credit portfolios.

While investors use CDS indices to trade large positions in credit names without having direct exposure to the underlying securities, these same instruments allow other participants, such as speculators and arbitrageurs, to take part in this market. Taking a long position in, say, iTraxx Europe – the main investment grade index of 125 equally-weighted names – without exposure to a cash bond position, offers upside potential in case of underlying credit deterioration.

Some credit indices are in tranched format. For example, the iTraxx Europe has five liquid tranches. The lowest tranche, or equity tranche, absorbs the first 3% of losses on the index due to defaults. As it is an equally weighted index of 125 credits, so the reference weight of each credit is 0.8% ($\frac{1}{125}$) of the notional of the index portfolio. Exposure to €30m notional of the equity tranche (0–3%) implies an exposure to €1bn notional of the underlying index and a €8m exposure to each of the individual index credits.

Thanks to the different iTraxx indices (Europe, HiVol, Corp), the sub-sectors (TMT, Autos, etc) and the maturities traded (five and ten years), it now became easy to execute 'curve' trades (i.e. taking advantage of changes in the shape of the yield curve) and relative-value trades between sectors. Also it was possible to trade within the same sector, buying or selling single names versus their sector, e.g. buying the technology, media and telecommunications (TMT) index protection and selling Telefónica, if it is believed the Spanish multinational will outperform the sector.

Tradable synthetic indices brought high volume, low margin trading to credit for the first time and provided a new way to take or hedge exposure to the broad credit market. But times moved rapidly on from simply trading synthetic indices to trading slices or tiers of credit indices and thereby trading or speculating on credit correlation.

Once CDS are pooled into a portfolio, the issue of correlation arises, between both spreads and defaults among assets in the pool. Correlation addresses the distribution of defaults throughout a portfolio and the likelihood of a single default causing a host of defaults. In an untranched portfolio, the correlation between credits defaulting has an effect on the value of the basket, but only when the whole market is performing poorly and correlation between names is high. However when portfolios are tranched the relative value of default correlation becomes important. Banks and hedge funds created a market for credit, based on the correlation between defaults, that is, correlation spread trading. Many investment banks or securities houses established a correlation trading desk as part of their credit trading activities.

A popular tranche trade in 2004, particularly for hedge funds, was to go long the equity tranche or 'first loss' tranche, as they were comfortable with the default risk. At the same time they would go short the mezzanine or senior tranches as they were more nervous about spreads widening. To hedge the spread risk they would buy protection on the mezzanine or senior tranches, which proportionally carried more spread risk than default risk compared to the equity tranche. Unfortunately the General Motors and Ford downgrades in May 2005 sparked turmoil in the tranche markets and investors learnt that equity and senior tranches reacted differently to single name shocks.

Another key product was the single-tranche collateralised debt obligation, where only one tranche of the capital structure is sold to an investor. Essentially, the value of the lowest tranches of a CDO increases as the correlation between defaults falls and decreases as default correlation rises. The more the defaults within a basket become correlated, the more the portfolio behaves like a single credit. The probability of the equity tranche being wiped out becomes similar to the probability of the most senior tranches being wiped out.

By delta hedging a single tranche CDO, a trader can eliminate most, if not all, of the sensitivity to individual credit spreads in the reference portfolio. What remains unhedged is the exposure to correlation.[5] The development of a bespoke tranche market made the pricing and risk management of correlation key. Some dealers managed their correlation risk by taking offsetting positions in tranches of the standardised credit indices. But with the names in the indices and those on a bespoke tranche likely to be different, the trader remained exposed to the possibility that default correlation might change differently in the two portfolios.[6] There was little consensus among players; each bank had its own model of how default correlation should be calculated and how it should be priced. Banks worked on formulating their own default correlation models. In terms of valuation of tranche CDOs, 'Mark to model' rather than 'mark to market' became the new mantra.

In the early days of the international bond market, traders typically had little formal higher education and some, allegedly, had honed their trading skills as 'barrow boys' in street markets. These new structured credit traders were required to have a PhD in mathematics and advanced C++ computing skills to devise and operate complex credit pricing models.

This all seems a long way from traditional Eurobond trading. However these developments in structured products had significant effects on the underlying bond markets and the pricing of credit. The demand by structured credit desks or credit correlation desks in both banks and hedge funds affected the price of credit yet had little to do with a true assessment of the credit quality of the underlying corporate or financial. With the pressing demand to create synthetic CDOs, either single or multi-tranche, correlation desks required exposure to a diverse spread of names. Top quality names were in short supply but were consistently required to balance out CDOs of lesser rated credits. This demand drove down the CDS prices on credits such as Nestlé or Unilever to just a few basis points. This price reflected excessive demand and lack of available deliverables, rather than their intrinsic credit quality.

A further consequence of the CDO boom was that structuring desks were typically sellers of protection in the CDS market, i.e. they wanted exposure to a range of credits. So CDS trading desks tended to be continuously buying protection with the consequent negative 'carry' (that is, paying the insurance premium if you like). To counterbalance this, the trader would hold numerous blocks of bonds on his book (perhaps $300–500m each) to provide regular income, which he was reluctant to sell. As a result the cash bond market became less liquid.

There were perhaps other less obvious consequences of the transition from bond trading to credit trading. If credit traders were now more frequently trading CDS than bonds, then the market was more the domain of ISDA rather than ISMA. Coupled with the demise of the Coredeal project, ISMA's Council of Reporting Dealers was proving to be less relevant to member banks and attendance at meetings started to fall away. ISMA needed to adapt to the new environment.

$$* \quad * \quad *$$

In late 2004 a group of the major investment banks, principally led by the US houses, circulated a letter to the financial trade associations in London requesting that they instigate talks with a view to possible mergers among themselves. The banks argued that they were members of too many associations, and some overlapped in their roles and their oversight. It was felt that, as the regulatory landscape was changing rapidly with the approaching implementation deadlines for the Lamfalussy Directives, fewer but larger trade associations representing more influential constituencies would be more effective in lobbying with the regulators in Brussels.

Certainly ISMA had been largely focused on building up the Trax business and electronic trading rather than the external challenges from Brussels. The association had a single advisor on regulatory matters who had been hired in 1999 as head of market supervision at Coredeal.

On the other hand, apart from the IPMA Match project, IPMA's focus had been largely on the external regulatory environment and in 2004 a further advisor was hired from the FSA to make up an entire staff of seven. But with a much smaller membership representing only the new issue houses, IPMA's overriding limitation was funding the work they were doing.

By year-end, talks were underway between three associations, ISMA, IPMA and the more equity market-focused London Investment Bankers Association (LIBA) with a view to a possible three-way merger. After some months of negotiation and mutual due diligence, LIBA withdrew from the talks, and in February 2005 ISMA and ICMA announced their intention to merge and to name the merged association the International Capital Market Association (ICMA). ICMA would have 'a broad franchise across the primary and secondary sectors of the international capital market. This merger will significantly increase the effectiveness of our advocacy work with the European Union and the EU member states, and in the United States and Asia. The timing is right as Europe works to create a single, integrated market for financial serves.'[7] The press release finished by inviting other associations to join ICMA.

By April things had moved on. It was announced that the Bond Market Association intended to now 'integrate their European based activities into ICMA and establish a global partnership between the BMA and ICMA'.[8] The Bond Market Association was a US trade body for the fixed income markets which had its roots in the US municipal bond market. They had embarked upon a global expansion strategy in 1997. Unfortunately this did not always sit well with the existing trade associations in geographical regions where the BMA set up their new offices. In Europe they targeted sectors of the European markets overlooked by ISMA. They established the European Securitisation Forum as an affiliate trade body for the asset-backed sector in Europe and the European High Yield Association similarly for the speculative grade bond market. In response to the notorious Citigroup/EuroMTS government bond trading incident in August 2004 they opportunistically established the European Primary Dealers Association to be a voice for that sector. Undoubtedly the call by the US banks for trade association mergers was particularly focused on the overlap of representation by the BMA and ISMA and IPMA. The tentative language of the April press release suggested the sensitivity involved in forging such a link between the bodies, but also its potential importance.

It was further proposed that Hans-Joerg Rudloff, by now Chairman of Barclays Capital, would become Chairman of ICMA, while the head of BMA International would become Chief Executive of the newly formed body.

In the fractious days that followed the announcement it transpired that not all parties had been consulted in the negotiations for this latest proposal. However it became apparent that the BMA's European presence was subsidised by its US operations and on the basis of insufficient funding for the new arrangement, the integration proposal was unfortunately abandoned. ICMA, the merger of ISMA and IPMA, officially started operations in July.

*   *   *

The bond markets opened cautiously in 2005 with worries of a weakening dollar, expectations of rising inflation and the consequent danger of higher rates and widening spreads from their historically low levels. They were wise to be cautious.

On 5 May, the Ascension Day holiday in Europe, S&P downgraded General Motors and its financing arm, GMAC, by two notches to BB and cut Ford and Ford Motor Credit one notch to BB+, with a negative credit outlook for all four entities. The US auto companies had been experiencing difficulties for some time, principally due to a loss of share in the North American market to Asian competitors. While spreads on their corporate debt had been widening as the companies' finances became more strained, the downgrade to junk status rocked the bond markets as Ford and GMAC paper were staples of many fixed income portfolios. The bond spreads immediately moved out by 100 basis points and the entire speculative grade bonds sector widened 1.5% to 2% on the concern that the size of the high-yield market was not sufficiently large to absorb all the outstanding paper issued by the two firms and their affiliates. However in the new trading environment it was the effects on the CDS market that were of greater concern to practitioners. The fear was that GM and Ford CDS featured in hundreds, if not thousands of CDO packages – and many investors might be unaware of their exposure. Synthetic CDO correlation trades (i.e. buying high risk tranches while selling low risk tranches) were particularly favoured by hedge fund investors so a further worry was that a number of hedge funds might face difficulties with the sharp downgrades.

In fact the panic was short-lived as within a month the spreads on the debt of both companies started to narrow after they both released restructuring plans. However the downgrades had served to alert the markets and the regulators about possible contagion effects in the now largely derivatives-based credit markets. The fact that the notional value of traded credit derivatives often far exceeded the amount outstanding of the relevant corporate bonds caused concern among the investment community. This came into sharp relief in October 2005 when Delphi, the largest US auto parts maker, filed for bankruptcy. The CDS on Delphi's debt in the market exceeded the value of its bonds tenfold. In fact, in this case, the market handled settlement of contracts quite efficiently. An auction was organised to set the reference price of the underlying bond and the CDS contracts were settled in cash relative to this reference price.

Of further concern as CDS trading proliferated was a growing settlement backlog. During 2005 just under a 150,000 CDS trades were executed monthly, while outstanding CDS confirmations exceeding 30 days approached 100,000 a month. In September 2005 the Federal Reserve obtained a commitment from 14 major dealers to upgrade their systems and reduce the backlog. Industry participants promised to introduce more electronic trading and confirmation systems.

Despite the turmoil in the CDS market and the settlement backlog the market continued to expand at a staggering rate. Outstanding notional principal had increased from $5.4trn in mid-2004 to $8.4trn at the end of 2004 to $12.4trn in mid-2005, a 128% increase.[9]

* * *

As part of the Financial Services Action Plan (FSAP) launched in 1999, EU Member States were required to have written the key securities Directives into their national law by 1 July 2005. It turned out that many countries failed to meet the deadline and Internal Market and Services Commissioner Charles McCreevy complained: 'Over the last six years we have made great strides towards a more open, integrated and competitive European financial market. However, some Member States are still lagging behind on the securities Directives. This is frankly very disappointing, bordering on the lamentable. This is going to hamper the efficiency of Europe's capital markets and the vital "single passport for issuers".'

The key Directives were the Prospectus Directive and the Market Abuse Directive. They came into effect in 2003, to be implemented in July 2005, and were both largely 'maximum harmonisation Directives', permitting no further amendments or additions by Member States. In addition the Transparency Directive and the Savings Tax Directive came into force in July 2005.

The purpose of the Prospectus Directive was to unify the law on what information must be disclosed when offers of debt or equity securities are made to the public in any Member State of the EU (in fact it applies to the wider European Economic Area (EEA), thus including Iceland, Norway and Liechtenstein). It harmonised the law on when a prospectus must be produced, what information it must contain and who approves the prospectus.

While the duty to produce a statutory information document in order to obtain admission to a securities trading market was not new, its introduction for public offers increased the regulation of the Eurobond markets. Under the Public Offers Directive, the predecessor of the Prospectus Directive, all 'Eurosecurities' fulfilling certain criteria were exempt, while a number of other exemptions were available.

The new Directive required the publication of a prospectus where securities were being offered to the public or admitted to a 'regulated market' – EU terminology for an organised and supervised securities trading market such as a stock exchange. It also listed situations where a prospectus was not required for a particular public offer.

The Prospectus Directive and a related Regulation prescribed in detail what information needed to be included in the prospectus for particular types of securities and issuers. The level of required information was greater for bonds with what was deemed a 'retail' denomination of less than €50,000 than for those with a higher 'wholesale' denomination (and, for both, is less extensive than that for equity securities). As of 1 January 2005, all EU issuers were required to adopt International Financial Reporting Standards (IFRS) or 'equivalent' generally accepted accounting principles. Information prepared according to other 'non-equivalent' standards must be restated. However there was no restatement obligation for offers of debt, derivative or asset-backed securities having a per unit denomination of at least €50,000.

The prospectus had to be approved by the regulator and made public before the offer could start or before the securities were admitted to trading. To facilitate a pan-European market, the Prospectus Directive also allowed a prospectus approved in one EEA member state to be used for a public offer or admission to trading in other EEA member states subject to 'passporting'. Prospectuses approved in the home jurisdiction were valid throughout the EEA on a passported basis for up to 12 months – provided they were supplemented with any significant new information.

In the case of issuance of an MTN programme the prospectus containing the pre-agreed terms was now termed a 'base prospectus'. For each issue under the programme, the issuer prepares only the 'final terms', little more than a term sheet specifying details of the issue and linking to the full description of the product in the base prospectus.

The implementation of the Prospectus Directive had an impact on the primary markets as borrowers brought forward issuance into the second quarter of 2005 ahead of its implementation. Issuance slumped in the third quarter and only picked up in the fourth quarter when issuance programmes had been updated in light of the Directive.

The EU Market Abuse Directive (MAD) replaced the old Insider Dealing Directive, and introduced a common EU legal framework for preventing and detecting market abuse and for ensuring a proper flow of information to the market.

Market abuse can occur as a result of insider dealing, i.e. acting on 'unpublished price sensitive information' (UPSI). The MAD defines inside information as information that is precise, non-public and likely to have a significant impact on the price of a financial instrument, i.e. information a reasonable investor would be likely to use in making investment decisions. The MAD imposes an obligation on issuers to disclose inside information as soon as possible, and issuers and their advisers are required to keep lists of persons who have access to inside information.

Market manipulation or 'price rigging' is forbidden under the Market Abuse Directive. Market manipulation comprises three forms: transactions and orders to trade that give false or misleading signals or secure the price of a financial instrument at an artificial level; transactions or orders to trade that employ fictitious devices; and distribution of information likely to give false or misleading signals. However the MAD permits market behaviour that might otherwise be viewed as manipulation, where the conduct in question is an accepted market practice in the market concerned and where there are legitimate reasons for behaving in that way. It is under this concession that primary market stabilisation practices are permitted.

Since stabilisation effectively involves creating an artificial market; it is allowed only under specific conditions which, if adhered to, provide a legal 'safe harbour'. It must be preceded and followed by detailed announcements and limited in time. In addition, all the stabilisation trades must be reported to the regulator. One limitation which had not been anticipated by the market was that syndicate managers would be restricted to an over-allotment of 5%. IPMA's Market Practices Committee were unhappy with this development having traditionally stabilised new issues to between 10% and 15%; they felt that a 5% limit would be insufficient in many cases to create an orderly primary market. In practice it transpired that certain regulators took the view that over-allotment may go higher if there is very good reason to do so. It remains an activity subject to close scrutiny by the regulators.

The MAD also required that those who produce or disseminate investment research must take reasonable care to ensure that information is fairly presented, and disclose their interests or indicate conflicts of interest concerning the securities to which the research relates.

Unlike the Directives above, the Transparency Directive was a 'minimum harmonisation' Directive allowing home Member States to impose additional requirements on issuers. The Directive was designed to enhance transparency on EEA capital markets by establishing minimum requirements on periodic financial reporting and on the disclosure of major shareholdings for issuers whose securities are admitted to trading on a regulated market in the EU. As with the Prospectus Directives it required the use of IFRS (or equivalent) for financial statements, except for issues with minimum denomination over €50,000.

The three broad areas covered under the Directive are the minimum content of annual, half-yearly and interim management statements; the notification requirements of both issuers and investors in relation to the acquisition and disposal of the major holdings in companies; and the method of disseminating and storing the required information on a pan-European basis. In line with Sarbanes-Oxley, annual and half-yearly financial reports now required management 'certification' confirming that the accounts were accurate and that management accepted liability for any errors and omissions.

The Transparency Directive also required immediate disclosure of any significant financial news, i.e. news that might reasonably be expected to affect investment decisions. In addition all regulated information needed to be stored and be easily accessible.

Throughout its history, the Eurobond market, with its tradition of bearer securities, enjoyed uneasy relations with European tax authorities. For 40 years the market lived in fear of the imposition of withholding taxes in one or more jurisdictions. In December 1997, EU Finance Ministers requested Brussels to come up with a scheme to prevent EU residents from evading tax by investing their savings outside their home countries. The following May, the European Commission published a proposal for new legislation, the 'Savings Directive', to ensure individuals within the EU paid the tax due on 'cross-border' interest payments. As initially drafted, Member States would have had to choose either to withhold tax at 20% on these payments or to provide the recipient's state with enough information about them to ensure that they could be taxed on receipt. After a barrage of lobbying, highlighting concerns about the possible impact on Europe's financial markets, and in particular the Eurobond market, a revised draft was tabled, based on the exchange on information between states, and was approved in July 2001.

In January 2003 European Finance Ministers reached political agreement that 12 states would implement arrangements for the 'automatic exchange of information' whereby each financial institution that acted as a paying agent would transfer information on actual interest payments to the authorities in the EU member country in which the final beneficiary was domiciled.

Although the Directive is based on 'automatic exchange of information', three EU Member States (Austria, Belgium and Luxembourg) initially opted to apply a withholding tax instead for a 15-year transitional period. Under the withholding tax option, banks automatically withheld tax (at a rate of 15% for the first three years, then 20% for the following three years, and 35% thereafter) from interest paid to individuals resident in other EU Member States. However no information regarding individuals was provided to the tax authorities either in the state in which the individual was resident or the state in which the bank account was located. It was the Bank's responsibility to pay the withholding tax on behalf of the customer. Under the withholding tax option the jurisdiction must also offer to customers automatic exchange of information and/or a system whereby the customer obtains from their local tax authority a certificate which details the source from which the interest payment arises.

During the transitional period in 2010 Belgium decided to give up the withholding tax option and joined the information exchange, while Luxembourg subsequently announced it would make the shift to automatic exchange in 2015. Both of these decisions were a testimony to how effectively the information exchange worked in practice.

Despite this raft of Directives being implemented there was no sense among securities market practitioners that the regulator's work was largely done. Eurobond houses now had to focus their attention on Brussels' plan to undertake a major overhaul of the Investment Services Directive (ISD) to adapt it to modern market conditions. The new Directive, which would be named the Market in Financial Instruments Directive (MiFID), was planned for implementation in November 2007. MiFID sought to introduce greater competition in the secondary markets, to extend the range of investment services and products that are regulated, and to harmonise regulations at a greater level of detail than hitherto.

*   *   *

Mergers and acquisitions, particularly cross-border M&A, was now experiencing a resurgence. For example, in October 2005 the markets were taken by surprise by Telefónica's audacious £18bn ($32bn) bid for O2. Telefónica's CFO maintained that favourable bank lending conditions were the single biggest factor in the timing of the offer. Telefónica raised the largest syndicated loan in Europe since France Télécom's record-setting €30bn ($36bn) loan in 2000, when it bought Orange. This was largely successfully refinanced in the bond markets over the next 12 months.

Meanwhile low rates continued to fuel the housing market in the US with real estate prices reaching new highs. Rising home prices led to rampant real estate speculation, and fuelled excessive consumer spending as people viewed their homes increasingly as a source of cash for discretionary purchases. With the ability to package mortgages into opaque CDOs and offload them to investors, banks were enticed to loosen their lending standards, lowering down-payment requirements, allowing more debt versus income, and offering mortgages with little to no income verification. Adjustable rate mortgages (ARMs) became popular with initial 'teaser' rates as low as 1% for the first year. The borrower believed, or was encouraged to believe, that as the value of his house would continue to increase, he would have plenty of equity to cover the increased mortgage payment when his adjustable monthly payment increased.

As 2006 dawned it was a case of 'God's in His heaven; all's right with the world!' The benign market conditions continued with new issuance records being broken around the world. In the equity market, the world's largest IPO was launched for the Industrial and Commercial Bank of China (ICBC). ICBC was simultaneously listed on both the Hong Kong and Shanghai Stock Exchanges in October 2006 with a valuation of US$21.9bn.

In the loan markets the largest ever syndicated loan was arranged for the German utility E.On, for an amount of $37.1bn to support its increased offer for Endesa, the Spanish electrical company. In fact the loan was later abandoned when E.On's bid fell through. In the US, Hospital Corporation of America, the largest US hospital management company, was the subject of the biggest ever leveraged buy out at $33bn, surpassing that of Kohlberg Kravis Roberts' for RJR Nabisco in 1989.

In the Eurobond market, against a backdrop of unprecedented issuance of UK mortgage-backed securities, Lloyds TSB made its debut by launching a £7.02bn deal, the world's largest ever securitisation. The deal, issued through its Arkle Master Issuer Trust Programme, was backed by £19.75bn of prime residential mortgages originated by Lloyds TSB's subsidiary Cheltenham & Gloucester, the UK's third-largest mortgage lender. The company considered a number of options, including covered bonds, before opting for the residential mortgage-backed securities (RMBS) market, preferring, according to a spokesman, a strategy of origination and distribution rather than origination and hold. Arkle attracted £10bn in orders from around 200 investors, including a single order of £2bn, which allowed the deal to be increased in size from an original £5.6bn. Barely a month later, Lloyds TSB launched a second Arkle RMBS offering for £3.256bn equivalent with a similar structure to the inaugural issue.[10]

2006 also saw the largest ever high-yield bond issue by a European company, NXP Semiconductors (formerly part of Phillips), denominated in both euros and dollars for an amount of €4.53bn equivalent; it was also the largest ever technology leveraged buy out in Europe. The transaction consisted of five separate bond tranches and a revolving credit facility in order to avoid the need for contractual amortisation or bank-style 'maintenance-based' covenants.[11]

US investment bank earnings reached a record $145.2bn in 2006 reflecting the surging stock and bond markets and the unprecedented level of takeover activity.[12] Goldman Sachs distributed a whopping $16bn bonus pool to its employees. And US government data showed that the average pay in investment banking was now 10 times that of all private sector jobs.[13]

However *Euromoney* pointed out that things were not so buoyant in the Euromarkets:

> *As a rule in the debt capital markets arena, fees are falling; where they are not, issuers are demanding more services, or they are asking for direct subsidies, as is very common in the financial institutions business. Even subordinated bank deals are becoming loss leaders. Structured finance has not been immune to this process. Residential mortgage-backed securities are now a completely commoditised business. Taking risk through principal finance or having proficiency in relatively opaque sectors such as CDOs is crucial to making any kind of money. Debt capital markets have become a commoditised world where the most efficient producer wins. There is*

no secret related business that makes it more profitable than it appears at face value.
It's a grind, pure and simple. Given that there is very little that can be done about
top line revenues, the focus must be on costs. And that means the bonus pools will be
getting smaller.[14]

In the pursuit of better margins, ABN Amro devised a new CDO-based product that appeared to achieve the holy grail for investors: a high margin instrument with a triple-A rating. The Constant Proportion Debt Obligation (CPDO) appeared at the peak of the market for structured products and was subsequently viewed as the poster child for the excesses of financial engineering in the credit market. The first CPDO issue, ABN Amro's Surf, was arranged in the summer of 2006, closed in November and was heralded as 'a breakthrough in synthetic credit instruments'. The Surf notes were rated triple-A by Standard & Poor's, yet offered a coupon of 200 basis points over Libor.

The CPDO was the latest in a long line of structured instruments which had started life many years earlier as principal-protected notes for retail customers. Buy a risk-free instrument to protect principal then invest in a particular risk sector to provide your returns. This concept developed into Constant Proportion Portfolio Insurance, which involved a degree of principal protection coupled with leveraged exposure to a risky credit portfolio. The CPDO did away with principal protection and in fact involved increased leverage if payments under the instrument could not be covered.

In a simplified description of the structure, firstly, the proceeds of sale of the CPDO notes are put into high quality collateral, a cash deposit or invested in a zero coupon bond paying par at maturity (typically 10 years). Secondly, the issuer sells protection (five-year contracts) on both the investment grade European iTraxx and the US equivalent Dow Jones CDX index referencing the 125 most liquid names, reset every six months. On the index roll date, the SPV must purchase protection on the off-the-run index and sell protection on the on-the-run index. By continually buying and selling derivatives on the underlying index, the administrator of the CPDO will be able to customise the amount of leverage it employs in an attempt to make additional returns off the index price spreads at any given time to generate the returns for the coupon and maturity payments during the CPDO's lifetime.

If a CPDO's net asset value (i.e. the sum of the value of the cash deposit and the mark-to-market value of the risky portfolio versus the present value of all future payments to be made by the SPV) deteriorates the arranger will take on additional exposure, by buying or selling index protection, in order to recoup his losses. This increased leverage as net asset value falls increases the structure's probabilities to pay coupons and principal and so earned CPDOs their high credit ratings.

Surf created a great deal of both interest and controversy when it first appeared, with some analysts dubious of the credit ratings assigned to the issue. In November 2006 S&P wrote a special report hailing the arrival of CPDOs. Interestingly in the months S&P had worked with ABN Amro, S&P had not developed a CPDO valuation model and had agreed to use ABN Amro's own proprietary model.[15] Other banks quickly copied ABN Amro's lead and around €2bn of CPDOs were sold by the end of the year.

In January 2007 *Risk Magazine* awarded ABN Amro's Surf transaction 'structured product of the year'. The great bulk of CPDO issuance, about $5bn, took place in late 2006 and spring 2007. At this time corporate credit spreads were at a cyclical low point and volatility in credit spreads had been subdued for three years. This would change dramatically in 2007 and the first CPDO default would be in November 2007.

In 2008 *Euromoney* mused: 'CPDOs are the apogee of the excesses of the credit bubble. Financial engineers created an instrument that combined opacity, complexity and leverage in spades. If a banker sat down with an investor today and offered them a structured product with a 200bp spread over a CDS index there would be a robust debate about its merits. If it was then explained that this yield was only attainable because the structure was 15 times leveraged, incredulity would probably turn rapidly to laugh-out-loud mockery.'[16]

* * *

With its new Chairman, Hans-Joerg Rudloff, ICMA set about reorganising the association to meet the needs of the modern market. In June 2006 news came that the US banks had pushed through a merger of the Bond Market Association (BMA) and the Securities Industry Association (SIA), the two largest securities associations in the US. The new industry group would be named the Securities Industry and Financial Markets Association (SIFMA). SIFMA became the new umbrella organisation for the European Primary Dealers Association, the European Securitisation Forum and the European High Yield Association in Europe.

Rudloff raised the profile of ICMA in the international markets by hiring René Karsenti in June 2006 as Executive President. Karsenti had been the longstanding Director of Finance of the EIB, the most prolific issuer in the Eurobond market, having been previously the first Treasurer of the EBRD. Bank mergers and acquisitions had meant that all financial trade associations had experienced declining membership with a resultant pressure on their finances. To offset this trend, Karsenti encouraged the association to open up membership to other constituencies. Over the next years, borrowers, investors and lawyers were all invited to become members or associate members of ICMA.

A refocusing of activities was also required. While the market services side of the association, notably Trax, had been a cash cow for many years, changes were afoot in the trade reporting space and revenues going forward would likely be under increased threat. Competing platforms were moving into the area with the result that the association was taking increased commercial risk. The aborted Coredeal experiment had already given the membership a taste of commercial failure. It was increasingly felt that, as a non-profit-making trade association, ICMA should exit 'market services'. In addition, with the implementation of MiFID little more than a year away, with its focus on pre- and post-trade transparency, it would be difficult to objectively advise member banks on price transparency when the association had its own proprietary reporting platform. So the Board of ICMA set in train the process of separating the market services division from the trade association and in 2008 ICMA Ltd became Xtrakter Ltd with a separate management.

One outstanding project on the IT side was the IPMA Match cross-market bookbuilding platform. The project had had a chequered history. The participating banks had been locked in for the initial three years of the project. As the third anniversary approached some banks were successfully using the service on a regular basis in live new issue transactions. Other issuing houses were continuing to experience glitches in the system and were uncertain whether to commit further after the initial period. In the end a small group of issuing houses pulled out of the system. Nonetheless this was sufficient to leave such a hole in the funding that IPMA, now ICMA, could no longer oversee the project. ICMA had to withdraw its participation. However the software provider offered to try to maintain the service with its modest finances for as long as they could. The renamed 'Issuenet' service continued and remains the only cross-market bookbuilding service to this day.

ICMA now invested heavily in developing the market practice and regulatory policy area of the association with key hires from regulators, law firms and other associations. This proved timely for the regulatory tsunami which lay ahead.

* * *

Owning your own home had long been trumpeted as the 'American dream'. The US housing bubble that began in 2001, fuelled by historically low interest rates, reached its peak in the second quarter of 2006 with house prices 132% higher than they had been in the first quarter of 1997. Between 2004 and 2006 US interest rates rose from 1% to 5.35%, triggering a slowdown in the US housing market. So from mid-2006 US house prices began declining but only modestly at first: just 2% from the second to the fourth quarter of 2006. There was no panic as people consoled themselves that US home prices had not fallen nationwide in any single year since the Great Depression.

Between 1980 and 2007, mortgage-related and asset-backed securities accounted for the majority of growth in the US bond market. By 2007, mortgage-related securities accounted for 25.3% of outstanding US bonds. The increased securitisation of home mortgage debt and the development of CDO technology had contributed to relaxed mortgage standards and the rise in 'subprime' mortgages. These are home loans given to people who are a poor credit risk and with weak documentation of income. Often they were 'ninja' loans, extended to those with 'no income, and no job'. Back in 1995 the subprime mortgage-backed market was around $65bn, by 2006 it was almost ten times that with issuance reaching $600bn, accounting for 20% of home loans. In the low-return bond market environment of 2006 and 2007, investors snapped up mortgage-backed securities of lower and lower quality, seduced by the high yields on offer.

Loan originators were less concerned about the credit standing of the individual mortgagee as the loan would be packaged with other loans of varying quality and sold to investors in a CLO or CDO structure. As long as house prices kept rising then subprime loans should have low default rates and high returns. Indeed banks looked to invest further into the lucrative subprime market. HSBC bought Household Finance in March 2003, then one of America's largest subprime lenders. In the first years after the acquisition Household generated about $10bn in profits for HSBC with the high rates it charged its customers. By late 2006 HSBC warned that the business was deteriorating and bad debts mounting. By early 2007 the US subprime sector accounted for about $1.2trn of issuance or 12% of all US ABS.

In 2006 Merrill Lynch bought a subprime mortgage business, First Franklin, for $1.3bn and Morgan Stanley bought Saxon Capital for $700m – everyone wanted a piece of the action. Euromoney was moved to comment:

> *Wall Street is praying that the US economy will land softly now that the Federal Reserve has pricked the housing market bubble, because it will be bad news for mortgage origination if house prices stall for long or, even worse, fall. Already there are early signs of credit deterioration in some of the riskier mortgage securitisations. It can only be a matter of time before subordinated CDO tranches start to take a hit … All the major banks are thinking about how to get access to mortgages because there are lucrative fees to be had from origination and then securitising those assets at a time when the US market has developed away from the traditional agency/CMO model.*[17]

While the Eurobond market was anxious about the health of the securitisation sector it was temporarily distracted by Moody's Investor Services announcement that they believed they had been under-rating banks for some time and they were revising the method of rating banks. Moody's had developed a new quantitative model based principally on the possibility of default rather than an analysis of the bank's creditworthiness. This 'joint default analysis' (JDA) emphasised the possibility of banks' senior unsecured ratings receiving external support from a parent bank, or a regional authority or national government by way of systemic support. On 23 February Moody's released new ratings for 23 banks in 15 countries in the Nordic, Benelux and CEE regions. Having previously only awarded four of these banks triple-A ratings, under their new joint default analysis, 16 banks were now rated triple-A. This was a remarkable outcome for the banks involved, some of which had only enjoyed an A1 rating previously.[18] Moody's subsequently upgraded J.P. Morgan, State Street Bank and Bank of New York on the basis that the US government would back the banks if they faced default.

Within days the market's scepticism was tested further when Moody's awarded triple-A ratings to the Icelandic banks on the basis of a 100% probability of government support. Surprise quickly gave way to scorn and ultimately ridicule, as bank analysts pointed out that the upgrades meant that the three Icelandic banks, Landsbanki, Glitnir and Kaupthing Bank now enjoyed a higher rating than ABN Amro. Yet in the market, investors required a yield spread on Icelandic banks five times larger than that on Aa1 rated ABN Amro.[19]

The barrage of criticism from both the market and the other rating agencies led Moody's to make a rapid and substantial revision to its joint default analysis, reducing their highest support assumptions and putting more weight on intrinsic financial strength. Moody's embarrassing climb-down did little in the long-term to damage its credibility, reflecting its oligopolistic position in the rating arena.

Euromoney used Moody's rating fiasco to comment on another concern with the rating agencies:

> *Structured finance is clearly a great business for the rating agencies and it is easy to see why. Structured finance involves not one asset, but many. Not only does the overall paper need to be rated and analysed but so does the collateral backing it. The structure also needs to be thoroughly stress tested and the tyres of the issuer and manager thoroughly kicked. Potentially, there are layers upon layers of fees. Structured finance is an area where the careful teasing apart of risk is absolutely vital. The alchemy of modern finance can turn sub-prime (aka high-risk) mortgages into triple A-rated CDOs. The alchemists are the investment banks. However, by providing opinions that put these products on a par with gilt-edged stock, the credit rating agencies are the sorcerer's apprentices.[20]*

By the end of the first quarter Eurobond market participants were getting increasingly unnerved by the developing deterioration in the subprime sector:

> *There has only been one topic of conversation in the structured finance market in recent weeks – and for once it was the same subject that everyone else in the financial markets is talking about – US sub-prime mortgages. Problems at originators such as HSBC, Fremont, Accredited Home Lenders and New Century Financial have generated negative headlines around the world. As far as the structured finance*

market is concerned, the key issues are what will be the impact on existing and future ABS and CDO transactions? ...

The sector has already experienced a sharp (and perhaps long overdue) spread widening that will have had severe implications for the growing numbers of ABS investors that mark to market. The first-loss investors in ABS CDOs are now hedge funds, proprietary trading desks and pension funds, all of which will suffer mark-to-market losses due to spread widening. Many credit hedge funds have typically gone long CDO equity and short the higher tranches of CDOs and they will suffer losses if not completely hedged. Many funds have also set up permanent capital vehicles to invest in RMBS and CDO equity and these vehicles will be particularly exposed to the downturn because of their concentration of exposure to the bottom end of the capital structure.[21]

According to the US Mortgage Bankers Association, in the first quarter of 2007, 5.1% of subprime loans were now in foreclosure and a worrying 15.75% were delinquent. The bad news now piled up. In February the Federal Home Mortgage Corporation, Freddie Mac, announced it would no longer buy the most risky subprime mortgages and mortgage-related securities. In April New Century Financial Corporation, the second largest subprime mortgage lender, filed for bankruptcy. In May UBS shut its hedge fund arm, Dillon Read Capital Management, after bad subprime bets led to a $124 million loss.

On 22 June, Bear Stearns investment bank, the second biggest underwriter of mortgage bonds, announced that it intended to bail out its failing Cayman Islands hedge funds, by extending to them between $1.6bn and $3.2bn in emergency loans. The funds had invested largely in CDOs, especially those of subprime mortgages. It was the biggest rescue of a hedge fund since LTCM, prompted by the need to avoid a meltdown in the mortgage-backed sector. They were too late. In a letter sent to investors in July, Bear Stearns Asset Management reported that its High-Grade Structured Credit Fund had lost more than 90% of its value, while the High-Grade Structured Credit Enhanced Leveraged Fund had lost virtually all of its investor capital. The two funds filed for bankruptcy at the end of the month.

In the same month Standard & Poors placed 612 securities backed by subprime residential mortgages on credit watch. By the beginning of August, American Home Mortgage Investment Corporation, the tenth largest retail mortgage lender in the US, filed for bankruptcy.

A sense of panic was beginning to grip the markets. Were Wall Street banks all loaded with toxic securities that could implode?

Was it only Wall Street banks?

NOTES

1. *EuroWeek*, Issue 841, 20 February 2004.
2. European Central Bank, *The Euro Bond Market Study,* December 2004, p. 44.
3. Ibid. p. 42.
4. *EuroWeek*, Issue 839, 6 February 2004.
5. Michael S. Gibson, *Understanding the risk of synthetic CDOs,* Trading Risk Analysis Section, Federal Reserve Board, July 2004 p. 21.
6. Thomas Belsham, Nicholas Vause and Simon Wells, *Credit Correlation: interpretation and risks,* Bank of England, Financial Stability Review, December 2005.

7. Press release*: IPMA and ISMA announce merger,* 2 February 2005.
8. News Release: *European Capital Markets Trade Associations Global Partnership to be Established,* 20 April 2005.
9. *EuroWeek*, Issue 923, *CDS notional more than doubles in a year,* 30 September 2005.
10. Risk.net, Risk Awards: Runner-up: Arkle, 1 December 2006.
11. *The Treasurer*, Deals of the year; High yield bonds: Silicon success NXP, January/February 2007.
12. *Reuters*, US Bank industry earnings highest since 2006: FDIC, 26 February 2013.
13. *New York Times*, Average pay in investment banking is 10 times that elsewhere, 2 September 2007.
14. *Euromoney*, The Death of DCM? June 2006.
15. *Risk Magazine*, Deceptive and Negligent: How the first CPDO got its AAA rating, 30 January 2013.
16. *Euromoney*, Obituary: the CPDO 2006–2008, November 2008.
17. *Euromoney*, Have Wall Street banks gone subprime at the wrong time? December 2006.
18. *Euromoney*, Has Moody's credibility been downgraded? April 2007.
19. *Bloomberg*, Moody's Blasted for Giving Icelandic Banks Top Rating, 26 February 2007.
20. *Euromoney*, Inside Investment: Sorcerer's apprentices, April 2007.
21. *Euromoney*, US sub-prime: ABS CDO pipeline dries up as sub-prime fears start to bite, April 2007.

CHAPTER 10

Busts and Bailouts

2007–2010

The complete evaporation of liquidity in certain market segments of the U.S. securitisation market has made it impossible to value certain assets fairly regardless of their quality or credit rating. In order to protect the interests and ensure the equal treatment of our investors, during these exceptional times, BNP Paribas Investment Partners has decided to temporarily suspend the calculation of the net asset value as well as subscriptions/redemptions, in strict compliance with regulations, for these funds.

This statement by BNP Paribas Investment Partners on 9 August 2007 referring to three of their funds, which had fallen 20% in value in less than two weeks, shocked European markets and is considered by many to be the trigger event which turned a developing US financial crisis into a global financial crisis that has embroiled the international markets for the last seven years. *The Guardian*'s economics editor commented: 'As far as the financial markets are concerned, August 9 2007 has all the resonance of August 4 1914. It marks the cut-off point between "an Edwardian summer" of prosperity and tranquility and the trench warfare of the credit crunch – the failed banks, the petrified markets, the property markets blown to pieces by a shortage of credit.'[1]

Fears of a broader credit squeeze developing prompted the European Central Bank and the US Federal Reserve to pump roughly $150bn into capital markets to boost liquidity. 'Everyone in Europe is now scared of the bank next door and what kind of losses it might be sitting on' said a bank syndicate official.[2] Issuance by financial institutions in the Eurobond market ground to a halt as secondary issues widened and CDS activity dwindled. Barclays Capital was an early victim of the rumour mill, suggesting possible serious exposure to structured investment vehicles (SIVs) and subprime losses. The rating agencies continued putting slews of CDOs on review for possible downgrade. Any new bond issues that did come to market were forced to offer pricing concessions. A UBS syndicate official commented: 'The machinery of fixed income is broken. There is a complete absence of bid-offer spreads in very large asset classes. There is disruption to bank-to-bank liquidity, overnight funding and commercial paper, and huge suspicion hangs over structured credit and mortgage-related asset classes in their entirety.'[3]

The asset-backed commercial paper (ABCP) market experienced a liquidity crisis as buyers were increasingly concerned about the quality of the underlying asset portfolio. As issuers found it difficult to fund their ABCP programmes they had to resort to their backstop liquidity facilities. Banks were finding it increasingly difficult to fund themselves and, where they could, started hoarding cash.

The mood deteriorated further when news emerged in mid-September that Northern Rock, a prominent UK mortgage lender, was forced to use the Bank of England's emergency lending facility, as its main sources of funding in the capital markets had dried up. Despite official reassurances that the bank was not bust, the news triggered the first run on a UK bank in 140 years. The UK Chancellor was forced to guarantee savers' deposits to stop the run and the Bank of England announced it would accept mortgage collateral for repo with UK banks. The UK government sought potential buyers for Northern Rock, but to no avail.

The Libor rate rose to its highest level since December 1998, at 6.8%, way above the Bank of England's base rate of 5.75%. It would be almost three months before a bank would brave the floating rate note market.

In the US the Federal Reserve started easing interest rates, but this proved too late to stem the flow of weak third quarter US bank results with their significant write-downs on CDOs and subprime. Merrill posted a record $7.9bn write-down. Chief Executive Stan O'Neal lost his job but managed to walk away with a severance package totalling $161m. Another rate cut in the US did not allay the market's fears that the financial institutions would have to announce further substantial losses in subprime. SIVs also came under pressure, with the first two to get into difficulties, Cheyne Finance and Rhinebridge plc, revealing their limited asset diversification and a strong bias towards the US housing market.

In Europe Ecofin, the Economic and Financial Affairs Council, comprising the Finance Ministers of EU Member States, announced a timetable for a review of different aspects of the markets functioning after the summer's turbulence, with a view to deciding whether regulatory action was needed. First on their list was a review of the role of credit rating agencies in their rating of structured finance instruments.

Towards the year-end Eurobond new issuance flows had reversed from their normal pattern, with corporate issuance heavily outstripping that from financial institutions. However a syndicate head noted: 'The secondary markets are basically non-existent as no bank seems willing to buy inventory. As soon as a new deal appears on the screens, people try to sell their paper and this completely destroys the market.'[4] Another syndicate official argued: 'Investors are in a dreadful position. They are asking for wide levels because they don't actually want deals to come and they're trying to put issuers off. They don't want to have to mark their portfolios at wider levels. Interest rate cuts in the major economies late in the year failed to lift the gloom.

By the end of the year concerns were being raised about the monoline insurers. These companies had increasingly moved away from their traditional municipal markets to higher yielding structured products. Inevitably this meant an involvement in CDOs where the monolines had built up an exposure of $78bn in US mezzanine and high grade ABS. The nightmare scenario was that if the monolines lost their triple-A status, $2.4trn of municipal securities would be downgraded.

Against this extraordinarily fragile banking background a consortium led by the Royal Bank of Scotland had finally won the battle to buy the Dutch bank ABN Amro for £49bn. The bid battle, originally involving Barclays as the potential acquirer, had dragged on for almost a year. The RBS consortium, which included Dutch bank Fortis and Spain's Santander, planned to break up the Dutch lender. Subsequent events would show the takeover to be an act of extraordinary folly.

*   *   *

In the middle of the financial maelstrom European market participants had to contend with the implementation of a core new Directive, the Market in Financial Instruments Directive, or MiFID. In reality most firms had been preparing for the changes since the Directive was adopted in April 2004. In November 2007 MiFID replaced the 1993 Investment Services Directive (ISD), with a view to increasing competition and consumer protection in investment services. MiFID reflected the developments in financial services since the ISD was implemented and it threw the regulatory net wider to capture more financial activities. It introduced more harmonised requirements for investment firms, particularly in relation to Conduct of Business and internal organisation, and for markets in relation to pre- and post-trade transparency.

MiFID enabled investment firms and 'regulated markets' to provide investment services or perform investment activities throughout the EEA on the basis of 'home state' authorisation, i.e. the passport. (Under the ISD a service had been regulated by the Member State in which the service took place.) But with MiFID the scope of the passport was extended to cover the provision of investment advice, which was promoted to a core service that could be passported on a stand-alone basis. MiFID introduced the operation of a 'multilateral trading facility' (MTF) as a new core investment service. (An MTF is a trading system that brings together buyers and sellers, according to a defined set of rules.) The Directive covered a wider range of instruments than heretofore such as credit derivatives, commodity derivatives and financial contracts for differences.

The Directive abolished the old 'concentration rule' in which Member States could require investment firms to route client orders through regulated markets (effectively the domestic stock exchange). MiFID encouraged competition amongst trading venues, allowing new trading venues to compete with domestic stock exchanges to try to break monopolies and help drive down the cost of trading. Oversight of trading venues was now extended from these regulated markets to include various types of trading platforms or multilateral trading facilities (MTFs) and firms dealing off their own books, which Brussels termed 'systematic internalisers' (SIs). Pre- and post-trade transparency obligations in equities were accordingly extended beyond exchanges to also include MTFs and SIs.

MiFID required firms to categorise clients as 'eligible counterparties', professional clients or retail clients (each having increasing levels of protection). Firms must categorise clients and assess their suitability for various investment products.

When handling client orders, MiFID firms must take all reasonable steps to obtain the best possible result in the execution of an order for a client. This was not just limited to execution price but also includes cost, speed, likelihood of execution and ease of settlement. Additional MiFID requirements included establishing and maintaining a written conflicts of interest policy which must be available to clients on request.

MiFID's impact was felt most acutely in the equity markets. It altered the structure of secondary equity trading in Europe. New trading infrastructures entered the market, resulting in a loss of share for the major stock exchanges, but having the effect of reducing trading costs. However surveys had shown that average trade size had fallen and in response to this, internal crossing of trades and trading through 'dark pools' (block trades away from the public market) had become more important.[5]

*   *   *

In December 2007 the US Federal Reserve, having already cut interest rates three times during the year, co-ordinated action by the five leading central banks around the world to offer billions of dollars in loans to banks. However the benefit proved only temporary. *Euromoney* reported:

> *Various losses, problems with SIVs and a contracting ABCP market have forced assets back onto balance sheets and stretched many banks' capital ratios. But with investors still wary, banks are paying huge premiums for the precious capital. UBS priced a €600m perpetual non-call 10-year issue just days after announcing a $10 billion, sub-prime related write-down. Investors placed over €3 billion of orders with the Swiss bank. But UBS was forced to pay a massive 245 basis points over mid-swaps, more than three times what it would have paid for a comparable deal before the summer … funding will remain cripplingly expensive for many financial institutions throughout 2008, and only prime names will find the essential capital readily available.[6]*

As the New Year dawned analysts announced the largest single-year drop in US home sales in a quarter of a century. The bank's fourth quarter results added to the gloom. Citigroup posted a fourth quarter loss of $9.8bn and $18bn in subprime-related write-downs. Merrill Lynch also announced a $9.8bn loss with a $14bn write-down, bringing their write-downs to $23bn in a matter of weeks. Many of the write-downs were, alarmingly, in super-senior exposures. Major banks now went in search of new strategic investors, particularly among the Middle Eastern and Asian sovereign wealth funds, who might be prepared to offer much needed capital injections. Meanwhile Bank of America acquired the failing Countrywide Financial for $4.1bn. In 2006 Countrywide had financed 20% of all mortgages in the United States making it the nation's largest mortgage lender.

On 18 January 2008, Fitch reduced Ambac's rating from AAA to AA, the first ever downgrade of a monoline insurer. Due to the very nature of monoline insurance this event signalled a simultaneous downgrade of bonds from over 100,000 municipalities and institutions totalling more than $500bn. After this event, many municipal and institutional bonds started trading at prices as if they were uninsured, effectively discounting monoline insurance completely. Bond insurers, like banks, desperately tried to raise capital to avoid further downgrades. Most potential losses for banks in the event of downgrades for the monolines would be through hedging arrangements that the bond insurers had provided on the least risky tranches of CDOs. According to S&P bond insurers had hedged $125bn of subprime-related CDOs.

The only buoyant area of the primary bond market was for top quality sovereign, supranational and agency (SSAs) issuers for short-dated offerings: symptomatic of a flight to quality by investors. Bank issuance was barely a trickle and only then for senior paper; the subordinated market had all but dried up. The floating rate note market was moribund. New issuance was now confined to short issuance windows when the market's tone improved briefly and conditions steadied temporarily. Issuers had to remain alert to capture these fleeting opportunities and focus on intra-day execution.

Primary market practices adapted to best protect against the volatility of the markets. Pre-sounding potential investors to assess their potential demand for an issue was common and price guidance needed to be set at attractive levels to entice investors quickly into the deals. Indeed such was the volatility of the market that syndicate desks would test out possible new issue price ranges before deciding on the public price guidance on a new offering. This became known as a 'price whisper'. However ICMA discouraged the terminology as it implied some form of non-existent confidentiality.

Another primary practice that increased during the volatile days of the crisis was the appointment of 'active' and 'passive' bookrunning lead managers on corporate transactions. This was heavily driven by a borrower's need to reward relationship banks for balance sheet usage. Capital was scarce, and if banks extended lines of credit to companies then they expected to be rewarded in other ways, such as involvement at a senior level in their capital market transactions, as 'passive' bookrunners. The active bookrunners are totally responsible for pricing and allocation decisions. The 'active' bookrunner will announce price guidance, build the order book, allocate the deal and finally price the securities. 'Passive' bookrunners would also be added to the top line but their role in the execution of the transaction will be very limited. They would typically receive the same underwriting commitment and fee as the active manager/s but would have a very secondary role with more limited access to the order book or 'pot'. The use of active and passive lead managers provided more control to key banks in a transaction and speedier execution, but allowed rewards for other relationship banks.

The method of syndication and distribution of new offerings was now very much in the syndicate participants' favour and underwriting risks accrued pretty much entirely to the borrower. Traditionally new issues were launched with fairly specific terms, distributed as much as they could be, and then closed, successfully or otherwise. The 'launch' of a transaction now took place when the offering had been placed with investors. The first indicative indication of a new issue to the market was the 'announcement'. This came to be expressed as a 'benchmark' offering for the borrower, rather than a specific amount, which gave flexibility to the syndicate should the deal struggle. Investors had their own interpretation of what a benchmark amount might be for a specific borrower. On, or soon after, the initial announcement, price guidance for the transaction would be given. Syndicate bank sales teams would then collect 'indications of interest' from investors and so build the book. At the height of the crisis, once the required level of demand was reached, the book would typically be closed. Markets were too volatile to leave books open in pursuit of additional demand. Bonds would then be allocated and then finally priced.

Setting price guidance was traditionally determined by outstanding bond issues and also CDS spreads. But in early 2008 the CDS market spreads kept widening. The technical problem in the CDS market was that there were very few natural sellers of protection and while there was continuous unwinding of structured credit products, there were no sellers to which to pass on the risk. This led to a decoupling of CDS and cash spreads with new issues priced well through CDS levels.

In January the Federal Reserve took the markets by surprise by slashing its key federal funds rate from 4.25% to 3.5%, the biggest cut in 25 years. Faced with the growing risk of recession, nine days later it reduced rates again to 3% and made it clear that it was prepared to take rates lower if the economy kept on declining.

Then out of left field came the news of the largest trading loss in banking history at the French bank, Société Générale. Jérôme Kerviel had been purchasing futures contracts on equity indices to the value of about €50bn. His role was to arbitrage the market and so he was required to hedge the position with sales elsewhere. However his hedge portfolio was fictitious. Like Leeson in the Barings scandal, Kerviel was experienced in back office procedures and covered up much of his activities. As the futures market fell, Société Générale had to meet margin calls. This alerted them to the open position, which they now looked to unwind, with a resultant loss of €4.9bn. Kerviel was prosecuted for dealing without authorisation although he persistently claimed he was innocent. The incident was a major embarrassment to the French bank for its lack of controls and risk management. In normal markets, news of such an extraordinary loss would have dominated the headlines for months. In 2008 it provided a curious sideshow in markets more worried about financial Armageddon.

The Federal Reserve had introduced its term auction facility (TAF) in December 2007 as a temporary 28-day borrowing facility for banks to avoid the stigma of having to use the Discount Window. In March the Fed increased the TAF by $40bn and created a new term securities lending facility (TSLF) for primary dealers (rather than banks), offering 28-day liquidity to try and keep the credit markets functioning. It also announced it was increasing and extending the swap lines it had put in place with the ECB and Swiss National Bank to enable them to offer dollar liquidity to European institutions.

The rumour mill was now working overtime. Rumours focused on Bear Stearns, the market leader in MBS, which was believed to be facing liquidity problems. This concern grew when the $22bn Carlyle Capital Corporation hedge fund, founded and still 15% owned by Bear, collapsed in early March. Clients and trading partners fled in droves over the following days fearing the company, with $46bn of mortgages and structured assets, would be unable to meet its obligations. As one executive said, it was '24 hours from solvent to dead'.[7] The US Treasury, Federal Reserve and the SEC became involved as Bear's position looked increasingly perilous. On 14 March Bear Stearns had insufficient funds to open for business and they approached J.P. Morgan, who managed their cash, desperately seeking funding. Morgan agreed, with the support of the Fed, to provide a 28-day bridge loan. Bear Stearns shares fell 50%.

A frenetic weekend of meetings and calls ensued between bankers and Treasury officials to avoid a banking failure. US Treasury Secretary Paulson insisted that a deal had to be done before the markets opened on Monday morning. J.P. Morgan argued that due to the large number of toxic securities on Bear's books it could not offer further support to the beleaguered investment bank without the participation of the Federal Reserve. Under duress, the Fed finally approved a loan of $30bn saying that it was necessary to avoid 'serious disruptions in the financial markets'. J.P. Morgan accordingly offered just $2 per share to purchase the bank, a huge loss for those whose stock had been worth $30 on the previous Friday and over $150 a year before. After much wrangling the purchase price was renegotiated to $10 per share by the end of the month.

Rumours continued to circulate on both sides of the Atlantic as to which financial institutions were next in line to experience severe liquidity problems. In the US, good quarterly figures from Lehman Brothers allayed growing fears as to their financial condition, while in the UK, fears circulated that Halifax Bank of Scotland (HBOS) might require emergency funding. In early April, UBS announced additional write-downs of $19bn, giving a total write-down of assets in 2007–8 of $37.5bn and so making UBS the biggest European casualty of the subprime crisis. Marcel Ospel, UBS's Chairman resigned.

Job losses of course were a logical corollary to the devastation in the markets. The Confederation of British Industry predicted 11,000 job losses in the City of London in the second quarter. Recruitment agency surveys showed that City traders' bonuses had been slashed by 40%, and bankers on Wall Street had seen their earnings contract by 60%. One beneficiary of the market gloom in New York and London was the Middle East. Investment bankers were migrating almost daily to take up roles in expanding institutions in Dubai, Abu Dhabi and Bahrain. The region's institutions had been much less affected by the financial crisis, but more importantly the effect of the crisis on the oil price, driving towards $150 per barrel, meant that wealth in the region was rising exponentially.

With public markets difficult to access and CDS spreads excessively wide, issuers became more active in private placements to meet their funding needs. Issuing private placements to specific investors at attractive spreads was preferable to public issues requiring substantial new issue premiums, which would simply serve to re-price outstanding debt wider. France Telecom noted in March: 'On average with a private placement you can price 20bp to 25bp through CDS, while if you're looking at a benchmark you're also looking at 20bp to 25bp over CDS. It's a win-win situation and execution risks are also limited in this type of transaction.'[8]

As well as jitters about the financial soundness of various bank counterparties, rumours continued to circulate amongst interbank participants as to whether banks were manipulating the Libor rate fixes. The British Bankers Association (BBA) set the Libor rate in London daily based on a poll of leading banks reporting where they believed the rates to be. It was not required for the rate fix that the bank should have transacted at the rate they reported. Accusations grew that banks were posting falsely low levels in the Libor fixing process to disguise their funding difficulties.

From as early as August 2007, the New York Fed admitted it had received emails suggesting that Libor submissions were being set below their true levels by the banks. In December, a Barclays employee informed the New York Fed that the Libor rate was being fixed at a level that was unrealistically low. In March economists from the Bank for International Settlements (BIS) raised questions about the accuracy of the Libor rates. A report headlined, 'Is LIBOR broken?' from Citigroup suggested that the current Libor rates probably understated where the true rates were by 20bps to 30bps. The *Wall Street Journal* picked up the story with an article entitled 'Bankers Cast Doubt on Key Rate Amid Crisis'. By mid-April the topic was being fiercely debated among market participants. Now the relevant regulators, the Federal Reserve and the UK's FSA, started to make enquiries of market participants. In early June, Tim Geithner, head of the New York Fed, sent the Bank of England a list of proposals to try to tackle Libor's credibility problem.[9] In the same month the BBA prepared a review of Libor and published a consultation paper. In August, in the light of feedback on the paper, the BBA concluded that the existing process for submissions would be retained. The issue had been brushed under the carpet – for now.

EuroWeek found the Libor debate irritating:

> *The Libor market may well be broken, but this should hardly be surprising. The financial markets as a whole are broken. Interbank rates are just one very important cog in the temperamental machine that is the financial system. Banks don't trust each other. That was always bound to affect the Libor rate – and did so long ago. Until there is full disclosure and full comprehension of exactly what risks are held and where, the credit risk in Libor is unstable. This is as it should be.*[10]

A sharp improvement in primary market conditions took place April and May 2008, largely led by the US market, encouraging some market participants to speculate that the worst of the crisis was now behind them. But these buoyant conditions were short-lived; with the ECB warning of inflation and possible recession in Europe, the market began to sell off again.

There was now increasing concern about the financial state of Lehman Brothers and talk of possible takeovers or mergers. Lehman had invested heavily in the mortgage-backed sector and as a result had posted record profits continuously between 2005 to 2007.After the Bear Stearns collapse, Lehman's stock had been dumped on fears it might be the next victim of the crisis. Rumours circulated of Lehman's needing to access the Fed borrowing facility. In June the firm announced a quarterly loss of $2.98bn, the first since going public 14 years earlier. In response the company raised $6bn via a heavily discounted equity offering. Lehman also revealed it had booked $17bn in write-downs since the beginning of the credit crisis. In the first half of 2008 alone, Lehman's stock lost 73% of its value.

Those bankers who did not take a summer vacation that year not only had to cope with the market rumour mill operating in overdrive but also with new proposals from Brussels signalling an impending regulatory backlash. The European Commission proposed an amendment to the Capital Requirements Directive (effectively the implementation of Basel II rules in Europe) hitting out at the 'originate to distribute' model which had become prevalent in the structured credit markets. The amendment (Article 122a) would prohibit banks from investing in 'credit transfer products' unless the originator or servicer retained at least 10% of the structure on their own books. The proposal was dubbed 'skin in the game', where the originator should align his interests with those of investors. This retention requirement was a vertical slice, that is, an originator would have to retain 10% of each tranche of a securitisation if it wished to distribute paper, significantly increasing the originator's capital requirement. The Commission's original proposal had been for a 15% retention but the market outcry had been such as to dilute the new proposal. The market was equally alarmed by the new proposal arguing that it would seriously disadvantage European market participants versus their global competitors. The Commission allowed just two weeks for the market's response. After intense lobbying later in the year, the Commission's proposal was reduced to 5% 'skin in the game'.

In mid-summer Merrill dumped $6.7bn of mortgage-related assets at just 22 cents in the dollar in a fire sale to Lone Star funds. The CDOs were backed in the main by super-senior high-grade bonds. AIG added to the dark mood when it announced $5.36bn losses for the second quarter and a write-down of its assets by more than $11bn. These losses primarily arose on billions of dollars of CDOs the company was asked to insure by banks like Goldman Sachs, Merrill Lynch and Société Générale. Goldman alone originated or bought protection from AIG on about $33bn of the $80bn of US mortgage assets that AIG insured during the housing boom.

In the Eurobond primary market the fragile conditions only left a window for the best supranational and European agency names. The EIB tentatively launched a $4bn three-year transaction at the end of August. Managers, Barclays, Citigroup and J.P. Morgan were surprised, and delighted, to see the book grow to $8bn in two hours with an all-time record funding level of mid-swaps minus 35bps. The flight to quality had driven EIB secondary paper to Libor less 55 bps. Other supras followed EIB's lead with central banks happily taking up the available paper. However government sponsored enterprises (GSEs), such as Freddie Mac and Fannie Mae, were definitely out of favour, tarnished by their position at the heart of the US housing crisis.

With US house prices falling, Freddie Mac and Fannie Mae had posted billions of dollars of losses with further losses expected. The market's concerns about their condition were realised in early September when US Treasury Secretary Paulson announced that the US government was taking control of the two companies under a 'conservatorship' plan. The Treasury would provide funds for the firms via preferred stock investments, lines of credit, and the direct purchase of mortgages. While Freddie and Fannie were pretty much insolvent with their $5trn of obligations, the market was still shocked by the US administration's pre-emptive intervention. Now the US taxpayer was on the hook. Staunch Republicans started accusing their own administration of 'socialist' policies.

Events over ensuing days would throw fuel on the fire.

In the European corporate sector investors were becoming more discerning about intrinsic creditworthiness, differentiating between cyclical and non-cyclical names and favouring names with strong cash flow and good local demand. In the first week of September French building materials company, Saint Gobain, and the German industrial gasses company, Linde, both with the same Baa1/BBB+ credit rating, launched similar deals but with spreads 190bps apart. Linde benefited from strong domestic demand. A year earlier both companies had launched offerings just 5bps apart.[11]

By early August Lehman's stock had improved marginally on rumours that the state-controlled Korea Development Bank (KDB) was considering investing in the company. But the sell-off began again in earnest after the Fannie and Freddie bailout and the announcement that the KDB was withdrawing from the negotiations. Lehman's stock plunged 77% in the first week of September and their CDS widened by 66%. The market was convinced that only an imminent sale could now save Lehman.

Last-ditch efforts over the weekend of 13 September between Lehman, Barclays PLC and Bank of America, aimed at facilitating a takeover of Lehman, were ultimately unsuccessful. Lehman's fate was sealed when the UK Chancellor refused to provide UK state guarantees for a takeover by Barclays. On Monday 15 September, the markets were stunned when Lehman filed for bankruptcy, with more than $600bn of debt and more than 100,000 creditors – the largest casualty of the global credit crisis.

Lehman's collapse also served as the catalyst for the hasty $50bn buy out of Merrill Lynch by Bank of America in an emergency deal announced on the same day. The fate of other big name financial institutions remained in doubt and stock prices plunged in Asia, Europe and the United States. In a forlorn attempt to stabilise markets, the SEC banned short selling in a wide range of financial stocks.

There now began three weeks of intense activity and emergency measures between governments, central banks and securities regulators, as the global financial system teetered 'on the brink of systemic meltdown' according to the head of the IMF.

Just two days after Lehman collapsed, the US government seized control of the giant insurer AIG via an $85bn bailout, which guaranteed the banks' multibillion-dollar exposure to subprime loans. Without a bailout, many more banks might have followed Lehman into bankruptcy. Lehman's collapse and the sale of Merrill Lynch reduced the number of independent firms on Wall Street to two: Morgan Stanley and Goldman Sachs. As it was feared that they also might be near to failure, the US administration changed their status into bank holding companies so that they could receive federal financial support. The Federal Reserve injected $70bn of funds into the banking system, more than it had at any time since 9/11.

In the UK on 18 September Lloyds TSB announced a takeover of troubled UK mortgage lender HBOS in a UK government brokered deal. The government pushed through the £12bn takeover of the country's largest mortgage lender and largest savings institution, to avoid a possible repeat of a Northern Rock-style bank run.

Some days later the focus moved back to the US where the largest bank failure in US history was announced. Washington Mutual, the US's sixth largest lender with about $310bn in assets, was seized by federal regulators and then rapidly acquired by J.P. Morgan Chase for $1.9bn. Speculation also focused on Wachovia, the leading adjustable rate mortgage (ARM) lender. In this case the Federal Deposit Insurance Corporation brokered talks between

Wachovia and Citigroup and Wells Fargo, in order to avoid another bank failure. Wachovia finally merged with Wells Fargo.

As each troubled day passed, Treasury Secretary Paulson was frantically negotiating to get his Troubled Asset Relief Program (TARP) accepted by Congress. The TARP programme would authorise the US administration to spend up to $700bn to purchase 'troubled assets' from financial institutions to strengthen the financial sector. Eurobond market participants followed every nuance of the debate hoping there might be conditions for the effective re-opening of the market. Most issuance had dried up with the collapse of Lehman. After much wrangling, Congress finally passed the financial bailout bill on 3 October.

European governments were also haunted by the possibility of European bank runs and bank failures. The collapse of Lehman Brothers had virtually frozen European lending and exposed serious capital shortages in key financial institutions.

In the UK the Treasury agreed to pay £42bn for Bradford & Bingley's ailing mortgage book. The Belgian-Dutch bank, Fortis, was given an €11.2bn equity injection by the governments of Belgium, the Netherlands and Luxembourg to boost its capital base. Then Dexia received a €6bn injection from the French and Belgium governments and major shareholders. The scene now moved to Dublin where Ireland's government, in response to banking shares losing more than 25% of their value, announced it would guarantee Irish banks' deposits and debts for two years. Amongst accusations of unfair state aid other European countries looked to prop up their ailing financial institutions and guarantee deposits.

Britain pioneered the bailout path in Europe as Gordon Brown's Labour government announced an unprecedented £400bn bank bailout plan to shore up its beleaguered banks. The Royal Bank of Scotland received £20bn from the government in return for a 58% stake in RBS ordinary shares and a tranche of preference shares. Lloyds TSB, which had agreed to take over HBOS, received a £17bn handout, giving the government a 43% stake. Alongside the £37bn capital injection, the UK Treasury announced plans for a £200bn bank guarantee scheme and a £200bn extension of the Bank of England's Special Liquidity Scheme. The bailout announcement coincided with an emergency interest rate cut by the Federal Reserve, the ECB, the Bank of England and three other central banks intended to ease pressure on the financial system.

Modelled closely on the UK plan, France, Germany, Spain, the Netherlands and Austria committed €1.46trn to guarantee bank loans and take stakes in lenders, racing to prevent a systemic collapse. Europe's central banks promised unlimited dollar funding in co-ordinated action with the US Federal Reserve. Unlimited access to cheap cash was at the heart of the ECB's efforts to support banks through the financial crisis.

Having observed the nature of European bailouts, the US reversed its former policy and agreed to also purchase equity ownership in major banks, and spend less funds on purchasing toxic mortgage debt.

Government support packages to prop up the international banking system typically comprised three core elements. Firstly, capital injections, secondly, asset guarantees or purchases – to reduce banks' exposure to troubled assets, and finally liability guarantees, both on customer deposits and bond financing. The issuance of government-guaranteed bank bonds (GGBs) to help banks retain access to wholesale funding was a key factor in re-opening the Eurobond markets to financial institutions.

A typical AA rated European bank could issue five-year bonds at about 10 basis points over the 90-day Libor rate before the crisis began. That rose to somewhere between 250bps and 350bps at the height of the crisis before government bailouts.

The various national guarantee schemes differed as to availability, size, term and cost. If financial issuers chose to go down the guaranteed route there would be a risk weighting advantage as this paper would be zero risk-weighted under Basel II.

On 6 October the European Investment Bank launched a $4bn three-year global bond at a record-breaking funding level of mid-swaps less forty basis points. The offering was oversubscribed within an hour. A week later SSA borrowers' issues were failing. The prospect of a deluge of government-guaranteed bank paper offered at cheap levels drove SSA spreads sharply wider. Barclays opened the floodgates with a €3bn three-year UK government-guaranteed transaction which was generously priced at 25 basis points over mid-swaps. The EIB's three-year global of only two weeks earlier moved sharply out to mid-swaps plus 20 basis points. An unhappy SSA syndicate banker raged: 'The Barclays deal has completely destroyed the public sector market. We have seen this brutal value destruction for issuers and investors have been decimated. I have never seen such a correction in the 12 years I have been in the markets. The widening we have seen has been across the board.'[12]

Unfortunately with an expectation that up to €200bn of GGB paper might hit the new issues market in the next six months to a year, spreads were unlikely to come in. Bank of Scotland soon followed Barclays with a guaranteed €3bn two-year offering and a £600m three-year sterling offering. From October 2008 to May 2010 close to 1400 GGBs were issued in the Euromarkets by approximately 200 banks from 17 countries for more than €1trn equivalent. Most GGBs had maximum three-year maturities but some countries extended this to five years. As well as government fees, issuers also had to pay the often hefty new issue spread demanded by investors. Certainly up until April 2009 each new deal had to be brought on a wider launch spread than the previous offering as investors knew there was plenty more supply around the corner. France avoided this through establishing the 'Société de Financement de l'Economie Française' (SFEF) which sold itself more as a traditional government agency borrower and would raise funds for French banks as required. All governments charged a fee for their guarantee, of course. In most cases fees levied were risk-based, with either historical credit default swaps or credit agency ratings being used as references. Typically European bank issuers had to pay their governments 50bps on top of their median CDS for the period 1 January 2007 to 31 August 2008. The average fees in Europe were close to 100bps, with Germany on the low side at 91bps, and the UK on the high side at 114bps, France being the exception with spreads as low as 50bps.

SSA bankers were concerned that the GGB market would eat into their traditional investor base of central banks, pension funds and insurance companies; in fact most GGB issuance found an investor base with bank Treasuries due to its attractive risk weighting.

2008 ended as it had begun, under a dark cloud. Still, it looked like Armageddon had been avoided, although the markets a year on were a shadow of their former selves. Bloomberg estimated that, as of the end of 2008, gross global financial institutions write-offs exceeded $1200bn. According to the BIS, cross-border lending by banks had shrunk by $4.8trn to $31trn in the nine months to December, the fastest fall on record. Business prospects for the bond markets in 2009 looked bleak, and market participants were facing end-of-year compensation rounds that might involve more redundancy pay-offs than bonuses.

With interest rates at historic lows, and economic activity weak, there was little opportunity for governments to lower them further. In this situation both the Federal Reserve and the Bank of England adopted the policy of 'quantitative easing' or 'QE'. QE involves the central bank making asset purchases, typically government bonds, and thereby pumping money into the economy. It was employed first by the Bank of Japan seeking to lift the country out of a period of deflation following its asset bubble collapse in the 1990s. The decision by the Federal Reserve in March to spend up to $1.2trn to buy government bonds and mortgage-related securities was designed to lower borrowing costs for home mortgages and other types of loans, and thereby stimulate economic activity. The Bank of England announced its first purchase of £75bn worth of Gilts also in March. This original figure was extended that same year, by £50bn in May, £50bn in August and a further £25bn in November.

*   *   *

As the markets were winding down for the Christmas break, Deutsche Bank managed to dampen any modest seasonal cheer that might have existed in the banking market. It announced that it would not exercise the call option on €1bn of subordinated lower Tier 2 bonds which would fall due in January 2009. With the seizing up of the interbank market, bank funding costs had risen to prohibitive levels. Indeed, for some time, funding levels had risen above the typical punitive step-up coupon on many Tier 2 floating rate notes. Yet banks had avoided breaking the market convention and extending the bonds, as it might upset the traditional investor base and cause reputational damage. Deutsche Bank was faced with an estimated cost saving of €100m to €150m if they did not call the notes. Deutsche's Treasurer argued 'It's difficult to justify to people who don't buy and sell financial institution bonds why these instruments should be called at par irrespective of the circumstances and to justify to regulators why the call date should be the the de facto maturity date.'

Measured by the Merrill Lynch Financials Sub-Debt Index, the nominal value of subordinated bonds outstanding in Europe was around €260bn at the end of 2008, of which €205bn had been issued for banks. Deutsche's move sent a shockwave through the subordinated floating rate note market. The Association of British Insurers (ABI) was the first official body to comment: 'We are disappointed and concerned at this action taken by Deutsche Bank, a leading global capital markets operator with no capital or liquidity issues. This is a severe setback for the stabilisation of banking markets and is likely to increase funding costs for banks generally.'[13] Subordinated issue prices fell across the board as the sector began to adjust to the new reality. But many subordinated issuers stubbornly insisted that they would be calling their paper on the appropriate date.

In January shares in Royal Bank of Scotland collapsed more than 60% after the bank warned its 2008 losses could reach £28bn. RBS's subsequent £24.1bn loss would be the largest ever corporate loss in the UK. RBS revealed that the UK government had increased its holding in the bank from 58% to 68% by converting its £5bn current preference shares into ordinary stock. This move again rocked the FIG sector and triggered a collapse in the price of hybrid Tier 1 subordinated debt, as investors feared coupon payments on hybrid debt would not now to be serviced. Investors avoided bank issuers and focused on the seemingly safer corporate sector. More corporate paper was issued in January 2009 than in the entire first quarter of 2008.

By mid-year, along with Deutsche Bank, issuers that chose not to call their subordinated offerings included Fortis, Belgium's KBC Bank, Spain's Banco Sabadell and Italy's Credito Valtellinese, whereas banks that had chosen to defer interest payments on their outstanding subordinated paper included Banca Italease, Depfa Bank and its parent Hypo Real Estate, Dresdner Bank, HSH Nordbank, and IKB Deutsche Industriebank. Bradford & Bingley joined this group as the UK government had altered the terms of its outstanding Lower Tier 2 issues enabling the bank to defer interest payments.[14]

In April S&P downgraded the hybrid securities of more than 80 European financial institutions due to the heightened deferral risk or cancellation of coupons on their hybrid securities. 'The downgrade reflects our assessment of the deteriorating financial prospects for the European banking industry in the worsening economic environment and our view that European governments and the European Commission over the medium term may be more willing than previously to encourage or force banks to suspend payments on hybrid securities to preserve cash and build capital,' the agency argued. Prior to the crisis the yield on bank bonds were stable at around 50bps over the Benchmark. With the crisis bank bond spreads started to fluctuate hitting an all-time high of 673bps in April 2009.[15]

As subordinated debt prices had plummeted to distressed levels in the secondary market, banks began buying outstanding paper back at deep discounts. This avoided the issue of calling paper or skipping coupon payments. More importantly, it directly added to their core Tier 1 capital. If subordinated paper could be bought at a price of, say, 50 cents in the dollar, then in the banks' accounts, cash would fall 50 cents on the buy-back, while liabilities would decline by 100 cents, with a resultant 50 cents' gain in core capital. The bank typically offered a slightly better price than paper was quoted in the secondary market leaving investors little choice other than to accept the offer or remain in a deeply discounted security with no certainty of a future call.

The EU authorities were by no means neutral on the question of calls and coupon deferrals, particularly in the cases where banks had received state aid. In July they made it clear that 'banks should not use state aid to remunerate own funds (i.e. capital) when their activities to not generate sufficient profit'. The abiding principle must be 'burden sharing', where creditors must accept their share of risk. Accordingly banks must not use taxpayers' money to repay equity and subordinated debt. The UK regulator, the FSA, informed RBS they must not exercise the call option on their hybrid securities whose call date was falling due. They also required that such banks should potentially defer or skip coupon payments on Tier 1 subordinated debt. The Commission's requirement encouraged banks further to look to buy back their subordinated paper via so-called 'liability management exercises' (LMEs).

Between January 2009 and April 2010 banks completed 54 discounted liability management exercises resulting in €58bn principal amount of bond issuance repurchased or issued in exchange offers. These transactions generated €19bn of pre-tax core capital.[16]

In November 2008 ICMA's inaugural Primary Market Forum discussed the outlook for the corporate markets after the demise of Lehman. The most optimistic among the Primary Market Practices Committee syndicate heads suggested there would no corporate bond market until at least 2010. They failed of course to consider the effects of the crisis on the loan market. For corporate borrowers the bond market proved a pragmatic alternative to loans, especially for longer dated funding. In 2007 loan market corporate volumes had reached $4.16trn, four and a half times the issuance of corporate bonds. In October 2009, Dealogic figures revealed that worldwide issuance of corporate bonds had outstripped the corporate syndicated loan market for the first time ever; $1.31trn of corporate bonds were issued against $1.08trn of syndicated lending. In Europe bond markets were outpacing loans by 61%.

Against people's expectation, 2009 was a record year for corporate issuance. Although bond spreads had widened to historic levels, absolute interest rates were much lower, so issuance was still attractive. For credit investors in bonds they were getting equity-risk like returns but only a third or fifth of the volatility. Due to the crisis many banks had run down their secondary market trading inventory and had little to offer investors, so the primary market was often the only place to acquire corporate paper in any size. Also, as banks slashed credit lines, the investor base changed from the ubiquitous hedge fund investor before the crisis, to a new predominance of 'real money' investors. Despite the supply, investors were lapping up deals which were often oversubscribed seven to eight times with spreads tightening by 30 to 50 bps. Investors, knowing allocations would be cut with oversubscribed deals, started inflating their orders. By the end of the year corporate bond issuance in Europe exceeded €250bn. The previous best was €200bn in 2001 when Europe was in the TMT M&A boom.

The escalating bank bailout costs for European governments were now beginning to take their toll on how the market was viewing underlying sovereign risks. In April the EU instructed France, Spain, the Irish Republic and Greece to reduce their budget deficits. Sovereign ratings were put under review with downgrades for Spain, Portugal and Greece. Domestic government bond spreads and CDS spreads in Italy Spain, Ireland and Greece were widening to record levels. Fitch reported that European governments' gross borrowing requirement would approach €2trn in 2009, a 45% increase on 2008.[17]

One area of the FIG market which might have been expected to fare better than most in the crisis, was the covered bond market, with its high credit ratings and jumbo issuance. However that was not the reality as investors shunned all bank paper and covered bond spreads widened. In May 2009 the ECB intervened with its covered bond purchase programme (CBPP.1) The objectives of the programme were: to reduce money market interest rates, to ease funding conditions, to encourage institutions to raise lending and to improve market liquidity. The covered bonds purchased 'had to be eligible for use as collateral in the ECB's credit operations'. The ECB made outright purchases of covered bonds in both the primary and secondary markets to the value of €60bn from July 2009 to the end of June 2010, a relatively modest programme in light of the €2.3trn of covered bonds outstanding in the European market.

There had been an increasing realisation in the crisis that existing hybrid instruments, particularly Tier 2 instruments, were largely ineffectual in preventing banks from going bankrupt. These instruments were largely now viewed as 'gone concern' instruments, that is, they would absorb losses only when bank-wide default was imminent. As a result, their benefit was largely limited to the subordinated cushion that they provided in bankruptcy and their longer dated maturities. The regulators looked more favourably on 'going concern' hybrid instruments – instruments that could absorb losses well ahead of a broad, bank-wide default and might help to stabilise an issuer and prevent such a default. In the FIG sector a number of banks were exploring the possible use of contingent capital products. These contingent capital instruments would be debt issues that would automatically convert into equity on some trigger event, such as a bank's core Tier 1 capital falling below a certain level. The contingent convertible or 'CoCo' was one such instrument.

In November Lloyds announced the largest ever liability management exercise by a European bank as part of a £21bn capital raising to exit the UK Government Asset Protection Scheme (a UK government insurance scheme for the bank's toxic loans). The plan was to exchange a whole raft of Tier 1 and Upper Tier 2 hybrid debt issues on which they were not permitted to make payments, and offer investors in exchange a contingent capital instrument. (Lloyds had been prevented by the European Commission from paying coupons on certain of its hybrid debt as a condition of its state aid.) The bank looked to raise £7.5bn of 'Enhanced Capital Notes' (ECNs) which would convert automatically to equity if the bank's core Tier 1 fell below 5%. The coupons, set 1.5% to 2.5% over existing hybrids, were non-deferrable and had a fixed maturity date of between 10 and 15 years. Commentators were sceptical about the new instrument. On the one hand they were concerned how a bank's equity share price might react if the minimum capital trigger point approached, and on the other hand, there were doubts that a natural investor base existed for such an instrument.

The Lloyds exchange was part of a wider fundraising including a £13.5bn rights issue. Despite the early misgivings, the pioneering offering was received enthusiastically by European investors resulting in the contingent convertible issue being increased from £7.5bn to £9bn. Whatever the future of the new instruments, the lead managers were certainly satisfied, pocketing a record-breaking £500m fee for the overall capital raising exercise. Unfortunately, in December the UK government imposed a 50% payroll tax on all discretionary bonuses over £25,000 for the following bonus round and raised the top UK marginal tax rate to 50%.

* * *

Governments and regulators had had an exhausting year; on the one hand trying to save the banking system from the brink of collapse, and on the other, laying plans to avoid such a catastrophic financial crisis ever happening again. By the end of the year a whole new international regulatory landscape was taking shape.

In April 2009 the UK's Prime Minister, Gordon Brown, invited the G-20 Heads of State to a summit in London to discuss the global financial crisis. The G-20, which included the key developing economies, now supplanted the G-8 as the preferred forum for international economic cooperation. The G-20 countries together pledged $5trn in stimulus to the world economy, to stem declining global demand and protectionist tendencies. The International Monetary Fund was confirmed as principal lender of last resort with pledges of $1trn dollars in additional resources from the G-20 countries and promises to strengthen its role. The G-20 leaders also agreed to establish a new Financial Stability Board (FSB) working with the IMF to ensure wider global cooperation. The FSB would monitor potential risks in the economy, especially those involving the biggest firms, and would conduct 'early warning exercises' and periodic reviews to spot potential trouble. It would report any possible threats to the stability of the global financial system to the G-20 Finance Ministers, the IMF and central bank governors. It would regulate all 'systemically important' financial institutions, instruments and markets (including the most important hedge funds). The FSB would establish a supervisory college to monitor each of the largest international financial services firms and encourage financial institutions to maintain contingency plans that could be used if the firm collapsed, i.e. the so-called 'living wills'.

The G-20 leaders met in more buoyant mood in Pittsburgh in September. The summit focused on the need for a globally coordinated response to the crisis. They agreed to maintain the stimulus to restore economic growth and create jobs. They agreed a process for economic cooperation and coordination to help avoid any return to serious imbalances that would undermine long-term growth. As regards the financial sector, the regulatory system for banks and other financial firms must rein in the excesses that led to the crisis. They agreed to act together to improve the quality and quantity of bank capital and to discourage excessive leverage and risk taking. Bankers' bonuses featured on the agenda but the leaders failed to agree on a cap, just a commitment to align compensation to long-term value creation. As regards derivative markets, it was agreed that standardised contracts should be cleared through central counterparties. There was also a commitment to investigate the possibility of a so-called 'Tobin tax' (a tax on financial transactions first proposed in 1972 by the Nobel-prize winning American economist James Tobin) on financial speculation to contribute towards the cost of future crises.

The mandarins in Brussels had not been slouching either. During the year the European Commission published Regulatory proposals on Capital Requirements (as mentioned above), Deposit Guarantee Schemes, Credit Rating Agencies and Alternative Investment Funds. The

EU Regulation on Credit Rating Agencies came into force in December 2009 and the use of credit ratings by EU authorised financial institutions was constrained from December 2010. It introduced a harmonised approach to the regulation of credit rating activities in the European Union and established a registration system for credit rating agencies. In order for a CRA to operate in the EU, it would have to be registered in the EU. CESR (later ESMA, see below) would be responsible for approving the registration of CRAs, their ongoing supervision, and taking appropriate enforcement action.

During the crisis it was noted that, despite the fact that financial institutions operated across borders using the single EU market, supervision remained mostly at the national level, was uneven and often uncoordinated. In May the Commission published a new supervisory framework proposal. A European Systemic Risk Board (ESRB) would be established and be responsible for the 'macro-prudential' oversight of the financial system in the EU. 'Macro-prudential' was very much the new regulatory buzzword, i.e. focusing on the risks to the financial system as a whole. It addressed the interconnectedness of individual financial institutions and markets.

The ESRB would assess risks to financial stability at national and EU level and act as an early warning system with powers to recommend preventative action to deal with possible systemic risks. It was proposed to instigate a European System of Financial Supervisors (ESFS), that is, a network of national financial supervisors working alongside a group of new European Supervisory Authorities (ESAs) The ESFS would allow greater harmonisation and consistency of rules applicable to financial markets in Europe and reduce the scope for regulatory arbitrage.

The ESAs would be adaptions of the existing EU supervisory committees but with extended powers. The European Banking Authority (EBA) would replace CEBS. The European Securities and Markets Authority (ESMA), with responsibility for the securities sector, credit rating agencies, clearing and fund management, would replace CESR. And the European Insurance & Occupational Pensions Authority (EIOPA) would replace CEIOPS.

On 17 December the Basel Committee for Banking Supervision (BCBS) announced a complete overhaul of the capital adequacy regime with its new draft proposals for a Basel III framework, described by the Basel Committee Chairman as a 'regulatory tsunami'. Basel III would entail profound changes in the way banks ration and employ capital. It struck at the heart of many of the weak links exposed by the financial crisis. The guiding principle behind the new framework was to raise 'the quality, consistency and transparency' of Tier 1 capital. It called for the phasing out of innovative hybrid Tier 1 capital as it was not sufficiently loss absorbing on a 'going concern' basis. The proposal stated: 'to be considered loss absorbent on a going concern basis, all instruments included in Tier 1 will, among other things, need to be subordinated, have fully discretionary non-cumulative dividends or coupons and neither have a maturity date or an incentive to redeem,' i.e. no step-ups. The framework required banks to hold buffers of capital above the regulatory minimum. If such buffers fell below a certain level then there would be constraints on payouts to shareholders and bank employees, as well as share buybacks. The Committee also proposed the use of a non-risk weighted leverage ratio for banks and a new global liquidity standard. The proposals would enter a relatively short consultation period finishing at the end of 2010 with full implementation tabled for 2012. As the new Basel III proposals were being debated traditional hybrid bond issuance in the market ground to a halt.

With the proposals from Basel announced, the European Commission launched a public consultation on changes to the EU Capital Requirements Directive (CRD), now CRD IV, to effectively incorporate the broad thrust of the Basel proposals. The regulatory workload going forward would be a heavy one.

There was a sense as 2010 dawned that the worst of the banking crisis was now past. Banks had written off swathes of their toxic exposure and had embarked on significant capital raising exercises. Reflecting the easing of strains on bank funding observed up to April 2010 many government guarantee schemes were allowed to expire at the end of 2009, e.g. those of the UK, France and Korea. Most remaining programmes were scheduled to be closed to new issues by the end of 2010.

* * *

Banking risk and sovereign risk are inexorably intertwined. Negative feedback loops between banks and sovereigns became increasingly apparent during 2009–2010. The bailout of the banking sector had raised sovereign indebtedness and sovereign funding costs. Government bonds formed a core part of many European bank portfolios. As sovereign spreads widened, losses accrued to the banks, weakening their balance sheets and so making bank funding more costly. Banks with significant exposure to the peripheral sovereigns, typically domestic banks, found it increasingly difficult to raise wholesale debt and deposits and so became more reliant on central bank liquidity and ECB funding. As the banks were reluctant to invest in more sovereign paper, the cost of sovereign funding rose; and so a vicious circle developed.

Monetary union in the Euroarea had not been accompanied by a full fiscal union, but by the Stability and Growth Pact (SGP) agreed at Maastricht. Under the SGP governments undertook to limit their budget deficits to 3% of GDP, but many fell outside this, and SGP was not enforced. After 2007, budget deficits rose substantially, raising levels of government debt and debt service. Between end-2007 and end-2010, average budget deficits in advanced countries increased from 1% to 8% of GDP and gross government debt rose from 73% to 97% of GDP.[18] With the concerns about future economic growth, there was grave concern over some countries' ability to repay their debts. In the Euroarea, governments do not issue their own currency nor stand behind each other's debts. So, in some peripheral Euroarea countries, government debt rose to unsustainable levels. Financial stability in the area was at risk from contagion from one debtor government to another and from one bank to another.

Sovereign concerns remained focused on the European peripheral countries – Greece, Portugal, Ireland and Spain. These concerns grew in November when Dubai announced that Dubai World, a government holding company, could not meet its obligations. In fact Dubai's debt difficulties were short-lived due to the deep pockets of neighbouring Emirate, Abu Dhabi.

In December a new government in Greece revealed that, contrary to previous government reports submitted to Brussels, their annual budget deficit now stood at an alarming 12.7% of GDP. Fitch and S&P downgraded the country to junk status. Greek sovereign debt now totalled €300bn, or 113% of GDP, almost double the Maastricht limit. In the bond markets weekly government bond auctions were monitored nervously as yields rose and CDS spreads widened. Greece opened 2010 with a jumbo offering of €8bn, which to everyone's immediate relief attracted €25bn of orders. But within days, as investors became more alarmed at the country's weak fiscal position and doubts about the sustainability of its debts, it had widened by 50bps. In February Greece unveiled an austerity plan aimed at curbing the deficit. The Eurozone and IMF agreed a safety net, or financial assistance package, of €22bn at punitive interest rates to help Greece if required. By April when Greece's borrowing costs had risen by 270bps in one month to 8.7% for 10 years, the financial assistance package was activated.

Up to €30bn in emergency loans was provided by Eurozone countries. But it was not enough. Finally on 2 May Eurozone states and the IMF announced a three-year bailout programme for Greece, totalling €110bn, initially comprising €80bn in bilateral loans and €30bn from the IMF. But the bailout came at a cost. Protestors took to the streets angry at the further austerity measures demanded in the bailout programme.

As Greece descended towards default, bond investors became increasingly alarmed about the nature of the Greek sovereign paper that they held. ICMA set up a help desk for investors. The euro complicated the situation. With the arrival of the single currency, domestic sovereign debt, which would previously have been denominated in drachma, and international sovereign debt had become blurred. Ninety per cent of European sovereign issuance was via auction: the traditional domestic market method of issuance. It was difficult to find the details of auction bonds, drafted under domestic law, and in many cases they were not defined. In addition, sovereign states were exempt from the disclosure requirements of the EEA Prospectus Directive so the level of investor protection was negligible. International or foreign law issues, on the other hand, were documented more fully and would typically include Collective Action Clauses (CACs). Later in the year ICMA called for sovereign issuers to standardise and publicise detailed bond terms and conditions in English on a public website during the life of the issue. They also urged sovereigns, even with domestically targeted deals, to comply with ICMA best practices.

In May 2010, in response to the Greek crisis, the 'European Financial Stability Facility' (EFSF) was agreed by the 16 Eurozone members. This was a €440bn fund to help Eurozone countries if they faced difficulties in accessing the capital markets. In return governments would have to adopt rigorous economic policies agreed with the IMF, the ECB and the European Commission. The Facility could be combined with loans of up to €60bn from the European Financial Stability Mechanism (reliant on funds raised by the EU Commission using the EU budget as collateral) and up to €250bn from the IMF, to create a total safety net of €750bn.

* * *

In the banking sector contingent capital was back on the menu. Rabobank launched a senior, unsecured contingent capital issue. As the bank is a cooperative with no publicly traded shares, bondholders would be subject to a 75% write-down of the principal payment on the bond if the bank's equity capital ratio dropped below 7%. (The Dutch bank's equity capital had averaged 10% over the previous 20 years.) The €1.25bn 10-year senior contingent notes attracted a €2.6bn orderbook from 181 investors and offered a return of 351 basis points over mid-swaps.

With the European Commission's clampdown on making coupon payments on hybrid instruments imminent in April 2010, the Royal Bank of Scotland (RBS) undertook a massive balance sheet restructuring exercise. RBS proposed £18.2bn equivalent of Upper Tier 2 and Tier 1 securities for either exchange or tender. Some of the Upper Tier 1 notes were to be exchanged for new senior notes while the Tier 1 securities were to be repurchased for cash. Much of the debt was trading at a discount of 60 to 70% of face value. Despite a somewhat subdued take-up by European investors, the liability management exercise succeeded in contributing £1.25bn to RBS's core capital post tax.

RBS was just in time. Investors shunned European bank paper as the Greek crisis reeled out of control and the ECB seemed to be unwilling to support the market. Bank issues dried up completely for almost a month. In July the market waited anxiously for the results of the first pan-European stress tests of the banking system by the Committee of European Banking Supervisors (CEBS). These inaugural tests involved modelling macro-economic and sovereign debt stresses over 2010 and 2011, and applying them to end-2009 capital levels. Only seven of the 91 European banks that underwent stress tests failed, with an aggregate capital shortfall of €3.5bn. Five of these were Spanish. While on the face of it this was better than the market expected, scepticism quickly grew as to the level of stringency used in the health checks and whether the bar had been set too low.

The Basel III rules, first published as proposals in December 2009, were the subject of intense lobbying and negotiation by banks, trade bodies, regulators and government authorities. The result of this process was the announcement by the Basel Committee of the transitional arrangements and key capital ratios in September 2010.

As things stood under Basel II, 50% of Tier 1 capital was supposed to qualify as 'core' equity, which was permanent, absorbed losses and gave the issuer freedom on whether to pay dividends or coupon payments. The rest of Tier 1 could comprise various types of hybrid instruments, which were subject to a patchwork of national laws. Basel III now unequivocally established core equity as king. The minimum requirement for common equity, the highest from of loss absorbing capital, would be raised from the previous 2%, before the application of regulatory adjustments, to 4.5% after the application of stricter adjustments. And this was to be phased in by 1 January 2015. The wider Tier 1 capital requirement, which includes common equity and other qualifying financial instruments based on stricter criteria, would increase from 4% to 6% over the same period. Tier 1 capital should be capital that enables a bank to remain a going concern.

Basel III now introduced two new buffers. Banks must maintain a buffer of capital at 2.5% above the regulatory minimum requirement, to be met with common equity that can be used to absorb losses during periods of economic and financial distress. This 'capital conservation buffer' required reduction in Tier 1 coupons, dividends and discretionary staff remuneration when the Core Equity Tier 1 (CET1) ratio fell below 7%. So when capital levels falls below the minimum CET1 requirement plus the buffer, banks should rebuild them through either raising private capital in the market, and/or reducing discretionary distributions of earnings (reducing dividend payments, share buy-backs and staff bonus payments). In addition a 'countercyclical buffer' in the range of 0 to 2.5% of common equity or other fully loss-absorbing capital would be implemented according to national circumstances. For any given country, this buffer will only be in effect when there is excess credit growth that is resulting in a build up of risk.

A non-risk based leverage ratio would serve as a backstop to the risk-based measures above. There was an agreement to test a 3% leverage ratio during the parallel run period to 1 January 2018. The proposed leverage ratio equalled common equity divided by reported assets with off-balance-sheet assets added back. The key difference with a risk-weighted ratio is that a leverage ratio does not risk adjust the asset.

Meanwhile the BCBS and the FSB were developing an approach to systematically important financial institutions (SIFIs), the 'too big to fail' institutions, which could include combinations of capital charges, contingent capital and bail-in debt. SIFIs would be required to hold extra capital based on a sliding scale linked to risk and size. The range was expected to be 1 to 3% of capital on top of a bank's minimum requirements.

The Basel Committee also devised two standards to address the acute liquidity problems experienced by banks at the start of the global financial crisis. Firstly, it expected banks to comply with a 'liquidity coverage ratio' (LCR) from the start of 2015, which would require them to hold sufficient high-quality assets to withstand a 30-day period of acute stress.

Meanwhile, a 'net stable funding ratio' (NSFR) would come into force from January 2018, designed to eliminate longer-term structural liquidity mismatches on bank balance sheets.

The LCR soon became a source of heated debate. In December 2009 when they first put the Basel III proposals out, the Basel Committee started from the idea that the only truly liquid assets were government bonds, following the traditional concept that the government rate was the 'risk-free' rate. However the events of May and June in the Eurozone now showed this to be something of an anachronism. There were increasing requests for the components of required liquidity buffers to be reconsidered.

In accordance with transitional arrangements under the Basel III framework, all bank regulatory capital instruments issued after 12 September 2010 had to comply with the new rules if they were to continue to qualify as capital after 1 January 2013.

Euromoney expressed exasperation at:

> the endlessly modified metrics and ratios now once again being concocted in Basel ... Banks have shown themselves incapable of safeguarding the system in which they operate. Intrusive, interventionist, expert, powerful, independent regulatory author- ities are the answer. Bankers can avoid tax, overpay themselves, and find their way around every rule and ratio. They must learn to fear the regulator's letter that begins politely: 'It has come to our notice that ...'[19]

While FIG issuance in EMEA dropped by 25% in the first nine months of 2010 compared to the same period in 2009, corporate bond supply was down almost 50% in 2010 on 2009 levels. This was largely due to considerable pre-funding by firms the year before and the low level of merger and acquisition activity. As investors had limited opportunity to secure exposure to the sector, yields were driven down further. As a result, corporate issuers benefited from some of the lowest ever costs of funding.

To avoid the volatility caused by the sovereign crisis many European borrowers had sought refuge in the US market with Yankee bond offerings. Forty per cent of US corporate bond offerings were for European issuers in the first half of 2010. In addition unrated European borrowers were attracted to the US private placement market, which saw record issuance. Apart from the attraction of reaching a wider investor base, the migration to the US market was also driven by the euro/US dollar basis swap which provided a favourable arbitrage opportunity for European borrowers. The negative basis swap spread benefited European issuers by lowering their effective cost of funding compared to issuing directly in the Euromarket. Dollar issuance could provide funding savings of as much as 60 bps over euro. Also the shape of the US yield curve remained relatively flat, which meant borrowers could extend maturity more cheaply than in euros. As a result the majority of European corporate issuance in the US was in the 10-year maturity.

But what had become of the securitisation sector?

The majority of securitisations structured since the collapse of Lehman Brothers had been retained in banks' balance sheets and repo-ed with, or funded by, central banks. Banks regularly issued senior tranches of securitised products for use as collateral in Eurosystem credit operations, or for liquidity reasons. Since the crisis began ABS was the largest single asset class in the composition of the collateral posted with the Eurosystem. Barclays Capital estimated that the amount of asset-backed securities placed with the European Central Bank and the Bank of England – roughly €1trn – was just below the total sold to private sector investors in the entire history of the European market.

A modest recovery in the European ABS market started in September 2009 when Lloyds re-opened the UK residential mortgage-backed sector (RMBS). RMBS was by far the most prominent asset class while commercial mortgage-backed securities (CMBS), credit card, auto loans and leases all experienced declines. Securitisation picked up in 2010 with €76.9bn of new issues (excluding retained deals); while not back to the frenetic years of 2006–7, it was a 300% increase on 2009. Seventy-nine percent of this supply came from the UK and Netherlands and almost all was prime AAA RMBS.

As a result of the crisis, regulators added a series of onerous requirements applying specifically to securitisation. In the EU, CRD 2 had added a 5% risk retention requirement (see above) for any structure that tranched risk, and required the originator of such a structure to carry out more detailed due diligence and risk assessment than hitherto. The CRD 3 proposal, which targeted trading book requirements, hit at re-securitisations (e.g. CDO^2) with a risk weighting of 1250%, effectively a dollar-for-dollar capital charge. (Although implementation of this latter measure was delayed from January 2011 to January 2012.)

The ECB also hit at the securitisation markets. They added tougher rating and transparency requirements for using ABS as collateral, while adding to the required haircut – up from 12% to 16%. ABS of all varieties sat in the highest haircut 'Category 5', below even senior unsecured bank debt. Any new issues had to be triple-A for repo with the ECB, and maintain two ratings with the lowest above A-/A3. Despite the higher haircuts and tighter rating requirements the share of ABS in the Eurosystem increased. In December 2010 the ECB decided to establish loan-by-loan level information requirements for ABS in the Eurosystem collateral framework to increase confidence in the ABS market.[20]

* * *

However the steadily escalating Eurozone crisis was never far from the headlines with other EU Member State debts coming under scrutiny. In June and July Moody's cut Greece's rating to sub-investment grade, Portugal to A1 and Ireland to Aa2. In August S&P cut Ireland's credit rating to AA- on concerns over the costs of shoring up the country's banking system. The following month the Irish central bank announced that the cost of bailing out Allied Irish Bank had ballooned to almost €35bn and other banks faced additional capital needs. Ireland's budget deficit was revised to 32% of GDP, the largest deficit since the euro was created. Fitch downgraded Irish debt to single-A.

In October, with the possibility of further sovereign bailouts looking likely, the French and German leaders agreed that private investors must contribute to future bailouts. The ECB, however, was concerned that forcing bondholders to take losses would serve to drive up sovereign borrowing costs. The debate continued at the G-20 meeting in Seoul, where the Finance Ministers of the largest European economies announced that any private sector involvement in bailouts would not apply to outstanding debt and would only come into effect from 2013. At the end of the year, the European Commission rattled the banking market with a proposal that bank bail-ins should include senior debt where necessary.

In late November, the Irish government finally applied for bailout funds from the EU and the IMF. Within a week a €85bn rescue package was agreed by European leaders in return for harsh austerity measures for the Irish economy. €35bn was designated to support the Irish banking system with the remaining €50bn to help the government's finances. An average interest rate of 5.8% was payable on the loans, above the 5.2% paid by Greece for its bailout. In response the Irish government announced the toughest budget in Irish history.

European leaders also agreed to establish a permanent crisis mechanism, the European Stability Mechanism (ESM), to safeguard the stability of the Euroarea. This would be a permanent replacement for the €440bn European Financial Stability Facility, which would mature in 2013. Any country with liquidity problems would be able to apply for emergency funding from the ESM, with strict conditions attached, without having to restructure its debt. The mechanism should force losses on private investors 'only on a case by case basis'. Greece was also told it could have an extra four-and-a-half years to repay emergency loans totalling €110bn to match the seven-year term offered to Ireland.

By year-end core Europe's combined government and financial debt stood at 164% of GDP; in the US, it was 191%; it was 213% for the UK and 214% for the European peripheral countries.[21]

Was Portugal next in the queue for a bailout?

NOTES

1. *The Guardian*, Financial Crisis: Timeline, 7 August 2012 reproduced with the consent of Guardian News and Media Ltd.
2. *EuroWeek*, Issue 1,016, ECB injects adrenaline to calm banks allergic shock, 10 August 2007.
3. *Euromoney*, Sub-prime fallout: Lessons of the market seizure, September 2007.
4. *EuroWeek*, Issue 1,031, Exportfinans pulls deal, lean times ahead, 23 November 2007.
5. Understanding the Impact of MiFID; City of London Corporation, October 2010, p. 5.
6. *Euromoney*, Bank Capital: Premium for protection, January 2008.
7. ©The Economist Newspaper Limited, London, *Bearing All*, 5 March 2009.
8. *EuroWeek*, Issue 1,046, European issuers spurn market opportunities, 20 March 2008.
9. Newyorkfed.org/newsevents/news/markets/2012/libor (page is no longer live – interested parties should contact the Federal Reserve Bank of New York).
10. *EuroWeek*, Issue 1,051, Libor may be broken, 25 April 2008.
11. *EuroWeek*, Issue 1,070, Tesco's €3bn leaves market in despair, 5 September 2008.
12. *EuroWeek*, Issue 1,077, Bank bond triumph massacres agencies, 24 October 2008.
13. *EuroWeek*, Issue 1,085, Sub debt market in turmoil, 19 December 2008.
14. *Financial News*, Crisis prompts rethink on gentleman's agreement, 8 June 2009.
15. Deutsche Bank Research, *Corporate Bond Issuance in Europe*, 31 January 2013, p. 8.
16. John Cavanagh, *Presentation on Liability Management for ICMA PMC,* Bank of America Merrill Lynch.
17. *EuroWeek*, Issue 1,089, Euro-peripherals, 30 January 2009.
18. BIS, Committee on the Global Financial System, Publications No. 43, *Impact of sovereign credit risk on bank funding conditions,* July 2011.
19. *Euromoney*, Regulation: The case for intrusion, October 2010.
20. European Central Bank, *Recent developments in securitisation*, February 2011.
21. *Euromoney*, Tensions run high over sovereign debt haircuts, January 2011.

CHAPTER 11

Sinking Sovereigns

2011–2013

The year began on an optimistic footing with an anticipated €5bn bond issue by the European Union on behalf of the European Financial Stabilisation Mechanism (EFSM). The EFSM on-lent the money to the Irish Republic as part of its bailout. With price guidance of mid-swaps plus 12–15bps the deal attracted €20bn in orders in under an hour and so final pricing was at the lower spread. Approximately 25% of the offering was placed with Asian central banks and sovereign wealth funds. Within days the bond tightened by 7bps.

This deal paved the way for the eagerly awaited inaugural transaction for the European Financial Stability Facility (EFSF) itself. This €5bn five-year issue attracted €30bn of orders before the book was officially opened. The borrower eulogised:

> *The book was covered almost nine times. We received more than 500 bids for a total of €44.5bn. That, we think is the biggest order book ever. The order books were officially open for only 15 minutes. All the big investors were present. There is no doubt that this huge investor interest is a vote of confidence in the strategy being adopted to restore financial stability in the Euroarea. It also shows that the EFSF's structure is suitable for it to execute its mandate. Particularly strong investor interest came from Asia. The Japanese government bought over 20% of the issue – they see this as a good investment and also contributing to European financial stability.*[1]

The initial price 'whisper' was tightened from an indicative 8bps to 10bps, to mid-swaps plus 6bps. Within days the offer price was below Libor. The European authorities were building their armory for further sovereign setbacks.

But the news bulletins in January diverted international investors' attention from the travails of Europe to developments in North Africa and the Middle East. In Tunisia a humble vegetable seller killed himself after being unfairly treated by police. The incident sparked protests that were brutally put down by the Tunisian authorities. As the protests escalated, Tunisia's leader was forced to flee the country. The so-called 'Arab Spring' had begun. Anti-government demonstrations, protests, uprisings and armed rebellions against dictatorial regimes and corrupt leaders spread across North Africa and the Middle East in early 2011. By February, Hosni Mubarak was ousted from power in Egypt after 30 years. In Libya the uprising against Colonel Gaddafi's regime triggered military intervention by NATO, driving the leader from power. Even Bahrain needed the help of the Saudi army to quell the rioting Shia majority. Violent protests persisted for months against the old ruling elites but opposition groups were often poorly organised and alternative political options proved difficult to determine. But the 'Arab Spring' had changed the mindset in the region and threatened international political stability.

The financial institutions sector was more interested in the Basel Committee's announcement of the principal features that bank capital instruments would have to include from 1 January 2013 to count as regulated capital for 'internationally active banks'. Common equity must form a majority portion of a bank's regulatory capital. Also going forward taxpayers must not be called on to bail out the banks. The Committee proposed that all bank capital instruments should be able to absorb losses at the 'point of non-viability' (PONV) before taxpayers are exposed to any loss, although it was not clear what constituted the PONV. Such loss absorbency was to be achieved by way of permanent write-down of principal of the instrument, or its conversion to equity.

Up to 25% of a bank's Tier 1 requirement may be made up of non-common Tier 1 instruments; this is 'Additional Tier 1'. In relation to 'Additional Tier 1' capital instruments, a bank must have 'full discretion at all times' to cancel dividends and/or coupon payments. Furthermore Basel III would require all Additional Tier 1 instruments to absorb losses on a 'going-concern' basis by either being converted to common shares, or by a principal write-down or write-off; in each case at a pre-specified trigger point.

Hybrid structurers, as ever, were not entirely satisfied with the proposals as many issues remained outstanding. What would be determined as the point of non-viability and how would it be applied? In the case of write-down of principal, could this not be write-down/write-up, to make it equivalent to the equity conversion option?

As FIG desks mulled over these issues, Crédit Suisse hit the market with a landmark $8.2bn contingent convertible, or CoCo, issue for themselves. This comprised a dual-tranche private placement and a public Regulation S offering. The bank announced the completion of $3.5bn and SFr2.5bn in private placements of Tier 1 capital notes to strategic equity investors, Qatar Holdings and the Olayan Group. The Swiss Financial Markets Authority (FINMA), the country's financial regulator, had taken the lead in endorsing CoCos a year previously and had worked closely with Crédit Suisse in defining appropriate terms for these 'Buffer Capital Notes' (BCN). Under proposed Swiss rules the major banks, UBS and Crédit Suisse, would have to hold 10% of core Tier 1 capital and 9% of contingent capital.

The Regulation S offering was for 30-year, non-call five-year (30NC5) Tier 2 notes. The exchange deal with Qatar Holdings and Olayan Group added a layer of structural protection to the Tier 2 instruments. If the minimum Core Equity Tier 1 ratio (CET1) of 10% is breached, dividends and coupons may be deferred or cancelled on their privately placed Tier 1 securities. But if the bank then were to breach the 7% CET1 ratio, the publicly offered Tier 2 notes would convert to equity. They could also be converted if Swiss regulators decide that the bank 'requires public sector support to prevent it from becoming insolvent, bankrupt or unable to pay a material amount of its debts, or other similar circumstances'.

Sceptics doubted there was a sufficient investor base for these innovative instruments. But they were proved wrong when the order book for the public issue exceeded $22bn, with orders from over 500 accounts. After extensive marketing the issue was priced at a yield of 7.875% and quickly traded up to 103. Institutional investors bought around half the issue with private banks taking a further third of the notes. The balance of placement was with convertible and hedge fund investors. The geographical distribution was roughly 70% in Europe, 20% in Asia and 10% with offshore US investors.

The Crédit Suisse issue was the first time a contingent convertible capital instrument was used to comply with the requirements for Tier 1 and Tier 2 capital under the new Basel III guidelines. With this issue attracting such substantial investor demand a growing consensus was developing in the market that CoCos should form part of the future toolkit for financial institutions. Would other regulators follow FINMA's lead in endorsing the instrument?

The market was disappointed when the Financial Stability Board (FSB) announced a delay in setting out guidelines for loss absorbent capital instruments until the end of the year. By summer the Basel Committee dealt a further blow to the contingent capital debate by announcing that the 'too big to fail' G-Sifi banks' extra capital requirement of 1 to 2.5% must comprise common equity only. With regulators in Europe reluctant, or unwilling, to commit to an acceptance of contingent capital instruments, the hoped for wave of issuance after the Crédit Suisse transaction did not materialise. In April the UK's Independent Commission on Banking made clear its strong preference for common equity over contingent capital instruments, suggesting a Core Tier 1 ratio of 10% for banks and for the bail-in of senior debt holders to protect bank depositors.

Euromoney remarked:

> *The proposal to bail-in senior creditors on non-viability of a bank has been the talk of the market ever since it was mooted last year and remains as unpalatable to investors now as it was then. Discussions centre on whether all senior unsecured issuance post-2013 should carry a bail-in provision or whether an entirely new class of senior bail-inable debt should be created. Existing issuance before 2013 will be grandfathered but the likelihood of the sector getting away with no bail-in language at all is diminishing by the day.*[2]

As concerns persisted about the health of Europe's banks, and the possibility of bondholder bail-ins, investors showed a marked preference for covered bond issuance over senior unsecured bank paper; jumbo issues increased by 37% in the first quarter of the year. In the more fragile peripheral countries of Europe covered bonds were now trading through the domestic government paper.

* * *

The storm clouds of the sovereign debt crisis were still overhead. In March the Portuguese Prime Minister resigned as opposition politicians rejected his proposed austerity budget. Government bond yields sky-rocketed and S&P and Fitch slashed the country's sovereign ratings. By April the country was forced to seek bailout funds. After three weeks of negotiation, Portugal agreed a three-year €78bn bailout with the European Union and the IMF. In return for the loan, which included €12bn of support for the country's banks, Portugal had to agree to a number of measures to increase tax revenue and reduce spending so cutting its budget deficit from 9.1% of GDP to 5.9% in 2011. With the Portuguese bailout, €256bn had now been spent to protect the Eurozone.

Despite the Portuguese bailout, sceptics acknowledged that some further form of debt restructuring for Greece was inevitable, even though officials publicly denied it would happen. Market participants now openly speculated whether Greece might leave the Eurozone; the so-called 'Grexit' option. In June, S&P downgraded Greece's sovereign rating to CCC – making it the world's lowest rated sovereign debt. Proposals for fresh budget cuts and austerity measures prompted fresh demonstrations in the streets of Athens.

Despite the deteriorating backdrop, the European Financial Stability Facility (EFSF) managed to issue a €5bn 10-year bond offering, attracting €8bn in orders from more than 100 investors at a minimal premium over existing paper. The reception for the deal prompted EFSF to quickly execute a follow-on €3bn five-year offering with the funds on-lent to Portugal. As with EFSF's previous two issues, Asian investors predominated.

In July the European Banking Authority (EBA) announced the results of their second round of stress tests for European banks. The tests were tightened up from the 2010 exercise with a tougher definition of capital and more extreme adverse scenarios, although the Core Tier 1 capital ratio requirement was reduced from 6% to 5%. The tests also increased capital haircuts for certain government bond holdings but fell short of including a scenario for sovereign default. Eight banks failed the test while another 16 came close to the minimum capital requirement, with Spanish banks making up the largest grouping.

July also saw the eagerly awaited new proposals for CRD IV from the European Commission. These fell broadly in line with Basel III. The Commission planned, however, to implement the key rules defining capital as a Regulation rather than a Directive, i.e. the Capital Requirements Regulation or CRR 1, to eliminate the risks of regulatory arbitrage and to establish a 'single rulebook' for the 8,000 banks in Europe. The accompanying Directive would allow national regulators to determine some aspects of the rules, such as the size of countercyclical buffers and further discretionary capital on an institution-specific basis under Pillar Two.

As they searched through the 600-page proposal, hybrid structurers were disappointed that the Commission did not elaborate on certain features of contingent capital instruments such as write-down/ write-up mechanisms and their prohibition of 'dividend stoppers' (mechanisms that stop dividend payments if coupons have not been paid). Rather the Commission charged the European Banking Authority (EBA) with developing technical standards for such instruments by the end of the year. As expected the trigger point for hybrid securities to be written down or converted to equity was set at 5.125% in line with the capital conservation buffer's 100% retention limit.

The CRD IV proposals hit the press just as European leaders announced a second bailout proposal for Greece amounting to €109bn. The deal, struck at an emergency summit of the Eurozone's 17 member countries, also involved support from the International Monetary Fund (IMF) and was conditional not only on the adoption of a new austerity package but also on private sector involvement in the bailout. Greece's loans were to be restructured on more generous terms. The maturity of the loans would be extended from the existing 7.5 years to a minimum of 15 years and up to 30 years, with a grace period of 10 years. Lending rates would be around 3.5%, close to the costs of borrowing for the EFSF. The maturities of existing loans from the first Greek bailout would be extended.

For the first time the bailout package involved a planned debt exchange scheme for private bondholders and banks amounting to €37bn. Germany in particular had pressed for the private sector to participate in taking a significant 'haircut'. The private sector involvement would take the form of a 'voluntary refinancing' with a 21% haircut, so as not to trigger a credit event under Greek credit default swaps (CDS). However this feature meant that the rating agencies viewed the situation as a 'selective default'. The haircuts on European banks could push some financial institutions in peripheral Europe to the brink, but any hoped for offer of support from the ECB was not forthcoming. However the role of the EFSF was to be expanded to help finance debt buy-backs and possibly intervene in secondary government markets. This second bailout package would become the subject of months of fraught negotiations and was only fully ratified by all parties in February 2012. The Eurozone agreement also eased the terms of bailout loans to Ireland and Portugal.

The market's immediate reaction was to rally strongly on news of the bailout proposal. The market's concerns now moved to Spain and Italy with the latter's government paper touching 6% yields. A leader in *EuroWeek* noted:

> *The way Italian bonds are behaving since the EU launched its contagion-busting Greek bailout is looking eerily familiar to anyone who has watched previous sovereign debt collapses of recent months. It didn't take long for the political rhetoric of solemn promises to pay back debts to wear thin. Barely two days of rallying prices turned into the sort of illiquidity-fuelled price crash that nudges 10-year yields up to the 6% figure that pushed Ireland, Portugal and Greece into seeking bailouts … Leaving it to the expanded EFSF is all well and good, but with the ECB unwilling to step in to backstop troubled sovereigns in the short term, there is still nothing on the table to help the Italians or Spaniards.*[3]

In fact in August the ECB announced it would reintroduce the six-month long-term financing operation, last used in April 2010 to support the European banking market. And under its Securities Market Programme the Bank began buying Italian and Spanish government securities and pushing yields down closer to 5%. Unlike primary market intervention, which was ruled out by the EU Treaty, the ECB considered that secondary market intervention was permitted. Also unlike quantitative easing (QE), ECB intervention is sterilised (that is, the ECB removes from the system elsewhere the same amount of money it spends, ensuring the programme has a neutral impact on the money supply).

Ideas had been circulating for some time on the possibility of the Eurozone issuing 'Eurobonds' to ease the sovereign crisis, particularly for the peripheral countries. This would be a government bond guaranteed on a joint and several basis by all Euroarea governments. The European Commission was charged with putting forward proposals for the issue of such 'Eurobonds'. These 'Eurobonds', it was argued, would make it easier for debtor governments to access the market at lower rates. Critics responded that 'Eurobonds' would increase rates for creditor governments; that the provision of guarantees might affect their credit ratings; and that budgetary discipline of ailing sovereigns would be reduced. In time, the confusing name, 'Eurobond', was dropped and the Eurozone joint government bond was referred to as a 'stability bond'.

With the sovereign debt crisis now at its height, September disappointingly turned out to be a month of warnings rather than action. The IMF urged European countries to 'act now and act together', while the US Treasury Secretary, Tim Geithner, urged Europe to create a 'firewall' around its problems to stop the crisis spreading. The meeting of finance ministers and central bankers in Washington called for 'urgent action'. With signs that Greece would fail to meet its budget reduction targets, the head of the European Union, José Manuel Barroso, warned that the EU 'faced its greatest challenge'. Remarkably in mid-month the European

Union, despite the dire outlook, managed to raise €5bn of 10-year money with the proceeds again being on-lent to Portugal.

Euromoney delivered a jaundiced view of the crisis. In the period since the subprime crisis it noted:

> *[W]e've been through unprecedented rounds of government intervention in the markets and levels of stimulus never before contemplated. We've been through the worst recession in nearly a century – and we might well still be in it. We've made fundamental changes to the banking system, to try to make it safer. We've done an awful lot. But the sad truth is we have achieved almost nothing. The sub-prime crisis turned out to be a precursor to the real issue in the economies of the developed world: there is far too much debt. And for all of the action, all of the emergency meetings, all of the policy initiatives, nothing has been done to successfully address that fundamental issue. Debt has been moved around. It's the most dangerous game of pass the parcel that has ever been played. Governments that spent well above their means for decades took on huge new levels of debt to bail out the banking system and spend their way out of recession. Now they are struggling to pay the bills, even through a period of historically low interest rates.*[4]

In October a further round of austerity measures from the Greek government caused violent anti-austerity protests in the streets of Athens. Greek CDS prices reached a level suggesting that the likelihood of a default over five years was now 95%.

The scheduled EU summit on the debt crisis was delayed by a week so ministers could finalise their plans to allow the next €8bn bailout payment to Greece and to consider an EU-wide bank recapitalisation plan. This proved timely as the Franco-Belgian banking group, Dexia, was on the brink of collapse. The bailout plan for Dexia came after German Chancellor, Angela Merkel and French President, Nicolas Sarkozy agreed Europe's crisis-hit banks needed to be recapitalised. With a balance sheet of more then €500bn, Eurozone governments viewed Dexia's rescue as vital to avoid greater market turmoil. The bailout included a €5.5bn capital injection by Belgium and France and state guarantees of up to €90bn to secure borrowing over the following 10 years. All this only weeks after the EBA 2011 stress tests had given the banking group a clean bill of health. The Dexia bailout yet again raised concern over the potential effect of bank recapitalisation on the indebtedness of individual sovereign states.

To ease pressures, the ECB increased the supply of short-term liquidity to banks in the Euroarea and eased the terms on which it was willing to accept collateral. They announced two operations in October – one for 371 days and one for 406 days. By 19 October the use of emergency overnight ECB lending had risen to €4.8bn. In addition, the ECB, Federal Reserve, Bank of England, Swiss National Bank and Bank of Japan announced they would provide dollar funding over the year-end. The ECB was now effectively adopting the role of the interbank lending market. Capital market funding opportunities looked expensive in comparison, particularly as senior unsecured paper issuance levels were widening on the anticipation of 'bail-in' legislation. Covered bond issuance revived for those institutions with available collateral although investors were becoming more wary about such issuance tying up a significant proportion of a bank's assets.

October's European summit also proposed expanded powers for the EFSF: to insure or absorb losses on government bonds, recapitalise the banks and extend the haircut on Greek government paper from 21% to 50%. This latter measure would provide €100bn of financing for Greece via a bond exchange. A proposal to expand the size, as well as the role, of the EFSF lifeboat fund met with reluctance from some sovereign creditors and contributed to EFSF's spreads widening in the secondary market in anticipation of expanded funding needs. A planned EFSF 15-year, then, 10-year deal in the primary market had to be postponed in early November. When it finally got the 10-year deal away a week later, the EFSF had to offer a spread of 104 basis points over mid-swaps and still the bonds widened in the secondary market.

In the light of the sovereign debt crisis the European Banking Authority (EBA) announced that the 70 biggest European financial institutions were required to reach a new temporary 9% capital ratio by end-June 2012, after stress testing for possible sovereign default. While the measure was widely expected, what was not expected was that, under certain circumstances, contingent capital instruments would be eligible for inclusion in the 9% limit. The EBA announced they were drawing up a common term sheet for the key characteristics of securities eligible under the arrangements.

Exactly 20 years after the meeting that resulted in the Maastricht Treaty, European leaders convened in Brussels in December for a summit to further the integration of Eurozone economies. The key measure was a 'fiscal stability union' or 'Fiscal Compact'. Under this Fiscal Compact Euroarea governments would undertake to limit their structural deficits to 0.5% of GDP and would be subject to penalties if their deficits exceeded 3% of GDP. The compact required changing an existing EU Treaty protocol and for this the unanimous approval of all 27 EU states was required. Despite the UK withholding their vote in protest at the proposed Financial Transaction Tax other EU countries pressed ahead with the Treaty changes.

Finally the ECB gave the markets the shot in the arm they so desperately needed. At year-end they announced a new Long Term Refinancing Operation (LTRO). Round one of the LTRO took place on 21 December supplying 523 banks across the Eurozone with €489.2bn of three-year funding. The loans were due to be repaid within three years at the modest rate of 1%, against a wide range of collateral, right down to single-A rated RMBS or SME loans. Unsurprisingly the biggest takers of the December LTRO were banks in the weaker Eurozone countries: Italy took €110bn, Spain received €105bn, France claimed €70bn, Greece asked for €60bn and Ireland €50bn. The loans helped spur a rally in Spanish and Italian debt, particularly among bonds that would mature before the ECB loans had to be repaid. A second long-term refinancing operation was scheduled for February 29 and the expectation was that this too would meet strong demand from banks, with estimates ranging up to €1trn of liquidity being injected into the banking system across the two operations.

* * *

While the sovereign and bank sectors of the Eurobond market had been pummelled throughout 2011, other sectors benefited from the record low interest rate environment. European corporate issuance in 2011 was almost exactly the same as in 2010 at about €213bn but the euro-denominated share of annual average issuance fell below 50% in 2011 for only the second time since the launch of the euro. (On average, 59% of corporate bond issuance had been in euros since 1999.) The dollar-euro basis swap had been favourable to European corporate borrowers issuing in dollars and swapping back into euros. Indeed the best European corporates were able to price bonds through the bank market and in some cases, even through their domestic sovereigns. Deutsche Bank calculated that 172 investment grade and high-yield companies issued bonds for the first time between the beginning of 2009 to end-February 2012.

One particular feature of the busy corporate primary market was the increasing number of bookrunners on deals. Passive bookrunners, who take little, if any, part in deal execution, became increasingly prevalent as companies needed to reward banks for ancillary services. *Euromoney* quotes DCM bankers comments at the time:

Borrowers are under pressure from the banks to reward them for the services they are providing. Banks need to make up for lost loan business or for providing very cheap loans below their own cost of funds. If a lender writes a loan at 50 basis points for a credit that is trading in secondary at 75bp then it is effectively subsidising that borrower's cost of funding by 25bp. So in return it wants to be on the DCM ticket.

Another commented 'In recent years the focus of all lending banks on ancillary revenues and particularly DCM business has become far more acute ... This is notable with the increasing involvement in primary deals of institutions that often have very limited bond distribution capabilities.'[5] A classic example was the €1.25bn $5\frac{1}{2}$-year issue for Vivendi, the French media and telecoms group, in January 2012, which had 16 bookrunners, of which four were active.

The first half of 2011 saw a surge in high-yield corporate issuance and a record year looked on the cards. European companies issued €38bn of high-yield bonds up to June, approaching 2010's record issuance of €51bn. Investors chased yields in the low rate environment and supply was forthcoming as many European companies couldn't get loans from deleveraging banks. The number and size of high-yield bonds issued in the first nine months of 2011 was up 43% from the same period in 2010 and hit the highest level since 2007, according to Dealogic. But only 12% of these junk bonds were issued in the third quarter as the Eurozone sovereign crisis was deepening and investors became increasingly nervous, shunning risky bonds despite their lucrative yields.

As the New Year dawned investors could not hide from the reality of the ongoing sovereign crisis. The failure of John Corzine's MF Global, and subsequent revelations about its significant exposure to European peripheral sovereign debt, renewed suspicion among banks regarding their actual positions in such debt. Standard and Poor's downgraded nine Eurozone countries, stripping both France and Austria of their triple-A ratings. Days later they downgraded the European Financial Stability Facility (EFSF). But what of the market's biggest issuer, the European Investment Bank (EIB), where France and Germany owned 16.2% of the subscribed capital? EIB also teetered on the edge of a downgrade but was spared the humiliation by the historical performance of its loan book. Respite was available for investors a few weeks later when Canada issued a comparatively rare $3bn five-year global offering. At only 8bps spread to the US Treasury and a coupon of 0.875% the deal nonetheless attracted over 200 orders totalling $9.5bn and subsequently tightened to 4bps spread.

The hoped-for momentum of contingent capital issuance after the Crédit Suisse CoCos did not develop. Rabobank launched two Tier 1 deals both exposed to permanent principal write-down rather than equity conversion. In mid-February UBS tested the market with a low-strike Tier 2 issue featuring a permanent principal write-down trigger. This was a dollar-denominated 10-year non-call five-year (10NC5) offering with a trigger of 5%. Investors who had shown enthusiasm for Crédit Suisse's earlier high-strike contingent convertible did not warm to the new structure; and with warnings of a possible Moody's downgrade of UBS, the deal immediately traded down.

Further hybrid deals were put on hold as the markets awaited the European Banking Authority's (EBA) consultation paper on technical standards for hybrids due in April. *EuroWeek*'s leader remarked: 'Now the European Banking Authority has a particularly thankless task ahead: drawing up the all-important fine print for bank hybrids. The details are dry and stuffed with jargon and acronyms, but what the EBA decides on how hybrids should write down, and potentially write up, in times of stress will determine the cost of capital for Europe's banks for years to come.'[6] When the EBA released its long awaited consultation in April it set out the proposals on write-down, write-up hybrid structures, putting such instruments more on a par with those converting to equity.

The second ECB LTRO auction in February saw 800 banks participate versus the 523 that took part in the first auction in December 2011. The ECB allotted €529.5bn, slightly higher than the €489bn allotted in December but some distance from the €1trn figure that was being speculated upon earlier. As a result of the cheap funding, peripheral government bond yields declined by as much as 1%. Of course to access the ECB's liquidity facilities, banks had to pledge more assets just as the amount of collateral also being pledged in covered bonds and repo transactions was increasing sharply. Fitch estimated median encumbrance of European banks to be 28% of funded bank assets (19% outside Europe), although there were wide national variations, with the largest increases being for those banks most dependent on ECB liquidity. According to RBS research, 'The LTRO will of course lead to a further encumbrance of balance sheets away from senior unsecured creditors, with our macro credit strategists recently estimating that the first LTRO alone forced unsecured bank bonds 1% lower down capital structures if looked at on a European industry-wide, aggregate perspective.'[7] Other commentators felt that the risk of possible bail-in legislation would eclipse the threat of encumbrance in subordinating bank bondholders. Banks would need to be just as concerned at what was below them in the capital structure as what was above them.

By March the majority of private bondholders had agreed to the Greek bond exchange, receiving a lower rate for a longer term on the new paper. To force the remaining bondholders to accept the exchange the Greek government decided to exercise collective action clauses. This action, forced on bondholders, now meant that a 'credit event' had occurred under ISDA credit default swap rules.

A notable feature in the bank market in the fourth quarter of 2011 and the first quarter of 2012 was banks undertaking liability management exercises. Banks took advantage of the depressed trading levels on their subordinated and hybrid paper to buy back bonds and thereby increase their Core Equity Tier 1 ratios. This contributed to banks successfully meeting the EBA's 9% Core Capital ratio by the end of June.

The bright light amongst the gloom for the first half of the year was the booming corporate sector. In the first week of the year BMW set the tone attracting €7bn of demand for a €2.5bn two-tranche deal. In the Yankee market SABMiller's $7bn bond in January was the largest corporate bond for three years, and BHP Billiton's $5.3bn issue was the largest deal from an Australian corporate on record. By early May 2012 $182bn was raised from 315 deals, compared to $118bn over the same period in 2011 from 259 deals and $126bn from 253 deals in 2010. The buoyant market brought with it high levels of oversubscription on new corporate issuance and consequently reduced investor allocations. Increasingly investors responded by inflating orders for deals to try and secure a reasonable allocation. ICMA's Primary Market Practices Committee spent much time discussing the problems and seeking to recommend best practice guidelines for both syndicate managers and investors.

* * *

But while the primary market was buoyant, the effects of the banking crisis were taking their toll on the secondary markets where liquidity had been draining away for a period of years. Traders had permanently reduced, or rather been forced to reduce, their bond inventories to preserve capital. At the ICMA AGM and Conference in Milan, Michael Ridley of J.P. Morgan noted that his bank traded 5,000 secondary Eurobond issues in 2011. Of the top 1,000 bonds, only eight traded more than three times a day, while 26 traded twice a day, 134 once a day and 832 traded just three times a week. Most notably he added that 145,000 bonds in the secondary market did not trade at all in 2011.

The story was similar in the US where corporate bond inventory at US broker-dealers was at a nine-year low. The February 2012 Federal Reserve's monthly dealer updates revealed inventories of US corporate bonds with over one year to maturity at just $45bn, compared to $93bn in February 2011 and $135bn in February 2006. As secondary markets contracted then the likelihood of institutional investors developing their own securities crossing networks was growing. In May a group of US investment managers called an emergency meeting with nine US investment banks to discuss the lack of liquidity in the secondary market.[8]

The debate over the separation of banking activities, which had raged since the beginning of the crisis, also had implications for secondary market-making going forward. The 'Volcker Rule' in the US, banned banks from undertaking proprietary trading. In the UK the Vickers Report proposed ring fencing banks' retail activities. In Europe the Liikanen Report in October 2012 recommended ring fencing banks' trading activities, leading to a scenario where a new bond issue would be launched by one banking entity but traded by a separate banking entity.

However most concern regarding the secondary markets was focused on the review of MiFID. In the light of the global financial crisis, the European Commission had decided to review the MiFID framework implemented in 2007. In October 2011, they adopted proposals for a revised Directive, MiFID 2 and a new Regulation, MiFIR. This continued the pattern of breaking out the key rules from Directives into a Regulation, adopted by every member state in an identical format. These were structural reforms aimed at establishing a safer, sounder, more transparent and more responsible financial system. The focus was on the less regulated and more opaque parts of the financial system, especially instruments traded over the counter (OTC). The proposals introduced a new 'catch-all' category of regulated trading venue, an 'Organised Trading Facility' (OTF). This would effectively be any facility or system operated by an investment firm not already regulated as a trading venue under existing MiFID rules i.e. a Regulated Market, an MTF or a Systematic Internaliser. The draft Regulation extended pre- and post trade transparency requirements for all trades (executed on a RM, MTF, or OTF) not just in equity but in bonds and structured finance products. It was these controversial proposals that had prompted the debate on bond market liquidity at the ICMA Conference. Traders argued that extending pre-and post trade transparency proposals to Eurobonds would not make the market more liquid. Traders would in fact be less willing to trade due to the increased vulnerability of any positions they took on in a thin market.

Other forces were at play reducing secondary bond market activity. The disappearance of the synthetic CDO market during the crisis led to a significant reduction in CDS activity. Since its peak of $58trn equivalent of CDS outstanding in mid-2008, the market had halved to roughly $29trn by the end of 2011. CDS spreads were more volatile and were no longer used as an indicator for spreads in the primary market.

In September 2011 there was a further blow for the secondary bond markets. The President of the European Commission put forward a plan to introduce a new financial transactions tax (FTT) in the EU 'to make the financial sector pay its fair share'. It was proposed that bond and share transactions be taxed at 0.1%. The tax would become chargeable for each financial transaction at the moment it occurred and would have to be paid by each financial institution involved in the transaction. Exchanges of financial instruments would be considered as two transactions for tax purposes, while repurchase and reverse repurchase agreements and securities lending and borrowing will be regarded as only one transaction.

Despite their cries for greater liquidity in the bond markets, the European regulators were now proposing to tax liquidity itself. The proposal created controversy from the start, with the UK in particular vehemently opposed to the plan. By October 2012, the Commission had to abandon plans for an EU-wide transaction tax after there proved to be insufficient support for the proposals. But, under the 'enhanced cooperation' procedure, a minimum of nine EU Member States were allowed to go forward with their own plan for FTT, and eleven participating member states proceeded under this process.

The securitisation sector had also failed to pick up in the aftermath of the crisis. The financial markets were keen to rebuild trust in securitisation which had suffered from its toxic tag since the beginning of the crisis. The Association of Financial Markets in Europe (AFME) launched its 'Prime Collateralised Securities' (PCS) initiative in June 2012. The initiative aimed to draw a line between pre-crisis securitisation, tarnished by US subprime lending, and post-crisis, clean, transparent low loan-to-value (LTV) lending. It was intended as a seal of quality or kite-mark for the best ABS and sought to persuade regulators to allow PCS-labelled securitisations into bank liquidity buffers, i.e. the LCR under Basel III, and to encourage the ECB to reduce the haircuts applied to PCS labelled ABS. However the multiplicity of securitisation structures across jurisdictions and asset classes would make the job of drafting standard rules challenging.

In June the behaviour of bankers came under the spotlight again when some Barclays traders were accused of attempting to rig the daily Libor fixing. The events referred back six years to 2007–2008, as the global banking crisis was developing. On 27 June, Barclays admitted to misconduct with regard to the rate fix. The UK's FSA imposed a £59.5m penalty although many accused the regulator of being asleep on the job and only re-alerted to the affair by legal moves in the United States. The US Department of Justice and the Commodity Futures Trading Commission (CFTC) imposed fines of £102m and £128m respectively, requiring Barclays to pay a total of around £290m. Despite a robust defence of Barclays' position, chief executive Bob Diamond was forced to resign and the already weak public perception of bankers and the banking industry deteriorated further. The regulators now began to scrutinise other banks for possible collusion in similar market manipulation activities.

* * *

After much speculation, in early June the Spanish government was forced to request a €100bn loan from the EU to recapitalise the country's banks. The Spanish authorities did not have the resources to bail out the troubled banking sector and bank funding levels in the capital markets were prohibitive. Some cynical observers wondered if, to all intents and purposes, this was an undercover bailout of the sovereign itself, without the accompanying austerity measures. But no sooner had a sticking plaster been put on Spain's woes than Cyprus asked for help. In June the Cypriot government requested 'external financial assistance' from the European

Financial Stability Facility or European Stability Mechanism. The country's economic plight was largely as a result of Cypriot banks' exposure to the overheated domestic property market and Cyprus's large exposure to the Greek economy restricting access to the capital markets.

Exiting the Eurozone was not an option. Mario Draghi, President of the European Central Bank, vowed that the ECB was 'ready to do whatever it takes to preserve the euro. Believe me it will be enough.'

Despite the developments in Spain, a month later the European Financial Stability Facility was able to launch the largest ever deal for a supranational borrower. The €6bn five-year offering at 50bps over mid-swaps proved a success attracting €8bn in investor orders, although some inevitably argued that it was too generously priced. This success may have been helped by a perception that any further bailout funds would more likely be raised by the new European Stability Mechanism (ESM). Indeed the market rallied through August and the primary market remained active.

The cause of the August rally was the ECB unveiling its Outright Monetary Transactions (OMT) scheme, in fulfilment of Draghi's promise made earlier in the summer. This was a programme where, under specific conditions, the ECB could purchase unlimited short-dated, one to three-year, sovereign bonds issued by Eurozone member states in the secondary markets. This would help bring down market interest rates and reduce debt-laden countries' borrowing costs. The OMT programme was dependent on a Eurozone government requesting a bailout and was subject to 'strict and effective conditionality' involving the EFSF or ESM. The programme would replace the original Securities Market Programme (SMP). While the programme was widely welcomed there was widespread frustration that the ECB had not come up with such a measure earlier. The *Financial Times*' Martin Wolf was moved to comment: 'By adopting OMT earlier, the ECB could have prevented the panic that drove the (bond) spreads that justified the austerity. It did not do so. Tens of millions of people are suffering unnecessary hardship. It is tragic.'[9]

September was most notable for bank bond buy-backs. As a result of deleveraging and restructuring, Royal Bank of Scotland (RBS) found itself with excess liquidity, as had Crédit Suisse and Lloyds before them. This was put to work in a substantial US and non-US cash tender offer targeting £16.6bn of outstanding senior notes across 19 different tranches. £4.2bn was subsequently successfully repurchased. Lloyds and Barclays followed suit taking the total debt targeted by UK banks to £41.4bn for the month. These exercises produced a tightening in financial institutions' senior unsecured spreads.

Later Barclays revived the faltering contingent capital market, with a high-trigger Tier 2 contingent convertible with full principal write-down. The UK authorities had offered no guidance so far as to whether contingent capital instruments would be acceptable in calculating UK banks' regulatory capital ratios, but with the launch of the Barclays CoCo transaction it was assumed the FSA had given its tacit blessing. The $3bn 10-year bullet instrument would be permanently written down, in full, if Barclays' Core Equity Tier 1 ratio falls below 7% of risk-weighted assets. The high trigger was much more to investors' liking, than the earlier low-trigger UBS offering, and after a global marketing campaign the lead managers built a $17bn order book, largely comprising Asian private banks, US institutional accounts and European investors.

Meanwhile the European regulators had been working overtime. The European Commission now set out its long awaited proposals for bank bail-ins, or more specifically for bank resolution regimes, the Bank Recovery and Resolution Directive (BRRD). The draft BRRD provided, inter alia, for regulators to have 'bail-in' powers, as part of the overall action taken to resolve a bank with minimum cost to taxpayers. These powers would allow the Resolution Authorities to compel the write-down or conversion of a broad range of liabilities of a failing bank or financial institution. These liabilities were proposed to include non-common equity Tier 1 instruments, Tier 2 instruments, other subordinated debt and most senior unsecured debt (excluding guaranteed deposits and very short-term debt). The BRRD, when enacted, is to be implemented by Member States by 1 January 2015, although implementation of the bail-in provisions may be delayed until 1 January 2018. In January 2013 the European Banking Authority (EBA) asked cross-border banks to draw up recovery plans by the end of the year to bridge the gap until the BRRD is implemented. The BRRD proposals opened up the opportunity for Tier 2 bond issuance with the point of non-viability (PONV) trigger requirement covered under the statutory framework.

In September the EU authorities added to the ever-increasing torrent of banking regulation with the Commission's ambitious proposals for 'European Banking Union'. Banking union was an inevitable consequence of the persistent fear of peripheral countries leaving the Eurozone, and the German government's steadfast rejection of the 'Eurobond' or 'stability bond' concept. Banking union would effectively provide support for Europe's weaker banks by pooling them with Europe's stronger banks. Under the proposals new powers would be given to the European Central Bank (ECB) as a common banking supervisor for major banks in the Eurozone. With a new 'Single Supervisory Mechanism' (SSM), as it was termed, ultimate responsibility for specific supervisory tasks related to the financial stability of all banks in the Euroarea would lie with the ECB. According to the EU proposals, the ECB will 'have direct oversight of Eurozone banks, although in a differentiated way and in close co-operation with national supervisory authorities'. As part of the banking union proposals the EBA would develop a *Single Supervisory Handbook* to preserve the integrity of the single market and ensure coherence in banking supervision for all EU countries.

EU Member States not in the Euroarea were invited to participate in the SSM, and it was expected that 17 Euroarea states plus seven other EU Member States would join (with the UK, Sweden and Czech Republic remaining outside). The ECB would be directly responsible for supervising large cross-border banks in the Euroarea and all other Euroarea banks with assets above €30bn of more than 20% of national GDP (i.e. around 150 banks in total). In December 2012 EU Finance Ministers agreed on the SSM although the implementation date was delayed to 1 March 2014 (or 12 months after the entry into force of the legislation). The Bundesbank lobbied successfully to exclude smaller retail and savings banks from the banking union proposals.

It was proposed that the SSM be accompanied by a 'Single Resolution Mechanism' (SRM). So if a bank anywhere in the Eurozone experienced difficulties, the ECB could intervene, and the process of bailing it out, or winding it up, would be managed by a common 'resolution authority', funded by a levy on Eurozone banks.

It was further hoped that a single European 'Deposit Guarantee Scheme' could be agreed for Euroarea banks in place of the various national schemes. So anyone with a bank account in the Eurozone would have their money guaranteed by a common Eurozone fund up to €100,000.

In the final quarter of 2012 the favourable currency basis swap between dollars and the euro and sterling encouraged a raft of US blue chip companies, such as AT&T, Pepsico and IBM, to tap the European markets for the first time in years, swapping back the proceeds to acquire attractive dollar funding. Corporate borrowing costs globally, but particularly in the Eurozone, were now at historically low levels, and likely to continue so in 2013 aided by substantial central bank largesse. Euro-denominated international corporate debt increased

69.5% in 2012, according to Thomson Reuters, making it the second largest issuance on record after 2009. Dealogic estimates European corporate investment grade bond issuance totalled $483bn equivalent in 981 deals. European high-yield issuance reached record levels as investors searched for yield. 2012 saw high-yield issuance approaching €70bn in almost 400 deals.

The rally in corporate bonds in the second half of 2012 pushed investor returns to a three-year high. In this low yield environment how did spreads compare to spread differentials going into the financial crisis? Deutsche Bank Research noted that the yield gap between AA and BBB rated corporate bonds was 49bps in January 2007, but stood at 158bps in January 2013. This suggested that yield-hungry investors were now more discriminating on risk than they were before the crisis.[10]

Unfortunately the loan markets had a torrid 2012. With their focus on impending Basel III regulation and their concerns about the Eurozone, EMEA syndicated loans fell by 33% during the year, while global syndicated loans contracted by 16%, according to Dealogic. European companies' outstanding stock of loans had shrunk and become shorter term while the stock of corporate bonds has grown from €1.1trn at the beginning of 2008 to €1.7trn by July 2012.

Late in the year the EU and IMF agreed an inevitable further bailout for Greece, writing off €40bn of debt and releasing further bailout funds of €44bn in order to avoid a Greek exit from the Eurozone. The bailout was conditional on Greece sticking with its austerity programme in full. Other measures agreed were a reduction in the interest rates on Greece's bilateral bailout loans, a decade-long suspension on interest on loans from the EFSF, and a pledge to finance a buy-back of Greek government bonds.

The New Year is traditionally a time for a flood of SSA issuance but January 2013 saw an explosion of issuance. There was more than €25bn of oversubscribed offerings in just one week. Even peripheral Eurozone sovereigns shared in the euphoria. Spain managed to success-fully launch a jumbo €7bn 10-year offering, marking a change in investor sentiment. Ireland, Italy and Portugal also launched syndicated deals that were quickly oversubscribed. In total there were 27 new euro and dollar SSA benchmark issues in January raising $91.1bn of new funding.[11] By March, Ireland confirmed its status as the fastest recovering patient among the peripheral sovereigns with its highly successful €5bn 10-year syndicated benchmark issue. This was achieved against a background of an election in Italy that effectively left the country with-out a government. Investor orders totalled €13bn and the deal tightened in the secondary market.

Was this the beginning of the long road to recovery?

In the ultra low yield environment, hybrid capital deals proved popular with yield-hungry investors. January saw as much corporate hybrid issuance as in the whole of 2012. The €6.2bn hybrid package for Electricité de France (EDF), more than three times larger than any previous corporate hybrid issue, proved a blowout. The success of the European tranches was immediately followed up by a blowout $3bn tranche. Copy-cat deals by other European utilities followed in the first quarter.

The Basel Committee added to the New Year cheer with a more pragmatic approach to banks' liquidity requirements. The Committee widened the definition of high quality liquid assets (HQLA) for the liquidity coverage ratio (LCR) by including so-called Level 2B assets, subject to higher haircuts and limits. Corporate debt securities rated A+ to BBB- and certain unencumbered equities could now be included subject to a 50% haircut. In addition, much to the relief of the ABS market, certain residential mortgage-backed securities (RMBS) rated AA or higher could be included with a 25% haircut. However the aggregate of these Level 2B assets, after haircuts, could not exceed 15% of total HQLA. The Committee also extended the deadline for full LCR adoption until 2019 with the minimum LCR in 2015 being 60% and increasing by 10% per year to reach 100% in 2019.

Investors in peripheral Europe were now faced with the widely expected news of a bailout for Cyprus in order to keep them in the Eurozone. After tortuous wrangling, a €10bn international bailout by the EU, the ECB and the IMF (the 'troika') was announced in March to recapitalise the country's ailing banking system. In return Cyprus agreed to close the country's second-largest bank, the Cyprus Popular Bank (also known as Laiki Bank). All lenders to Laiki Bank had their investments wiped out, including senior, unsecured bondholders – a first for a Eurozone bailout. All deposits over €100,000, totalling €4.2bn, would be placed in a 'bad bank', implying they could be wiped out entirely. Smaller depositors at Laiki would have their accounts transferred to the Bank of Cyprus, the island's largest commercial bank. The Bank of Cyprus survived but investors not protected by the €100,000 deposit guarantee would suffer a major 'haircut' on their investments of up to 40%. This agreement had to be enforced in Cyprus by the imposition of capital controls – but an embarrassing exit from the Eurozone was avoided. *EuroWeek* commented: 'As far as the Eurozone and the SSA market is concerned, Cyprus is a controlled explosion isolated from the volatile substances of the Italian and Spanish economies.'[12] Indeed, post the Cyprus agreement, Italian and Spanish sovereign offerings continued to enjoy lower yields as fund managers piled into periphery paper. In April the ECB cut its main refinancing rate by 25 basis points.

In March the Bank of England identified a £25bn capital shortfall among UK banks. Just ahead of the Easter break, Barclays launched a further contingent capital transaction much along the lines of their November 2012 Tier 2 offering; a 10-year non-call five-year issue (10NC5) with a 7% core equity Tier 1 trigger with full principal writeoff. The smaller $1bn offering attracted $3bn of demand and was accompanied by a tender offer for two outstanding subordinated $ issues. The CoCo transaction was notable as the first to include specific bail-in language in its documentation.

*   *   *

In April, Apple smashed all market records with a blockbuster $17bn corporate bond offering – as if heralding the imminent 50-year anniversary of the cross-border bond markets. The order book for the deal reached $52bn within three hours. The company, recently rated Aa1/AA+, managed to raise $1.5bn of three-year fixed rate bonds at 20 basis points over US Treasuries and $4bn of five-year fixed bonds at 40 basis points over. In the floating rate market the company issued $1bn of three-year notes at 5 basis points over Libor, and $2bn of five-year floaters at 25 basis points over Libor. These short-dated issues were topped off with a record-breaking $5.5bn 10-year issue at 75 basis points over Treasuries with a 2.4% coupon and a $3bn 30-year tranche at 100 basis points over Treasuries or 3.5%. A notable feature of the deal was the appointment of only two bookrunning lead managers, Goldman Sachs and Deutsche Bank, who earned underwriting fees of $53.25m between them.

But did Apple need money?

Apple is the world's most valuable company, and has a cash mountain of $145bn and, up to that point, no debt. Aswath Damodaran, Professor of Corporate Finance at Stern School of Business, explained in the *Financial Times*: 'By borrowing from the capital markets, Apple can pay dividends to shareholders more cheaply than if it used the money stored outside the country, while getting a tax deduction for interest expenses. This decision has angered those who like to inveigh against "tax avoidance" and "corporate greed". But the culprit is not Apple, it is the over complex US tax system.'[13]

John Kay added his comments:

> *Apple is raising money because its money is in the wrong places and it would face tax bills if it repatriated the money to the US. The transaction illustrates a paradox in the modern relationship between business and finance. Companies have never had so little need for capital nor so much engagement with capital markets ... A modern company, such as Apple, is knowledge-based, outsources its manufacturing and has little need of any tangible capital at all ...*
>
> *When Apple borrowed, it did so not to raise funds for its business but to return to its shareholders cash secured from operations. Capital markets are no longer mechanisms for putting money into companies, but mechanisms for getting money out.*[14]

So as the 50-year anniversary of the Eurobond market approached, market participants were coaxed into imagining they were back in the good old days before the crisis. The primary markets were booming and DCM desks were enjoying a record year. DCM revenues in the first half of 2013 were running 12% ahead of the same period in 2012. The heady central bank cocktail of quantitative easing (QE), long-term repurchase operations (LTROs) and Open Market Transactions (OMT) was keeping the party in full swing. High-yield, emerging markets and even peripheral Eurozone sovereign paper was meeting strong demand with issues oversubscribed.

Emerging market issuance exceeded $250bn in the first half, according to Dealogic, marking an issuance record. This was helped by an $11bn six-tranche deal for Petrobras breaking the record as the largest ever emerging market transaction, attracting an order book of $43bn.

Even the outlook for ABS was looking brighter. There had been renewed signs of life in both the CMBS and the CLO sectors. Michel Barnier, Commissioner for Europe's Internal Market, released a green paper in April 2013 suggesting a range of measures to promote long-term financing of the real economy including the 'reshaping' of Europe's securitisation market. The paper proposed developing new securitisation instruments for small and medium enterprises and the creation of 'European labels' for structured credit vehicles. The Commission was also reviewing whether capital requirements under the proposed Solvency II Directive for the insurance industry should be adjusted down to remove barriers to investment in assets such as debt securitisation. Mario Draghi, ECB President, also joined the call for reviving the securitisation market.

The only sector not joining the party was the war-torn banking sector, as market participants sought to get their heads around the landslide of regulation. In May the European Parliament's ECON Committee detailed its negotiating position with regard to bank 'bail-in'. An agreed EU 'bail-in' scheme should be operational by January 2016 at the latest. They insisted that insured deposits, below €100,000, can never be subject to bail-in, while uninsured deposits can only be subject to bail-in as a *last* resort. In addition, funds from deposit guarantee schemes must not be used to help pay for bank resolution measures, and taxpayers' money should only be used after *all* capital has been written down to zero.

Meanwhile the ECB argued for the protection of all deposits, not just insured deposits, and believed bail-in powers should only be used to maintain an institution that has reached the point of non-viability as 'a last resort'.

In June EU Finance Ministers agreed on their bail-in plans. Owners, creditors and depositors – in that order – should cover the expenses of bailing out or winding down failed banks. Insured deposits, secured liabilities, employee liabilities, interbank and payment liabilities under seven days would be excluded. Insured deposits would be completely protected, and the preference given to SMEs and individuals deposits. Governments would be allowed to inject funds but only after minimum bail-in of 8% of the total liabilities of the failing bank, although such intervention should be capped at 5% of the bank's liabilities. The ESM can also inject funds but only after all unsecured bondholders are wiped out.

But the fragility of the markets was revealed in June when Ben Bernanke, Chairman of the Federal Reserve, repeated his comment that the US might consider gradually reducing its asset purchase programme and possibly run down (or 'taper') quantitative easing (QE) by the first half of 2014. Markets fell, Treasury yields rose and the new issue pipeline froze temporarily. With concerns about tapering, the 30-year tranche of the recent Apple offering fell to a price of 88 by the end of June, while the 10-year tranche fell to 92 in the secondary market. Still corporate borrowers had never had it so good. According to Barclays indices, average borrowing costs on European investment grade corporate bonds had fallen from 2.8% in the previous summer to just 1.8% in June 2013.

The bond markets now dominated corporate funding. Just less than half of the €495bn total new debt funding for European companies in the first half of 2013 had been from the loan markets, which is the smallest ever proportion and down from 60% in 2012, according to Fitch. Total funding from new bank loans was only €238bn in the first half, suggesting a full-year total below €500bn for the first time in a decade. Bond financing accounted for 82% of the average corporate debt structure, according to Fitch, up from 68% in 2008 – this is a higher ratio than issuance data suggest, because most loans are just unused standby facilities.

So as the 50th anniversary of the Eurobond market was reached on 1 July 2013 the corporate bond markets were in the rudest of health even if propped up by central bank life support systems. The European sovereign bond markets appeared to be on the road to recovery, albeit a fragile one, and the financial institutions sector was acquiring greater clarity on the way forward in a new world where traditional concepts of debt ranking were being turned on their heads.

And here our narrative should stop. But as investment bankers returned to their offices after the summer break there was a bond issue of such significance that it makes a more fitting end to our story.

Corporate finance records were blown apart with the announcement of a $49bn eight-tranche transaction for Verizon, financing its purchase of Vodafone's 45% stake in Verizon Wireless. The deal was almost three times larger than Apple's record-breaking offering. The four lead managers had firstly underwritten a record $61bn 364-day bridge loan to finance the $130bn acquisition. The bond issue refinanced 80% of the bridge loan just 10 days after the acquisition from Vodafone was agreed. The deal included two floating rate tranches, $2.25bn maturing in three years and $1.75bn maturing in five years. In addition there were six fixed rate tranches, $4.25bn three-year, $4.75bn five-year, $4bn seven-year, $11bn 10-year, $6bn 20-year and $15bn 30-year.

The transaction originally targeted an amount of $20–25bn but attracted $101bn of orders from some 1200 investors enabling the $49bn issuance. The paper tightened 60 basis points in its first two or three days of trading. Some market participants felt the deal had been priced too cheaply, while others just grabbed what they could. Indeed the new issue premium (NIP) was around 30% over the overall secondary market spread. However the borrowers' priority was to finance the maximum amount of paper in the shortest possible time as Verizon, rated Baa1/BBB+, already had $47bn debt outstanding. Their aim was to avoid anything more than a one-notch rating downgrade as a result of the financing. In addition the company and the lead managers were nervous that the Federal Reserve might announce tapering plans in its mid-September FOMC meeting which could upset market rates.

The deal of course was a bonanza for the underwriters both in terms of fees and league table standing. The four active bookrunners on the deal shared fees of $166.57m. The seven passive bookrunners shared fees of $89.1m. In addition two co-managers earned $4.7m each, bringing total underwriting fees to $265m. Overall fees were 54 basis points of the amount raised in the issue.

This deal provides a fitting climax to our story. This single transaction for Verizon exceeds in volume the total Eurobond issuance in the first twelve and a half years of the cross-border markets, from mid-1963 until end-1976 – a quarter of the Eurobond market's life.

NOTES

1. *EuroWeek*, Issue 1,189, 28 January 2011.
2. *Euromoney*, Will the bank bail-in make bond investors bail out? June 2011.
3. *EuroWeek*, Issue 1,215, 28 July 2011.
4. *Euromoney*, Why nothing can prevent the next global financial crisis, September 2011.
5. *Euromoney*, How to earn a crust in debt capital markets, June 2012.
6. *EuroWeek*, Issue 1,246, 16 March 2012.
7. *EuroWeek*, Issue 1,243, 24 February 2012.
8. *Financial Times*, Fears grow bond rush will turn to price rout, 22 November 2012.
9. *Financial Times*, The sad record of fiscal austerity, 26 February 2013.
10. Deutsche Bank Research, *Corporate Bond Issuance in Europe*, 31 January 2013, p. 9.
11. *EuroWeek*, Issue 1,290, SSA's market's January party quietens down as secondary fizzles, 1 February 2013.
12. *EuroWeek*, Issue 1,297, A controlled explosion in Cyprus, 22 March 2013.
13. *Financial Times*, Unlike America's tax code, Apple is perfectly rational, 8 May 2013, p. 13.
14. *Financial Times*, Business loves capital markets – but it doesn't need capital, 8 May 2013, p. 13.

Postscript

On 24 June 2013 the International Capital Market Association invited over 300 market participants, both past and present, to a black-tie dinner at The Savoy Hotel, London, to celebrate the 50th anniversary of the Eurobond market. The dinner was addressed by an eminent group of market veterans. Peter Spira, originally of S.G. Warburg, spoke most poignantly, as the sole survivor of the team at Warburgs that organised the original Autostrade transaction. Stanley Ross, in his own inimitable forthright style, spoke of the late 1960s bond settlement crisis and the foundation of the AIBD.*

Eugene Rotberg, formerly Treasurer of the World Bank and a party to the first ever swap transaction gave the most pithy presentation of the evening; a condensed history of market developments and, somewhat tongue-in-cheek, responses as to how the industry adapted to cope with them. He gave a version of a speech he had delivered on a number of occasions:

We made mistakes. How did we hide them?
Answer: Off balance sheet trades or we didn't mark to market….

How to avoid reporting losses?
Answer: For banks, keep lending to a non-paying borrower so it could pay interest. The principle was straightforward. 'A rolling loan gathers no loss.'

How to lend without fear of the capacity of borrowers to repay?
Answer: Securitise. Package the asset. Get rid of it fast. Not to worry about prudential lending.

How to compete?
Answer: In the US, repeal Glass Steagall, and, develop an asymmetrical compensation system which rewarded success but hardly penalised failure.

How to avoid disclosure completely?
Answer: Form a hedge fund.

How to increase return on capital?
Answer: Leverage. Or manage other people's money – or both if the client permitted it.

How to avoid all regulation?
Answer: Hire financial wizards – mathematicians/ physicists. The regulators will never figure it out or catch up. They still haven't:

---

*Stanley Ross died on the 23rd July 2014.

But despite these wondrous things, risk didn't disappear. It was simply hidden or unreported, or passed on, or securitised, but in a world of increased leverage, risk was to be ignored only at one's peril …

But I cannot leave you on such a down note because, despite everything I have said, the people in this room, our predecessors and those who follow, have changed and will change the world. Very simply, you permitted capital, in all of its ordinary and arcane forms, to be available to the private sector, to governments and to multinational institutions. You were bridges to success, you created access, you were the catalyst for globalisation and while you did not invent cross border financing – you honed it, polished it, adjusted it, made it fit the circumstances and the demands of investors.

Hans Joerg Rudloff picked up on the theme of leverage and risk, but went on to say:

I do not want to talk about that; I want to tell you how privileged I feel that I have been able to be part of the extraordinary development of this market. It is a market I always believed in and it is a market where I do believe that there cannot be better mechanisms to allocate capital around the world … We have created – as Gene explained – a complex and complicated machine, but which was, and is, able today to raise trillions of dollars and allocate those across the world. We clearly have helped, after the defeat of the Soviet Union, to bring a new economic and political model to many countries in this world. We have taken the risks, sometimes frivolously, as has been said today, sometimes though with great courage, to spread what we believed in: market economies and market allocation of scarce resources.

Stanislas Yassukovich concluded:

What of the future? I am not very optimistic … we unfortunately live with a political class that has some difficulty learning the lessons of history. All of you here know that the Euromarket was driven to London by capital controls imposed in the United States. The secondary market was driven from Switzerland to London by a transaction tax, known as a stamp tax at the time, in Switzerland. What are we talking about these days? Transaction taxes. We have already seen little hints of capital controls, so the environment is not favourable. On the contrary, it is extremely unfavourable. No doubt there will be a similar gathering 50 years from now. I am not absolutely certain it will be in this time zone. It may actually be in the Pacific region.

Should we call into question the survival of the cross-border bond markets over the next 50 years? The key attributes of the cross-border bond market are its bearer status and its freedom from withholding taxes at source. Is this bearer status, with its concomitant opacity, sustainable in a world where we have experienced a massive financial crisis triggering a landslide of new regulation and a requirement for greater transparency? Possibly not. The adoption of the pot system in the Eurobond market with its required 'name give-up' provided the first significant nail in the coffin of bearer status. Transparency requirements by regulators may well force the market towards greater disclosure including a requirement for the registration of securities. That in itself should not be a deal-killer and the market should survive any such development.

The question of withholding taxes is a trickier one. History does not support the long-term maintenance of fixed currency agreements. Evidence is rife, from the gold standard to Bretton Woods, that fixed currency agreements between widely differing economies eventually break down. The euro will need to defy history if it is not also to succumb to such pressures. The danger is that if any major European currency re-alignment is found to be necessary, if it is acrimonious, then trade barriers will be raised, and withholding taxes may well be introduced. This would strike at the heart of the cross-border markets. Solving the issues around the single currency in Europe is imperative for the survival of the cross-border market we have built over the last 50 years.

The global financial crisis has its roots firmly in the debt markets; but is there, as some claim, too much debt? The average debt levels of industrial countries were 165% of GDP in 1980 but had risen to 320% of GDP by 2010. This is an annual average increase of more than 5%. Adjusted for inflation, corporate debt has risen three times; over this period, government debt has risen four and a half times and household debt six times, and all are still rising. But why have debt levels risen so far? Yves Mersch, Governor of the Central Bank of Luxembourg in 2011, gives the principal reasons as the liberalisation of credit markets since the late 1970s and the introduction of (complex) financial innovations.[1] This is very much part of our story, so should the Eurobond market be shouldering some of the blame?

From a corporate financing perspective, debt is cheap compared to equity. Financing with equity has attractive attributes; the money does not have to be returned to shareholders and the company has the flexibility, if it wishes, not to pay dividends. But from the perspective of the shareholder these attributes contribute to higher risk and therefore the shareholder will naturally seek a higher return. This raises the cost of equity funding. That in itself is sufficient to promote a preference for debt funding over equity.

In addition, borrowing is considered a basic cost of doing business and in most jurisdictions the interest that a company pays is treated as a tax-deductible expense. Dividends and retained earnings are not. With this 'tax shield', as the corporate finance academics term it, the respective government subsidises the company's borrowing. Corporate tax rates around the world vary between 10% and 40%, with the majority of jurisdictions in the 20–35% bracket.[2] This represents a considerable benefit for the company to pursue, and a major incentive towards debt financing.

If the financial authorities believe we have excessive levels of debt then the simplest approach to address this surfeit is to reduce or remove this tax subsidy. This does not appear to have been seriously considered in the current crisis.

Perhaps the issue is not that absolute amounts of debt are excessive but that there are weaknesses in the financial system that create excessive debt spikes at different points of the cycle.

In a capitalist society, greed is the one constant; both corporate greed and individual greed. The dogged focus on shareholder returns in the last decades has promoted a system prone to excess. If the business cycle turns down we still expect companies to perform against the odds, and the financial press singles out and condemns the under-performers. But if we demand strong returns in difficult markets then companies and banks will resort to excessive risks, and more than likely, excessive leverage.

The extraordinary achievements of the first half-century of the cross-border bond markets are plain for all to see, but so also are the mistakes. We must learn the lesson so simply articulated in a BIS Working Paper entitled 'The Real Effects of Debt':

> *Debt is a two-edged sword.*
> *Used wisely and in moderation, it clearly improves welfare.*
> *But when it is used imprudently and in excess, the result can be disaster.*[3]

NOTES

1. *The Challenges of Excessive Indebtedness,* Yves Mersch, Governor, Central Bank of Luxemburg, address at Euro Finance Week, Frankfurt, 15 November 2011.
2. KPMG Corporate Tax Rates Table, 2013.
3. *The Real Effects of Debt,* BIS Working Paper No. 352, Stephen G. Cecchetti, M.S. Mohanty and Fabrizzio Zampoli, September 2011.

Glossary

This glossary focuses on the instruments, practices and the jargon of the cross-border bond markets. It does not seek to explain the relevant regulatory bodies and regulatory measures relevant to the capital markets, which would probably fill a volume on their own.

Account A client or customer.

Account X A client order in a pot syndication where the client's identity is not revealed.

Active bookrunner A bookrunner on a corporate bond issue charged with arranging, pricing and allocating the issue.

Amortisation Debt repayment by way of instalments over a scheduled period.

Asset stripping The process of buying an undervalued company with the intent to sell off its assets for a profit.

Back office A securities firm's accounting, clearing and settlement operations.

Bail-in When banks are in difficulty bondholders forfeit part or all of their investment to 'bail in' the bank before taxpayers are called upon.

Basis points or 'bps' or 'bips' One hundredth of one percent, i.e. 1 bp = 0.01%.

Basis risk The risk that the relationship between the differences (spread) of the price or rates of two closely linked financial instruments will change over time.

Bear squeeze (or short squeeze) A bond rising in value having been subject to a substantial level of short sales forcing traders to take losses.

Bearer bonds A bond owned by whoever is holding it, rather than having a registered owner.

'Bells and whistles' Additional features of a security designed to attract investors and/or reduce issuer costs.

Benchmark Underlying (government) bond or swap of similar maturity against which spreads are calculated. Most bonds are priced relative to a benchmark.

Benchmark issue An issue of normal, liquid size relevant to the type of borrower.

Bid-ask or bid-offer spread A two-way price comprising a bid, or the price at which a trader is willing to buy, and an ask (or offer) at which a trader is willing to sell.

Bond covenant A legally binding term of an agreement between a bond issuer and a bond holder. Bond covenants are always incurrence rather than maintenance based.

Bookbuilding Investors indicate to the underwriter how many bonds they would like to buy in a new issue and these indications are accumulated in order to assess demand and set the price of the issue.

Bookrunner A lead manager in a bond issue with the responsibility, in whole or part, for managing the P&L of the transaction. Bookrunners are always lead managers, but lead managers are not always bookrunners.

Bought deal   The lead manager(s) buys a whole bond issue on predetermined terms and price and then looks to place the bonds with investors, i.e. final issue terms are agreed between the lead manager and borrower prior to the issue's launch.

Brady bonds   Bank debt to developing countries converted into negotiable bonds backed by US Treasuries under a scheme introduced in 1989 by the then US Treasury Secretary Nicholas Brady.

Bridge   The automated interface or link between the ICSDs, Euroclear and Clearstream (formerly Cedel).

Bullet   A bond which pays a fixed rate of interest and is redeemed in full on maturity. Sometimes called a 'straight' or 'vanilla' bond.

Bunds   German government bonds.

Buy-side   Institutional investors who buy investments on behalf of others.

Call feature   The issuer has the option to redeem (i.e. call) the bond on specified dates and prices prior to maturity.

Cap   The highest interest rate that can be paid on a floating rate security.

Capital adequacy   Measure of the financial soundness of a bank, usually calculated as a ratio of its capital to its assets.

Carry trade   A transaction where money is borrowed at a low interest rate to finance the purchase of a security with a higher one.

CD: Certificate of Deposit   A money market instrument issued by a depository institution as evidence of a time deposit – typically less than one year.

CDO: Collateralised Debt Obligation   A securitised interest in a pool of loans or debt instruments typically divided into tranches. It may be a collateralised loan obligation (CLO) if it holds only loans or collateralised bond obligation (CBO) if it holds only bonds.

CDO^2   A CDO structure where the underlying portfolio is made up of other CDOs (also called a 'resecuritisation').

CDS: Credit Default Swap   A credit derivative where the seller agrees, for an up-front or continuing premium or fee, to compensate the buyer when a specified event, such as default, restructuring of the issuer of the reference entity, or failure to pay, occurs.

Central Counterparty or CCP   CCPs place themselves between the buyer and seller of a transaction and effectively guarantee the obligations under the contract agreed between the two counterparties, both of which would be participants of the CCP.

CMO: Collateralised Mortgage Obligation   A bond backed by multiple pools (or tranches) of mortgage securities or loans.

CoCo: Contingent Convertible   Hybrid capital securities that absorb losses when the capital of the issuing bank falls below a certain level. They automatically convert into equity on some trigger event, such as a bank's core Tier 1 capital falling below a prescribed limit.

Collar   Upper and lower limits (cap and floor, respectively) on the interest rate of a floating rate security.

Collective action clauses   Contractual provisions that enable a sovereign issuer to approach bondholders with a proposal to modify key terms of the relevant bond(s). If certain specified quorums are reached, then the modifications are binding on all bondholders.

Commercial paper   Short-term financial obligations with maturities ranging from 2 to 270 days, issued by banks, corporations and other short-term borrowers. They are unsecured and usually sold at a discount.

Convertible bond   A bond containing an option that permits conversion to the issuer's common stock at some fixed exchange.

Coupon   The rate of interest on a bond. Eurobonds always pay interest annually.

Covered bond Senior, secured obligations of a regulated financial institution. The bonds are secured by a pool of mortgage loans or public sector debt and they offer investors a preferential claim over these assets.

Credit card receivables Asset-backed securities collateralised by credit card repayments.

Credit derivative An OTC derivative designed to transfer credit risk from one party to another.

Credit enhancement A variety of provisions that may be used to reduce the credit risk of an obligation.

Cross default Repayment of a bond issue can be accelerated if a borrower defaults on any of its other debts.

Currency swap A swap that involves the exchange of principal and interest in one currency for the same in another currency.

Custodian A bank or other institution that holds securities on behalf of investors. The custodian's tasks include: the safekeeping of securities, delivering or accepting traded securities and collecting principal and interest payments on held securities.

DCM: Debt Capital Markets The bond new issues department of a bank or securities house.

Delivery against Payment, or Delivery versus Payment (DvP) A settlement system that stipulates that cash payment must be made simultaneously with the delivery of the security.

Delta The delta of any derivative instrument tells us the relation between its price and that of the underlying security. In other words, for a change in the underlying price, the delta represents how much of the change will be reflected in the price of the derivative.

Delta hedging An options strategy that aims to reduce (hedge) the risk associated with price movements in the underlying asset by offsetting long and short positions.

Due diligence The process of researching a borrower's fitness to issue bonds in the international capital markets.

Event of default A borrower declares itself bankrupt or is forced into voluntary liquidation.

Event risk The risk that an event will have a negative impact on a bond issuer's ability to pay its creditors.

FIG: Financial Institutions Group The origination group or desk in DCM servicing such borrowers.

Final terms A term sheet specifying details of an issue under a debt programme and linking to the full description of the product/issuer in the base prospectus.

Fixed price re-offer The lead manager distributes bonds to the management/ underwriting group who place them with clients. The managers agree to sell to investors at a fixed price, agreed in advance, until syndicate is 'broken'. Syndicate is broken by the lead when most of the issue has been placed at the fixed price.

Force majeure A contractual clause in an underwriting agreement which gives new issue managers the right to suspend an offering in the event of major disruptions in the markets caused by external circumstances.

Foreign bond A bond offered by a foreign borrower to investors in a domestic capital market and denominated in that nation's currency. A foreign bond issue in the US is a 'Yankee' and in Japan is called a 'Samurai bond'.

Forward Rate Agreement or FRA An agreement between two parties who agree on a fixed rate of interest to be paid/received on a fixed date in the future.

Fungible An asset perfectly interchangeable with any other of the same type, class and issuer. A fungible bond is a new issue that has all the same specifications as an existing issue, other than price.

Futures   Transferable, exchange-traded contracts to buy or sell a standard quantity of a specific currency, interest rate, debt instrument or financial index at a future date at a price agreed between the two parties.

Global bond   A bond eligible to trade in both the domestic and the Eurobond market via special settlement arrangements.

Grey market   The pre-issue market. The trading of bonds immediately after an issue is announced. Sales are made, as per the ICMA Recommendation, on an *'if, as and when issued'* basis.

Haircut   The percentage by which an asset's market value is reduced for the purpose of calculating capital requirement, margin and collateral levels.

Hedge fund   A private investment vehicle that uses strategies such as short selling, leverage and derivatives to reduce risk and enhance returns.

High-yield bonds   Typically corporate bonds that are rated below investment grade by the major rating agencies – sometimes called 'junk bonds'.

Hybrid   A security having features of both debt and equity instruments.

Index linked   A bond with a coupon rate that varies according to some underlying index (typically CPI or RPI).

Initial Price Thoughts (IPT)   Tentative price indications for a proposed issue on which managers are seeking feedback. Unlike formal price guidance they may involve several successive iterations that may widen as well as tighten. The process is also termed 'Price discovery'.

Inter-dealer Broker (IDB)   Specialist financial intermediary that facilitates transactions between traders.

Interest rate swap   A contractual agreement between two counterparties to exchange interest rate cash flows, based on a specified notional amount; from a fixed rate to a floating rate (or vice versa) or from one floating rate to another.

Inverse FRN   An interest rate swap where the floating rate has a coupon which rises when the underlying floating rate falls. Thus when the market floating rate falls the payout increases.

Investment grade   Bonds that are rated at or above 'Baa' by Moody's, or 'BBB' by S&P.

IOIs: Indications of Interest   Non-binding orders to purchase securities.

IPO or Initial Public Offering   The first sale of equity by a private company to the public.

iTraxx Indices   A family of credit derivative indices, where the underlying reference entities are a defined basket of European credits.

Lead manager   A senior or main underwriter of a new issue. Where there is more than one lead manager, they are referred to as Joint Lead Managers or JLMs.

Leveraged Buy Out (LBO)   The acquisition of another company using a significant amount of borrowed money (bonds or loans) to meet the cost of acquisition.

Liability management   Transactions enabling issuers to restructure or retire their debt as their business strategies and/or goals evolve.

Libor: The London Interbank Offered Rate   The rate banks charge each other for short-term Eurodollar loans. It is the benchmark used to price many capital market and derivative transactions.

Long bond   The 30-year US Treasury bond; considered one of the benchmark indicators of interest rates.

Mark-to-market   The process of daily adjustment of a financial instrument's value to reflect its current market value as the prices go up and down in the market.

Market-maker   A firm or person that is actively involved in making simultaneous bid and offer prices in certain securities to facilitate trading and provide liquidity.

Master agreement   A standard agreement used in over-the-counter derivatives transactions.

Medium-term note   A debt security issued under a programme that allows an issuer to offer notes continuously to investors through a panel of dealers.

Mezzanine   The tier between the junior, or equity, tier and the senior tier in a tranched CDO.

Mid-swaps   The average of bid and offer swap rates for euros used as a benchmark or reference rate over which euro-denominated bonds are priced.

Monoline insurers   Specialists in providing insurance against the risk of a bond default on a timely basis.

Mortgage-Backed Security (MBS)   A security that is secured by home (i.e. Residential or RMBS) and other real estate loans (i.e. Commercial or CMBS).

Negative carry   A situation in which the cost of holding a security exceeds the yield earned.

Negative pledge   A clause in a bond agreement, which prevents a borrower from pledging assets to other lenders if by so doing bondholders' security would be reduced.

Netting   Instead of swap agreements leading to a stream of individual payments by either party, payment flows are offset against each other so that only one net payment is made.

Note   A short-term debt instrument, typically with a maturity of between one and 10 years.

OATs   French government bonds (Obligation Assimilable de Trésor).

On-the-run   The most recently issued US Treasury bond or note of a particular maturity. 'Off-the-run' refers to Treasury securities that have been issued before the most recent issue and are still outstanding.

Optional redemption   A right to retire all or part of an issue prior to the stated maturity during a specified period of years, often at a premium.

Origination   Solicitation of potential borrowers for new debt offerings.

OTC: 'Over the Counter'   (Also called 'off-exchange' trading) is any trading performed without a formal exchange. Traders negotiate directly with one another over computer networks and by phone.

Pari passu   Ranking equally.

Passive bookrunner   A bookrunner without any role in organising and distributing a new corporate bond issue. Passive bookrunners typically get a full underwriting commitment plus fees and access (eventually) to the pot.

Pass-through   A security representing a direct interest in a pool of mortgage loans. The pass-through issuer or servicer collects payments on the loans in the pool and 'passes through' the principal and interest to the security holder on a pro rata basis.

Paying agent   Place where principal and interest are payable, usually a designated bank.

Perpetual (or 'perp')   A floating rate note that has no final maturity and therefore has no arrangement for repayment of principal. With no repayment the note assumes equity characteristics.

Petrodollars   A term prevalent in the 1970s to describe the abundance of dollars held and invested by members of OPEC and other oil producing countries.

Pot syndication   All or part of a new issue is set aside to be allocated to investors out of a central order book (i.e. the 'pot') run by one or more bookrunners. Other syndicate members contribute orders to the pot, but do not control the final allocation or distribution of bonds. Pot issues require syndicate members who are putting orders into the pot to disclose the names of their investors ('name give-up').

Praecipium   The part of the management fee of a new issue formally paid to the lead manager.

Prepayment risk   The possibility that the issuer will call a bond and repay the principal investment to the bondholder prior to the bond's maturity date. A particular feature of RMBS.

Price discovery   (See Initial Price Thoughts.)

Price guidance   The price range formally indicated for a proposed issue at or immediately after announcement.

Price tension   Competition between underwriters on price.

Primary market   A financial market where the first sale of a financial instrument by the original issuer is sold.

Principal write-down   A write-down of part or all of the principal of a bond upon the occurrence of a particular trigger event (common in CoCos).

Protection   A guarantee of a minimum allocation of bonds to an underwriter.

Protection buyer   The credit default swap counterparty that pays another counterparty to compensate them in the event that the reference entity suffers a credit event.

Protection seller   The credit default swap counterparty that takes on credit risk of a reference entity in return for appropriate compensation.

Put   A security that provides a purchaser with the right, but not the obligation, to sell an underlying asset at a specified price at or for a specified period of time.

Quanto   A type of derivative in which the underlying is denominated in one currency, but the instrument itself is settled in another currency at some fixed rate. Such products are attractive for speculators and investors who wish to have exposure to a foreign asset, but without the corresponding exchange rate risk.

Re-allowance   The portion of an underwriting fee passed on to other distributers.

Receivables   Debts or other monetary obligations owed to a company by its debtors or customers.

Red herring   US term for the preliminary prospectus or offering circular of a new issue, which may be used to obtain an indication of the market's interest.

Regulation S   The rules governing sales of bearer securities to US investors outside the US.

Re-offer   Offer of securities from the underwriters or management group to investors (whereas the 'offer' is between the issuer and the management group).

Repo   A Repurchase Agreement. An agreement between two parties where one party sells a bond to the other party for a specified price with the commitment to buy the security back at a later date.

Repo rate   The interest rate in a repurchase agreement in which an asset is sold by one party to another in return for collateral.

Retention   Underwriting banks take up an allocation of bonds but do not disclose where the bonds are distributed.

Road show   A series of presentations by an issuer of securities to potential investors in different financial centres.

Rule 144A   The rules governing sales of bearer securities to US-based investors.

Secured debt   Debt backed by specific assets or revenues of the borrower. In the event of default, secured lenders can force the sale of such assets to meet their claims.

Securitisation   The process of grouping assets or debt together in order to convert them into marketable securities.

Selling concession   The compensation in an underwriting agreement paid to members of a selling group.

Selling group   Distributers in a syndicate with no underwriting obligation.

Selling restrictions   Rules governing the selling of securities in different jurisdictions.

Sell-side   Firms that sell investment services to investors.

Short sale   A trade involving the sale of a security by an investor who does not actually own it, with the intention of buying the security at a lower price at a later date to earn a profit.

Sinking fund   Mandatory prepayments made by a borrower to redeem a certain amount of a bond issue, thus reducing the principal amount due at maturity.

SIV: Special Investment Vehicle   A pool of investment assets that attempts to profit from credit spreads between short-term debt, i.e. issuing commercial paper, and investing in long-term structured finance products such as asset-backed securities.

Spread   The spread of a bond refers to the difference between the yield of the bond and the yield of, say, a government bond of comparable maturity. Since government bonds are traditionally considered risk-free, the spread reflects the risk premium of the bond. The spread is expressed in basis points ($\frac{1}{100}$ of 1%).

SPV or SPE: Special Purpose Vehicle/Entity   A legal entity created by an originator, or seller; typically a major bank or finance company. An SPV's operations are typically limited to the acquisition and financing of specific assets. The SPV issues bonds that are backed by the cash flows of income-generating assets.

Stabilisation   The process of supporting the price of a new issue by means of over-allotment and then the management group buying the bonds for a limited period of time in the aftermarket.

Step-up   Bonds with coupon payments that increase ('step-up') during the life of the security. In many cases, step-ups become callable by the issuer on each anniversary date that the coupon resets after an initial non-call period.

Straight bond   (See Bullet.)

Structured product   A security created by combining underlying instruments such as bonds with derivatives. The resulting product is designed to choose the most acceptable risk level and return requirements for the investor.

Subordinated bonds   Bonds with a promise to pay that cannot legally be fulfilled until payments on certain other obligations have been made, e.g. secured and senior unsecured.

Subprime   The term used for lending to borrowers at a higher rate than the prime rate as they have a higher risk of default. Subprime borrowers typically have low credit scores due to prior bankruptcy, missed loan payments, home repossession etc.

SSA: Sovereign, Supranational and Agency   The origination group or desk in DCM servicing such borrowers.

Super-senior   The highest tier of a tranched CDO with highest credit rating and the lowest exposure to risk. A 'super-senior' tranche is often defined as one that is senior to a AAA rated tranche.

Supranational   International development organisations owned by groups of sovereign states, e.g. the World Bank.

Swap spread   The difference between the swap rate for a specific maturity and the yield on a Treasury with the same maturity.

Synthetic CDO   A CDO created from the securitisation of a portfolio of credit default swaps.

Tax gross-up   Eurobonds are structured so that they are free of any taxes imposed by the country of the issuer. If withholding taxes are imposed then it is the responsibility of the issuer to make gross-up payments to ensure the investor receives his full return.

Thrift   A savings and loan institution (similar to a UK building society) in the US.

Ticket   A securities trade. The term comes from the ticket that records all the terms, conditions and basic information of a trade.

Tombstone   An advertisement announcing an underwritten bond offering that includes the name of the issuer, amount and basic terms of the bonds. Traditionally it included a list of underwriters ranked in order of seniority.

VaR: Value-at-risk   A statistical measure which calculates the maximum loss that any financial instrument or portfolio may be expected to suffer over a defined period with a specified confidence level.

Warrant   An option on an underlying asset which is in the form of a transferable security.

Waterfall or 'cascade'   Payment allocation of principal and interest cash flows to debt holders in order of priority in a multi-tranche security such as a CDO.

Withholding tax   A tax levied on income (interest and dividends) from securities owned by a non-resident.

Wrap   An unconditional and irrevocable guarantee of timely interest and principal payment on a security by the guarantor (typically a monoline insurer).

Yield curve   A graph showing returns of bonds with the same bond ratings but differing maturities over the same period of time.

Yield to maturity   The calculated return on investment that an investor will get if they hold the bond to maturity. It takes into account the present value of all future cash flows, as well as any premium or discount to par that the investor pays.

Zero coupon bonds   A bond that does not pay any interest during its life, but is initially sold at a discount and pays the face value at maturity.

ABC *see* Arab Banking Corporation
ABCP *see* asset-backed commercial paper
ABI *see* Association of British Insurers
ABN Amro 200
ACE (AIBD, Cedel and Euroclear) 114
Ackroyd and Smithers 92
ACS *see* Asset Covered Securities
active bookrunning 211
ADB *see* Asian Development Bank
Additional Tier 1 instruments 230
adjustable rate mortgages (ARMs) 199
adoption of fungibility 38
ADSL *see* asymmetric digital subscriber lines
advanced internal ratings based approaches 188
AFME *see* Association of Financial Markets in Europe
African Development Bank (AfDB) 138
AGMs 84–85, 88, 105, 114
AIBD *see* Association of International Bond Dealers
Alpha Finance Corp 148–149
Alternative Trading Systems (ATS) 173
Ambac Financial Group 153
Amsterdam 1, 2–4
Angel Trains 146
Arab Banking Corporation (ABC) 54
'Arab Spring' 229–230
Argentina 178–179
ARMs *see* adjustable rate mortgages
Asian Development Bank (ADB) 138
Asian economies 138, 154–155, 167, 199
Asset Covered Securities (ACS) 182
asset-backed bonds 76, 146–147
asset-backed commercial paper (ABCP) 208
asset stripping 110
Association of British Insurers (ABI) 181
Association of Financial Markets in Europe (AFME) 239

Association of International Bond Dealers (AIBD) 40–41
1963–1969 39
1970–1979 52, 55–56, 62–65
1979–1984 79–80, 84–86, 88, 89, 92
1985–1989 103–104, 113–115
oil 62–63
pre-1962 15
asymmetric digital subscriber lines (ADSL) 169
ATS *see* Alternative Trading Systems
Austria 4–5, 8, 114
automatic exchange of information 198
Autostrade 23–24, 26
Ayatollah Khomeini 69

BAA airports operator 181
back-to-back loans 68
Bahrain 57
Bahrain Monetary Agency (BMA) 57
bailouts 207–228
Bancomext 119
Bank of Amsterdam 2
Bank of England 9, 13–14, 18, 24, 30–31, 61
Bank of International Settlements (BIS) 55
Bank of London and South America (BOLSA) 35, 40
Bankers Trust 125–126, 140
Bankers Trust International (BTI) 49, 50
Banking Act 1933 11–12
Banking Regulations and Supervisory Practices 112–113
Bank Recovery and Resolution Directive (BRRD) 240–241
Barclays bank 92–93
Barings merchant bank 3–4, 141–142
Basel Committee 187–189, 225–226, 231, 242–243
Basel Committee on Banking Regulations and Supervisory Practices 112–113

Basel Committee on Banking Supervision
(BCBS) 188, 222
BBA *see* British Bankers' Association
BCBS *see* Basel Committee on Banking
Supervision
Bear Stearns 85, 160, 204
Beatrice Foods 183
Belgium 8, 29–30, 38
Berlin Wall 121
bespoke tranche markets 192–193
Beta Finance Corp 148–149
'Big Bang' 92–93, 102
Black Monday 109–110
Black Wednesday 135
Black-Scholes model 80
BMA *see* Bond Market Association
BOLSA *see* Bank of London and South
America
BondBook 173
Bondclear 38–39
Bond Market Association (BMA) 174, 201
Bondtrade 35
bookbuilding systems 160–161
bookrunning 211
Brady bond exchanges 154
Brazil, oil 69
Bretton Woods conference 13
British Bankers' Association (BBA) 152
British Telecom (BT) 106
British Treasury 9–10
Broad Index Secured Trust Offering (BISTRO)
150–152
BRRD *see* Bank Recovery and Resolution
Directive
BTI *see* Bankers Trust International
bubble economy 130
bulge brackets 74
busts 207–228
buy and hold investors 109
buy side firms 87
BZW 3-way merger 92–93

CACs *see* Collective Action Clauses
Campbell Soup 74
Canada 74
Capital Adequacy Directive (CAD) 137
Capital Requirements Directive (CRD) 189, 214,
222–223
'carry' trade 137
CDO *see* Collateralised Debt Obligation
CDS *see* Credit Default Swap

CEBS *see* Committee of European Banking
Supervisors
Cedel 42, 114, 118–119, 131–132
Central Bank of Iran 47–48
Central Capital Market Committee 91
Centrale de Livraison de Valeurs Mobilières 42
CESR *see* Committee of European Securities
Regulators
CET1 *see* Core Equity Tier 1 ratios
CFTC *see* Commodity Futures Trading
Commission
chemical zeroes 83–84
Chicago Mercantile Exchange (CME) 80, 110
China 138, 199
Citibank 59
Citicorp 69, 92–93, 111
Citigroup 148–149
Citron 140–141
Clearstream 118
client relationship management (CRM) 161
CLN *see* credit-linked note
CLO *see* collateralised loan obligation
CMBS *see* commercial mortgage-backed
securities
CME *see* Chicago Mercantile Exchange
CMOs *see* collateralised mortgage obligation
Collateralised Debt Obligation (CDO) 190–193,
195, 198–200, 202
Collateralised Loan Obligation (CLO) 147, 148,
150, 151–153
Collateralised Mortgage Obligation (CMO) 94,
95
Collective Action Clauses (CACs) 178–179, 224
commercial mortgage-backed securities (CMBS)
227
Committee of European Banking Supervisors
(CEBS) 224–225
Committee for European and New York
Settlements 40
Committee of European Securities Regulators
(CESR) 164, 173
Committee for Liaison with the Issuing Houses
40–41
Committee for Standard Market Practices 40
Committee of Wise Men 164
Commodity Futures Trading Commission
(CFTC) 239
.com's 163–185
conduits 149
Confederate States of America 6–7
cons 163–185

Constant Proportion Debt Obligation (CPDO)
200, 201
contagion, Asian 154
Control of Borrowing Order 1958 61
convergence 145–162
Core Equity Tier 1 (CET1) ratios 225, 230
cotton bonds 7
County Bank 99
Court Jews 4
covered bonds 181–183
CPDO *see* Constant Proportion Debt Obligation
CRD *see* Capital Requirements Directive
credit 145–162
Credit Default Swap (CDS) 150–153, 190–193,
195, 232–234, 238
Crédit National 76
credit rating agencies (CRAs) 177
Crédit Suisse Financial Products (CSFP) 126–128
Crédit Suisse First Boston (CSFB)
1970–1979 60
1979–1984 74–76, 82–85, 87–88, 90
1985–1989 106
1999–2004 169
derivatives 126, 141
Crédit Suisse White Weld (CSWW) 15, 58, 60
credit-linked note (CLN) 151–152
Cresvale International 106
CRM *see* client relationship management
CSFB *see* Crédit Suisse First Boston
CSFP *see* Crédit Suisse Financial Products
CSWW *see* Crédit Suisse White Weld
curve trades 192
CUSIP numbering systems 160
Cyprus agreement 243

Datastream 86
DCM bankers 236
deferred purchase bonds 76
Deficit Reduction Act 1984 (DEFRA) 89
Delaware subsidiaries 36
delivery versus payment (DvP) 42
delta hedging 192–193
Deltec 35
Denmark 99
Deposit Trust Company (DTC) 119, 121
1999–2004 180–181
derivatives 125–144
Deutsche Bank 91, 128
Deutsche Bank Capital Markets 101
Deutsche Morgan Grenfell (DMG) 127–128
deutschemark 28–30, 35, 78, 91, 132

Discount Bonds 112
Dominion Securities 35
Dow Chemical 91
Dow Jones CDW index 200
Dragon bonds 138
drawdowns 102
Dr Evil trade 174
Drexel Burnham Lambert 110
DTC *see* Deposit Trust Company
Dutch East India Company 1
DvP *see* delivery versus payment

EARNs *see* Euro Area Reference Notes
EBA *see* European Banking Authority
EBC *see* European Banking Company
ECB *see* European Central Bank
ECBC *see* European Covered Bond Council
ECNs *see* Enhanced Capital Notes
Economic and Monetary Union (EMU) 104, 133,
135–136, 164–166
Economist 39
Ecu *see* European Currency Unit
EDC *see* Export Development Corporation of
Canada
EDGAR databases 180–181
EFSF *see* European Financial Stability Facilities
EFSM *see* European Financial Stabilisation
Mechanism
EIB *see* European Investment Bank
EIOPA *see* European Insurance & Occupational
Pensions Authority
EMU *see* economic and monetary union
Enhanced Capital Notes (ECNs) 220
Enron 175–176
equity tranche trades 192
ESAs *see* European Supervisory Authorities
ESCS *see* European Coal and Steel Community
ESFS *see* European System of Financial
Supervisors
ESM *see* European Stability Mechanism
ESRB *see* European Systemic Risk Board
e-trading 172
EUA *see* European Units of Account
Euro Area Reference Notes (EARNs)
158
Eurobond Guide, 1979–1984 86
Euroclear 38–39, 42, 114, 118–119
euro-deutschemark 29, 35
Euromarkets 14–17, 25
1963–1969 25, 27, 30–31, 33, 37–40
1970–1979 47–51, 64

Euromarkets (*Continued*)
  1979–1984 81, 91–92
  1985–1989 101, 103–105, 117–118
  1999–2004 167–168
  2004–2007 197–198, 199–203
  IRI 23
  oil 61
  pre-1662 13, 14–17, 18
Euromoney
  1979–1984 84
  1985–1989 111
  1999–2004 165–166, 169, 171, 177
  2004–2007 199–203
  convergence and credit 158
  derivatives 129, 134
European Bank for Reconstruction and
  Development (EBRD) 131–132
European Banking Authority (EBA) 222, 232,
  235, 237, 241
European Banking Company (EBC) 51
European Central Bank (ECB) 233–234, 237,
  240, 241, 243, 244
European Coal and Steel Community (ECSC) 23
European Covered Bond Council (ECBC) 183
European Currency Unit (Ecu) 67, 82
European Financial Stabilisation Mechanism
  (EFSM) 229
European Financial Stability Facilities (EFSF)
  224, 229, 232–236
European Insurance & Occupational Pensions
  Authority (EIOPA) 222
European Investment Bank (EIB) 61, 158,
  164–165, 236
European Monetary System (EMS) 67, 82, 132
European Monetary Union (EMU) 67
European Mortgage Federation 183
European Recovery Program 13
European Securities and Markets Authority
  (ESMA), busts and bailouts 222
European Stability Mechanism (ESM) 228, 240
European Supervisory Authorities (ESAs) 222
European Systemic Risk Board (ESRB) 222
European System of Financial Supervisors
  (ESFS) 222
European Units of Account (EUA) 26, 29
Eurotrade 35
EuroWeek 63, 156
Exchange Act of 1934 11
exchange-traded contracts 80
executive search consultants 85

Export Development Corporation (EDC) of
  Canada 74
Exxon Valdez oil tanker spill 149–150

Famous Artists Schools 42, 43
Fannie Mae (Federal National Mortgage
  Association) 94, 95, 158
FASB *see* Financial Accounting Standards Board
FDIC *see* Federal Deposit Insurance Corporation
Federal Deposit Insurance Corporation (FDIC) 12
Federal Home Loan Mortgage Corporation
  (FHLMC) 94
Federal Home Mortgage Corporation (Freddie
  Mac) 158, 204
Federal National Mortgage Association (FNMA)
  94, 95, 158
Federal Reserve Book (FRB) Entry system 119
Fedwire 118
FGIC *see* Financial Guaranty Insurance Company
FIMBRA *see* Financial Intermediaries, Managers,
  and Brokers Regulatory Association
Financial Accounting Standards Board (FASB)
  175
Financial Futures and Options Exchange (LIFFE)
  133
Financial Guaranty Insurance Company (FGIC)
  153
Financial Intermediaries, Managers, and Brokers
  Regulatory Association (FIMBRA) 103
Financial Security Assurance Inc. (FSA) 153
Financial Services Act 1986 102
Financial Services Action Plan (FSAP) 163, 195
Financial Stability Board (FSB) 221, 231
Financial Times 54–55, 63, 67, 95–96, 102, 103,
  121
financial transactions tax (FTT) 239
FINSIDER 23–24
First Interstate Bancorp 101
first loss tranche trades 192
First National Bank of Boston 12
First National City Bank of New York 59
First World War 8, 9–10
fiscal stability union (Fiscal Compact) 235
Fixed Price Reoffer systems 116–117
Floating Rate Certificate of Deposit (FRCD) 59
floating rate notes (FRNs)
  1970–1979 50, 59, 60, 69
  1979–1984 82–83
  1985–1989 99–102, 113
  2004–2007 189

FNMA *see* Federal National Mortgage
   Association
Foreign Fund markets 5
Foreign Targeted Treasury Notes 90
forward rate agreements (FRAs) 128
foundation internal ratings based approaches
   188
France 3
Frankfurt Kassenverein 42
Franklin National Bank 55
FRAs *see* forward rate agreements
FRB *see* Federal Reserve Book Entry system
Freddie Mac (Federal Home Mortgage
   Corporation) 158, 204
FRN *see* floating rate note
FSA *see* Financial Security Assurance Inc.
FSAP *see* Financial Services Action Plan
FSAP (Financial Services Action Plan) 163, 195
FSB *see* Financial Stability Board
FTT *see* financial transactions tax
Fulham borough 128
futures contracts 80
Futures Trading Commission (CFTC) 239

G-20 (Group of Twenty) 221
G-30 (Group of Thirty) 129
GAAP *see* Generally Accepted Accounting
   Principles
Gang of 26 180–181
General Electric Capital Corporation (GECC) 138
Generally Accepted Accounting Principles
   (GAAP) 11
General Motors Acceptance Corporation
   (GMAC) 76–77, 101, 159–160, 179, 194–195
German-Jewish emigrants 21–22
Germany
   1963–1969 28–29, 30, 35, 41–42
   1979–1984 77, 91
   1985–1989 121
   convergence and credit 158–159
   derivatives 127–128, 132–135
   Deutsche Bank 91, 128
   Deutsche Bank Capital Markets 101
   deutschemark 28–30, 35, 78, 91, 132
   Deutsche Morgan Grenfell 127–128
   Frankfurt Kassenverein 42
   pre-1962 4, 7–10
   Zurich 15
GIB *see* Gulf International Bank
Gibson Greetings Inc. 140

Ginnie Mae (Government National Mortgage
   Association) 94, 95
Glass-Steagall Act 11–12
Glen International 108
globalisation 99–123
Global Landmark Securities (GlobLS) 158–159
Global Master Repurchase Agreement (GMRA)
   131
GMAC *see* General Motors Acceptance
   Corporation
GNMA *see* Government National Mortgage
   Association
golden handshakes/hellos 86
gold-plating 163
gold reserves, Bank of England 9
gold standard 7–8, 9, 11
Goldman Sachs 130, 138, 181, 199
Government National Mortgage Association
   (GNMA) 94, 95
Gower Report 102
Gracechurch Personal Loan Finance 146
Grand Duchy 38
Great Depression 10–12
grey markets 62, 65, 106
Group of Thirty (G-30) 129
Group of Twenty (G-20) 221
GRS Holding Co. 146
Grupo Ferrovial construction and infrastructure
   181
Gulf International Bank (GIB) 54

Halifax 109
Hambros Bank 27–28
Hammersmith borough 128
'hard' commission houses 85
headhunters 85
hedge funds 108, 192–193
Herstatt Bank 55
Hewlett Packard 79
high quality liquid assets (HQLA) 242
*History of Railroads and Canals in the United
   States* 6
Holy Alliance 4–5
Hong Kong 167
Hope and Co. 2–4
host states 136
HQLA *see* high quality liquid assets
HSBC bank 202
Hutchinson Whampoa 167
hybrid bank issuance 189

IBM 78
IBRD *see* International Bank for Reconstruction and Development
ICBC *see* Industrial and Commercial Bank of China
Icelandic banks 203
ICMA *see* International Capital Market association
IDB *see* inter-dealer broker firms
IET *see* Interest Equalisation Tax
IFR *see International Financing Review*
IFRS *see* International Financial Reporting Standards
IMF *see* International Monetary Fund
IMF, 1999–2004 178–179
IMI *see* Instituto Mobiliare Italiano
IMRO *see* Investment Management Regulatory Organisation
IMS *see* Innovative Marketing Systems
The Independent 92, 135–136
indications of interest 160
Industrial and Commercial Bank of China (ICBC) 199
ING 142
Inland Revenue 24
Innovative Marketing Systems (IMS) 87
Insider Trading Directive 137
Instituto Mobiliare Italiano (IMI) 48
Instituto per la Riconstruzione Industriale (IRI) 23
inter-dealer broker (IDB) firms 65–66
Interest Equalisation Tax (IET) 26, 30
internal ratings based (IRB) approaches 188, 189
Internal Revenue Service 90
International Bank for Reconstruction and Development (IBRD) 77
International Capital Market association (ICMA) 194, 201–202
International Financial Futures and Options Exchange (LIFFE) 133
International Financial Reporting Standards (IFRS) 196
International Financing Review (IFR) 63
International Investor 108
International Monetary Fund (IMF) 12, 154, 156, 232–234, 243
International Organisation of Securities Commissions (IOSCO) 177
International Primary Market Association 88

International Securities Identification Numbers (ISIN) 160
International Securities Regulatory Organisation (ISRO) 103
International Stock Exchange 103–104
International Swaps and Derivatives Association (ISDA) 79, 164
Investment Management Regulatory Organisation (IMRO) 103
Investments Services Directive (ISD) 136–137, 173, 198, 209
Investors Overseas Services, Ltd (IOS) 43, 44
IOSCO *see* International Organisation of Securities Commissions
IPMA
  1979–1984 89
  1985–1989 102, 105, 115, 121
  1999–2004 164, 167, 171, 178–179, 181
  2004–2007 194, 201
  convergence and credit 159, 160
  derivatives 130
Iran 47–48, 69
Iraq 69
IRB *see* internal ratings based approaches
IRI *see* Instituto per la Riconstruzione Industriale
Iron Curtain 121
ISD *see* Investments Services Directive
ISDA *see* International Swaps and Derivatives Association
ISIN *see* International Securities Identification Numbers
Islamic revolution 69
ISMA
  1985–1989 119
  1999–2004 164, 167–168, 173–174
  2004–2007 193–194
  convergence and credit 148, 153, 157
  derivatives 130–131, 135–136, 137, 142–143
ISRO *see* International Securities Regulatory Organisation
ISS Global 181
Issuenet service 201
Issuing Houses Sub-Committee 40–41
Italian Motorways 25
iTraxx 191–192, 200

Japan 27, 31, 77, 91–92, 100–101, 106–108, 130
Japanese government bonds (JGBs) 141–142
J.C. Penney 74, 77
Jewish emigrants 21–22
JGBs *see* Japanese government bonds

joint default analysis (JDA) 203
J.P. Morgan 15, 127, 129, 149–151
'jumbo' straight bond issue 101
junk bonds 110

KDB *see* Korea Development Bank
Keynesian economic theory 53
KFTCIC *see* Kuwait Foreign Trading Contracting and Investment Company
KfW development bank 158–159
KIC *see* Kuwait Investment Company
Kidder Peabody 60–61
KIIC *see* Kuwait International Investment Company
KKR *see* Kohlberg Kravis Roberts
Kohlberg Kravis Roberts (KKR) 110
Korea Development Bank (KDB) 155, 215
Kuwait City 58
Kuwait Foreign Trading Contracting and Investment Company (KFTCIC) 57
Kuwait International Investment Company (KIIC) 57
Kuwait Investment Company (KIC) 57

Lamfalussy Process 164
Latin American economies 69, 80–82, 112, 119, 141, 154, 178–179
LAUTRO *see* Life Assurance and Unit Trust Regulatory Organisation
LBO *see* leveraged buy out
LCRs *see* liquidity coverage ratios
Legal and Documentation Committee (LDC) 89, 105, 111, 112
Lehman Brothers 138
leveraged buy out (LBO) 110–111
liability management exercises (LMEs) 219
LIBA *see* London Investment Bankers Association
LIBOR *see* London Inter-Bank Offered Rate
Life Assurance and Unit Trust Regulatory Organisation (LAUTRO) 103
liquidity coverage ratios (LCRs) 225–226, 242–243
living wills 221
Lloyds TSB 199, 215–216, 220–221
LMEs *see* liability management exercises
loan-to-value (LTV) ratios 239
London 3–5, 8, 18, 24–27, 34, 38–39, 92, 102–103, 128
London Inter-Bank Offered Rate (LIBOR) 48, 69, 99–100, 213

London International Financial Futures and Options Exchange (LIFFE) 133
London Investment Bankers Association (LIBA) 194
long only investors 109
Long-Term Capital Management (LTCM) 157–158
Long-Term Refinancing Operation (LTRO) 235, 237, 244
Lotus Software 79–80
Louisiana Purchase 3
LTV *see* loan-to-value
Luxembourg 24–25, 29–30, 36–37, 38, 42

Maastricht 132–135
MAD *see* Market Abuse Directive
Mahathir Mohammad 154
Market Abuse Directive (MAD) 196–197
Market in Financial Instruments Directive (MiFID) 198, 200, 238
MarketMaster 87
Market Practices Committee 89
mark-to-model systems 187–205
Marshall Plan 13
Master Trust structures 152
matching of participants processes 38
MBIA *see* Municipal Bond Insurance Association
MBS *see* mortgage-backed security
medium term notes (MTN) 101, 158
Mellon Securities Corporation 12
Mexico 80–82, 112, 119, 141
Midland Bank 13–14, 92
MiFID *see* Market in Financial Instruments Directive
millennium bug 168
Ministry of Defense (MoD) 146
Mississippi Bubble, Paris 3
Mitsubishi Chemical 106
MoD *see* Ministry of Defense
monoline insurers 153
Moody's Investor Services 203
Morgan Grenfell 27
Morgan Guaranty 38, 51, 77
Morgan Stanley 82, 90, 116, 130, 134, 202
mortgage-backed security (MBS) 95, 109
Mortgage Bankers Association 204
The Mortgage Corporation 146
MTN *see* medium term note
multilateral trading facilities (MTF) 209
Municipal Bond Insurance Association (MBIA) 153

NAFTA *see* North American Free Trade Agreement
National Association of Securities Dealers (NASD) 113–114, 169
National Home Loans Corporation 146
National Westminster (NatWest) Bank 99, 146, 147–148
Nazi Party 21
Nestlé 106
Netherlands 1–2, 36
net stable funding ratios (NSFR) 226
new issue premiums (NIP) 170
New York markets 36–37, 40, 55, 59, 75, 95
New York Stock Exchange (NYSE) 110, 174
New Zealand 60–61, 116
Nikkei stock price index 107, 141–142
ninja loans 202
NIP *see* new issue premiums
'no action' letters 120
Norges Kommunalbank 27–28
North American Free Trade Agreement (NAFTA) 141
Northern Rock 208
North Sea oil 61, 67–68
Norway 27–28, 114
NSFR *see* net stable funding ratios
NXP Semiconductors 199
NYSE *see* New York Stock Exchange

Observer 93
Office of Foreign Direct Investment (OFDI) 36
offshore banking units (OBUs) 57
OIE *see* overseas investment exchange
oil 47–71, 88
oil exporting countries, 1979–1984 80
OMT *see* Open Market Transactions; Outright Monetary Transactions
one-off bonds & FRNs 102
Open Market Transactions (OMT) 244
Organised Trading Facilities (OTF) 238
Organisation of Petroleum Exporting Countries (OPEC) 53, 59, 69
Orion Bank 51, 68
Osaka Exchange 142
Oslo AGM 114
OTF *see* Organised Trading Facilities
Outright Monetary Transactions (OMT) 240
overseas investment exchange (OIE) 104
over-the-counter (OTC) markets 16–17, 80, 238

paper money 7–9
parallel loans 68

Par Bonds 112
Paribas Capital Markets (PBCM) 134
Paris 3, 9–10
Parmalat 183
partly paid bonds 76
passive bookrunning 211
passports 136, 195
pass-through issuance 94–95
PBCM *see* Paribas Capital Markets
PCAOB *see* Public Company Accounting Oversight Board
PCS *see* Prime Collateralised Securities
People's Republic of China 138, 199
perpetual FRNs 99–101
personal computers 79–80
peso 80–81, 141
'Pfandbriefe' system 181–182
'Phibro' Corporation 87
Philipp Brothers 87
Phoenix Inns 145–146
point of non-viability (PONV) 241
PONV *see* point of non-viability
pot systems of syndication 159–161
pound sterling 8, 10, 11, 30, 135
premium dollars 17–18
pre-payment risk 94
pre-pricing 61
price rigging 197
primary bookbuilding systems 160–161
Primary Market Committee 63, 88
Prime Collateralised Securities (PCS) 239
printing money 7–9
Procter and Gamble (P&G) 139–140
programme-trading 109
Prospectus Directive 137, 196
Prudential Bache 85
Prussia 4–5
Public Company Accounting Oversight Board (PCAOB) 177
Public Offers Directive 196
Public Securities Association (PSA) 131
put Eurobonds 81–83

quantitative easing (QE) 217–218, 233, 244
Quantum Fund 135
Quotations and Yields 63, 86

RBS *see* Royal Bank of Scotland
recognised investment exchanges (RIE) 103–104, 173
regulated markets 136, 196
Regulation S 120–121

relative-value trades 157, 192
remuneration packages 85
'repo' market 130–132
residential mortgage-backed securities (RMBS) 146, 199, 227
restricted securities 121
retractable Eurobonds 81–83
Reuter Monitor Bond Service 86
reverse enquiries 102
RIE *see* recognised investment exchanges
Risk Magazine 157, 200
RJR Nabisco 110
RMBS *see* residential mortgage-backed securities
rogue speculators 154
rogue traders 141–142
ROSE Funding 147–148
Rothschild family 4–5, 21
rouble-denominated debt 156
Royal Bank of Canada 68
Royal Bank of Scotland (RBS) 218, 224, 240
Roylease 68
Rule 144A 120–121
Rule 415 101–102
Russia 4–5, 8, 156–157

sale and repurchase agreements (repo) 130–132
Salomon Brothers 76, 78, 87, 90, 95, 138, 157
SAMA (Saudi Arabian Monetary Agency) 56–57
Samurai markets 61
SAPs *see* structural adjustment programmes
Sarbanes-Oxley Act (SOX) 176–177
Saudi Arabia 56–57
Savings Directive 197–198
Savings Tax Directive 195
SBC Glacier Finance 152
SBC Warburg 151–152
SDRM *see* Sovereign Debt Restructuring Mechanism
SEA *see* Single European Act
SEC *see* Securities and Exchange Commission
Secondary Market Makers Association (SMMA) 89
Second World War 12
Securities Act of 1933 11, 120
Securities Association (TSA) 103, 104
Securities and Exchange Commission (SEC) 11
   1985–1989 101–102, 120
   1999–2004 164, 169, 175–177, 180–181
Securities Industry Association (SIA) 201
Securities Industry and Financial Markets Association (SIFMA) 201
Securities and Investment Board (SIB) 102–103

Securities Market Programme (SMP) 240
securitisation 146–150
Self-Regulatory Organisations (SROs) 11, 102–103, 104
Seligman Brothers 21–22
sell-side firms 87
Serbia 8
Settlement Committee 42
SGP *see* Stability and Growth Pact
shelf registration 101–102
Sheraton hotel 58
SIA *see* Securities Industry Association
SIB *see* Securities and Investment Board
SIFMA *see* Securities Industry and Financial Markets Association
SIMEX 142
Single European Act (SEA) 104, 132–133
single passport for issuers 195
Single Resolution Mechanisms (SRM) 241
Single Supervisory Mechanisms (SSM) 241
single-tranche collateralised debt obligation 192
SIVs *see* structured investment vehicles
Smithsonian Institute 51
SMMA *see* Secondary Market Makers Association
Smoot Hawley Tariff Act 10–11
SMP *see* Securities Market Programme
Societa Finanzaria of Warburg (FINSIDER) 23–24
South American economies 69, 80–82, 112, 119, 141, 154, 178–179
South Sea Bubble, London 3
Sovereign Debt Restructuring Mechanism (SDRM) 178
Soviet Union 13, 121
SOX *see* Sarbanes-Oxley Act
Specially Targeted Treasury Notes 90
special purpose entities (SPEs) 175
special purpose vehicles (SPV) 94, 146, 147, 150–152
speculative investment securities 12
SRM *see* Single Resolution Mechanisms
SROs *see* Self-Regulatory Organisations
SSM *see* Single Supervisory Mechanisms
Stability and Growth Pact (SGP) 223
Stamp Office 24
stand-alone bonds & FRNs 102
Standard Oil 31–32
sterling *see* pound sterling
sterling bloc 11
Strauss Turnbull 15, 16–17
streaker bonds 76–77

structural adjustment programmes (SAPs) 155
structured investment vehicles (SIVs) 148–149
substantial US market interest (SUSMI) 120
super-equivalence 163
Sweden 99
Swiss Bank Corporation (SBC) 131–132
Swiss franc, 1979–1984 78
Swiss National Bank 27
Switzerland
  1979–1984 74–75
  Bank of International Settlements 55
  CSFP 126–128
  CSWW 15, 58, 60
  oil 60, 61–62
  pre-1962 17
syndication 159–161
systematically important financial institutions
  (SIFIs) 225, 231
systematic internalisers (SIs) 209

TAF *see* term auction facilities
TARP *see* Troubled Asset Relief Program
tax
  FINSIDER 23–24
  IET 26, 30
  Savings Tax Directive 195
  streaker bonds 76–77
  Swiss federal tax 17
  United States banks 17–18
  US-Netherlands tax treaty 36
Tax Equity and Fiscal Responsibility Act 1982
  (TEFRA) 90
TBMA *see* Bond Market Association
Tecnost 166
TEFRA *see* Tax Equity and Fiscal Responsibility
  Act 1982
telecommunications companies 169–171, 176,
  179, 198
Tequila Crisis 141
term auction facilities (TAF) 212
term securities lending facilities (TSLF) 212
Texaco oil 88
The Bond Market Association (TBMA) 174
The Economic Consequences of the Peace (1919)
  9–10
The Mortgage Corporation 146
The Securities Association (TSA) 103, 104
thrift institutions 94
tiger economies 138
Tiger Fund 108
Tobin tax 221
Tokyo stock market 106

tombstone advertisements 31–32, 48, 62
'too big to fail' institutions 225, 231
Toyota Motor Credit Corporation 115
TradeWeb 172
tranche trades 192–193
Transparency Directive 195, 197
Trax system 114–115
Treaty of Versailles 9
tri-party repo 131–132
Troubled Asset Relief Program (TARP) 216
TSA *see* The Securities Association
TSLF *see* term securities lending facilities

UMTS *see* Universal Mobile
  Telecommunications System
"uncles" 21
United Kingdom (UK)
  1979–1984 86, 92–93
  1985–1989 100
  Audit Commission 128
  Building Societies Act 109
  busts and bailouts 208, 215–216, 220–221
  convergence and credit 145–152
  derivatives 128, 133–135, 141–142
  pound sterling 8, 10, 11, 30, 135
  pre-1962 3–4, 7–8, 18
United States (US)
  1963–1969 30–31, 35–36
  1979–1984 76, 80–82, 89–91, 94–95
  1985–1989 101–102, 110, 113, 118–121
  1999–2004 174–176
  busts and bailouts 208, 215–216
  convergence and credit 159
  derivatives 130
  federal/foreign tax 17–18
  Mortgage Bankers Association 204
  oil 57–58
  pre-1962 6, 9, 10
  US-Netherlands tax treaty 36
Universal Mobile Telecommunications System
  (UMTS) 169–170
unpublished price sensitive information (UPSI)
  196

value-at-risk (VaR) 125, 129
Venezuela 15
Vienna AGM 114
Vietnam War 30
Voluntary Foreign Credit Restraint Programme 30

war on terror 174
Weedon & Co. 35, 38

White Weld 15, 16, 18
wireless (wi-fi) technologies 169
Wise Men Committee 164
World Bank 12, 77–78, 117–118,
  130
World Trade Center 174

Y2K 168
Yankee bonds
  1963–1969 25
  1970–1979 55
  1985–1989 117–118

1999–2004 167–168
pre-1962 14–17
see also Euromarkets
10-year non-call five-year (10NC5) offerings 236,
  243
30-year, non-call five-year (30NC5) Tier 2 notes
  230
yen-denominated Eurobonds 91–92

zaiteku (financial engineering) 107
zero coupon bonds 76–77
Zurich 15